You Send Me

You Send Me

THE LIFE AND TIMES OF SAM COOKE

Daniel Wolff

with S. R. Crain, Clifton White,
and G. David Tenenbaum

WILLIAM MORROW AND COMPANY, INC.
NEW YORK

It is the policy of William Morrow and Company, Inc., and its imprints and affiliates,
recognizing the importance of preserving what has been written, to print the books we
publish on acid-free paper, and we exert our best efforts to that end.

LIBRARY OF CONGRESS CATALOGING-IN-PUBLICATION DATA
Wolff, Daniel.
You send me : the life and times of Sam Cooke / Daniel Wolff with S. R. Crain . . .
[et al.].—1st ed.
p.   cm.
Includes discography (p.), bibliography (p.), and index.
ISBN 0-688-12403-8 (acid-free paper)
1. Cooke, Sam. 2. Soul musicians—United States—Biography.
1. Title.
ML420.C665W65 1995
782.42164'4'092—dc20
[B]   94-3547
CIP

Printed in the United States of America

2   3   4   5   6   7   8   9   10

BOOK DESIGN BY BRIAN MULLIGAN

For my parents

CONTENTS

Prologue

The brand-new cherry-red Ferrari purred softly in the parking lot. It was empty except for a bottle of whiskey on the floor and a copy of the Black Muslim newspaper, *Muhammad Speaks*, on the backseat. Above the idling car, in the darkness of the December night, a neon sign read "Hacienda Motel." Beside it, hand-painted: "$3–Up."

Inside one of the motel rooms was the owner of the car. A black man, he was wearing an overcoat, one shoe, and nothing else. A .22 caliber bullet was lodged in his chest. It had passed sideways through his left lung, the left chamber of his heart, and then on through his right lung and rib cage. On his head was a two-inch lump where he had apparently been struck with a hard object. He was sitting on the floor, his back against the wall. He was dead.

The room belonged to the motel manager, a stocky fifty-five-year-old black woman named Bertha Franklin. When the police arrived, Franklin told them the dead man had checked in around 2:35 A.M. with a young woman. "First, he wrote his name, just his name down, and then I told him . . . I saw her coming, and so I told him, 'You will have to put "Mr. and Mrs." ' " The couple had gone off to their room, and about twenty minutes later, Franklin heard a knock at her door. She was on the phone with the motel owner, so she excused herself and went to the door. It was the same man, looking for his "lady friend."

"No! She's not in here."

At about this time, the police operator at the local precinct, the 77th, got a call from a young woman. "Hello. Will you please come down to this number? I don't know what street I'm at. . . . The telephone number is PI 7–9984. That's the telephone booth. . . ." The police operator asked what the problem was. "Well, I was kidnapped."

Back at the Hacienda Motel, Bertha Franklin was still talking to her boss when she heard a car drive up from the rear of the parking lot. There was another knock; it was the man again. Mrs. Franklin, looking through the barred window where guests registered, could only see him from the waist up. He seemed to be wearing a jacket with no shirt underneath.

"Is the girl there?" he asked.

"I didn't see no girl," Franklin answered.

"Let me in to look then." Franklin told him the police were the only people who could come in. "Damn the police!"

With that, he started working at the locked door, banging at it with his shoulder. The frame quickly ripped loose, the latch gave, and he was in. The man, bare legs showing, strode past Franklin straight to the kitchen and then searched the bedroom. When he came out, he grabbed Franklin by the wrists and demanded to know where the girl was. The middle-aged woman fought back, and the two of them fell to the floor.

"He fell on top of me. . . . I tried to bite him through that jacket—biting, scratching, biting, scratching, and everything. Finally, I got up, when I kicked him. . . . I run and grabbed the pistol off the—grabbed the gun off the TV, and I shot. . . . At close range. . . . Three times."

"Lady, you shot me!"

It didn't seem to stop him; he ran at her again. "So, I got this stick and hit him with that. In the head. It was very flimsy . . . the first time I hit him, it broke." The phone was still off the hook; now Franklin got back on and told her boss to call the police. Outside, in the parking lot, under the flickering neon sign, the red Ferrari continued to idle.

The first cop on the scene kept everything as it was until the detectives could arrive. The apartment was a mess, and there was blood all over Mrs. Franklin's turquoise dress, but she appeared to be unharmed. The gun was on a table next to the TV with three live bullets in it and three empty casings. The broken stick was on the floor.

A half block away, in a phone booth, the police discovered a twenty-two-year-old Eurasian named Lisa Boyer. She had long, straight black hair and a round, slightly babyish face. She showed the police where she had thrown the dead man's clothes under a nearby stairway. And then she was taken to the precinct to tell her version of the night's events.

Lisa Boyer said she'd met the man for the first time that evening at a dinner party in Hollywood. He'd offered her a ride home; she'd accepted; but they'd decided to have a drink at a nightclub first. Though the man did not appear to be drunk, at the club he got in a heated argument with another gentleman who had begun to chat Boyer up. "I was quite shaken," Lisa told the police, "and I asked him, 'Please take me home.' " They'd left the club at two in the morning as it was closing, but instead of turning north toward the motel where Lisa Boyer lived, the man had headed down Santa Monica Boulevard to the Hollywood Freeway. As he gunned the sports car, she asked again to be taken home. "Don't worry now. I will. I just want to go for a little ride." She kept asking, but he just kept racing the Ferrari and talking to her as he drove: "You're a lovely girl, you know that? I'm mad about you, baby. Such pretty long hair."

He'd pulled off the freeway onto Figueroa Street in a tough section of south Los Angeles. "Please!" Boyer said she cried. "Take me home." Instead, he drove into the motel, slammed the car door, and walked, fast, toward the glass window, where Bertha Franklin registered him. Boyer followed, asking in a loud voice to go home, but "he dragged me into that room."

Latching the door behind him, the man pushed Boyer onto the bed and pinned her there. "We're just going to talk," he said.

"He pulled my sweater off," Lisa told the police, "and he ripped my dress off. . . . I knew that he was going to rape me." According to Boyer, the man undressed, and when he went into the bathroom, "I picked up my clothes, my shoes, and my handbag, I opened the latch, and I ran out."

The first thing Lisa Boyer did, she said, was knock on the manager's door. Not getting a quick enough answer, she left. She pulled on her sweater and walked up the block, then dumped the rest of her clothes on the ground and got fully dressed. Tangled among her clothes were the man's shirt, sport jacket, and pants. She left them there, ran into a phone booth, and called the cops. "I had no idea that someone had shot [him]."

To the police, it was a routine incident: "Another dead nigger on the south side," as one observer later put it. They took the body to the county medical examiner's, where it was logged in at 4:15 A.M. Negro male, approximately twenty-five years of age, measuring five feet ten in length, weighing 162 pounds, with black hair, brown eyes, and dark complexion. At around six, they notified the family. The widow greeted them with hysterics—"Is it true? Is it true?"—as two young children were rushed out of earshot. An autopsy was performed at eleven that morning; the blood test showed 0.14 percent ethanol (drinking alcohol), which, according to the examining doctor, might have affected the man's judgment. There was no sign of narcotics. The body was then placed in crypt 19 until it could be claimed.

The headlines in the papers that Friday morning, December 11, 1964, were about the release of nineteen white male suspects in the killing of three civil rights workers in rural Mississippi. The second lead was Dr. Martin Luther King's acceptance of the Nobel Peace Prize. "I accept this award with an abiding faith in America and an audacious faith in the future of mankind. . . . I refuse to accept despair as the final response to the ambiguities of history. I refuse to accept the idea that man is mere flotsam and jetsam in the river of life unable to influence the unfolding events which surround him. I refuse to accept the view that mankind is so tragically bound to the starless midnight of racism and war that the bright daybreak of peace and brotherhood can never become a reality."

By midafternoon, the dead man's body had been transferred from the morgue to the People's Funeral Home on South Central Avenue. There, a friend discovered that "he wasn't fixed up. . . . His hands were up like this, and his fingernails was all ripped up. They didn't put his hands behind him; they didn't do anything to change his position. His skin was black because he had laid so long before he was embalmed. If you know anything about that, the blood will turn a dark person blacker: real, real black. He looked bad! Pain and all that grimace was on his face. . . ."

That evening, the LAPD got a clue that this was not just another shooting. Dozens of teenagers began milling around the scene of the killing—playing music, singing songs, refusing to disperse. Soon, the 77th Precinct announced that both Lisa Boyer and Bertha Franklin had passed lie detector tests. There was a hurried, two-hour coroner's inquest, which found the shooting had been in self-defense. Then the case was officially closed.

The next day, banner headlines in one of the Negro papers in Los Angeles declared that the ruling had "enraged" thousands. An estimated eighty thousand people—most of them black, most of them crying—viewed the body. Of these, a funeral director reported to the papers, "none seems to believe the story behind the killing."

The funeral at L.A.'s Mount Sinai Baptist Church was "infested," one woman recalls. "The entire area was covered, a sea of people." As the mourners left the church and walked down the rainy streets, music came rolling out of hundreds of ghetto apartments. "You Send Me," "Only Sixteen," "Wonderful World," "Chain Gang," "Cupid," "Twistin' the Night Away," "Having a Party," "Bring It on Home to Me," "Another Saturday Night." The songs raged against each other in a great mess of sound, the only thing holding them together the common thread of an extraordinary voice: intimate, slightly rough, with a characteristic quaver to it, almost a yodel.

A business associate issued a press release describing the deceased as "a happily married man with deep religious convictions . . . not a violent person" and added that the official version of his killing was "entirely inconsistent with the type of person he was." Baltimore's *Afro-American* announced a "cover-up" in the shooting. New York's *Amsterdam News* had a front-page article full of specific questions about the night's events. The *Forward Times* in Houston revealed that Lisa Boyer was a call girl, "Blanchie" Franklin had been arrested several times previously, and over $1,500 was missing from the dead man's sport coat. And the *Chicago Defender* began a five-part series on what it called "the mysterious death."

Subsequent events only heightened suspicions. A month after the shooting, Lisa Boyer was arrested in a vice raid on a Hollywood motel and charged with prostitution. Two months after the death, the widow applied for a marriage license to wed an underage friend of the deceased. Rumors flew: the dead man had been set up by the mob, or by his jealous wife; the shooting had actually taken place elsewhere.

The more time that passed, the more convinced the dead man's friends became that the official version of the death was a lie. Personally, politically, financially, the man had been right at the brink of realizing his enormous potential when he had ... not fallen. You couldn't convince those who knew him of that. You couldn't convince them that all his charismatic power had ended with an unclaimed corpse, hands upraised, fingernails ragged, a look of terror on its face. This man had a name; he had a past and a purpose. To believe that he was just another dead nigger was to deny all that—was to deny history—was to say that nothing had ever changed or ever could.

Chapter

1

At three in the afternoon, in the year 1895, in the parlor of a good Christian's home in Jackson, Mississippi, the Reverend Charles Price Jones had a vision. He had locked himself in early that morning to pray and meditate on a passage from Deuteronomy: "Lord, give me power to convince my people and my generation of the beauty of holiness and the advantages of righteousness." Reverend Jones, a light-skinned, distinguished-looking Negro, was in the midst of a religious crisis. A staunch Baptist who had pastored churches in Alabama and Arkansas, he yearned for "spiritual assurance, heart peace, rest of soul, the joy of salvation." He was worried that his people—the colored people—wanted to advance in the world. He knew that worldly advancement was only a snare. What they needed—what he needed—was to find salvation in God.

It's hard to believe advancement presented much of a temptation to the colored population of Mississippi in 1895. The brief hope of Reconstruction had ended. Slavery had been replaced by the perpetual debt of sharecropping, and Mississippi was enacting one of the most repressive eras in its repressive history. Lynchings were commonplace. The state legislature had begun passing laws to reinstate strict segregation everywhere from railroads and trolleys to public rest rooms. Coloreds and whites had separate schools, hospitals, prisons, even chain gangs. Jackson's few Negro policemen had been fired, and the remains of a colored secretary of state, buried during Reconstruction in a white cemetery, would soon be moved to the "nigger burying ground" across town.

Praying in the hot, still parlor, Reverend Jones sought some way out of this oppression. If this was all the world could offer his people, then it made sense for them to renounce it, to seek salvation elsewhere. He fasted and prayed and meditated until three in the afternoon, when, exhausted, he collapsed on a sofa. There he suddenly began "laughing and crying and verily kicking like an infant for holy delight." He had been touched, and it lifted him above the parlor, beyond Jackson's crowded nigger town, beyond the smell and taste of grinding poverty, above the state of Mississippi itself with its thousands of miles of cotton rows, like lashes on a dark back. But instead of rising forever, the Reverend was brought back to earth by the voice of the Spirit that had touched him. It spoke not about preaching or forming a church or even feeding the poor. No, the Spirit said, "You shall write the hymns for your people." And with that, Jones recalled, "I got up and went to the organ in the corner of the room, wrote a song titled 'Praise the Lord,' ruled off a tablet, set it to music, and sang it before I left the room."

The Reverend C. P. Jones would go on to found a new church and write more than a thousand songs of inspiration and salvation. He claimed he never meant for such a thing to happen. "I had no idea at all of taking up holiness as a fad, or an ism, or a creed, or the slogan of a 'cult.' I just wanted to be personally holy." But as he spread the word of his new vision, others became interested. It was happening all over the South—especially the colored South. Between the economic panic of 1893 and 1900, twenty-three Holiness denominations sprang up. "Never before in the history of the nation," one historian has remarked, "had so many churches been founded in so short a time." In a time of despair, when people needed a new beginning, the Holiness movement was the religious equivalent of William Jennings Bryant's populist agrarian revolt; it offered a fresh chance.

By February 1897, Jones and another former Baptist missionary, C. H. Mason, were holding their first Holiness revival in an abandoned ginhouse in Natchez, Mississippi. Jennie Watson was healed of a "helpless" affliction; sixty new members signed on. But if you could be made whole by this new faith, it also placed you in immediate danger. That same night in Natchez, someone fired five pistol shots and both loads of a double-barreled shotgun through the window. When Jones called for a Holiness convention in June of 1897, a circular, purporting to have come from Jackson's "SIMON PURE BAPTISTS," ordered Jones and his "holy rollers" out of their church and out of town.

It was Reverend Mason who was elected leader of the new denomination—called the Church of God in Christ—and Mason who had the business sense to incorporate the church in Memphis, thus making it the first legally chartered Southern Holiness denomination. That meant that its ministers could perform marriages (and be paid for same), ride the railroads at discount rates, and get all the other benefits the clergy of older organized religions did. One astonishing result was that, at the height of the Jim Crow South, the Church of God in Christ drew white ministers looking to get out of their own brand of poverty and also unable to get licensed through the older denominations. Jones himself had once hated the white race; his grandparents had told him how they were whipped "till the blood ran down." But now, saved, he claimed he "loved that race as he loved others." While the congregations appear to have remained segregated, the clergy of the Church of God in Christ had a strikingly interracial membership.

The new church's most important break with Baptist dogma was over how one acquired faith. Baptism was not for newborns but for young adults who could knowingly accept the Spirit—and it alone was not enough. The second step to becoming a "saint" was to receive the Holy Ghost—to have a personal vision—the way C. P. Jones had. You were supposed to feel the actual, healing Power. No wonder the Church of God appealed to the poor and the disenfranchised; it was a vision without patience—a vision of God walking this earth—of miracles and healing and, above all, change. In the economic and social prison of the Black Belt, the Holiness movement attracted those most in need, most desperate.

One of the early converts was Hattie Cook. Hattie and her husband, Alex, were tenant farmers just outside of Jackson. Both had been born in Mississippi right after the Civil War, and their parents had been born there, too, as slaves. The couple was married in 1887, and Hattie had had a child every two years since. That November of 1897, not long after the Reverend Jones held his first Holiness convention, Hattie had given birth to her sixth child, a boy they named Charles. The Cooks, like almost all their immediate neighbors and three-quarters of all the Negro farm families in Mississippi, lived as best they could under the sharecropping system. They owned no land. While the tenant families might show some small profit come fall harvest time, they were inevitably penniless by Christmas—their savings spent at the company store, their food, clothes, mules, and plow bought from the Man on credit. While Hattie could read, her husband, Alex, couldn't, and the children worked in the fields as soon as they were old enough, so they were lucky if they got a month of schooling a year.

Hattie joined Mount Olive Church, founded by J.L.I. Conic, a young minister who would go on to become a bishop in the Church of God. Not only did all the Cook children from baby Charley up attend each Sunday, but Hattie became such a dedicated member she took to stopping by the Conic home to help out. Mother Cook—as she was known to the Conic children—washed, cleaned, did whatever was needed. Hadn't one of Hattie's fellow converts had her vision this way? Bent over, scrubbing, she'd become filled with the Holy Ghost when she'd asked the Lord to "cleanse her heart and make it as pure and white as the floor."

Hattie's husband, Alex, took a somewhat dim view of her devotion. "He wasn't saved," Charley would remember years later and then add with a laugh, "but he was a friend to the saved folk." He also couldn't have been very surprised: Hattie's whole family was religious, and her brothers were deacons in various churches. "All of them was good singers," Charley recalls. "And pray, man? They was some praying folks, I'm telling you!" Charley, however, would be the family's first full-fledged preacher. A smart, verbal boy, he was baptized and officially saved when he was eight—with Reverend Conic as his godfather.

Two years after Charley's entrance into the church, in 1907, the founding fathers had a falling out. Reverend Mason attended a revival meeting in California where, he would write, "a flame touched my tongue which ran down to me. My language changed and no word could I speak in my own tongue. Oh! I was filled with the Glory of the Lord!" It was his own, separate vision, and Mason became convinced that speaking in tongues was the one true sign of conversion. Back home, Reverend Jones didn't buy it, and the new church split over the issue (and, perhaps, over the more worldly question of sharing power). Mason turned out to be an even more charismatic preacher than Jones and an astonishing organizer. After the break, he kept the name, and his Church of God in Christ (or COGIC, as it's often known) went on to become the largest Negro Pentecostal sect in the world, with a massive temple and headquarters in Memphis. Jones reincorporated the original church a few years later as the Church of Christ (Holiness). It was quickly overshadowed by and often confused with Mason's COGIC.

Hattie and her children stayed loyal to Jones. Charley was particularly pious. At age seventeen, he left Jackson for his first job, making concrete posts for the railroad; seventy-five years later, he'd still remember it as an early test of his belief. Charley was a tall, thin kid who looked older than he was. The man who had come to Jackson to recruit laborers had promised Hattie her underage son would stay in his home, where the wife was a devout Holiness believer. But when Charley and sixteen other young men arrived in Kentucky, the man arranged to farm them out to a local boardinghouse run by a pair of "high yellow" sisters. Something about the setup didn't sit right with Charley, and he was adamant. "You told my momma you was gonna keep me at your house; you gonna keep me there. Or else I'm going back home. I'm not a dog, man! I got a home." Home, mother, and religion were what separated men from dogs, and a colored in Mississippi had to stand by that distinction, because there were a lot of people out there ready to tell you there *was* no difference.

Around 1918, Charley began working in Mississippi's so-called Delta area, a narrow strip of land that ran along the Mississippi River between Memphis and Vicksburg—not that far from Jackson. Over the centuries, spring floods had deposited up to thirty feet of topsoil here, and the warm, moist climate made it perfect for growing cotton. The Delta had become "cotton obsessed, Negro obsessed, and flood ridden," according to one historian, "the deepest South, the heart of Dixie, America's super-plantation." When Charley moved into the area, the World War had pushed cotton prices to record highs, and wages were up as much as 30 percent. As the famous bandleader and composer W. C. Handy put it, "Everybody prospered in that Green Eden."

Age twenty-one (for real this time), Charley found work in Shelby, near the Big Sunflower River, which flowed out of Clarksdale. One day around Christmas, he was helping a man build a chimney when a bunch of young girls walked by. One of them caught his eye— "They didn't get no prettier!"—and within twenty minutes, Charley remembers, he'd told her they were going to get married. Cook and his first wife, Rosetta Johnson, lived on a plantation fifteen miles outside of Clarksdale, between Sumner and Tutwiler. There he and his new brother-in-law sharecropped cotton, but Charley's main interest was still the church.

One day, he headed down the road to Greenville, where there was a revival. "That was my first church," Cook recalls, "where I preached my first sermon and everything." He spoke more than once, and he was good at it, with clear diction, a strong singing voice, and a way in the pulpit—a way of moving his hands gracefully in the air as if describing the very flight of angels—that drew crowds. Folk archivist Alan Lomax has recorded a sermon from the Delta area that gives a feel for the hypnotizing rhythm, repetition, and congregational call and response that made for a successful preacher.

Oh, Jesus (Oh, Jesus), my rock
In a weary land (Yes),
Our shelter
In a time of storm.
Please have mercy tonight (Yes)
Oh, Lord (MORE HIGH-PITCHED AGONY, SHRILLER), Lord (Lord),
Lord (Lord), Lord Jesus (SCREAM) (Howdy) (WOMAN SHOUTS)

I know you heard me one Sunday morning
When I was in sin.
(. . . FIRST STRONG RESPONSES FROM WOMEN, AS SHOUTING FERVOR
BEGINS)
You got on my side.
You cut loose my stammering tongue,
Set my heart on fire.
(LONG PAUSE, FILLED BY THE CLEAR-VOICED "OO-OO" OF WOMEN)

On and on it went—as much singing as talking—the crowd responding to every twist of phrase, every change in modulation as the young, sharp preacher stared them down or looked dramatically to the ceiling to beseech God. The whole point was to bring the Spirit into the room—to evoke the kind of experience that had overcome Reverend Jones in the parlor—and a good preacher went on building the tension till the women and men were up on their feet or rolling in the aisle, lost in a divine frenzy.

At the end of the revival, Cook recalls, the Reverend came up to speak to him. "They tell me the Lord done called you to preach?"

"Yeah. Here I am."

"Well, I've got something to offer you. . . . It take me five years to get sixty folks, and you done come in in three weeks now, and you got eighty some-odd. . . . I'm gonna get out of the way and let you pastor. . . ."

It was not only the Christian thing to do; it was also practical: the more people who came, the larger the offering. From Charley's side, preaching was one of the few prestigious colored jobs around. (Colored male jobs, actually: preachers were overwhelmingly men, their congregations preponderantly women.)

The Holiness movement was still spreading rapidly, and every little town, plantation, crossroads seemed to set up its own meeting. By 1937, there would be over eighty Negro churches in and around the Delta town of Clarksdale, most with fewer than eighty members. With more churches than preachers, it was common for reverends to go circuit-riding: Jones's organization allowed a preacher to pastor up to four different congregations. Charley was young and eager to travel, and his first expansion after Greenville was down to Leland, Mississippi, fourteen miles away. There he made a deal with the pastor: "You take all the money that's raised on your two Sundays, and I'll take all the money that's raised on my two Sundays." It was a preachers' battle, head to head, to see who could convert more souls. Cook spoke to local mothers, persuading them to come in and bring their brood; he had relatives in the area and brought them out to the church. "I went over there and fired the money up! I paid all the expense and everything; put the money in the treasury."

Now, Charley had two Sundays busy. Then one of the church bishops sent him up to Morehead, another twenty miles east of Leland. Morehead's congregation was just beginning—a mere four people— and they met in a local Baptist church. That first Sunday, they raised only thirty-five cents for the Reverend Cook. When the service was over, he walked across the street to the established Methodist church, where the pastor greeted him like an answered prayer.

"I asked the Lord to send me a preacher this morning, 'cause I'm not able to preach. Reverend?"

"Yes, sir?"

"Do you feel like preaching?"

Charley always felt like preaching. He reached an agreement: in return for speaking, he could invite the congregation to join his church. He then went back across the street to try and make the same bargain with the Baptist minister.

This was a little more difficult, since the Reverend Jones had, after all, been drummed out of the Baptist organization for his heretical Holiness beliefs. But Charley ran into a stroke of luck.

"Cook?" said the Baptist minister. "Cook? That name seem familiar to me. You wouldn't happen by any means be kin to Alex Cook and Hattie Cook?"

"No," Charley said, "they just be my father and mother."

The ice broken, the young man made his proposal, and the Baptist accepted. "I had the go-on," the Reverend Cook recalls, "and the sense to operate."

Soon the twenty-two-year old was pastoring three congregations, and all three had some cash in their treasuries. "Listen: You do right," Cook would recall years later, "God will bless you! I know all about it. And money? Well, money ain't never been no question with me. 'Cause, see, if it could be made, I'd go out there and make it."

The Reverend Cook didn't become rich preaching, but the work had a degree of prestige he couldn't find anywhere else. The Delta sometimes seemed to be nothing but cotton. In the fall, the ground was as white as snow, and across the dead-flat horizon, colored people pulled long canvas sacks as they separated the soft cotton from the sharp husks. It was backbreaking, dawn-to-dusk work, and almost everyone did it: mothers carrying babies, children old enough to walk, great-great-grandparents permanently stooped by a lifetime in the fields. The very air you breathed was cotton—wisps of it blew across the dirt roads—and the only break was Saturday night and Sunday morning: Saturday night to cross those flat fields in the dark and congregate in what they called a juke joint, someone's shack where there'd be corn whiskey and maybe a bluesman beating an old guitar. And Sunday morning when you met in church, sang the old hymns, and tried to imagine a different world. No wonder Charley loved to preach: a man who could call up something better in the middle of all this—now, he had something! Charley liked getting all dressed up, standing before a different church each Sunday, and feeling both the power of the Lord and the passion of the congregation. He liked the excitement, he liked the traveling, and he believed.

His belief helped sustain him over some hard times. Two months after his first son, Clemmie, was born, Rosetta died. The baby was sent to his maternal grandmother to be raised. Around this time—as the World War ended and many colored veterans returned home ex-pecting justice—racial repression grew worse. In 1919, there were twenty-five riots across the country in seven months. Chicago may have had the worst: a thousand families burned out of their homes and twenty-three people killed. But the South did its part. Mississip-pi's Governor Thomas Bilbo announced that the state's record number of lynchings was the only way to deal with "the attempt of the negro race to seek social and political equality." And in Charley's hometown, the *Jackson Clarion-Ledger* didn't mince any words: ". . . [T]his is a white man's country to be ruled by white men as white men see fit." The reaction of a lot of colored people was to leave. Between 1910 and 1920, Mississippi lost almost 150,000 Negroes to the North.

Charley decided to stay in Clarksdale for the time being. A few years after his wife's death, while preaching at a Holiness convention, he spotted a pretty teenager singing in the choir. Annie May Carl (or Carroll—the spelling differs depending on the document) was five years younger than Charley. Her mother had died in childbirth, and she had been raised by an aunt in Mound Bayou, Mississippi, where she worked as a cook in a private home. The courtship wasn't as lightning-quick as it had been with his first wife, but soon enough Charley had made the trip out to see her kin and propose. The two were married on November 15, 1923.

Annie May was a patient, devout, hard-working teenager who must have considered her preacher husband a catch. While he was lively, verbal, eager to make his way in the world, she was quiet and steady: a bulwark, as the church would put it. Both exhibited a kind of inner confidence hard to come by in a land where they were often treated as less than human. But Annie May had been raised in one of the South's foremost centers of racial pride.

Mound Bayou had been founded in 1887 as an all-colored town: a "self-conscious experiment in race building." There were about six hundred people in the town proper and four thousand, mostly cotton farmers, outside it. "Everything here was Negro," one native-born resident recalled, "from the symbols of law and authority and the man who ran the bank down to the fellow who drove the road scraper. That gave us kids a sense of security and pride that colored kids don't get anywhere else." Booker T. Washington often cited Mound Bayou as his race's brightest model for the future, and Teddy Roosevelt called it "an object lesson full of hope for the colored people."

Eventually—inevitably?—the experiment failed. By the time Annie May was school-age, the town's foremost symbol of prosperity, its mill, had been turned into a dance hall. And around when she got married—as cotton prices fell drastically in the early twenties— Mound Bayou looked like just another Delta town filled with tenant farmers and domestics. But a fierce sense of history and pride re-mained. To have been raised in Mound Bayou was to have lived in one of the few places in the South where colored people had at least felt the possibility of independence.

So, Annie May and Charles shared more than an unwavering reli-gious faith. And with their racial pride also came a belief in the im-portance of family. Annie May Cook would work hard her whole life making sure the home stayed together. In the rough, debilitating world of the Delta—where men left looking for decent wages and never returned, where women routinely died in childbirth, and chil-dren were expected to hold their own as soon as they were big enough to drag a cotton sack—the family often collapsed under the pressure. It's a testament to both of them that the couple proceeded to forge a home that protected and sheltered for almost forty-five years.

One of their first decisions was to take in an orphan. Willie B. was Annie May's first cousin. His parents had both died, and the three-year-old was being raised by his widowed grandmother over in Pine Bluff, Arkansas. "I didn't have no children," Reverend Cook recalls, "and I liked children." So, the newlyweds began their life together with a baby—and then proceeded to have more. Mary was the first-born, followed by Hattie (named after Charles's mother) and then Charles Jr.. The Cooks were a long way from rich, but Charley was managing to provide. By 1930, he listed himself as doing "public work" (probably on the roads), and he soon found himself a job as a houseboy for a white family and moved his growing brood into Clarksdale proper.

Chapter 2

amuel Cook, Charley and Annie May's fourth child, was delivered by a midwife in Clarksdale at 2:10 in the afternoon on January 22, 1931. This made three generations of Sam Cooks, including the Reverend Cook's older brother and one of his deacon uncles on his mother's side.

Sam's birthplace had begun as a sleepy town on the Sunflower River, but because Clarksdale didn't flood like the cities directly on the Mississippi, it had become a stop on the railroad line between New Orleans and Memphis. "We wasn't in no country," Sam's brother, Charles, recalls proudly. "We were in the city!" By the time Sam was born, Clarksdale was the center of the northern Delta. At the end of the week, the colored population would pour out of the giant plantations that surrounded the city and head for the colored part of town: a thriving, active city-within-a-city called the New World. Here the streets were lined with stores and bars, whorehouses and churches, ready to absorb what little money the sharecroppers made.

Out of these elements—a large colored population, a little spending money, the exhaustion of picking cotton and the exhilaration of cheap whiskey—came a music historians have called the Delta Blues. Legendary practitioners like Robert Johnson, Charley Patton, and Skip James were drawn—like the Reverend Cook—to the relative prosperity of Clarksdale. Here they traded licks and lyrics and played all-night dances, till the music reached a zenith of moaning double-entendres, secret protest, and contagious gut-bucket beats. Here a whole blues culture thrived, typified by the hoodoo symbolism of Robert Johnson supposedly becoming a guitar genius by going to the crossroads at midnight and striking a deal with the devil.

In the year Sam Cook was born, the music was starting to pass through the culture on thick black 78-rpm records. Portable recording units had been set up in Memphis as early as 1927, and "race" records like Patton's 1929 "Pony Blues" had surprised white label owners with how well they sold. The records captured the sound of King Cotton—the juke joints and the porch swings—just as that rural life was beginning to fade. But the social and cultural swirl of Clarksdale produced more than the "devil's music." Its twin was the church song: the spiritual.

"You ain't supposed to cross them," one bluesman told author William Ferris, ". . . something bad can happen to you. That's what you call going too far wrong. You can't serve the Lord and the Devil, too." Yet, Delta bluesmen as seminal as Patton, James, and Blind Reverend Gary Davis did just that, switching back and forth. During the late 1920s, recordings of sacred music outsold blues. Preachers were especially popular. The Reverend J. C. Burnett's "The Downfall of Nebuchadnezzar," for example, sold eighty thousand copies while the great blues singer Bessie Smith was selling about a quarter that many. Which helps explain why Blind Lemon Jefferson—author of blues hits like "Black Snake Moan" and "Match Box Blues"—also recorded as Deacon L. J. Bates and why blues pianist "Georgia Tom" Dorsey switched over to the religious field. A year after Sam was born, Dorsey composed his classic "Precious Lord" and helped usher in the modern gospel era. And the trade-off went both ways; by 1929, a sanctified minister would be recording on the Victor label with a jazz band. Often only the lyrics seemed to distinguish the sacred from the profane.

The Holiness sects played a special role in this mix. Down in New Orleans, at around this time, the young Mahalia Jackson noticed that her own Baptist congregations sang sweet, but when she really wanted to be moved, she hung around outside a Holiness church. "Those people had no choir or organ," the future queen of gospel music would recall. "They used the drum, the cymbal, the tambourine, and the steel triangle. Everybody in there sang, and they clapped and stomped their feet, and sang with their whole bodies. They had a beat, a rhythm we held on to from slavery days, and their music was so strong and expressive. It used to bring tears to my eyes."

The Reverend Cook's churches would have been no exception. Not only was he a fine singer, but Reverend Jones's vision in the parlor had not been forgotten. The founding father was still writing hymns, still sending them out to his pastors, still advocating his "Ministry of Music." Because the Holiness movement was a new beginning, it threw away the musical restrictions imposed by the Baptists. The cymbals, drums, and tambourines were let into the Holiness churches specifically to produce that rhythm that brought on ecstatic visions. So, at the same time a reverend like Charles Cook might denounce the devil's music, his own church was relying heavily on a hand-clapping, foot-stomping beat. To the outside observer, the height of a Spirit-raising service looked a lot like a juke joint on a particularly hot Saturday night.

Sam Cook grew up in the middle of all this. Annie May carried the nursing baby to church, and as she sang in the choir, one of his older sisters held the infant in a room pulsing with sound. The streets were nearly as loud. The Cooks didn't go down to the clubs on Issaqueena Street—not a reverend's family—but all you had to do was go to market to hear the vendors singing the praises of fresh vegetables and catfish, the blind musicians playing guitar on the corner, the preachers leading an impromptu hymn for whoever would stop and join in. It's no wonder, then, if Sam's father can't remember a time the boy didn't sing. "Where I lived," says the Reverend, "I had a paper-shell pecan—I had two trees in my backyard. That boy would get him some sticks . . . under the shade tree; he'd get him a lot of sticks and throw them about. And then he'd sing to them sticks! . . . He was just a kid; he was a child! . . . Didn't nobody teach him no singing. He was born with that gift."

The Cooks were renting a place at 2303 7th Street in what was known as the Brickyard section of Clarksdale. The house was typical of the area: a one-family shotgun, long and narrow, with a porch in the front, a little backyard with the pecan trees, an outhouse. There was no running water. All Clarksdale's coloreds lived east of the railroad tracks; Brickyard housed what there was of a Negro middle class, even if it was, as one historian puts it, "more by education and attitude than by money."

Here, the Reverend Cook was a well-known, respectable member of a community that included teachers and shopkeepers. As he headed toward work, it would be "Good morning, Reverend" and a polite "Yes, sir" from the children he'd pass. Compared to other Mississippi cities, Clarksdale was considered liberal, but once he crossed to the white side of town, the Reverend Cook became "Charley" or "boy." There he was supposed to address a white as "sir" or "ma'am," avoid eye contact, and get off the sidewalk when they walked by. Any lapse could lead directly to jail, and jail could lead anywhere. In the clinical language of a sociologist of the period, "lynching or the possibility of lynching is a part of the culture pattern."

The Reverend Cook's job as a houseboy was a relatively prestigious one. The man he worked for, Edwin John Mullens, was an embodiment of the fortunes to be made off cotton—and off those who picked it. At the height of Mullens's prosperity, he'd had five thousand acres in cotton and been "rated for above a million dollars in his assets." The Mullens house at 2410 4th Street in northwestern Clarksdale was only a few blocks from where the Cooks lived, but the contrast was striking. The fifteen-room Victorian mansion had bathrooms upstairs and down, and hardwood floors, and was stuffed with fine imported furniture. Off to the side was a fifty-by-ninety-foot swimming pool complete with brass hardware and toy submarines, a "natatorium" that had cost the millionaire $10,000 in 1918. It was a world of cars shipped in from England and hand-tailored silk shirts, where colored houseboys crept into the big, drafty bedrooms early in the morning to light coal fires lest any of the Mullenses should wake in a chill. One of those houseboys was Charley Cook—still a servant to King Cotton but once removed, at least, from the backbreaking fields.

As it turned out, the prosperity the Mullenses represented was more fleeting than it looked. In a one-crop economy, a price drop could spell disaster. One fall, when his son was out East to pick up one of those imported cars, Mullens had to wire him to take the bus home: their fortune had been lost. The Depression stunned Clarksdale, and it was particularly difficult for the colored population. Despite the migration North, more than three-quarters of the nation's Negroes were still in the South, the vast majority tenant farmers, living without electricity, their children going to school in run-down, overcrowded shacks where they read from a few tattered and ancient books.

So, as his toddler son sang under the pecan trees, the Reverend Cook got ready to leave 2303 7th Street and the South. The reason was simple—he wanted to better himself—and the destination obvious. By this time, Annie May had given birth to another son, L.C., and was pregnant with a sixth child they'd named Agnes. "I decided . . ." the Reverend Cook begins and then corrects himself: "Well, the Lord told me to come to Chicago. . . . I left Clarksdale with thirty-five cents in my pocket. . . . I had a car, I had a hog—and I sold all of that and left the money with my wife. And I and another preacher hoboed all the way up here. . . . We just caught trucks that hauled grocery, you know. We'd catch a truck and go as far as the truck went."

The two preachers weren't alone. The roads were crowded with colored families heading north. They poured into Chicago from Mississippi and all over the South. Between the end of the First World War and the start of the Second, the city's colored population nearly tripled. Some came cold, but most had family or friends who'd already made the trip. You arrived, as Charley Cook did, fresh from the country, awed by Chicago's skyline and the miles of low, teeming neighborhoods that stretched away from the lake. Whether you hoboed or took the train that dropped you at 12th Street, you eventually found your way to the neighborhood they called Bronzeville.

When the complexions got darker, the buildings more crowded, the smell and sounds more familiar, you knew you'd made it. An eight-mile-long, mile-and-a-half-wide city-within-a-city (or, more accurately, town-within-a-city, because the country folk brought a lot of the farm with them), Bronzeville held 90 percent of the colored population. It was the first major Negro urban center in the United States.

Reverend Cook came with connections. The Church of Christ (Holiness) had been firmly established in the center of Bronzeville for almost two decades. A prayer meeting had started back at the time of the World War; within a couple of years, the congregation had grown enough to move into a building at 3243 Cottage Grove Avenue. Under the leadership of the Reverend William Webb—a charismatic preacher who'd been converted to the faith by C. P. Jones himself—the church eventually bought what was known as the Christ Temple Cathedral at 44th Street and St. Lawrence. It was an imposing brick building that cost the then enormous sum of $55,000. So the Reverend Cook had a local Holiness community to plug into, and he was also connected at the national level. Charley's godfather, J.L.I. Conic—the man whose house in Jackson Mother Cook had cleaned—had become vice president under Jones and one of five national bishops.

Soon enough, Reverend Cook had been made an assistant pastor of Christ Temple. He also found work. Like three-quarters of the colored men in Bronzeville, he ended up doing unskilled labor: long, hard hours in Chicago's stockyards. Charley—now pushing forty—felt lucky to find it. He took a quick trip back to Clarksdale, and, with the Depression raging, made the move to bring his family North. They landed at 33rd and State Street—Bronzeville's Broadway—and soon moved a couple blocks north to an apartment in the Lenox Building at 3527 Cottage Grove Avenue.

The Lenox Building was a solid three-story brick structure, one of hundreds that had gone up around the turn of the century to house stockyard workers. Though the area had changed from suburban to working class, it was still mostly white. In 1929, a family named the Murphys lived in what would become the Cooks' building; their neighbors were the Levinskys and the Shapiros and the Kohns. But by the time the Cooks arrived, the Southern migration had changed all that. "Something of the community's past grandeur still remains," a local "fact book" commented, "but it is fast disappearing under the blight of economic decadence." Across the street from the Cooks, Ellis Park was seen as a symbol of this slide: "once a promenade for the elite . . . but now a playground for Negro children."

Sam Cook was one of those children. At five and six years old, he used the park as a backyard, skipping rope and playing ball with his brothers and sisters. They knew all the local shopkeepers, and everyone knew them. There was a grocery store downstairs at 3527, Daniels's cleaners up the block, and then Nezbitt and Wallington's printing shop. Families like the Cooks lived above these mom-and-pop operations, and nothing much happened on that corner of Cottage Grove that someone didn't observe and comment on. A local can remember Herbert Daniels coming out of his cleaning establishment to swat a sassy child's butt; never mind whose child.

Objective statistics of the time make the area sound miserable: the people who lived around Ellis Park earned less than folks in other parts of the city, were more likely to get syphilis and TB, received substandard educations, were more likely to get in trouble with the law, and died younger. Cottage Grove and the surrounding neighborhood had the city's highest proportion of families on relief—40 percent—and half the people packed into little apartments like the Cooks' were getting some kind of government aid. But as one local put it, "We didn't know we were poor until 1960." While the Cook children had little to no money in their pockets, neither did any of the other kids. The Reverend Cook drew a decent wage—better than he'd ever heard of in Clarksdale—and Mrs. Cook made sure the kids were washed, well dressed, and fed.

One of the distinct advantages to living at 3527 Cottage Grove was that Doolittle Elementary School was just down the block. All Sam had to do was cross the street and follow the crowd of giggling, bright-faced children into Doolittle's red-brick entranceway. The elementary school was hopelessly overcrowded and understaffed; during the years Sam went there, it had to run on two shifts—one from eight till noon and another till four. Although it served a population that was 85 percent colored, thirty-one of its thirty-three teachers were white. But compared to the school-shacks the Reverend Cook had grown up with in Jackson, compared to what was available in Clarksdale at that time, Doolittle Elementary was paradise. The nationally known *Chicago Defender* had used pictures of schools like Doolittle as a prime lure to get families to move North. All the Reverend and Mrs. Cook needed to know was there was indoor plumbing, a playing field, a separate desk for each student. They made Sam and all the children go faithfully, pay attention, and learn.

While there was some fooling around at Doolittle and some hooky-playing, Sam's parents were too serious about education and the community was too close-knit for him to get in much trouble. As one contemporary recalls, "In church on Sunday, your teacher was over there, and your mom was here, and the preacher was there, and the policeman was in the back row!" It was at Doolittle that Sam learned the neat, careful printing he used all his life. It was there that he got his first chance to sing a solo—during a school program in the fifth or sixth grade: "And boy," he'd later recall, "did I have stage-fright!" And it was at Doolittle that he made his first friends and had his first schoolboy crush. The friends he would continue to stay in touch with as long as he lived. The sweetheart was one of the pretty Campbell twins, both with quick smiles and flashing brown eyes. Two decades later, Barbara Campbell would become Sam's second wife.

As far as the Cooks were concerned, however, church was where Sam got his most important education. Within about a year of his arrival in Chicago, Reverend Cook was made pastor of a small congregation in Chicago Heights. Christ Temple Church (Holiness) had been founded in 1919, and in the eighteen years since, it had had—by the Reverend Cook's count—seventeen preachers. "The preachers couldn't do nothing with them!" Among them had been J.L.I. Conic; now, as bishop, Conic helped make his godson pastor.

The small Chicago Heights congregation had been meeting in a basement at 1610 Shields Avenue. "I worked up to one hundred and twenty-five [people]," Reverend Cook says proudly. "I filled the church up. You had to be sure you come there on time if you wanted a seat; if you didn't, you'd have to stand around the wall!" Under Reverend Cook's pastorship, the congregation built its two-story wooden church—the cornerstone bears his name—and he kept them busy. There were weekday services, prayer meetings, Sunday school, and a young people's department. The Reverend commuted the sixty-mile round trip from Cottage Grove. For Sunday service, he'd bring Annie May and the kids; all of them sang in the choir.

Because the Church of Christ modeled its service on the Baptist, what happened in Chicago Heights was a lot like what went on at the larger West Point Church right across the street from where the Cooks lived. (When the Cook children didn't make it down to their father's church, they sometimes attended West Point.) The day began with a 6:00-A.M. prayer service, followed by Sunday school at nine. Dressed in his best clothes, Sam would sit with his sisters and brothers in absolute silence and be drilled in the Good Book. There was no giggling, no fidgeting, just an hour and a half of concentrated learning. At eleven, the main service began with a devotion—the congregation singing a song or two, a reading of scripture, and a prayer. Then Sam would rise with the rest of the choir and sing a few special selections. Following that, the Reverend Cook would preach, and Sam would watch the congregation amen his father's every word. In the evening—after a home-cooked meal provided by the church ladies—there would be youth programs, and at eight, a final night service.

It was a long day, but there was nothing special about it. By the end of the Second World War, some 65,000 of Bronzeville's 300,000 people were in church Sunday morning; 60,000 kids attended Sunday school. "Rows of automobiles, freshly polished, line the streets around all the larger churches, and many of the smaller ones," an observer writes. " 'Church mothers,' their little gray caps perched on their heads and secured by chin straps, mingle around the door with the younger folk clad in their stylish Sunday best." For Sam—as for many of his neighbors—the church was the center of the community.

It was there he learned how a man should and shouldn't behave, and it was there he got the education he cared most about—his musical education.

"I guess he'd been singing all his life," recalls Sam's brother Charles. "From the time, I guess, he could talk. He loved to sing! He just had a pretty tenor voice." Around the start of the Second World War, the Cook kids decided to form their own group. Teenagers Mary and Charles sang lead, while the small ones—L.C., Hattie, and Sam (aged about ten)—harmonized behind them. Sam was "just a tenor singer," Charles remarks. "He always wanted to lead, but we wouldn't let him. . . ." They called themselves, appropriately enough, the Singing Children, and at first they just appeared at their father's church. If the Reverend Cook visited some other congregation on church business, he'd sometimes carry the children with him, but it was mostly around Chicago Heights and in Harvey.

As they got better, the Singing Children would go across the street to West Point when a gospel program was going on. People would see the Cook kids—all dressed up and respectable and eager in their pew—and invite them up to do a number. It was usually a spiritual like "Swing Down, Sweet Chariot," some old song that everybody knew, and they sang it in a respectful, slightly old-fashioned style. But they got over. It was more than just their youth, because Bronzeville was flush with talented kids singing together. And it was more than their good looks, though Sam, especially, was a disarmingly cute kid. No, as Albertina Walker recalls (she grew up on Cottage Grove and would go on to found the legendary gospel group the Caravans), "They all *could* sing!" Eventually, they even got a manager, a friend of their father's, and began arranging programs and charging admission: ten cents a ticket. The five of them might take home $12 or $14 to split among themselves. As well as being the Lord's work and something both Cook parents approved of, it brought in real money.

"My family was poor," Sam would admit years later, and then, choosing his words carefully, add, "but my father provided me with all the necessities. He tried to raise us the right way." The Reverend Cook soon left the stockyards and found himself a better job out at the Reynolds Metals plant in McCook, Illinois. It was grueling work—in charge of two furnaces, skimming off hot metal—but it was a union job, CIO, and the Reverend soon held a union position. The Cook children had clothes, food, a roof over their heads. Anything more than that was luxury. As one visitor to Cottage Grove put it: "It was a slum neighborhood. That's all to that. [The Reverend Cook] wasn't a maneuverer. He was trying to be an honest man, and he had a whole lot of mouths to feed. . . . He could have done better if he had have been crooked. But he just wasn't."

It was a source of pride that his wife didn't have to get a paying job. Sam's mother washed and fed and cleaned up after an apartmentful of kids. A good cook, she never seemed to go too far from the sink and the stove. She had grown into a large woman, seemingly as wide as she was tall, and her sharp eyes now glittered in a big round face. The kids thought she looked like an Indian squaw, and, in later years, Sam would sometimes wrap a blanket around her shoulders and laugh at the resemblance. Annie May was the reassuring center of home life, and she spoiled the children as best she could, until Sam became something of a momma's boy: praised, a little pampered, self-confident beyond his years. With that came a clear set of values. As one of his friends observed, "His religious background, his training, his father's teaching—they were always present with him. Whether he did what he taught him or not. It was always with him."

Sam literally walked a straight line: down the stairs of the Cottage Grove apartment, past the West Point Baptist church, to Doolittle Elementary, and back. In Bronzeville, in the midst of the Depression, poor but honest parents like the Cooks would tell their children that all they needed could be found in these institutions: the home, the church, the school. But the truth was you barely survived walking that line. You got the necessities, as Sam put it. If you wanted even a little more, you had to stray. "We used to tear down fences," Sam would laugh, years later, "and sell them back to the people for wood." Or better yet, you could sing for your supper.

As a grade-schooler, walking home from Doolittle, Sam strayed —or, rather, lingered—at the corner of Cottage Grove and 35th. The streetcars changed there, so you usually got a good crowd of people. And if you waited till closing time, there would be even more: factory workers and women coming back from being maids and cooks in the white people's houses. Sam would climb up on a tub he'd lug to the streetcar stop—maybe have a friend bang on a guitar—and he'd sing. Not church songs—not the Christian music that the Singing Children performed—but the pop tunes of the day: "I Don't Want to Set the World on Fire," "Because," "I'm in the Mood for Love." The crowd was amused by the little kid with the sweet, thin tenor and the wide smile. Then he'd launch into his big tune, "South of the Border," number one on the Hit Parade in 1939. "His eyes would light up," according to a later article in the *Chicago Defender*, "and from the swing of his small body, persons waiting for their streetcars knew he was enjoying his singing as much as they were and would toss him an extra few pennies or even a nickel."

From there, it was a short step into Redmond's. The tavern sat right at the end of Sam's block. In the morning, when he passed it going to school, Redmond's would be quiet and shuttered, as if the building itself had a hangover. But at dusk, when Sam would sneak in, the men and women would be settling down for their first cold beer, and the jukebox would be pouring out Duke Ellington, Billie Holiday, the big-band sounds of the time. Sam would have to sing over the records and the chatter, but here, with people's money already out on the bar, it was a better payday. The slender, smooth-skinned boy would go from stool to stool, table to table. It wasn't the straight line Reverend Cook had in mind—home, church, and school—but it was better than stealing wood.

The Reverend Cook didn't consider himself a stern father, certainly not compared to the way he'd been raised. "I'd let them go to a moving picture two days of the week, when there wasn't any school . . . but, boy, on a Sunday, they were in church!" And to Mrs. Cook, Sam was just a "wonderful boy. As a youngster," she recalled, "he was sweet and thoughtful, always doing things for me. Whenever he made any money, he would come home and offer it to me before spending a penny." Nobody had to know exactly how he made each penny. Sam learned early on that if you went to church, if you didn't talk back, if you treated your elders respectfully—with a yes-sir-no-ma'am politeness straight from the Deep South—it smoothed over a lot. The Reverend Cook was an honest, God-fearing man, but he was a practical one, too. A little extra change helped; the streets of Chicago offered lots of worse temptations than singing for pennies; and Sam was a good boy.

In 1942, age eleven, Sam Cook was baptized at his father's Christ Temple Church. Having announced that he would take Christ as his personal savior, Sam rose that day and, with the elders shouting "Amen!" and the family proudly looking on, was immersed by his father in a large tub at the front of the altar. Sputtering, a little scared no doubt, Sam came out of the water a member of the Church of Christ (Holiness). In the credo of that church, he was not yet a "saint"—to be a saint you had to cut yourself loose from the world and follow Christ—but he was on his way.

The Holiness movement—Reverend Mason's COGIC in particular—was continuing to grow spectacularly, especially among the urban poor. Basically conservative, it could offer its believers familiar, down-home values and still be flexible enough to respond to the shock of what people were beginning to call the ghetto. But even in the midst of this religious explosion, the Reverend Jones's Church of Christ (Holiness) was going through a crisis. Jones was getting old and sick; he would attend his last national convention in 1944. Reverend Cook's mentor, Bishop Conic, had died in 1939, and the church as a whole was entering what its historian called "the beginning of the end of [the] fellowship."

Not long after his son's baptism, the Reverend Cook went to Cleveland to pastor a church there. When the family returned to Chicago, after a year or so, the Reverend's work changed for good. He became what the church called a "national evangelist." It meant he didn't have his own congregation but went from town to town, church to church, preaching revivals, setting up special "soul-saving" meetings. It was more like the old days back in Clarksdale, when he'd stormed into town and out again, a visiting celebrity.

According to Bishop Conic's son, M. R. Conic, who had also become a bishop of the church, Charley became "a kind of a . . . wanderer. . . . People liked him! That's what saved him, carried him as far as he went. . . . He'd show up periods of time, and you'd wonder: where had he been? He was just kind of a freelance fellow." Once again, Charley was free to ramble, making his own money based on whatever the church raised while he was there preaching. As often as he could, he took his family with him. In the beginning, that was a shock to the churches, because it was their responsibility to house and feed a visiting evangelist. The Reverend Cook would show up with his wife and seven kids, including the new baby, David. "I wouldn't mind," parishioners would say, "but all them children!" Soon enough, they learned that the Reverend Cook brought all his own food, that his wife made a first-rate meal, and that the children—the Singing Children—were an enormous asset to any revival.

"Brother, I made my money!" the Reverend laughs. "I took care of that church—all the expenses of that church—*and* my money! And I kept a car and everything." The Singing Children would warm up the congregation till they were primed and yelping, then the Reverend Cook would step to the pulpit and preach them toward Jesus— and generous donations. In the summer, when school was out, they'd travel as far as Washington, D.C., and California. "The road was just getting good," says Reverend Cook. "They done graveled them, and they just went to concrete them."

For Sam, entering adolescence, it was one big education. He watched how his father meeted and greeted. He learned how to behave with the deacons and the church ladies. And he studied how best to put over a song. Mary and Charles still wouldn't let him sing lead, but he worked on his harmonizing, and the kids got to where no other group intimidated them.

Well, almost no other group. The exception, according to brother Charles, was back in Chicago. One evening, the Singing Children went to the big church at 44th and St. Lawrence to hear and join in on a gospel program. The five Cooks sat together, primed and ready for their number. Then they heard the headliners: a male quartet called the Soul Stirrers that sang Thomas Dorsey's compositions and other gospel tunes with a sweet harmony and a light but absolutely insistent drive. Charles listened a little and then told the rest, "I'm not getting up there to sing tonight." The Stirrers had Old Man Harris fluting out the lead like a bird, J. H. Medlock trading raw shouts, and S. R. Crain driving the group along as he beat time with a clenched fist in his palm. "No, I'm not singing tonight." Sam turned from the quartet to his brother and back again. "Them Soul Stirrers," Charles remembers, "they come out of Texas; them Soul Stirrers was bad! We all was just amazed at that harmony they had. Could beat anything else we'd ever heard."

By the war years, Bronzeville had become the center of a new, evolving musical culture: an outgrowth of the northern migration. As author Joseph R. Washington notes, "It was only in the urban milieu that one could put together Holiness dogma, Pentecostal answers, black music, and the deepest depression into a whole shape and sound limited neither by tradition nor fears of being put down by wise fools or foolish wisemen. . . ." The city was home to the Soul Stirrers, Mahalia Jackson, Sallie and Roberta Martin, and Thomas Dorsey, just to name a few.

In addition to this gospel music, there was also a new kind of electrified blues and jumpy urban dance music. All Sam had to do was walk south on Cottage Grove from his house to pass some of the classier nightclubs: the Rhumboogie, El Grotto, Club Trianon. If he stood outside the door of the Macomba, for example—just a few blocks down from the Cooks' at 39th—he might hear the ultrasmooth Billy Eckstine, the young Ella Fitzgerald, or jazz tenorman Gene Ammons. Not that the Reverend Cook would have approved. The Macomba was a late-night place: "a hangout for pimps, whores, dope dealers, jazz musicians," said to be under the protection of Al Capone.

"The people are going astray," one reverend commented at the time. ". . . All [young people] think about is doing some kind of dance where they draw up like a cold cricket." But some pastors became famous for supposedly being able to "see" lucky numbers and passing them on to their congregation. And soon enough, entrepreneurs saw the potential in what was going on in the neighborhood. When it came to what Bronzeville called "clean" jobs, only the church, the post office, and the mortuary provided more than music. By 1948, the owners of the Macomba—a pair of Polish immigrants named Leonard and Phil Chess—would establish their own record label with offices at 52nd and Cottage Grove. Chess Records became famous by distributing the electrified blues of artists like Muddy Waters, Howlin' Wolf, and Little Walter. All this floated around Sam's neighborhood, as if the sound of Clarksdale had followed the Cooks north and settled on their block. Which, of course, it had.

Bronzeville's culture was in its own way just as isolated as Clarksdale's. When Sam stepped out the back of the Lenox Building, for example, he stood on the edge of the white community that clung to the turn-of-the-century mansions along Ellis and Lake Park Avenue. "You couldn't get over that way, really," says Sam's neighbor Albertina Walker. "All back from 39th on back to 35th, wasn't too many blacks on the other side of Cottage Grove." But if, on the other hand, Sam stepped out the front door, he entered a world almost exclusively colored. "The astonishing thing," one observer wrote, "is that segregation so severe could have sharpened steadily for thirty years." It wasn't quite so astonishing when you realized how hard some elements worked to keep it that way.

As Bronzeville had expanded, so had Chicago's Ku Klux Klan. By the time the colored population had reached 150,000, there were twenty "klaverns" with more than fifty thousand members of the "Invisible Empire" of white, native-born, adult male Protestants. The Klan had helped put into place "restrictive covenants": agreements, usually among neighborhood associations, to keep out the colored by promising not to sell or rent them either land or houses. Far from a fringe movement, this red-lining approach was endorsed by Illinois Bell, Commonwealth Edison, and Chicago's rapid transit company, among others. In 1927, a standard form had been created for city-wide use, and the policy would last for the next twenty years, stringing a kind of legal barbed wire around Bronzeville.

Sam grew up understanding that while he might make spare change singing at Redmond's, if he tried it a block east, he would be lucky if he was only thrown out. During the hot Midwestern summers, Cottage Grove crackled and people sat out on the wooden

porches that stretched like scaffoldings over the back of the tene-
ments. But if Sam and his friends wanted to swim in Lake Michigan,
they had to be careful to pick one of the colored bathing areas. Chicago's major race riot in 1919 had started when a colored boy had
crossed the black/white line at the 29th Street beach. Thirty-eight
people had ended up dead, and any kid with any sense knew that
nothing much had changed.

Interracial activities seemed "unnecessary and almost 'unnatural' "
to much of Bronzeville. It had become a city unto itself: a larger, less
deliberate version of Mound Bayou but with some of the same sense
of pride and self-sufficiency. While the restrictive covenants kept
them in, many didn't so much want out of the South Side as they
wanted the right to expand upon it. The war economy had broken
the back of the Depression; with the jobs had come hope. "The
quicker the war is over," the *Defender* had editorialized, "the sooner
this danger will be passed, and our strong virile youths can return to
help buttress the fight for our full rights." As Sam left Doolittle Elementary for high school, Bronzeville seemed rich with possibility.
The way author Richard Wright put it, the challenge of the times
was whether the Negro could "find a meaning in his humiliation and
make his slums and his sweat-shops his modern cathedrals out of
which will be born new consciousness that can guide him towards
freedom. . . ."

Chapter 3

Wendell Phillips High School was a ten-minute walk from Cottage Grove, down to Pershing Road and over. Getting there, however, was quite an achievement for Sam and the Cooks. Sociologists of the era called the South Side "essentially a community of sixth-graders." For Bronzeville families, sending a child through high school was something like sending one through college a generation later: it meant sacrificing a wage-earner for four years and banking on a future where what a child learned might actually be more important than skin color. Yet education was, in a lot of ways, the payoff to the move north, and Wendell Phillips had been a symbol of this dream since it opened in 1904. While you could still go through the entire system and never have a colored teacher, for Phillips to have *any* Negro teachers was a mark of distinction. A poll of students found general agreement that their segregated schools were "more satisfying" than integrated ones, and Sam's classmates remember Phillips as the pride of the neighborhood, its students highly motivated and disciplined.

Like Doolittle, the school had had trouble coping with the great influx of Southern migrants. A city report of the thirties had scored it lowest among the four high schools, "slightly above 'abandon all hope.' " In response, the city had built a trade school—DuSable High—to try to relieve some of the pressure, but Chicago's colored population grew by another 80 percent in the forties, and when Sam came to Phillips, it and DuSable combined had three thousand more children than their seating capacities. Phillips ran on double shifts—twelve periods a day—and still could barely cope with the crush.

Discipline was strict. One look at a portrait of the white principal, Mrs. Maudelle B. Bousfield, tells it all. Lips pressed tight, pince-nez over a sharp nose, sitting upright in a hard chair, "the First Lady of Phillips" had a stern, uncompromising look that brooked no nonsense. The counselor and senior teachers for Sam's class of 1948 were all white, mostly middle-aged, and 90 percent female. They were overworked and underpaid, and the simple fact is that many of them didn't want to be there. A study done four years after Sam graduated found that Chicago's public school teachers, as a group, felt that "all Negroes" were "lower-class . . . difficult to teach, uncontrollable and violent in the sphere of discipline, and morally unacceptable on all scores, from physical cleanliness to the spheres of sex and 'ambition to get ahead.' "

Sam, with his January birthday, was among the youngest in his class. Faced with this attitude from the teachers and the contradictory pressure from his parents to succeed, he all but disappeared into the mass of Wendell Phillips High. Many of his fellow students barely remember him. On the class hay ride, he sat alone, hardly speaking. "I had a real high shrill little voice then," Sam would recall. He sang with the a cappella choir, but doesn't seem to have been featured, and it wasn't till his junior year that he got to solo in glee club: "The First Noel" during the Christmas program. His teachers would remember him as a good student with a special interest in architectural drafting. He had a good eye, a steady hand, and the ability to make detailed, meticulous drawings. In his yearbook, the class poem imagines what everyone will have achieved by the far-off future of June 1965. While other children are named as potential bankers, doctors, and businessmen (and some of Phillips's graduates did go on to fulfill these promises), Sam Cook isn't even mentioned. And while the captions under other graduating pictures list achievements from class president to varsity football to debating society, Sam's simply says, "Bookroom helper—Draftsman."

Still, there are some signs of his personality. In the yearbook's list of unimaginable occurrences—like Joseph Mills growing taller than four feet nine and Janette Newell without her big belts—there's mention of Sam Cook "not being able to make a person laugh." The school records described Sam as "personable and aggressive," which—given the prejudices of his teachers—probably meant confident.

He had good reason to be. Outside of school, he was able to make people do a great deal more than laugh. By the time he graduated, Sam was leading one of the two or three top young gospel quartets in the city. He was mesmerizing crowds, sending grown-ups into fits of religion, and drawing flocks of young girls with his smooth voice. That none of this shows up either in his fellow classmates' recollections or in the chatty yearbook may be the most revealing aspect of those years. Apparently, along the straight line of church, family, and school, Cook was already perfecting an ability to maintain discreetly separate lives. The cathartic church programs were a long way from the rooms full of chalk dust and stern white teachers. You disguised the one from the other with the power of personality, that contagious smile of his, the ability to make people laugh.

By Sam's sophomore year, the Singing Children had disbanded. Charles Cook, Jr., went into the service, and sister Mary had decided she was "too old to be getting up there singing: you know how girls will change." She would soon marry a Sunday school teacher from across the street at West Point. Sam may have been ready for the family group to fold. He not only yearned to sing lead, but felt adolescence kicking in. The way he remembered it, he "noticed the girls and . . . left the group to return to his singing in the streets. . . ."

It wasn't anything formal. Sam, Johnny Carter, James "Dimples" Cochran, and some other kids got together and "tried to sound like the Ink Spots. We would sing around places and have fun," according to Cook. The Ink Spots were crooners who had taken church harmonies and refined them to slide smoothly into the pop market. As Johnny Carter (who went on to sing with the Flamingos and the Dells) puts it, "All of us sung more than one kind of music, but we all learned in church. That was the school—and the graduation—and the college!" "Dimples" would eventually take the "sepia croon" of the harmonies and cut classics like 1954's "Goodnight Sweetheart, Goodnight," with the Spaniels. "We used to sit down in the basement at night," Carter remembers, "and tell jokes by the furnace: all kinds of jokes that little boys ain't supposed to tell! Then we'd strike up some tunes: pop or whatever. All we needed was a lead singer and then the baritone—or whoever had the lowest voice—sung bass. . . . We sung everywhere."

It was a time of change for the Cooks, what with Mary and Hattie coming of age, Charles in the service, and the adopted son, Willie, in his own apartment. They moved just around the corner to 724 East 36th street: a half block closer to the lake. And it was a time of change for Bronzeville, too; the streets Sam and his buddies hung out on were getting tougher and tougher. When the war ended, men returned to reclaim jobs, and a new wave of immigrants arrived. South Side housing, built to hold 110,000, was crammed with triple that number. Apartments were being divided up with flimsy partitions; many had no running water. Flash fires would tear through the tiny rooms, and there was a growing plague of rats and disease.

The year the Cooks switched apartments, there were large-scale housing riots in Chicago, and the following summer thousands of whites gathered around the Fernwood Park Homes between 98th and 110th streets, where they beat colored people at random and overturned cars. At least one Negro community organization offered explicit resistance: "We are out to fight to the finish to see that Hitler who has been defeated in the war will not be victorious here at home." As the violence increased and a new, less patient postwar generation emerged, Bronzeville's transplanted rural values began to change, too.

About the time the Singing Children broke up, Sam joined the Junior Destroyers: more a social club, he would later insist, than a gang. Compared to the guns and drugs to come, that was certainly true. On the other hand, he admitted, "We used to fight quite a bit," and "We had to belong to a club to go to school." All the Cook boys had their "clubs": Charles was a member of the older, stronger Dea-

cons, and L.C. was in the Nobles. Johnny Carter, also a Junior De-
stroyer, shrugs off the violence. "They wasn't a lot of firearms and
things in those days. If you went into a fight, you fought with your
bare hands or maybe a knife fight—every once in a while, a little zip
gun or something. Yeah, everybody had their little territory." And
Jerry Butler, another of Sam's contemporaries, agrees. "What else
were you going to do? We weren't robbing and stealing or sticking
people up or anything. When we got together, it was to sing and
have a good time and play basketball and all that. But we also had
to take care of ourselves in case anybody wanted to get bad. So we
wore our little jackets."

Sam hung with the Junior Destroyers, sang on the streets, and
flirted with the girls, but his main ambition was musical, and it was
too large to be satisfied by the glee club or his Ink Spots imitation.
He needed something like the Singing Children but more professional, and, in a neighborhood full of kids forming and disbanding
groups, it wasn't long before he got his chance.

The way Sam told it, he was standing in his living room, singing
to himself, and four neighborhood kids happened to hear him. They
rang the Cooks' doorbell to be introduced. Others put the meeting
on the street, around 36th and Rhodes: the route home from Phillips.
In that version, Sam happened on a group of kids working on their
a cappella gospel harmony. They didn't sound bad—not bad at all—
and when he joined in, the mix was an instant pleasure. "They just
all fell in love with him singing," says his brother Charles.

Lee Richardson sang lead for the group, his brother Jake bass,
Creedell Copeland was the baritone (his father coached the boys), Gus
Treadwell was the tenor, and Marvin Jones second baritone. Taking
on Sam meant adding a second lead singer, but that wasn't as radical
a move as it sounded. After all, Chicago's premier quartet—those
Soul Stirrers who had stunned the Singing Children—already had
that alignment.

Sam took to the quartet style immediately. A couple years older than
the other boys, he brought a confidence (some might even have said an
arrogance) and the experience of his time on the road with his father.
This was different from the Singing Children, however. They'd been a

"gospel" group—like the famous Roberta Martin Singers and the Robert Anderson Singers: a style that mixed male and female voices and often used piano or organ accompaniment. Quartets, on the other hand, sang with no instruments, and the vast majority were male.

The gender difference was important. Gospel groups reflected the largely female church congregations. When someone like Roberta Martin came forward, the sisters heard one of their own; many found gospel groups more intensely religious—and more innovative. The quartets, like the Soul Stirrers or their chief rivals the Famous Blue Jay Singers (whose office was right around the corner from the Cooks at 3609 Cottage Grove), functioned more like male preachers: cocks in the henhouse. They tended to dress sharp, turn a harmony till the church ladies squealed, and generally strut their stuff. "Believe it or not," declares the Reverend Sammie Lewis, who began his gospel career with the Roberta Martin Singers, "there is a gap. . . . The gospel singers stayed with the gospel singers, and the quartet singers stayed with the quartet singers."

Sam's new group decided to name themselves after their local Highway Baptist Church and became the Teenage Highway QCs. Why QC? "Nobody knows," Sam shrugged, years later. "We just added it to Highway. We had planned to figure out something for the Q and the C too, but after we got to singing we forgot all about it." And they did get to singing. The QCs were a little too young to think about going professional—they were all in high school, after all—but there were still bragging rights and the female attention that came with them. Like the older quartets, the boys stood in a line and relied on straight, heart-rending a cappella harmony behind Sam's and Lee's leads. The key was practice. They'd rehearse a couple of hours in the evening, two or three times a week—and then catch brief moments on the street. When big brother Charles came out of the service, he was shocked by how far the kids had come and how fast. "He told me one night to come go hear him sing. So I said okay. I went to hear him, and I was really amazed that he could really sing like he did! 'Cause he had me in tears, almost."

Soon, the QCs were part of the quartet circuit: Ebenezer, St. Paul, Church of God in Christ, 44th Street Baptist Church, Tabernacle

Baptist Church. "All the groups that came out of Chicago," recalls Spencer Taylor, then with the Holy Wonders, "they basically ran the same little trail: round and around." And Lou Rawls, traveling the same route with his group, the Kings of Harmony, laughs over "our little programs. Naturally it would be for the collection, whatever they'd take up. You might have five guys in the group and the collection would turn out to be twenty dollars. But, of course, we were kids. That was big money." The ultimate proving ground for the young quartets was 3838 South State Street: Quartet Headquarters.

3838 was a storefront that the newly formed National Quartets Union had transformed into a meeting hall. The union had been started by the city's top quartets: the Blue Jays and the Soul Stirrers, whose lead, R. H. Harris, served as its national president. It was patterned after the Baptist choir convention and had a similar aim: to "professionalize" the groups. The annual meeting featured workshops that trained the quartets in "how to meet people, how to address an audience, how to perform, how to dress, and, really, how to sing"—as well as how to manage money and make booking contracts. All of that, while helpful, was a little beyond the Teenage QCs. For them, the union meant 3838 South State, where they got to face off against their contemporaries. "Yep," says Leroy Crume, member of the Crume Brothers at the time, "when you get good enough you can sing with the big boys: you can go to 3838. That was a step up!"

Lou Rawls remembers a "Battle of the Quartets" every Thursday night. "You didn't win nothing. And you never knew who won, 'cause it wasn't even put on like a contest. The people would come 'cause there was *good* stuff!"

3838 could pack in around two hundred people. For an advertised program, there might be a seventy-five-cent charge at the door. But "where we'd get our pay," Crume adds, "is from the people enjoying us. Even if it was our concert and we took an offering, none of the money would go in our pockets anyway. It would all go towards uniforms or some kind of expenses: traveling around here and there." The uniforms—according to Rawls—were a status symbol. "You got five dudes comin' in, none of them over eighteen, all dressed *alike*?

That's big-time, man! We even had shoes alike. Of course, the first time it rained, it was over for the shoes. The soles split in half and they started crying. They called them West Side Specials. And don't let your suit get wet. Your pants would run up your leg."

The QCs made it to 3838 South State pretty quickly, considering their age. Within the first year, they were being asked up to sing and were clearly holding their own. In fact, Crume used to hate to see them coming. "What would happen is the Crume Brothers would have a concert and then just up pops the QCs! . . . Sam was so durn popular! The Crume Brothers, without Sam coming around, we had the young girls, you know. But when Sam came around, oh man! That was it. Everybody flocked to Sam: 'Sam Cook! Sam Cook!' I just didn't like that!" Occasionally, members of the big-time groups would drop by Quartet Headquarters, but mostly it was the better-known locals, and the competition was fierce. The more ambitious began to see their goal as more than just bragging rights. "We were, I guess you'd say, the farm team," says Rawls. "Like in baseball. . . . We were considered like the replacements. At least, that's what we were saying!"

Sam was one of the ambitious ones. As he got closer to graduating from Wendell Phillips, he was determined to build on the attention he got at 3838, and the way to do that, all agreed, was to get the group a trainer. It wasn't about originality, after all. There was a long tradition of quartet singing in the city, and teenagers apprenticed themselves to it—the same way a young bluesman like Muddy Waters studied under Son House. Trainers were older men, members of established groups, who could show you the ins and outs of the music, and, because the QCs wanted the best training around, they naturally turned to the Soul Stirrers—who not only ruled Chicago but ranked as one of the two or three top quartets in the country.

The Stirrers had begun as a teenage gospel group back in 1922 at the Mount Pilgrim Baptist Church in Trinity, Texas. When a choir trainer described the eleven-year-old boys as soul-stirring, their leader, Senior Roy Crain, had latched onto the name. That group eventually broke up, and when the Depression hit, Crain headed south to Houston, where he managed to get work in the rice mills.

There, in 1933, he met a quartet that needed a baritone, and S.R. agreed to join with one proviso: they take that Soul Stirrer name.

Around this time, quartet singing had begun to loosen and change. From slave gangs to chain gangs, black people had strung together harmonies so tight and complex you could almost see them in the air—almost lean on them. In the twenties and thirties, while the posture remained the erect, responsible one of a God-fearing churchman and the delivery clear and dignified, the jubilee style had evolved. Quartets took the old hymns and swung them. It's the style that was adapted by early pop harmonizers like the Ink Spots and the Mills Brothers. The most famous jubilee singers, the Golden Gate Quartet, started coming down even harder on the beat, giving up some dignity for the sake of urgency and drive. As Willie Johnson, the founder of the Gates, explained the change to gospel historian Doug Seroff: "[T]he main churches that got to me were the Holiness churches, because they sang with a beat. And whenever I got around to training the group, I'd give our things a beat, upbeat it you know."

While some preachers saw it as sinful entertainment, the congregations loved what Johnson called this "vocal percussion." "It was just like a drumbeat but it had notes to it, it had lyrics to it you see. And you had different beats, you had different accents. Like a bunch of guys beating a tom-tom somewhere. . . . It all had to be done sharply and together, along with the harmony, we sang simple chords."

By the late thirties, according to one historian, "the entire country was fired up with groups of extraordinary power and quality," and the Soul Stirrers of Houston would prove to be one of the most powerful. Crain sang baritone, O. W. Thomas bass, Edward R. Rundless lead, and the Reverend Walter LeBeau tenor. When LeBeau started getting interested in preaching, they added A. L. Johnson. Johnson not only had managed his own group and knew the gospel highway, but—a great advantage in those hard times—he had a car to drive it. His addition rearranged the group. Johnson sang baritone (the part he knew from his former group), Crain took over tenor, and LeBeau became a second, high lead with Rundless. The double leads would revolutionize the quartet sound (so called not for the number of members but its four-part harmony).

Library of Congress field recorder Alan Lomax taped the Stirrers in 1936 and called their sound "the most incredible polyrhythmic music you ever heard." LeBeau, on the high lead, featured an earsplitting falsetto, while behind him, Crain and the others constructed a remarkably light, tight harmony. They hit the beat, no question, but with a crystal-clear touch. It was a distinctive sound, distinctively Texan, some thought, like the light feel fiddler Bob Wills incorporated into Western swing a decade later. Crain says it came about by mixing styles. Back in Trinity, with the first Stirrers, the boys had sung wherever they could; that meant going to the Sanctified church once a month and driving the songs home and then singing in a sweeter, more dignified style next Sunday in the Baptist church. The two approaches had eventually merged.

The Soul Stirrers became one of the first professional quartets. With the help of Johnson's car, they started going from town to town, depending on the donation plates for what little money they made. Gradually, the Houston members dropped away, and Crain replaced them with friends from up in Trinity. Jesse (J. J.) Farley took over the bass duties in 1936, and then when Rundless left to pastor, Rebert H. Harris took over the high lead role in 1937. That year the group moved its base to Chicago, where the Soul Stirrers' distinctive style met the new, bluesier gospel compositions of Dorsey and others. By 1938, record labels had caught on to the trend and were issuing fifty quartet records a year. The Stirrers cut a version of Dorsey's "Precious Lord," as well as R. H. Harris's "Walk Around," and the records helped increase the group's popularity. By 1940, the Stirrers were appearing on radio station WIND every Sunday morning.

But just as gospel seemed about to take off, the Second World War came. The Stirrers had toured all forty-eight states by then, but the war's recording and travel ban stopped the movement in its tracks. While Crain kept them together—adding baritone T. L. Bruster (yet another childhood friend from Trinity) and, in 1943, R. B. Robinson—the demand for the music built. Although the major labels (and the white world generally) didn't know or care about it, V-J Day was the beginning of a long-delayed surge in gospel music's popularity. At the same time Bronzeville was pushing at its edges—its people able to afford and beginning to demand decent housing—there was an increased market for what was called "race music": blues, pop, and gospel. That welled-up demand was just kicking in when Sam and the QCs asked R. B. Robinson to train them.

Robinson was a tall, slender, good-looking man with a neat mustache and a receding hairline. He and his young wife, Dora, were living in an apartment not far from the QCs' basement practice hall. As Crain recalls it, he, R.B., and the bass singer, Farley, showed up at a little neighborhood church on the spur of the moment, and Cook was there. "We got Sam to sing lead," says Crain. "We was at the program being friendly, so we went up there and got a homeboy. Well, that was Soul Stirrers' strategy, you know: we pick up a homeboy and this makes all his friends our friends." It was the first time Crain heard Sam, and he remembers the song—"In That Awful Hour"—and the whispered reaction among the other teenagers: "You know they let Sam sing with them last night? Man, Sam sang a song with them Soul Stirrers last night!" Crain heard something in the thin teenager's voice—an urgency behind the smooth delivery—and no doubt R.B. did, too. When Sam asked Robinson to train the QCs, he agreed.

Essentially what R.B. did for the boys was take apart the quartet sound from the inside out. Say they were looking at the Soul Stirrers' arrangement for "Steal Away," the group's first single on the Aladdin label in 1946. R.B. would show young Jake Richardson just how Farley sang the bass line, show Copeland how to do his baritone part, and so on. Then, once the kids had the harmony, he'd also coach them on tempo: how to get that light swing that was the Stirrers' trademark. And, of course, he trained Sam on lead. In some ways, that was the most difficult, not only because Rebert Harris had an extraordinary voice to try to mimic, but also because the lead singer improvised more than anyone else. The best R.B. could do was point Sam in Harris's direction and hope the boy would carry it from there.

Mostly, the boy did. Dora Robinson remembers that soon it was all R.B. would talk about. "Dora, you don't realize. Those guys, they could have it made! And Sam—he's really, really good." The more he worked with them, the more the QCs sounded like their trainer's group, till they were sometimes billed as the Soul Stirrers Juniors. It was, initially anyway, an immense advantage. "The people really loved that," says Crume. "And Sam was a young guy—handsome dude. And the girls, oh, they just flocked to him." Almost like a cover band, the teenagers could do all of the Stirrers' hits: songs like "Canaan Land," "Remember Me," and "He Knows How Much I Can Bear."

R. H. Harris has said he trained Sam personally. "I brought him into my home and set him down and gave him pointers how he should control his voice, how his personality should be onstage." Whether or not that ever happened—family and friends deny it— Sam was clearly modeling his style on Harris's. In fact, there wasn't a quartet lead in Chicago who didn't owe a debt to "Old Man Harris." But Sam brought along his own personality, too. A scrawny adolescent with wide eyes, that big smile, and a clear, open face, Cook had an intensity that came through his modest, aw-shucks manner. Soon the QCs were good enough to be official stand-ins: Spencer Taylor (who would later lead the group) can remember that when the Stirrers were out of town, the QCs would sometimes sing in their regular 7:35 A.M. spot on WIND. There were adult quartets that would have liked that kind of exposure. For a sixteen-year-old like Sam to step before a mike and know his voice was going out all over Chicago was heady, heady stuff.

No wonder he didn't focus on being a big shot at school; he was already showing signs of success in another, adult world. In the face of teachers who thought of their students as "morally unacceptable," Sam simply hid his achievements and his ambition. He took pride in how he dressed, making sure that with next to no money, he still looked spotless. And he developed a style that let him fly under his teachers' prejudice. He told jokes; he charmed; he learned how to appear innocent. Respectful and good-humored, he passed through Phillips as he had Doolittle, without leaving much of a ripple. While his diploma never helped him much, Sam was proud of it; fifteen years later, he'd still be listing his high school graduation in biographical sketches. The Reverend and Mrs. Cook were delighted by their son's achievement: a culmination to their move north.

And then he did ninety days in the Cook County jail.

Chapter

4

Sam graduated in June of 1948, age seventeen. While in school, he'd had a part-time job at the Blue Goose, a neighborhood grocery and butcher store over on 37th Street, but his main focus had been the QCs. The group was getting small out-of-town dates, mostly in the suburbs around Chicago, and they were doing fine at 3838 South State, but it didn't, finally, amount to much. You certainly couldn't live off it. In May, they'd appeared as part of a big Mother's Day program at the Holiness Community Temple at 55th and Indiana. It included Mahalia Jackson, the smooth gospel crooner Robert Anderson, and a young singer named Clay Evans, who would go on to found the influential Fellowship Baptist Church. But at the same time on the same day, just down the road at DuSable High, the Soul Stirrers had been hosting *their* annual Mother's Day program with nationally known quartets like the Pilgrim Travelers, the Norfolk Singers, and the Richmond Harmonizers. For a young quartet that wanted to get ahead, that was the place to be—and the QCs weren't likely to be invited as long as they kept sounding so much like the Stirrers.

It was around this time—"just when he got out of school," as S. R. Crain recalls it—"when he got into a little trouble." He still seems to have been seeing Barbara Campbell. She lived on Lake Park—next block over from the Cooks' place on Ellis—and Johnny

Carter, who lived in between, can remember Sam going back and forth. Barbara had grown into a pretty teenager, and when she and her twin, Beverly, rode their motor scooters around the neighborhood, heads turned. But Sam was—even then—not a one-woman man. There were the girls who hung around 3838: the ones drawn by his voice and the group's popularity. And there was at least one other fairly regular girlfriend, Georgia.

One night, Sam went by Georgia's house and brought along a little something to spice up the evening. In those days, cheap pornography came in the form of smudgy one-page "fuck stories," pretty primitive stuff and probably more a joke than a turn-on. Somehow, the story ended up in Georgia's little sister's hands, and she took it to school the next day. It's easy to imagine the giggling and the whispering, the teacher coming down the aisle to ask what all the nonsense was about, and then the long moment as she stood there, reading. "Young lady, where did this come from?"

Eventually, the kid sister told, and the trail led back to Sam. Either the school or the girl's parents called the cops, and the cops came to the Cooks' apartment. In a family where the Bible ruled supreme—where no one was allowed to curse, never mind read pornography, never mind carry it over to your teenage girlfriend's house—all hell must have broken loose. But the first priority was their boy. Though he hadn't been in any trouble before, Sam got ninety days on a morals charge. For a colored boy without money or connections, Cook County law enforcement was more than just humiliating; it was dangerous. Everybody knew what had happened out in Morgan Park just a few years before. Two cops, responding to a call, had come upon a teenager Sam's age and color. Their official report said the kid picked up a rock, and one of the cops, "in order to protect himself," shot in the air and accidentally killed the boy. Everybody in Bronzeville also knew that the police had escaped without punishment.

In later years, Sam hardly ever talked about his time in jail. It certainly wasn't part of the clean-cut, Christian image he was already cultivating. That image, his self-confidence, and his charm helped pull him through. Somehow, he persuaded the white warden to let him organize a gospel group. And he drilled them till they sounded like something. When his time was up, the warden actually invited Sam to come back and sing. Still, the jail time must have showed him how easy it was to fall off the edge—to slip out of the protection of family and church—and just keep falling. In Bronzeville, one slip was all it took.

When Sam rejoined the QCs, instead of being the sweet-faced son of Reverend Cook with that innocent look and angelic voice, now the young man singing the praises of Jesus was a felon, and on charges involving the morals of a minor. Luckily, the church was built on forgiveness. It was a mean world, and they knew everyone strayed now and then; plus, there was something about the Cook boy when he started to sing—his smile, his voice, the way he held his hands up to the light—that won a congregation over. Didn't the whole incident, in a way, even deepen his singing? Now, when he cried out he'd been tempted, when he spoke of the Devil, it wasn't just a teenager repeating the words to a song, but real testimony. Sam worked at winning them over, beginning to understand how much his voice and his personality could erase, and more determined than ever to make something of himself.

The training with R.B., the pushing to get on local programs, the long rehearsals finally began to pay off. The QCs' break came on September 26, 1948, when they appeared on a big quartet program with the Soul Stirrers, Nashville's Fairfield Four, and the Flying Clouds out of Detroit. Sam's group, by far the least known, opened the program and then sang a few other numbers later in the second half. The crowd, as always, reacted positively. These were, after all, local boys. There was the gasp of recognition as the teenage QCs hit the harmonies that the Soul Stirrers had made famous: the sort of thrill that, years later, the Jackson Five could evoke by doing the Temptations. James Hill of the Fairfield Four remembers the QCs as "a little local group" and Sam as still tender but "a real good singer which struck the attention of everybody."

In the crowd was a friend of R.B.'s, Louis Tate, who had driven up from Gary, Indiana, to hear the program. Tate, married and with nine children, was about to turn thirty-four years old. He was working in one of the steel mills, but he'd had some experience managing gospel acts and was a longtime fan of the music. In the late twenties, while living in Louisiana, Tate had run into the Harmonizing Four, a tight, melodic jubilee group out of Bessemer, Alabama. "That was the time," Tate recalls, "when you went around and sung on the corner, passed the hat around. I heard them sing a couple places, then I carried them around the city: drugstores and what have you. And they'd sing and I'd pass the hat around." Because he knew all the little towns in the area, the teenage Tate was brought in as the group's temporary manager. It had given him a taste, and, now, twenty years later, he knew talent when he heard it.

"I just sat there," Tate says of that night at Phillips, "and I was spellbound. 'Cause I didn't know no kids could sing like that!" After the program, when he told Robinson how good the boys sounded, R.B. jumped at the chance: "Tate," he said, "that's a good group. They need a manager. Ain't nobody got 'em."

Impressed as Tate was, it was still a difficult decision. He knew managing the QCs would mean a lot of traveling: the boys had to get out of Chicago, where they would always be second bill to the Soul Stirrers. Even if he concentrated on the Midwest, it still meant leaving his family for long stretches. And he'd be staking his livelihood on a bunch of teenagers, only one of whom—the fresh-faced lead with the sweet tenor voice—was even out of high school. But he didn't stop to consider very long. "This is something I always wanted to do, and I always was tied up with it. I loved it!" And, looking back on the decision after forty-five years, he'd say, "There it is; here me is."

For the QCs, it was a much easier call. Going out on the road as a professional gospel quartet meant adventure; it meant a chance to make a name; and—if Mr. Tate could be believed—it might even mean cutting a record. For Sam, wondering about his future, the offer was an open door out of Bronzeville. All he had to hear was "Would you—" and he leapt.

At the program that night, Tate was already feeling out the Flying Clouds about sponsoring the QCs in Detroit. Then he went to the boys' parents and, presenting himself as the God-fearing responsible man he was, asked their permission to take the children on the road. For all but the Cooks, it meant giving permission to drop out of school. On the other hand, what did their boys have to look forward to at home? That summer, one reporter had described Chicago as a "ghetto where health, cleanliness and safety are impossible; our great Loop department stores and business where the only Negro is one who swings the broom; the mobs that set upon Negro citizens for the crime of buying a decent home; the 'white only' signs carried in the Help Wanted advertisement of Chicago newspapers; the newspapers themselves that put Freedom in headlines, yet hire no Negroes."

All but the Copelands agreed to let their children go. (The baritone part was taken by Marvin Jones until Creedell graduated.) Reverend Cook was downright enthusiastic, and he overrode any doubts Annie May had. Hadn't Sam been on the road with the Singing Children—and wasn't the road what helped feed them all? Charley, "the wanderer," helped Tate get a car, and, in the early part of the new year, the manager set out with a bunch of teenage kids, five dollars in his pocket, and nothing much else but promises. "Them ain't our childrens now," the parents had told Tate; "them your childrens."

They didn't even make it to their first stop in Detroit before the money ran out. "When we got—I don't know where it was: a pretty good piece down the road—we went in a nice filling station. And we start getting a little gas, you know?" The only question was how they'd pay. "So I had Sam to hit a number," Tate continues, and they passed the hat. Before the tank was full, they'd paid for it, the locals in rural Michigan delighted with a little entertainment on another cold winter's day. Consider it Sam's professional debut.

The official program was that Sunday, February 20, 1949, at the Forest Club. Tickets were $1 in advance, $1.50 at the door, and the proceeds were split among the young QCs, the veteran Harmony Kings of St. Louis, and "Detroit's own" Flying Clouds. Tate took out his own ad in the local Negro newspaper with a picture showing the six teenagers lined up neatly, each wearing a dark jacket, white shirt, and dark tie. "Back then," Tate recalls, "they didn't recognize you if you didn't have a uniform on you." Sam, the oldest and tallest, gazes out at the gospel world with a look of serious, sober attention, while

Tate poses in front: the elder leading the boys into their first big "three-way song battle."

As in all gospel battles, no winner was declared, but the QCs did well enough to draw the attention of a young Baptist preacher by the name of C. L. Franklin. After the program, Franklin invited the boys to stay in Detroit. If, as the Reverend Franklin would later declare, "raising money in church is an art," he was one of the premier artists. Franklin had moved to Detroit from Buffalo a few years earlier with his young family, including an infant daughter, Aretha. When he took over the New Bethel Church, it was in a dilapidated former bowling alley, but that soon changed. Franklin's church quickly got a reputation as one of the city's gospel centers. Music drew people; people—under the magical power of Reverend Franklin's words— gave money; money built a new church. By that early March of 1949, it was already working. New Bethel had increased its membership by a thousand; soon, Reverend Franklin's home would become an important gathering place on the gospel circuit. In their living room, his daughter would hear all the greats from the Ward Singers to James Cleveland.

So for a little while, Sam and the QCs had a chance to work with one of the master fund-raisers and charismatic leaders of the gospel world: not a bad start for a group that had just been singing for its gas. Then one day, Tate was paged at Franklin's church; it was a call from radio station WDIA in Memphis asking the boys to come down and sing over the air. "I got up the next day and went to Memphis."

Despite the arrangement with Reverend Franklin, the QCs couldn't afford to pass up radio exposure. Nashville's Fairfield Four was a case in point. The quartet had been on the enormous, 50,000-watt WLAC since 1942, and it had profited both the station and the group. "Now, I'm not saying that Fairfield sounded any better—or as good," chuckles their bass singer, Isaac "Dickie" Freeman. "All I'm saying is it's what people would go for. [Lead singer Sam] McCrary had one song that he would hit: 'Remember Me.' The [radio] theme, man! People would go wild. You know why? Because they'd hear it all over the country. Guys all down in Mississippi, Florida, Alabama, Georgia . . . Sam would get up and say, 'Reeeee—'

and the crowd would just go up! Like you threw gas in there!" Just the possibility of radio was enough for Tate to leave Detroit and make Memphis the QCs' new base.

Like Chicago, Memphis had been transformed by the urban migration. When the boys arrived, the city's "negro population" (the local white papers kept the "n" deliberately, blatantly small) was 40 percent—over 150,000 people—and growing fast. There was a severe housing shortage, and Tate first lived in a hotel, then after about a month moved with them to a private home, and eventually out to one of the projects that had gone up to try to house the newcomers. In all these moves, of course, they never left the colored part of town: the city's notorious Edward H. "Boss" Crump made sure of that.

The QCs were used to colored people eating in separate establishments, going to different schools, getting haircuts and attending churches exclusively among their own. But Jim Crow down South had its own twists. During Sam's last year in high school, for example, the Freedom Train had stopped in Chicago. Painted red, white, and blue, it had been touring the country that election year carrying the Declaration of Independence, the Bill of Rights, and other historic documents. The *Chicago Defender*'s reaction was to urge its readership to go visit as a reminder of how the current Congress had "failed repeatedly to even reach a vote on fair employment, poll tax, and lynching." Boss Crump, on the other hand, had canceled the train's Memphis stop altogether because of the threat it posed to segregation. "A custom of 150 years can't be sidetracked in a day or a year and made workable," Crump told the papers. "It would be a regrettable mistake—a costly mistake to have the whole crowd, whites and colored, men and women, and children, surging through at the same time—what a gamble—a desperate gamble, and it must be avoided. . . ."

Crump's policies even extended to gospel music. The first big out-of-town concert in Memphis had been a decade before when the Blue Jays had been booked into the auditorium on Main Street. According to promoter James Darling, the hard-singing quartet had the potential to draw a large white crowd, so Crump "gave them orders not to come"—and no whites showed.

Unlikely as it seemed, one of the main forces in breaking that seg-regation would be WDIA, the tiny radio station that had summoned the QCs to Memphis. Not long before Sam arrived, it had been trans-formed from a failing business into the "Mother Station of the Ne-groes." White-owned, white-managed, and white-supervised, the station had hired local celebrity Nat D. Williams as the first publicly promoted black dj in the South. Williams described his employers in his newspaper column: "They are businessmen. They don't necessar-ily love Negroes. They make that clear. But they do love progress and they are willing to pay the price to make progress." By 1950, Negro buying power in Memphis would be estimated at around $100 mil-lion and nationally at a potential $10 to $12 billion, and WDIA was an immediate hit. Suddenly, listeners in Memphis (like the fourteen-year old Elvis Presley) could hear the forbidden music over the anon-ymous airwaves. Half the station's programming was devoted to gospel (low-budget and respectable), and the owners were soon out looking for more acts and more personalities to fill their dawn-to-dusk airtime.

None of the disk jockeys the station hired for this new format proved more popular than Dwight "Gatemouth" Moore. It was Moore who put the QCs on his one-o'clock program, *The Light of the World,* where they did a regular ten to fifteen minutes a day. A former blues singer with local fame "to rival the great [W. C.] Handy," Gatemouth had suddenly heard the call early in 1949. "Walked out on the stage to sing the blues," he recalls, "and instead of singing blues, I don't know what happened: I started singing an old song, 'Shine on Me.' Right in the nightclub! The people thought I'd lost my mind."

Moore may have switched fields but he stayed a showman. Accord-ing to author Louis Cantor's history of WDIA, the Reverend once an-nounced over the air that he would walk on water and even set a time for the great event. Throngs of listeners showed up by the banks of the Mississippi, only to hear Gatemouth's pronouncement that the waters were troubled, and "Reverend Moore cannot walk on troubled waters!" Part of his promotion was always music. Gatemouth saw the great religious quartets—like the Soul Stirrers or the local Spirit of Memphis—as "not only unique singers but master showmen. They could get that emotional out from the audience."

Moore judged Sam and the others according to this sly mix of entertainment and enlightenment, the blues and the gospel. Sam, he concluded, "was never a great singer. 'Cause I come up under singers. But he had a great, unique tenor voice with the peculiar delivery that was fascinating and outstanding. And he had a beautiful personality! His diction was good. And he looked the part: youthful."

The arrangement proved a blessing all around: a savvy show-business type promoting the group, a charismatic young quartet to draw listeners to Gatemouth's show, and a hit for WDIA. In Gatemouth's own modest estimation, "I was the hottest thing. I was the only thing!" He booked the QCs on his "Spiritual Midnight Rambles" Friday nights at the Palace Theater. Tate cemented the relationship by becoming first deacon at Moore's little storefront church. And the boys moved in near Moore and "lived between Tate's house and my house," according to Moore. "They were stranded. . . . And I liked them. And my children were there, so I let [them] come and eat at my home. Plenty food!"

Plenty food was just what the QCs needed. "A lot of time," Tate recalls, "all seven of us had to share two hamburgers." While their radio time helped them book three or four local programs a week, WDIA's policy was not to pay for on-air appearances; the free publicity was pay enough. At live shows, there was usually no admission but "goodwill offerings," the congregation giving whatever it could. That was then split among the groups who performed—and each group's part was further split to pay for gas, food, rent, and any other expenses. Plus, there was the stiff competition of the Memphis gospel scene. Reverend Mason had made the city home for COGIC, and by 1945, the denomination had built the $400,000 C. H. Mason Temple, the largest Negro-owned convention hall in the nation. It had quickly drawn the best in professional gospel artists. Where groups in Memphis had once sung—as the title of one local song put it—to be "happy in the service of the Lord," now, if you didn't look good, move good, and sound good, there was no way you were going to hold your own against the likes of the Dixie Hummingbirds, the Blue Jays, or the Soul Stirrers.

Sam and the QCs learned from all this competition. At the top of the pile of the city's local quartets was the Spirit of Memphis, which also sang over WDIA. With the thunderous lead of Silas Steele and the keening tenor of Wilmer Broadnax (known as "Little Axe"), the quartet released a record on the local Hallelujah label in the fall of 1949. Suddenly, the air play gave them a national reputation, and soon they were on tours from San Francisco to Newark. Tate, Sam, and the rest of the QCs took note: eventually, they were going to need a record. As well as performers, Memphis boasted one of the finest gospel songwriters in the country: the Reverend W. Herbert Brewster of the East Trigg Baptist Church. Brewster also appeared on WDIA, but he was best known for his elaborate biblical pageant plays that featured his own extraordinary compositions, like "How I Got Over," "Surely God Is Able," and "How Far Am I from Canaan." Though not as well known as Thomas Dorsey, Brewster was an equally great composer—as melodic and often more dramatic. Mahalia Jackson would help turn Brewster's "Move On Up a Little Higher" into a million-selling record, and Brewster recalled how the young Cook would come around to be "lectured" on composition.

It wasn't always easy to book programs in this hotbed of talent, but the QCs pieced together an itinerary within WDIA's range: the smaller nearby towns in Tennessee and just across the river in Arkansas. None of the boys had day jobs—that was the deal Tate had struck with their parents—"and most of the time we just, you know, laid around till we got something." Still, they did all right. As Bob Weaver, a contemporary of Sam's who grew up in Memphis remembers it, ". . . [T]hey were so good we used to keep them for weeks. He was such a nice, lovable guy, and everyone liked him, young and old." Weaver and Cook would daydream about the future, and Sam was never modest about his goals: "I want to be great like [Nat] King Cole one day."

In May, the QCs took a trip out of Memphis to Indianapolis, where Tate had been made head of Indiana's Quartet Union. For the first program of the year, he brought the QCs, the Harmony Kings of South Bend, and a bunch of local groups to the Antioch Baptist Church. It was a big enough deal to advertise: a picture of the group with a caption warning Indianapolis, "Fail to hear this great program, and you will miss the treat of the season."

To see a portrait of the QCs at this point—clean-cut teenagers in identical blue uniforms with neat white handkerchiefs peeking out of their top pockets, hair combed, hands carefully folded—was to see an advertisement for good Christian living. After two months on the road, banging back and forth from one gospel program to the next, living catch-as-catch-can, they all look delighted with themselves. They were, after all, away from home, seeing the world, and sometimes actually getting paid to sing. According to Tate, none of the teenagers cursed or drank, and they were all very religious. "Now women," Tate chuckles, "Sam couldn't get away from them women. . . . I didn't keep him away, but when I thought he'd did his thing long enough, I'd kind of—'Life is like this. And you take life easy. And you—' Well, I taught him."

Indianapolis gives a good idea of how gospel music was expanding. A typical Sunday featured ten to fifteen programs all over the city. The variety was immense, the staged competitions fierce, and this was only local groups. All the big names passed through town, too. In this competitive field, Tate's Quartet Union connection helped a lot. Locals were springing up all over the Midwest and South, and as state president, Tate would travel from Fort Wayne to Evansville, naturally making sure his group appeared on the programs.

This became the QCs' pattern: based at WDIA, playing what out-of-town gigs they could secure, and then dropping back into Memphis until another small tour could be arranged. Soon Sam was breaking into other cities—Milwaukee and Cincinnati—without even an invitation. There was the time the group drove into St. Louis, for example, in the early part of 1950 to see Mother Ross, who had a late-night radio program. They knocked, introduced themselves, and in the tradition of the gospel road, were invited in to do a number. They ended up staying in St. Louis a month or two. "We was eating and sleeping," Tate says. "She gave us a place to stay and she fed us good. She give up a little money, but like I said, there wasn't a whole lot of money there to get. Money was kind of scarce." Instead, they gained a connection. Mother Ross took to Sam—he called her Mom—and Mom made sure the young group got the best gospel publicity in St. Louis. (Years later, Sam would record her daughter, Jackie Ross, on his label.)

And every few months, they'd get back to Chicago, see their families, go down to 3838 South State, and brag a little about their adventures on the road. "Yeah," Sam's brother Charles recalls, "he was making good money with the QCs."

That was certainly the impression they wanted to give. The reality was that they were barely getting by, headlining small programs but lucky to get a chance to open for the really successful quartets. What they needed, all agreed, was a record. Tate tried; he tried in Detroit, Memphis, Cincinnati, at a couple of places in Chicago—just about every tiny independent label that recorded gospel music and some of the larger ones. "But all the record companies was saying that they was too young, that their voices would change. They all had their excuse. And they sounded too much like the Soul Stirrers." That was the killer. R.B. had done his job too well. While the resemblance to the Stirrers brought them work, it also kept them at what Lou Rawls called the minor-league level.

Sam, in particular, worked at changing all that. "He'd eat it, sleep it, walked it, talked it. Singing," in Tate's words, "was his life." And it wasn't just the singing; Sam was writing, too. It was as a QC that Sam first understood how important it was to have your own songs. If the group couldn't have a totally original sound, it was at least possible to have original material. And it was as a QC that he fixed the habit that would stay with him all his life: writing whenever and wherever he was.

As the group beat their way across the Midwest and South, Sam kept coming up with ideas: new songs and arrangements he'd try out on the others. Cook and Tate roomed together, until the eighteen-year-old's drive to be gospel's best got to be too much for his manager. "He'd wake up at twelve, one o'clock, two o'clock, and say, 'Tate-i! Listen at this! How this go?' " Maybe he'd have dreamed a

melody or worked out a new verse to a song. Tate had to hear it right
then, and when the sleepy manager would mumble something about
how it was fine, yes, yes, Sam would wake the group—make them
get up in the middle of the night and practice harmonies. As if singing on the radio and at programs and then rehearsing as they drove
from gig to gig wasn't enough. Sam might appear totally relaxed in
front of a congregation, and he sang as if the words just floated out
with no effort, but, as Tate recognized, "He studied music."

Still, as hard as Sam worked at it, there was no getting over. The
group as a whole just wasn't making it, couldn't get past the resemblance to the Stirrers. They would perform with major acts in Memphis, help pack the seven-thousand-seat Mason Temple as Gatemouth
emceed, but come Monday morning, the QCs would have little to
show for it. Despite signs of a growing reputation and a professional
sound that had deepened during the year and a half they'd been on
the road together, the bottom line was that Tate was going broke.
He'd grown close enough to the boys to name his tenth child, a girl,
SammieLee after his two lead singers, Sam and Lee Richardson, but
it couldn't last. "I had carried them as far as I could. . . ."

Chapter 5

By mid-1950, R. H. Harris had had enough of the gospel road. He'd been singing lead with the Soul Stirrers for thirteen years. The day he knew it was over was when he came back home to Chicago on one of their infrequent layoffs, walked through the front door, and discovered his infant daughter—a poppa's girl—suddenly unsure who he was. "Like to cut my heart out."

The group, and Harris in particular, were at the peak of their powers. Though they had just lost James Medlock, the second "hard" lead, his replacement was working out great. Paul Foster, a round-faced, highly religious man, had first met the Stirrers some years before when he'd been singing around Houston. Late in 1949, he and his group, the Houstonaires, had shared a program with the Stirrers at Wheatley High School. Medlock was threatening to quit; Foster knew the Stirrers' style and material; and R. B. Robinson was especially convinced he'd "fit in good." Three weeks later, the Stirrers grabbed Foster, and soon he was sharing lead at his first major program in Cleveland.

The sound of Harris and Foster worked out immediately. A song like "By and By," an old Charles Tindley hymn arranged by Crain and Harris, highlights how the two leads played off one another. It was cut just a few months after Foster had joined. The tune opens with sweet barbershop harmony—the group assuring us we will understand by and by—and the first solo has that same, soothing quality. But by the second verse, Harris has taken off. His insistent voice, climbing higher, calls up doubt even as he promises, "My God will lead us." As the rest of the Stirrers turn the words over and over like some well-tuned wheel, the level of urgency keeps rising. Gospel expert Anthony Heilbut has called Harris's lead here an "art almost immune to criticism." Part of what pushes it forward is Foster's deeper, driven voice. "By and By" passes from describing the milk and honey of a promised land to the sound of doubt being overcome: a drama the Stirrers enacted through their traded, escalating leads.

For the Soul Stirrers to lose Old Man Harris, then, was nearly unthinkable. To all appearances, he was the heart of the group—surely his keening leads were their signature. But on Sunday, September 24, 1950—at the end of a program at DuSable with the Pilgrim Travelers and the Fairfield Four—Harris stepped forward and shocked the audience by announcing he was leaving the group. "It was like a bomb dropped," says Harris, as the 2,300 people who filled the auditorium buzzed with the news. Behind him, the Soul Stirrers weren't doing much better. They had just signed a new recording contract with a label on the West Coast and—the economy buoyed by the Korean War—were bringing in their best money ever: the payoff for years of scrambling from town to town. They'd just managed to survive one loss by finding Foster; now twenty years of work was disappearing before them, unless they could find a replacement for the irreplaceable Harris.

The immediate need was a lead for the bookings already in place, and they picked up Leroy Taylor. Taylor, according to the group's manager, S. R. Crain, was "a very spiritual boy. I was satisfied with him. . . . He was doing all right, but all right wasn't enough. You had to do good." On top of that, Taylor had a secure and fairly well-paying job as a cab driver in Chicago and wasn't convinced it was worth giving up for the uncertainties of the gospel road. For a while, Paul Foster did all the lead work himself, but it proved too much. Foster began to suffer from migraines; in his own words, "I needed someone to help me sing. . ." It's not hard to imagine the panic among the Soul Stirrers at this point.

Crain readily admits it was R. B. Robinson's idea to listen to the QC's young lead, Sam Cook, and that most of the Stirrers doubted it would work. This was, after all, a kid not yet twenty. "I wasn't worried about him singing," Crain says. "I was worried about him being too young. I didn't know if his parents wanted him to go out on the road. And the responsibility. It's a big responsibility to take on your shoulders when you carry a child from his parents out on the road." The responsibility went both ways. No other top-ranked gospel group had a lead this young. The Stirrers, veterans of the road in their forties, were used to playing to congregations of about the same age. What would it do to their credibility to have some boy leading them? And could the teenager make the jump from the minors to the majors? How big were *his* shoulders?

R.B. had no doubts. "Those guys are crazy!" he'd tell his wife. "Sam is *just* the right one to take Harris's place." And clearly the group had to do something. Finally, Crain—who had, after all, heard Sam sing and recognized his talent—was ready to consider the impossible. "Go get that little fellow," Crain told R.B., "and let's try."

The test was a sing-off. Sam and Leroy Taylor went to the manager's house, where Crain, in his phrase, "carried Sam over a song": Reverend Brewster's "How Far Am I from Canaan." In the quiet room, with the gospel veterans looking on and the nineteen-year-old standing nervously in place, Crain sang the first phrase of the hymn, "I'm standing on Jordan." Cook repeated it, pitch-perfect. "Gazing cross the swelling tide," sang Crain, and on the first note, instead of simply hitting pitch as Crain had, Cook bent it, undulating the note in a swell that matched the lyrics.

"He did it precisely and better," Crain recalls, "and with his own style! I couldn't hardly train him. And the boys looked at him, grinning." (Whether it was actually Sam's "own" is a question. This is the song Reverend Brewster says Sam came out to East Trigg in Memphis to learn. But it was certainly a distinctive style.) Taylor sang, too, but there was no comparison and no call-back. "That's my boy!" Crain told Robinson and Foster. Cook smiled. "You want to go with us, son?"

Sam could barely contain himself. The impossible had happened:

the thing he'd been training for and hoping for since—when? Since he was a child, really. He was going to replace the great R. H. Harris. He was going to go back out on the gospel road, and this time he'd see the world in style: with money in his pockets and good clothes on his back. He'd watched the Stirrers stride to the front of a church in their pure white custom-made suits with the wide lapels, those carefully knotted, black ties with big white polka dots, their hair slicked back, their shoes gleaming. The Stirrers ruled the quartet world. And Crain was asking if he wanted to sing lead for them!?

First, Sam had to approach his father and mother about the switch. Charley Cook didn't even hesitate. "Man, anytime you can move up higher, move up!" Annie May was more cautious. "You gonna—you telling him to leave the Highway QCs?" The Reverend Cook brought the discussion back to basics. Hadn't he supported his family from church to church? There was a distinction to be made here, and the father and son understood it, plain as day. "Listen," said Reverend Cook. "The man making a living! He ain't singing to save souls! He's singing the spiritual song, but before they'll go anywhere and have a program . . . someone will say, 'Well, we'll give you five hundred dollars for this program. And then you can have all over!' "

It was the same discussion they'd had about Sam going with the QCs. Crain clinched it (as Louis Tate had) by promising Mrs. Cook that he'd be personally responsible for Sam's well-being, but as brother Charles Cook puts it, "My daddy never did interfere with whatever we wanted to do. He may have given his opinion, but he didn't interfere."

The QCs were a different story. When they learned they were losing their lead, they came around the Cooks' house, angry and miserable and trying to get Sam's parents to change their son's mind. "Naturally," says Charles, "they didn't want their best singer to go somewhere else." But Sam was determined and ambitious, and there was no question in his mind that the future lay with the Soul Stirrers. It may have been the first, but it certainly wasn't the last time in his life he would choose "moving up higher" over personal loyalty. The only possible stumbling block was Louis Tate, who did, after all, have a contract to manage Sam.

Tate remembers it was a Sunday night, about two in the morning, when someone knocked on his door. He rolled out of his bed and hurried downstairs, worried that there was some emergency. There stood Sam and Tate's old friend R.B. Robinson, both dressed up and looking serious. "Goodness! What you-all doing here this time of night?" Sam and R.B. came in and sat down, and Sam began the conversation by saying all the QCs were mad at him. And their families were, too. "About what?" Sam looked to R.B. for support and then broke the news.

"The Soul Stirrers want me to go with them. And I want to go with them. But . . . now . . . you are the person who's got to let me go with them. If you don't . . . let me go with them—I . . . can't go with them."

As he stumbled to the end, Sam knew—and so did Tate—that what he was asking probably meant the end of the Highway QCs. The teenager may not have understood the sacrifices that "Tate-i" had made for them, but nearby slept little Sammie Tate, Sam's goddaughter, a living reminder of the bond they had. It was harder in many ways than asking his real father's permission. Sam hated that idea—hated leaving anyone behind—and told Tate-i they'd still be in touch. The two older men and the boy all looked at each other for a moment, and then the one still in his pajamas made a little speech.

"Well, Sam. I would be less than a man to tell you not to go with them. Far as that contract I got, you can just forget it. . . . I done carried you as far as I can carry you without a record. You're with the number-one group, and if I don't let you go with them, I just think I'm less than a man. Far as I'm concerned, you get with them!"

After two years and hundreds of miles, it was officially over. They shook hands. The QCs would eventually find another lead, the young Johnny Taylor, and go on to record and tour nationally, but not with Tate. He'd manage other gospel and even some rock & roll groups. Now, he went back to bed, and Sam drove north to Chicago to become a Soul Stirrer.

Of course, there was still no telling if the kid could do the job. The first test was scheduled to be right at home in a program at his own Wendell Phillips High School. The Soul Stirrers rented the auditorium, charged a quarter to get in, and invited the people to hear the new lead for themselves. "Harris," in Crain's words, "was the champion born, the pioneer. What was on the streets was 'He can't do nothing with Harris.' " It was like the head-to-head gospel battles Sam was used to at 3838 South State, except this time he was up against an invisible opponent. Crain, as manager of the group, talked the kid up and appealed to people's sense of fairness: "He didn't join us to do nothin' with Harris; he joined us to sing!" But most remained unconvinced: "We gonna see, we gonna see. We want him to sing now, Crain! 'Cause we gonna pay our money, we want some singing!"

The Soul Stirrers had exactly one rehearsal with Cook. They went over their arrangement of "Canaan," making sure Sam had the pitch right. In the end, they had to lower their arrangement a full octave from where it had been for Harris's astonishing range. But if the boy didn't have the old man's voice, the rehearsal reassured the veterans that he knew how to make a song his own. They were fairly confident the day of the program as Sam's family, a lot of his classmates, and the QCs settled into their seats. "They all come to see how Sam was going to do," Crane recollects. Backstage, the kid began what the Stirrers soon recognized as a characteristic show of nerves: clasping his hands now in front of him, now behind, then wringing them as if to wash the fear away. Otherwise, he appeared remarkably cool.

When the Soul Stirrers came out, Crain had Robinson, the group's baritone, do a couple of his songs first. They included "Elijah," an up-tempo number that was sure to get the crowd going. "After he got through with that," Crain recalls, "I turned to Sam." He was deliberately saving Paul Foster, the powerful lead with the proven ability to move the crowd. "We'll do our little shouting after a while," Crain figured.

With Sam standing there, wringing his hands behind his back, Crain began his introduction. "Now, give the little fellow a chance. Just give him a chance. You gave us a chance, didn't you?" And the hometown crowd filling the Wendell Phillips auditorium responded with amens. "I'm not gonna say he's good," Crain went on, "but the Soul Stirrers are good! Aren't we?" And again it was "Amen, amen!"

Then they lit into their tight arrangement of "How Far Am I from Caanan," and the new lead singer stepped forward.

It didn't take more than a line of lyrics before the crowd knew he was good. "Sing, Sam!" someone shouted. And then someone else joined in. And then, Crain recalls, "some little girl that liked him" stood up and declared, "That's my baby! Sing, baby!" and it was all over. "Ain't no use in calling Paul," Crain chuckles, "because Sam shouted them! That little boy up there! That baby! And we old men made him look still younger."

The old men's amazement and delight were just beginning. "After the concert," Crain remembers, "I didn't get much of a chance to say much to him. Because the audience had him surrounded. But I said to my bass singer, 'Farley, that boy's phenomenal! Don't you see all those people around him? You see what he's gonna do? Ain't never been that much around Harris.'" People kept coming up to Crain and the other members and pumping their hands, too, saying, "Crain, I knew you'd do it." As if it were Crain who had done the singing. The crowd understood the chance the Soul Stirrers had taken using a "baby." Sam's success guaranteed theirs; his failure would have done the same. Crain reflected on the moment, years later, "If you do well, everybody knows you; if you do bad, nobody know you." The other Stirrers were a little stunned. T. L. Bruster, the baritone, watched the crowd around Cook and said, "We don't get a chance to please nobody, that boy's so popular." To which Crain could just grin and reply, "That's the most popular man I ever seen in my life."

A triumph at your old high school, in front of your family and friends, with no competition, was one thing. Going out on the road and facing not just the memory of Harris but the other gospel stars was quite another. There were no harder singers anywhere—not in the nightclubs or the honky-tonks or the back-country jukes. And in his first out-of-town program with the Stirrers—in Pine Bluff, Arkansas—Sam would face the best of them. "My battle," as Crain would say, "had just begun."

First off, there were the Fairfield Four. They had the immense advantage of those broadcasts over WLAC in Nashville. Sam McCrary sang a dramatic tenor lead where he'd grab a note and hold it like a bulldog, the group pumping away behind him. And they sang in a modified jubilee style, so those in the congregation who wanted that "old-time religion" were naturally won over by the Four. As James Hill, manager of the group, laconically defines Sam's problem at the beginning, "Well, he had to make a way for himself."

Then there were the Jackson Harmonaires, also and better known as the Five Blind Boys of Mississippi. They were led by Archie Brownlee, "the out-singingest blind boy on earth!" according to Crain. "Ray Charles mocks him a little. That's all he could do: mock him. He can't sing like him." Brownlee was a light-skinned black man who wore round, metal-framed dark glasses, but the mild exterior hid an insatiable, devoted performer. All the gospel leads could scream, but Brownlee had an aching crack to his voice that they all stepped back and admired. One of the Blind Boys' specialties was the slow testimonial: hardly a song at all, more a series of deliberate chords, as if the typical gospel intro was extended and extended. Brownlee's shrieked asides would propel the number slowly forward. He'd shake under the power of the music as he sustained a strained note across the length of the turnaround at the end of each verse. Years later, when Sam wanted to reminisce, he'd play Blind Boys records, and though he was never one to show his emotions much, he'd get tearful. As he told a friend, "He's the only one who could do that—to move me like that."

If their singing wasn't enough, the Blind Boys' theatrics tore the house up. At the start of the program, the five of them would be led to the front, each with a hand on the shoulder in front of him. Something about the blindness always touched a nerve in the crowd, and they were primed for the miraculous before a note had been sung. Then, once it began, Brownlee would rush the stage with a fervor, helped along the aisles when he needed it, or weaving his own way among a gasping, yelling congregation. There was nothing, nothing, he wouldn't try. "I seen him at Booker T. Auditorium," recalls one observer, "jump *all the way* off that balcony, down on the floor—*blind*! I don't see how in the world he could do that. People would just fall out all over the house!"

The other major group on the program was the Pilgrim Travelers.

The Travelers, like the Soul Stirrers, were originally out of Texas and used the same double-lead technique. They had a particularly strong pair of singers to put it across. Kylo Turner was the R. H. Harris of the group; his soothing baritone had something of a crooner's quality, till it jumped to falsetto. Tall, slim, fine-looking, Turner would set the house for Keith Barber, who'd then bring it down with his growled solos. Jess Whitaker sang a gorgeous quartet baritone, and if that wasn't enough, the group's manager, James W. Alexander, made sure their showmanship ranked with the Blind Boys'. "They used to call us Texas cowboys," Alexander told author Anthony Heilbut. "Turner would hoist his leg, shake his skinny hip and holler. The people couldn't stand it." Behind him, Alexander had choreographed the other Travelers to "circle the mike, dip, run"—all this in some of the most stylish, urbane matching suits of any quartet.

The Travelers' material leaned to an almost Victorian sentimentality, as in their most popular release, "Mother Bowed," which milked a congregation shamelessly. Turner's lead begins all sincerity and nostalgia, while the rest hum sweet chords behind him. By the chorus— "Mother bowed and she prayed for me"—Turner's voice has frayed, and when it rises to declare he can see her kneeling there, the "see" is a falsetto note meant to carry the congregation back to their own idealized mommas. They were formidable gospel opponents.

Among these groups, the Stirrers' young lead didn't have much of a chance that night in Pine Bluff. As J. W. Alexander recalls it, Sam "was accepted, but the competition—it was like a rookie coming into the big leagues. He didn't bring down the house." And the other quartets did: they "shouted the house unmercifully," in Crain's words, "all over Sam, me, Paul. We done learnt a song to sing; we got our little applause; and then the program's over."

Afterward, the Travelers and the Blind Boys took turns ribbing the rookie, calling him a "lightweight." But both veteran managers, Crain and Alexander, could see Sam had it in him. It was a question of overcoming his fears, for one thing, and understanding his talents, for another. Alexander asked Crain's permission to speak to the boy, give him a little advice about coming up against the likes of Archie Brownlee. "Sam, I smoke Camel cigarettes," J.W. said obliquely. "If you go into a store, and I want you to bring me a packet of Camels, I must make it plain. Otherwise, you might bring back Lucky Strikes. Well, if you can't sing loud enough, just be sure they understand what you say."

Crain, meanwhile, had noticed something else: what had happened at Wendell Phillips was happening again. "They're not around Archie; they wasn't around Turner; they wasn't around Sam McCrary. They was around Sam Cook: leader of the Soul Stirrers!" And this wasn't his hometown crowd; this was the critical gospel audience, who took their church deadly seriously. Bass singer J. J. Farley came over and watched a moment. "Now, why is that?" "Man," Crain answered, "they like the boy! You can't help but people like him! That's gonna pay off," Crain told Farley. "When he learn, he gonna run over that mess you see yonder," gesturing toward the Travelers. "He'll get them. I'll see to him getting them! Don't worry."

S. R. (Senior Roy) Crain would turn out to be Sam's foremost singing teacher. A tall, handsome, dark-skinned man with hair neatly parted in the middle, Crain had held the Soul Stirrers together over two decades with a combination of guile and integrity. He could be a stern disciplinarian, but behind that righteous stare there was a twinkle. He understood a man needed to have some fun. Crain had a great ear for arrangements, wrote well, and had a no-nonsense approach to quartet singing. You rehearsed till you knew your part in your sleep; then you presented the song in a straightforward, church-like manner; finally, you paid attention to what your audience did and didn't like and adjusted accordingly. Crain was a lot like Sam's father, and he quickly became a new, fixed point in Sam's moral universe. Cook would later tell a reporter that Crain was "the guiding force" in his coaching, stage presence, and style.

Sam, with his pitch-perfect ear, learned quickly. The Stirrers toured for about a month—Camden, Hot Springs, Little Rock, a series of one-nighters fairly close together, so you could sleep late in the day and still make the next eight o'clock program. For Sam, it was the beginning of the dream. "I had a wonderful time," he'd say years later, "a wonderful life. I was doing the thing I liked best and getting paid for it. The fifty dollars or so a week I got at the beginning seemed like a fortune. It was one church after another on the one-nighter trail, [but as a teenager] who cares about inconveniences?" There was about a month of this in-battle training, and then Sam headed west to cut his first record with the group.

First, there was a big Los Angeles program at the Embassy Auditorium on February 11. The Pilgrim Travelers and the Sallie Martin Singers were appearing with the Stirrers, and if you went by the publicity, so was R. H. Harris. The main colored paper in town, the *Los Angeles Sentinel*, ran an old picture of Harris snapping his fingers with pleasure as the quartet signed a contract with Specialty Records owner Art Rupe. So far, the Stirrers were keeping Rupe in the dark about their new, untested lead singer.

Art Rupe was a thick-lipped white man with large black glasses and a receding hairline. Though he didn't look hip, he ran one of the most influential independent labels in the country, which would soon feature early rock & roll greats Little Richard, Larry Williams, and Lloyd Price. Specialty was, in Little Richard's words, the Motown of its day, though it isn't as well known as some of its competitors like Chess in Chicago and Sam Phillips's Sun Records in Memphis. That's partly because Specialty was on the West Coast, and rock & roll history has tended to focus on the Mississippi River: from the romantic vision of Robert Johnson playing raw country blues around the Delta plantations through Muddy Waters' migration to Chicago and on to rock's central article of faith surrounding Elvis in Memphis. The story is, of course, much broader than that, and Specialty is right in the middle of it.

In 1930, there were only eighty thousand Negroes in California, almost two-thirds of them concentrated in the Los Angeles area, and most of those clustered around Central Avenue. Around the time Sam Cook was born, L.A.'s colored area was a community of shady pepper-tree-lined streets and leisurely Sunday-afternoon strolls from church. All this disappeared when the nation launched its "preparedness" campaign for the Second World War. California's proximity to the Pacific theater and its year-round good weather created a defense-industry boom; in four years, the state's workers increased by 70 percent.

At first, that didn't affect Negroes. Instead, it provided the unwritten sequel to *The Grapes of Wrath:* on the theory that even they were better than the coloreds, the ostracized Okies were finally given work. But by 1942, the labor shortage was so severe that the aircraft and ship builders had no choice but to hire Negroes. An incredible era of prosperity set in; in June 1943, between ten thousand and twelve thousand Negroes entered the city, the majority coming out of Texas and Louisiana. The colored district spread south to Watts and Compton and west across Crenshaw. If Central was no longer quite as central to the nearly half a million Negroes in the area, it was still studded with nightclubs and after-hours joints. There was the Club Alabam, the Swanee Club, Ivy Anderson's Chicken Shack, Club Alimony. The scene drew the "territory bands": small dance combos that bounced around the Southwest. It convinced two brothers, Otis and Leon René, to form one of the first black-owned record labels, Excelsior/Exclusive. And it drew the young Art Rupe.

Rupe had been raised in McKeesport, Pennsylvania, close enough to a Negro Baptist church to hear the choir singing. "Particularly," he recalls, "in the summer when the church windows were open." He'd come to California, along with thousands of others, to get into the motion picture business. As a graduate student in business administration at UCLA, however, he soon became interested in the independent record business. Rupe got a few months' experience with a small label before graduating. Then, with $600 he'd saved, he decided to go into business for himself.

He began by going to Watts and buying—in tiny, hole-in-the-wall record shops—the ghetto's best-sellers. For a couple of weeks, he listened to the 78s over and over again. "Some of this music moved me so much it brought tears to my eyes," he told author Arnold Shaw. But the business graduate in him was working too, and, stopwatch in hand, he tried to analyze which records clicked and why. As he told Shaw, "I looked for an area neglected by the majors and in essence took the crumbs off the table of the record industry. The majors kept recording what we call country blues. The black people, particularly the black people I knew, never lived in the country. They looked down on country music. Among themselves, the blacks called country blues 'field nigger' music. They wanted to be citified."

It was a crucial distinction. Sam Phillips, for example, has often claimed that his moment of epiphany was seeing the rough-voiced Howlin' Wolf, fresh from the fields, still wearing his overalls, shouting out the blues. "When I heard him," Phillips has testified, "I said, 'This is for me. This is where the soul of man never dies.' " It was an aesthetic Phillips stuck with throughout. You can look long and hard through the Sun catalog without finding anything that might be called sophisticated. And the Chess brothers, too, found in their star, Muddy Waters, a way of selling records by appealing to a nostalgia for the South and exactly the kind of field music (albeit electrified and modernized) that Rupe avoided. But Specialty got its name because Rupe planned to specialize in citified Negro music: "a big-band sound, expressed in a churchy way . . . a little more sophisticated, a little more disciplined, a little more organized and closer to the American, popular, Tin Pan Alley structure. . . ."

The economics of the big band scene was now collapsing under its own weight. (The orchestras of Benny Goodman, Woody Herman, and Charlie Ventura would all fold within a three-week period late in 1946.) Out of the ruins, musicians like Louis Jordan were starting smaller combos. As a white, Rupe admitted he felt like "a freak of some kind" to be fooling around with this other culture's music. But if he had doubts about its commercial potential, they must have been quieted by Joe Liggins's "The Honeydripper." The record had exactly the kind of sound Rupe was looking for, and there it sat—late in 1945—at #1 on *Billboard*'s race charts.

Rupe found his version that same month at the Cobra Room on First Street where Roy Milton's Solid Senders played. "RM Blues" was an instant success and stayed on the "race charts" for twenty-six weeks. As Rupe later put it in a radio interview, it "made two institutions, Roy Milton's Solid Senders and Specialty Records." None of this was by chance. Rupe had followed up his business-school analysis of what made a hit with painstaking rehearsals. Since each three hours of studio time cost him nearly half of his starting capital,

Rupe simply couldn't afford to have the band screw up. And that remained his working method: a market analysis of what "race" records
were selling, finding the artists who could produce that sound, and
then intense preparation to make sure he got what he wanted with a
minimum of time and expense. Rupe characterizes himself as a better
record producer than he was a businessman, but he had to be both to
survive off the "crumbs."

Art Rupe's love for religious music turned out to be a real advantage in the cutthroat world of independent labels. "Actually," he's
said, "I dug gospel music more than rhythm and blues," and Specialty's catalog bears that out. By the time Sam Cook came to record at
the beginning of 1951, the label had released about 120 singles.
These included r&b hits by Milton, Joe Liggins and his brother
Jimmy, and the great balladeer and songwriter Percy Mayfield
("Please Send Me Someone to Love"). But fully a third of Specialty's
releases were aimed at the religious market. Rupe says what he loved
was "the fervor, raw intensity, and sincerity" of the music. "Gospel
was the real thing, and r&b was its child, a derivative and offshoot. . . ." While gospel didn't sell as well on the jukeboxes, it never
seemed to stop selling: a 78 like the Pilgrim Travelers' "Mother
Bowed" would still move briskly years after it was cut. What's more,
the artists were cheap, used to working for little to no wages, and
most of them were incredibly polished: quartet harmonies, worked
out over long hours on the road, were often ready to go as soon as the
group entered the studio.

In 1950, when Rupe first learned the Soul Stirrers might be available, they were already stars, and their recordings on Aladdin were
selling well; Art had a bunch in his personal collection. According to
S. R. Crain, the Mesners at Aladdin "was paying us what amounted
to three or four times more than anybody else was getting. They was
giving us six hundred dollars a session. Man, we thought we was
rich!" But there was trouble getting the money due. Rupe offered the
same flat fee—plus royalties of one cent a side. The Stirrers were delighted. "One thing about Art," Crain says, "he might not have offered you too much, but whatever he offered you, he paid you!"

The Stirrers' first 78 on Specialty, Harris's "By and By," had sold

27,000 copies: a major gospel hit. Late in 1950, their "How Long" had done even better. When Specialty put out a fifth single at the end of January 1951, Rupe wrote Crain, ". . . this kinda makes the well kinda dry. . . . May I suggest you work on as much original and new material as possible . . . at least six sides." So, on March 1, 1951, the group showed up at the Universal Recorders studio in Hollywood with some new songs—but without their best-selling lead.

"Where's Harris, Crain?"

The manager looked at his boss with as little expression as he could. "We don't have Harris no more, Art."

Rupe could see that, and he was shouting angry. As his wife and business partner, Lee Rupe, put it, "You sign the lead"—that's what identified a quartet. What's more, the group had deliberately hidden the change from the record owner: Harris had put his name on their contract renewal just a month before, even though Sam had taken his place.

Crain explained. "I don't want Harris, Art. He quit. He retired. He's a grown man; he's supposed to do what he wants to do. . . . I got a man here in Harris's place." Crain gestured over to Sam, who was sitting to the side, not saying a word. Rupe took one look. "That kid?"

"Yes, sir. He can sing!"

Rupe then turned to his gospel advisor, J. W. Alexander. "Can he sing?" The expensive studio time was ticking past. "Yes, he can sing," J. W. said.

By this time, Crain was losing *his* patience. He couldn't blame Rupe—Harris had the prettiest voice this side of heaven—but you didn't check with Alexander about the new kid. If Crain said he could sing, he could sing. "Art, let me tell you something. I tell you now: don't you ever ask nobody about the Soul Stirrers but me!" Crain was pounding his fist for emphasis, looking at both Alexander and Rupe. "Don't you do that!"

Art surveyed Crain and the rest of the group, the kid in the corner, and then Alexander. "Okay," he said, "I'll allow you one mistake."

As the rest of the Stirrers took their places, Sam stood stiffly and discreetly massaged his hands. The group had decided to begin with one of Thomas Dorsey's tunes, "Come, Let Us Go Back to God," but as Sam sung his first "Oooh!"he threw his head back, and the note carried up and over the mike. Rupe stopped the session; he couldn't even hear the kid. They repositioned and did a second, satisfactory take, but if, as Crain says, Sam left Rupe "at awe. He awed Art Rupe!" the label owner didn't show it. The way he judged a record was how it sold, not how it sounded. Plus, too much studio time had already been wasted. All business, Rupe moved them right on to "Peace in the Valley," a crowd favorite in the Southwest, probably because the Stirrers modeled their version of the Dorsey tune on country-western singer Red Foley's. Paul Foster took control of most of the lead, with Sam adding only one shouted verse.

Eventually, they got to "Christ Is All," a tune the Stirrers had cut with Harris back in July. Written by Kenneth Morris, a Chicago-based songwriter and publisher, "Christ Is All" had a "pop" feel to it. In Harris's version, the group had sung a remarkable, bubbly backup like some old steam calliope. Over that, the Old Man had delivered a sincere, lifting lead up high in his range. For Sam, the group left the arrangement pretty much alone. Though that meant it was pitched almost too high for the boy, he used that to his advantage. When he rose to join the others on a blended note—"He's all!"—the obvious effort came across as fresh and innocent. There's a choirboy quality coupled with a sophisticated rhythmic sense: as the background percolates along, Sam skims and darts among the Stirrers like a boy playing with waves at the beach.

Rupe was turning Cook's recording debut into a marathon eleven-song session, but he fought against doing what turned out to be the biggest hit. "The kid wanted to record a song," J. W. Alexander recalls, "called 'Jesus Gave Me Water.' " It was a tune that Alexander's Pilgrim Travelers had recorded for Rupe a couple of years before. That spring, the song was being featured as part of a five-record package over WLAC in Nashville. "So Art hit the ceiling," recalls Alexander, who tried to reassure him that it was okay: the Travelers had plenty of songs. Plus, the kid did it differently. The Travelers' version started at a solemn pace with smooth group harmony. When Kylo Turner took lead, the song stayed slow and kept the hushed, reverent quality of some of the old spirituals. It seemed a suitable pace for the biblical story of the Sumerian woman who met her Savior at the well. The young Sam Cook's take on the tune is an early indication of the qualities that would identify him for years to come.

First of all, the group had rearranged the tune at double the tempo, so it jumped along. Sam starts it with a soaring "Oh, Jesus," and then the backup chants "gave me water": a contagiously optimistic sound. Where the Travelers found the story awe-inspiring, Sam approaches it with all the enthusiasm of a kid jumping up and down telling a crowd of friends about what happened down at the well this morning. Cook was never considered to have one of gospel's best voices, but he did become known as a great storyteller, and "Jesus Gave Me Water," is his first masterpiece in that vein. By this, their eighth number, he's worked out his mike problems and every word is clearly enunciated. The sweet Mississippi accent he got from his parents dwells on each syllable and calls for attention. The third time through the chorus, Sam lets the group start and, by coming in a beat later, kicks up the excitement. And when he sings "I want to let His praises swell," Sam's voice does just that. If Art Rupe didn't know he had a hit here, he wasn't listening.

Finally, the session also produced the first recording of one of Sam's own songs, "Until Jesus Calls Me Home." Finding new material was a constant struggle for all gospel groups, and the Stirrers were delighted if their new lead brought his own songs. Crain says, "Sam could do it. You either got it or you don't got it. Sam had it. . . . He was a genius so far as melody was concerned. He'd just whistle a melody." In this case, the tune offers some insight into the songwriter. "Why should I worry?" it begins. "I'm gonna find consolation in God's sweet Zion songs." We should sing, it goes on, "till Jesus calls. . . ." If there are echoes of the Reverend Cook and Gatemouth Moore—music as entertainment—Sam's also declaring that one way to cope with the world is through the sheer beauty of the human voice.

Art Rupe has said his first impression of Sam Cook was of a "very intense guy. He didn't give an appearance of being nervous, but when you'd talk to him he'd really study you; he'd really look and listen like he was taking impressions with his pores as well as with his eyes and with his ears."

He was also studying the business. One of Sam's early lessons would come when he learned that in order to record his tune, he had to sign a writer's contract that called for Cook to publish any and all of his songs with Rupe's Venice Music Incorporated. That meant 50 percent of the receipts went to the owner. Controlling an artist's publishing was standard practice for both independent and major labels at the time—which helps explain why executives who never sang or wrote a note ended up making most of the money. Crain, a productive songwriter himself, recalls, "We would put it in his publishing. We didn't know no better then. . . ." For Sam, just turned twenty, the chance of having one of his songs released as a record was a dream come true; the rest must have seemed like details. But the contract would come to haunt him.

Rupe took a while to release the new material. A month after the session, on April 8, when the Stirrers were back in Chicago on a program with Brother Joe May, Crain was pushing for some action. "Yes," Art reassured him, "you are about due for another release," and added with mixed enthusiasm, "I think you have got something." But another month later, from Florida, Crain was still trying to convince Rupe: "I am sure that the people will like and buy my records with the young feller (Sam)."

The Soul Stirrers made their real money not from their penny-a-record royalties but from live performances. They needed a successful record to draw big houses, and that was especially true with their new lead. Right after the recording session, for example, the Stirrers had done a Sunday-morning radio broadcast to promote an Oakland program. When the promoter had realized that Harris was gone, he'd panicked and wanted to back out. Likewise, major gospel stops in the Midwest and South didn't want to book them with the new kid. They couldn't get a program in Birmingham, where the group was used to earning $700 to $1,000 with Harris. Instead, they ended up in Bessamer—a great gospel town but eleven miles outside Birmingham with decidedly smaller crowds. They needed a record with 'Sam on it to get over, and finally, late in May, Rupe released "Peace in the Valley"/"Jesus Gave Me Water."

Specialty's were some of the finest-sounding 78s of the era; Rupe not only insisted on using the best studios but he had also turned out to be a first-rate producer. "Where Art was good," Crain remarks, "he was good on mastering. Master mean when you get the tape in there, when you go to mastering, you know how to pull the lead singer in. Put the background back and pull the lead in. He knew that. He was genius at that!" Usually, the gospel sides didn't take much fiddling: there was minimal instrumentation, and the material had been honed to a sharp edge on the road. The other place Rupe was good was on the original recording. He treated gospel, as he says now, "as an art form" and pushed his singers. "The expression I used in the studio was 'Let's put more church in it!' The artists knew what I meant, and generally delivered." Finally, he had a good ear for what would sell and worked hard at promotion.

With all that, he was apparently as surprised as anyone by "Jesus Gave Me Water." It hit as no Soul Stirrers single ever had before: within a couple of months of its release, it had sold nearly seventeen thousand copies. Harris's biggest hit on Specialty had sold about ten thousand more than that, but then, in the next quarter, "Jesus Gave Me Water" doubled its sales. For the first time ever, the Soul Stirrers earned back their recording advance and got some royalties. The record single-handedly made Sam Cook's reputation and started the group on its most popular and profitable period. Sam was ecstatic, the Stirrers delighted, and Rupe—once he'd seen the figures—was finally convinced. "[We] want to thank you for suggesting that we put out 'Jesus Gave Me Water,' " he wrote Crain that September, "and keeping on us until we did it. . . . What do you think we should release next?"

Chapter

6

I t all turned on Sister Flute. That's what the Stirrers called her, a name they'd first heard around New York City. There was a Sister Flute in every congregation: the archetypal church mother, the one who started the shouting. When she fell out—when she danced the holy dance and locked rigid with the Spirit, so caught in the throes of possession that the deacons had to come and wrestle her back into the pew so she wouldn't hurt herself, her eyes rolled up, her heels pounding the hard wood floor, her best Sunday hat crushed and forgotten beside her—once Sister Flute got to moaning and amening, the rest would follow. And then the Stirrers triumphed. Because when you got Sister Flute, you got the house, and when you got the house, the offerings were larger and the crowds in the next town a little bigger. It was said that the tradition of spirit possession went back to the ring dances of the slaves and, beyond that, to Africa, but for Sam and the Stirrers it was a question of the here and now—of Sister Flute.

With "Jesus Gave Me Water," Sam had a calling card, but he still had to learn how to turn the crowd, and the only school was one-nighter after one-nighter. The Stirrers might do only twenty to thirty minutes a program—a couple of songs during the first half, a few more at the end—but they booked programs six days a week, ten months out of the year. "It's a wonder we lasted so long as we did,"

Crain reflects. "Run ourselves to death!" Every successful gospel group had to do it. The Pilgrim Travelers' itinerary for April 1950 gives some idea of the intensity. The quartet played twenty-two dates that month, starting in Philadelphia and cutting down through South Carolina, Georgia, Alabama, Tennessee, and Mississippi, till they ended up in Monroe, Louisiana. They then got a day off to get to New Orleans, but mostly it was booking on top of booking and glad of it. In one week, for example, they played a different Alabama town every night: Huntsville, Talladega, Decatur, Montgomery. And you were supposed to get Sister Flute every night in every town.

For Sam, there was the added burden that she came expecting to hear R. H. Harris. Because the gospel circuit was fairly set, Sam kept having to sing in the same churches and before the same crowds that Harris had. In April, for example, the Soul Stirrers hosted their annual Mother's Day program at DuSable High. The program included the Travelers and Sam's old radio mates, the Spirit of Memphis. The crowd was fine, but Harris's new group—the Christland Singers— had appeared in the same place just a week before, and most people in the gospel world couldn't help but hold the younger man up against the older.

After Mother's Day in Chicago, the Stirrers usually had an Easter program sponsored by the Reverend C. L. Franklin in Detroit. During the good spring weather, they'd hit the Deep South and maybe swing up through the Northeast. They'd go to Newark (where the gospel crowds tended to be bigger than in New York City), then down through Philadelphia—a solid Stirrers town—and Washington. Then, during the summer, they might be anywhere. In August 1951, they played Texas, and if the ads for the program at the Sam Houston Coliseum are any indication, Sam's hit record still hadn't made the difference. The Travelers, the Blind Boys, and the Spirit of Memphis all listed their current hits and ran pictures of their famous leads. For the Stirrers, on the other hand, the promoter used a shot of Paul Foster and advertised Harris's number "By and By."

In September, the group usually sponsored another all-star program in Chicago and then tried to hit the Carolinas in time for the tobacco harvest, when their fans had money in their pockets. In the dead of winter, they'd be in Florida—St. Pete, Tampa, Miami; Christmas back at home; then out to California for another bout of recording in February. That first year, as Sam did the circuit, Sister Flute listened, she even nodded her approval; but it wasn't Rebert Harris—and she didn't budge.

Looking back, S. R. Crain believes the difference between Harris, "the gentleman," and Sam Cook was the difference between the forties and the fifties. "Harris was a fanatical Christian," Crain recalls. "Sam was not." You could joke with Cook about the church ladies getting off on their harmonies, about the shady ministers and promoters, about the sexual shenanigans going on in the various churches. Harris would hear none of it. It isn't, according to Crain, that Harris didn't have gospel groupies himself, but he "had to try and get the do, where Sam was running away from it."

Quartet singers, arriving in their long cars and dressed in their slick city-tailored suits, had always attracted women. But the war years, with their dramatic increase in working women, marked a real change. The way Harris put it to author Anthony Heilbut, "Women became more far-ward, they came to the front faster, they were more open in their push." Harris didn't like it. The Old Man believed deeply in not just the gospel highway, but the Gospel Path. For him, the Soul Stirrers were messengers, traveling from town to town, setting an example, and his rectitude (he avoided even being around anyone who enjoyed a social drink) spoke well to his generation. In 1945, he ran for mayor of Bronzeville—a popularity contest dreamed up by Chicago's colored papers to boost circulation—and won walking away with over 400,000 votes.

Harris's attitude translated directly into the way he sang. Starting in the late forties, leads like the Dixie Hummingbirds' Ira Tucker had begun charging the aisles, running down through the center of the church to confront Sister Flute face to face, urging her on, daring her not to respond to the divine Presence in the room. The Soul Stirrers didn't play that. "R. H. Harris used to stand right there, flat-footed," says Crane, "and he'd kill the world!"

Though Sam had grown up in the Holiness church and had seen the outrageously great Brownlee and Tucker in action, he'd been trained to stand just as still. In fact, thanks to R.B. and the years with the QCs, Cook could do a creditable enough impression of Harris to please Sister Flute. But an impression was all it was. "Sam had the best tone," Crane states, "but he couldn't outcry Rebert Harris. Harris's daddy was the best tenor in Texas. Sam wouldn't tackle any song the least bit too high. Sam used his head; Harris would tackle any note." Even after the Stirrers lowered their pitch, Sam hit anything over high C with what they called a false tone.

In Crain's estimation—and the recordings bear this out—Harris was flat-out a better singer than Cook: a larger range, a sweeter tone, and a pioneering way of phrasing that Cook could only study. It tore right into Sister Flute. His style was perfect for the thirty-to-sixty-year-olds who came to church after a long week's work and wanted a reminder of the old-time, countrified religion. Harris's aching tenor—learned, he has said, by listening to the songbirds out on the Texas plains—spoke directly to the congregation's recent past. In the first few months after Sam took over, the change was obvious. The Stirrers might hear an occasional shout, but people didn't get up and walk across the pews to the front of the church, yelling and carrying on, as they had with Harris.

What the Stirrers noticed instead was a startling change: the children started coming forward. Though the quartet had been on the road for decades, it had never seen anything quite like this. Girls in their teens and younger, normally flirting in the back pews or waiting patiently beside their parents and grandparents for the service to be over, suddenly pushed to the front—and shouted. It wasn't Sister Flute, but it was something. What popular music was just beginning to see—the empowerment, some say the invention, of the teenager—began happening in gospel around Sam Cook.

In a way, it wasn't surprising. After all, the era's top female singer, Bronzeville's own Dinah Washington, had learned how to get a house as one of Sallie Martin's gospel singers. And the summer's #1 hit, the Dominoes' "60 Minute Man," may have had street-corner lyrics—how to keep doing it for an hour at a stretch—but musically, it was bathed in quartet singing. The group's organizer, Billy Ward, had founded the Dominoes to sing gospel, and Clyde McPhatter, their lead, had come up with the Mount Lebanon Singers in New York City. In fact, their first appearance at the Apollo Theater, they'd sung spirituals—opposite the Orioles, whose double leads and hummed backgrounds also sounded awfully familiar to any Stirrers fan.

Meanwhile, in the gospel world, singers like Sister Rosetta Tharpe kept pushing the music closer to pop entertainment. When Tharpe married her road manager in July 1951, 25,000 paying customers watched the ceremony at the baseball stadium in Washington, D.C. Rosetta, never one to disappoint her fans, wore a $1,000 white nylon lace gown with a sequin-trimmed three-foot train. Newspapers began noting the "current fad in the hinterlands for gospel singers who team showmanship and religion."

All of this worried members of R. H. Harris's generation. In August, Thomas Dorsey issued a warning: "If the words are not clearly heard, much of today's gospel music can be confused with the 'blues.' We sincerely hope that this bad practice will cease now. Let us always, please, keep our gospel music as it was intended—a music of reverence and worship." Solemn as that sounds, it was spoken by a man who, two decades earlier, had been known as Georgia Tom, a blues pianist whose biggest hit, "Tight Like That," steamed with risqué lyrics. The criticism he was now leveling at gospel was exactly what he and Mahalia had faced in the thirties, and Dorsey would have no more luck drawing the line between sacred and secular than anyone else.

What Cook had going, as Crain puts it, was "youth, education, presentation." He still hadn't filled out, and his thin, graceful body was a lot like the young Sinatra's. His smooth features (the word people always used for him was "pretty") seemed to catch fire when he smiled. Plus, he worked at getting the house. Lorenza Brown Porter, leader of the Argo Singers out of Chicago, remembers seeing the Stirrers in Atlanta one time when Sister Flute stayed dead cold. No matter what the quartet did, the congregation wouldn't respond, until, finally, Sam stepped away from the others, sat down on the edge of the slightly raised altar area, and just kept "singing, singing, singing," till he won them over. Porter calls it "sincerity" and adds, "Through bad times or good times, his voice had hope."

That was another difference between Cook and Harris. Harris's voice had rung with the sound of want, but, as Sam took over, the country was finally coming to believe the hard times were done. Though the recession of 1947 had been worrisome, its mildness had ended up convincing many that the economy might survive peacetime. Business had begun to boom. Between 1947 and 1957, the country's real gross national product would increase by 45 percent; Americans would move in droves to their own homes in the suburbs; new cars and television sets would become commonplace instead of luxuries. It's true that throughout this period, Sam's colored congregations stayed in about the same economic relationship to whites as they'd been in during Harris's day—but everyone's lot was improving.

Instead, there were a new set of worries. In March 1947, President Truman had issued an executive order to find "infiltration of disloyal persons" in the government. Now, Senator Joe McCarthy was waving lists of alleged communists, and leading Negroes from W.E.B. Du Bois to actor/singer Paul Robeson (whose concerts featured spiritual singing in the old, pre-gospel style) were being effectively silenced. The gospel world was part of this "battle." The *Los Angeles Sentinel*, for example, donated a full page to the First Congregational Church's ad entitled "Deliver Us from Evil." "America has lost her way," it began. "Our boys are dying in Korea. Our people at home are disillusioned, confused and frustrated. . . . Only the Communists seem to know where they are going. . . . [and] the Communist challenge can only be met with the help of Almighty God." In January, the Pilgrim Travelers had recorded a J. W. Alexander song, "Jesus Is the First Line of Defense," that promised prayer would defeat the Reds.

Sam's approach was more subtle. His second Soul Stirrers single was "Come, Let Us Go Back to God"/"Joy, Joy to My Soul," released in late 1951. Crain calls "Joy" a pop song: "We had the thirteenth notes and all like that." From Sam's first, sweet reading of "I'm blessed" to Farley's almost minstrel-like bass lead, the tune is all light and air. Though it goes back to an earlier era for its exquisite barbershop harmonies, the song's assurance fits the times. As he'd written in his first recorded composition, singing was the answer to worry, and "Joy" finger-popped along much the same lines. Art Rupe calls Sam more "mellifluous" than Harris, with "more control"; the same adjectives might be used to describe the new decade compared to the old.

When this second single began to fade early in 1952, the Stirrers arrived in Los Angeles to cut more material. The recording session on February 22 was neither Sam's nor the group's finest hour. A major problem was the accompaniment. Though master engineer Bunny Robyn signed the recording sheet, Art Rupe okayed the drummer that was added to all seven songs they cut. Quartets were beginning to realize—as "gospel" groups like Rosetta Tharpe's had long since—that a little instrumentation helped put a number over, but the Stirrers' arrangements were clearly worked out a cappella. On "Jesus Paid the Debt" and "Jesus Will Lead Me," the thumping bass drum and heavy-handed high hat drag the beats.

They did better on "How Far Am I from Canaan." When Sam ad libs, "I can hear—I can hear the saints, child—singing," it nestles into the Stirrers' arrangement as if it had been practiced hundreds of times—which it had been, all along the gospel highway. But on the first single released from the session, "It Won't Be Very Long," Sam is mostly second lead and, in trying to match Paul's intensity, does a mediocre R. H. Harris. If this is how he'd been coping with Sister Flute's expectations on the road, Cook was getting the Old Man's urgency by raising his voice to where it sounded ready and rough. "Just Another Day," written by Sam, hits some of the same snags. It's a sign of how hard Cook was battling Harris's ghost that Foster, the shouter, actually sounds the more relaxed.

Finally, Crain had arranged "Let Me Go Home" in a quiet, intimate style. Home, in this case, is "up yonder." The song tugs on a lot of the same heartstrings as the Travelers' songs about Mother—with not quite as much schmaltz. Foster's reading of the line "I want to be home with my Father" is convincing; his earthly father, after all, had passed just before Paul joined the Stirrers. But when it's Sam's turn to talk about his visions of his family "around the old fireside at home," it sounds forced. He had no experience of the rural life they're trying to evoke (the Cooks were more likely to be around the radio in their South Side apartment), and he tries to compensate by pushing his voice. Still, there's one moment that gives a hint of things to come. When Cook sings how he hears his family "calling for their children," his voice breaks on "calling." It's the beginning of the "yodel" he would later make famous. It doesn't quite fit the song; it doesn't have the smoothness of later years; but there it is, in early 1952: the trademark that would help shape his career.

The other thing that may have made "Let Me Go Home" tough for Sam to sing convincingly was its sentiment. While he came from a strong family and was extremely loyal to it, this first year on the gospel highway was dedicated to sowing wild oats. Though he went out of his way to present himself as a clean-cut, well-mannered Christian, he was also young, attractive, and on the loose. Sam Moore (who went on to fame singing with Sam and Dave) grew up in a highly religious home in Miami. He remembers the first time Cook came into town with the Stirrers for a program at his high school: "When I first saw this man and heard him, I said, 'Oh my God! Look at him!' This man was so smooth, so good, and such class! ... You gotta understand: a pretty boy that's got class! I mean, I've seen women just pass out wanting to get to him!" It wasn't just women, either. Miami's premier gospel promoter was, in Moore's words, "an open gay. We're talking flaming! He was a little bit more than Little Richard . . . very stylish, but there was no secret." There was a lot of homosexuality in gospel—some of the greatest talents, male and female—and, in Moore's words, "many who were welcomed into [the Miami promoter's] bed." Moore doesn't pretend to say Sam was one of them, "but I know [the promoter] loved himself some Sam Cook."

Unknown to his gospel fans, by 1952, Cook, age twenty-one, was going to be a father. Barbara Campbell, the pretty twin who had been his grade school sweetheart, was pregnant. In April 1953, she would have a baby girl: Linda. Fatherhood came as Sam was trying to grow into the role of lead singer for the most famous quartet on the road. Inevitably, that meant shedding some of the old neighborhood. For example, one afternoon he showed up for a program with his face all banged up. It seemed he'd been in a little gang fight, nothing serious. But Crain, the quartet's manager, made it clear that

Cook could either be a member of the Soul Stirrers or the Junior Destroyers—not both. Barbara Campbell was part of that past, of what a twenty-one-year-old might call his "youth." No one seems to remember exactly what caused the split—maybe it was a fight, maybe it was simply that he was on the road all the time, maybe it was the child—but a friend of both Barbara and Sam recalls, "Barbara had to raise the baby alone. She did everything she could to try to keep jobs going. And she told me that she worked in factories, and, if she was sick one day, they'd dock her. And all she got was thirty-five dollars a week anyway. . . . I don't know why he didn't marry her." But he didn't; he stayed in touch, he offered some support, but he didn't get married.

Between the February recording session and that August when the Stirrers returned to Los Angeles, Cook was on the gospel circuit almost full-time. The premier gospel attractions were starting to make relatively good money: Mahalia's three-month "Gospel Train" headed out that March for what the *Defender* called "a juicy $3,000 weekly guarantee." Clara Ward and the Ward Singers played Carnegie Hall in April and drew thirteen thousand in a hometown appearance at Philadelphia's Convention Hall. The Stirrers were in a particularly strong position to capitalize on this. Through the forties, they had played an informal network of churches, schools, and auditoriums, arriving in town a little early to pass around handbills or maybe hang out at the local barbershop to make sure folks knew they were there. It had been a courtesy system: one group booked a program with out-of-town acts, and the favor would be returned a few months later. Then, late in 1949, Art Rupe had started Herald Attractions. "I felt a gospel booking agency would serve my artists and boost their earnings vis-à-vis the haphazard way they were booking themselves." Rupe didn't need to add that it would also boost his earnings by giving him a cut of the action and helping to promote the records.

The move placed Specialty in the forefront of the industry in more ways than one. Rupe hired a Negro woman, Lillian Cumber, to manage Herald Attractions. "[T]his company, Specialty, is the only one that has ever attempted to create a position for a Negro," Cumber wrote around the time she was hired. "The others just don't seem to care. . . ." Specialty, she added, "will not tolerate a distributor who is prejudice [sic] even if it means the loss of sales. Mr. Art Rupe is a young liberal who doesn't preach liberalism, he practices it." As a PR woman, Cumber may have been prone to exaggeration, but her hiring and the whole concept of Herald Attractions made quite an impact in gospel; it created a Specialty package program of the Stirrers, the Travelers, Brother Joe May, and, occasionally, the Swan Silvertones. Though the circuit was still chancy going—promoters would back out of programs, or hold them and refuse to pay, or pay less than promised—at least the Stirrers didn't have to do it all themselves the way Mahalia, for example, would continue to do for years to come.

In August, they swung through Los Angeles for the annual National Quartet Convention. In an all-star program at St. Paul's, they appeared with R. H. Harris's new group, the Christland Singers. It wasn't a head-to-head between Cook and Harris—that would come later—but it was certainly a summit meeting. Ten days later, Lil Cumber sent the group out on the most intensive stretch of touring Sam had yet seen. Along with the Travelers and Archie Brownlee's Blind Boys, they would play 101 cities over the next three months. Cumber started the tour with a press release saying they were expected to sing to over fifty thousand people.

By now, Sam had the routine pretty well down. Programs usually began at seven or eight in the evening. They started with a prayer, followed by a local minister reading from the Bible. If no minister was available, one of the singers would do the honors. "We ain't here for no entertainment now," someone usually had to say. "We're here for church!" The warning was needed when you looked out over the congregation. The youngsters were oohing and aahing at their first sight of Sam; Sister Flute was all done up in her Sunday best; and the deacons sat in their dark suits carefully checking that their ties were still knotted just so. But no one looked sharper than the quartets. The Soul Stirrers traveled with two sets of tux and tails (one black and one white), at least one other tailored suit with those wide lapels and the big, loosely flowing trousers, and a pair of brightly shined shoes to go with each outfit. Their hair was processed and slicked back, and Sam had grown a neatly trimmed pencil-thin moustache to match the older men's. All the singers sat up at the front of the church like visiting dignitaries, applauding the little local groups who usually opened the show.

Each night they would rotate the order of appearance. In the first half, each group would make sure to sing their current single and maybe one other tune. So, in that summer of 1952, after Archie Brownlee had issued some of his trademark shrieks on "Precious Memories," the Pilgrim Travelers would do "Lord, Help Me Carry On," an ideal vehicle for Kylo Turner's vocal acrobatics. And the Stirrers would let Sam slice through "Canaan" just to give everyone a taste of what was to come. Then there'd be a half-hour intermission. The groups would come down to mingle with the congregation and sell autographed 8 × 10s. The Specialty acts never hawked their records at live appearances; Art Rupe kept track of inventory back in L.A. Still, Crain can recall years when the Stirrers met their car payments on the proceeds from the souvenirs alone. If the programs weren't entertainment, they were certainly business.

In the second half, each group would knuckle down to get Sister Flute. Though they might do only a couple more tunes each, the men would stretch them out. Now was the time for Kylo's leg kicks and for Brownlee to wander between the pews. By now, the Stirrers had adjusted to what their young lead could and couldn't do. On a line like the one from Dorsey's "Someday Somewhere"—"I may be next on program to go"—Sam couldn't quite bring off the required sense of foreboding. He was too young, and he didn't have the voice for it. But give him something hopeful, something uplifting, and he soared. Sister Flute got swept up by the young man's sweetness, and the other Soul Stirrers saw the future unfold before them.

The programs usually ended around eleven. Then, depending on how far the next stop was, they'd either push on or decide to spend the night. Staying at a church sister's meant a home-cooked meal and a comfortable bed, when too often the alternative was sleeping in the car and eating what was known as "quartet chicken": bologna and bread. By the early fifties, there were Negro hotels in the bigger cities, and the Stirrers would settle down to relax before bed. Sam, the rookie, would always be bouncing after a program. As in his QC days, he was ready to try out new material or work on arrangements. And he loved to talk. He'd chatter on about current events or music, anything and everything, till his roommate, Foster, just had to go to bed. Then he'd go bother someone else.

"He'd come knock on your door anytime," recalls Albertina Walker of the Caravans, "two, three o'clock in the morning. He couldn't sleep. He'd come knock on my door—not just mine but others as well. I'd be asleep or whatever. 'Tina! I got a joke. Girl, let me tell you. I got a joke you got to hear. I can't keep it to myself. You got to hear this joke, Tina! Tina! . . .' And, Lord, the joke wouldn't be funny at all. I'll be wanting to kill him. But what would make you laugh was him. It would tickle him so bad, you'd be laughing at Sam!"

Or the rookie would head out to explore whatever town they were in. That's how fellow gospel singer Johnnie Morisette met Cook. One night in Mobile, Alabama, Morisette was walking into the Twilight Cafe, a gospel hangout, when a skinny kid jumped the fence. "I hear you're a singer," Sam said. (Morisette was lead with a girl group, the Harmonious Harmonettes.) "Well, I'm a singer, too." The two cocky youngsters hit it off, went on to hear a program together, and, as Morisette told journalist Tim Schuller, "We stayed out the whole night long. . . . Sam and me was runnin' round Mobile in a big old Packard, we was *ridin',* Jack! I was introducin' him to the girls. . . . and the Harmonious Harmonettes—they was pretty!"

Although all the singers had their special friends whom they'd visit each time they came through town, Sam was proving himself quite a ladies' man. He had a seemingly bottomless appetite, and it wasn't just sexual. He loved the companionship. He loved talking with women, trying out new songs on them; he loved just hanging out. And they, in turn, loved him. Sam never appeared to be hitting on anyone; he didn't have to. His big smile and smooth brown skin, the way his body arched when he stood on tiptoe to reach a note, were more than enough. The women would flock around him, and his courteous son-of-a-preacher's manners welcomed them all.

When day broke, the six men would load up their bags and pile into the car. Each year, the group would rack up some 100,000 miles on a Buick or Cadillac, then buy a new one. On the dusty highways, they'd practice their harmonies or just nod off in the back till the next town, where the same thing started all over. Johnny Fields of the Alabama Blind Boys recalls how "on those long, boresome trips riding, we would stop through town. [Sam] would run in and get a couple of books. He was a good reader. He would ride with the Blind Boys for miles and read different westerns to us."

The groups lived in such close proximity that, as Jesse Whitaker of the Travelers put it, you had to "try to treat each other like brothers. And that's the only way a group can get along—you got to be like brothers, and you got to be businesslike." The Stirrers had strict rules of behavior, setting fines for missing rehearsal or being late to a program, and Sam mostly followed them—at least as a younger man. "We were spiritual singers, you see? That's a different thing than when you're in show business," says Crain. "There has to be a oneness to make it in spirituals. Because the money isn't there, so you got to have that oneness between each other to make it."

In December, when the 101-city tour finally ended, the Soul Stirrers just kept traveling. On the 14th, they were in Cleveland, where they shared a program with the Spirit of Memphis, and, as a special guest, the Negro first baseman for the Indians, Luke Easter. Here, Sam first met the Womack Brothers, a local family group, which must have reminded him of his own Singing Children. The kids' father, Friendly Womack, was a tenor lead for a couple of the city's gospel groups, and when he heard the Stirrers were in town, "[h]e went down and hit on the manager," recalls Bobby Womack, "to see if we could open the show." Crain was understandably skeptical: Friendly Jr., the oldest, was all of eleven, Bobby was eight, and the baby, Cecil, was four. According to Bobby, Sam tipped the scale. "Go ahead," he encouraged Crain, "give the boys a chance." As Cecil Womack climbed up on a fruit box in order to reach the mike, Sam grinned: "Take it easy on me now, little fellow! Don't give me too hard a time." Their debut set the Womacks on a trail that would eventually lead to a contract with Sam's record label—and that was the least of it. Bobby would end up stepfather to Sam and Barbara's child, Linda—who would, in turn, grow up to marry Cecil.

While in Cleveland, Sam also learned he was going to become a father again. His relationship with Marine Sommerville dated back to when Reverend Cook had pastored a church in the city: the Sommervilles had lived on 87th Street, the Cooks one street over. Later, Marine had gotten reacquainted at one of the programs, something that happened all the time, according to Crain. "They'd hear Sam, and they'd just bowly-bowly-bowl over him! Marine," he goes on, "came to Chicago for a while, messed around there, and got big." That December, 1952, she was five months big. Their daughter, Denise, was born in April, and though this child didn't slow him down, either, he recognized her as his own, gave the mother some money, and stayed in touch. Years later, when his income had soared, Marine would sue him for child support. At the moment, he was young and irresponsible and apparently bewitchingly attractive enough to get away with almost anything.

When the Stirrers returned to Chicago for Christmas, Sam was still living with his parents at 724 East 36th Street. It made sense, given how rarely he was home—and how little cash he managed to save. He was the only unmarried Stirrer, the only one not paying rent, and he was still constantly broke. It was part of the rookie's personality, and the others must have figured he'd outgrow it.

But even if Sam had wanted to find his own place, it would have been difficult. That November, as Dwight Eisenhower was elected President, Chicago's enforced segregation was pushing the housing situation in Bronzeville past the livable. A few years earlier, the Supreme Court had ruled that restrictive covenants were illegal, so white citizens' groups had turned to other means. During the summer of 1951, a Negro couple had tried to move into the all-white suburb of Cicero. A mob of six thousand whites, many of them teenagers, had taken to the streets. For two days, the police did little more than observe the rampage. Finally, five hundred National Guard troops were brought in. "I keep asking myself why all this just to keep Johnetta and me from moving into the apartment," Harvey

Clark asked, but Bronzeville knew why. As the young NAACP law-yer Thurgood Marshall put it a few weeks before the Cicero riot, "We don't want equality next year or in the next decade or the next generation; we want it now."

Similar things were happening across the country. On Christmas night, 1952, a bomb went off under the bedroom of one of Florida's leading civil rights crusaders, killing him instantly. In the winter months, as Sam toured the South, the FBI cracked down on the Ku Klux Klan, arresting thirty-one members. At the same time, Marshall was presenting five separate challenges to the school segregation laws in the hope that the Supreme Court would rule segregation not only unfair but unconstitutional.

Maybe the older Stirrers couldn't sense it, but Sam's generation was beginning to force a change. You could hear it in the music. In Cleveland, a white disk jockey named Alan Freed sponsored some-thing called a "Moondog Matinee" that headlined the Dominoes and drew a big, racially mixed teenage audience. In Los Angeles, the lead-ing r&b store was reporting that 40 percent of its sales were to whites. Even Art Rupe's Specialty broadened. Drawn to New Orleans by the rolling piano sound of Fats Domino's "Goin' Home," Rupe and his wife, Lee, discovered a singer so shy he auditioned from be-hind a curtain. But with Domino and his band backing him, Lloyd Price did a number called "Lawdy Miss Clawdy" which eventually went to #1 r&b, stayed on the charts six months, and changed Rupe's mind about who bought his records. A line from the Dominoes' "60 Minute Man"—"I rock 'em and roll 'em all night long"—was begin-ning to resonate through the culture.

Chapter 7

I t's not surprising that S. R. Crain and J. W. Alexander can pinpoint the moment Sam Cook made his breakthrough. After all, it changed their lives, too. That the two men disagree on exactly where it happened isn't surprising, either, given the number of dates they shared. Both place it at the beginning of 1953 in California: Alexander recalls the town as San Jose; Crain remembers a school auditorium in Fresno. But both describe a single moment of transformation, and they agree on how the "accident" happened.

The song, Crain says, was that same "How Far Am I from Caanan?" that had been Cook's audition number. The Soul Stirrers would still occasionally forget and pitch "Canaan" up where Harris used to sing it. At this program, when Cook tried to reach for the highs, he couldn't make it. "So, in trying to dodge one of those high notes," Alexander remarks, "he did a whoa-whoa-whoa type of thing." Or, as Crain puts it, "He just floated under."

It's a technique Cook had used before. Tate recalls it from when Sam sang with the QCs. Gatemouth Moore, speaking of Sam as a teenager in Memphis, says, "He could yoooo! He could yodel into them notes!" The Reverend Sammy Lewis thinks he even recalls the technique when Sam was with the Singing Children: "He would make those—what we'd call curlicues?—with his voice; people would just fall out!" And Alexander adds, "The note-bending was a thing that had been done with gospel even before Sam. Harris was a note-bender. [But] Sam had a particular note-bending style." When Sam took hold of a note that night in California, it wasn't the traditional, nonverbal moan that Holiness congregations were used to. It wasn't a cry of pain. Instead, he decorated the note, embellishing the melody till it hung, fragile as lace, in the air over the congregation.

Whatever you called it, the technique fit in beautifully with the Soul Stirrers' tight, light harmonies. It was, compared to the shouting of Archie Brownlee or the Stirrers' own Paul Foster, an urban sound: cool, sophisticated, and yet shot through with emotion. Sam's looks alone were drawing a younger crowd, but this was the aural equivalent: the sound of a new generation, based on what the gospel pioneers had done but replacing the emphasis. As Johnny Fields of the Blind Boys of Alabama puts it, "It was a certain joy in his singing. Even when he was singing about Mother, it was not a thing where you'd run off and tuck your head. And when people would shout, it wasn't from sadness; they would be shouting from happiness." Both Alexander and Crain were savvy enough to hear something new and different and know, almost immediately, its potential. "Sam," S.R. told him after the breakthrough program, "that sound good to me!"

Cook put on a little modesty: "Well, I had to do that, Crain, 'cause it was too high."

"Yeah," Crain answered, "just keep doin' it."

The next program, Sam tried it again, and thirty years later, S.R. can still remember the audience's excitement as the kid swooped through his leads, testing and expanding on this new sound he'd come upon. "Amen!" it began. And then as Cook strung out another syllable, bending and leaning on the note, it was "Hallelujah!" This was God's work, this exquisite new sound that echoed around the church. "Thank you, Jesus! Thank the Lord!" Old women rose in their Sunday best and waved folded fans in the air; men slapped each other on the back and chortled; and the young girls got wide-eyed and steely with attention. "Sing, boy! Help yourself! Thank you, Jesus!"

"It's a fire," says Crain about such moments. "A fire that burns. If you're serious about this thing, as a singer, it *will* burn. You'll catch

on fire, and it'll burn everybody!" Cook had turned out a crowd before, but never like this—never just by hitting a note and hanging
there, bending it, finding the melody behind what the older men
were harmonizing. Almost instantaneously, he knew and the congregation knew something special had happened. "One heart," says
Crain, "touched the other one."

You can hear the change in parts of the Specialty session of that
February, 1953. It happened that Rupe couldn't make this session:
the Soul Stirrers' first in a year. He wrote Crain, "I have all the confidence in the world in you, Roy," and added that he was very particular when it came to letting groups record on their own: "You and
the fellows should consider this a very high honor. . . ." So Alexander
was the session's official producer. He dutifully noted to Rupe that
the group arrived a half hour late for the 9:00 P.M. date. They then
did four not very successful takes of "Christ Is All," a tune they'd
tried the year before, too. After that, it was a one-take on Crain's arrangement of "End of My Journey." In the opening verse, Sam rises
to a quavering falsetto, but after Paul's chorus—when he declares he's
"singing whoa-oh-oh-ah-oh"—you can hear Sam's first uncertain
stabs at his new technique.

"He'll Welcome Me," written and arranged by Crain, was an up-
tempo shouter with the first lead given to Foster, and Sam's answer
rasped out in the old style. It would prove to be Crain's biggest in-
performance song—"my national anthem"—and it delivered the hard
gospel Soul Stirrer fans had come to expect. But by the time they get
to "He's My Friend Until the End," Sam is sailing into new territory.
The first-person pronoun achieves four or five syllables— "I-yi-aye-i!"
—while Farley's bass boom-booms steadily along as if the lead's acrobatics were perfectly normal. ("Sam started as a bad imitation of Harris," the bassman would later tell author Heilbut, "and wound up
with his own yodel. After that, he could sell what he had better than
any other member of the Soul Stirrers.") Unexpectedly, repeatedly,
Cook takes notes and, in a breath, explores their alternatives, their
nuances. Certainly, it owes to R. H. Harris, but there's also some Billie Holiday there, some jazz improvisation. By the end, Sam is almost
tra-la-la-ing as he scats out of the song.

"He's My Friend" may have scared Art Rupe. He had a tendency to stay with a good thing, to have his acts put out like-sounding records once one had proved a hit. The first Stirrers single Rupe released in 1953 was from the session before, and when he finally put out another, late in the year, it featured the "old" sound of Crain's "End of My Journey." By the time "He's My Friend" was released, well into 1954, not just Sam but the whole Stirrers sound was changing yet again.

Bruster had left the group to join R. H. Harris in the Christland Singers, and Crain had replaced the baritone with Bob King. King, from Philadelphia's Bells of Joy, not only sang well, he played the guitar. As audience demand had pushed quartets toward a more driving sound, they'd gradually begun to use more instrumentation, most often the guitar, since its rhythmic clang-a-lang updated the old harmonies without changing them all that much. Starting in '53, the Soul Stirrers deliberately chose to modernize, building the guitar into both their recordings and live programs.

It wasn't an easy transition. On July 8, 1953, they took their new sound into the studio and laid down three tracks; two days later, they came back in and cut the same songs again. "Asked Art to let us make it over," says Crain, "'cause we could do better. And that's what made Art such a famous record man, 'cause he would go along with it. You tell him you feel the spirit, old Art would try it!"

The only cut released from this session was "Come and Go to That Land," arranged by Cook. It begins with King's strumming, then the rest of the group sets up the brisk pace by chanting. "To that land." With Cook and Foster trading off leads, there are at least three major rhythms working, and Crain was frankly dazzled that King could find breathing space. "See, the Soul Stirrers were hard to play for, 'cause we had practiced a cappella and practiced our harmony and had it so close there wasn't no room in there for no music." After seven takes, they finally got it, with King chording softly behind, adding the occasional high lead. Rupe left the guitar so far back in the mix it was barely there and, instead, brought the drums way forward.

Compare the final result to the Orioles' pop hit at the time, "Crying in the Chapel," and it's clear the Soul Stirrers had many of the same components: drums, guitar, tight harmony backup, and a sexy lead. The lyrics of "Come and Go to That Land" may prefigure the Dell-Vikings' 1957 hit "Come Go with Me," but there was too much sound out there to untangle direct sources. Maybe it's enough to say that as the Stirrers went from city to city, everybody was listening to everybody else. And the technique—Sam shouting "Joy!" seven times, on and off and all around the multirhythms behind him till Sister Flute had to wave her hands with pleasure—the technique was much older than anyone singing.

Sam was also expanding his note-bending. At the same session with King, as he enters the chorus of "I Gave Up Everything," Cook slides all the way down the scale on a wordless "whoa" that's plain devastating. The effect of six months of touring is obvious. Cook's voice has gotten stronger, more confident, and he unleashes the "yodel" with the air of a man who knows what he can do. As Crain puts it, "We was in our power then."

Sam was not only in his power; he was also suddenly and seriously in love.

The Sunday before this 1953 recording date, the Stirrers had played up in Fresno, California, in what Herald Attractions billed as the "First Annual Gospelcade." Along with the Travelers and the Spirit of Memphis, it featured the Blind Boys of Alabama. (Any confusion with Archie Brownlee's Blind Boys was probably intentional. Brownlee was signed with one of Rupe's main competitors: Don Robey's Peacock label out of Houston. These Blind Boys, led by Clarence Fountain with Johnny Fields on bass, were signed to Specialty.) The Gospelcade, Lil Cumber proclaimed, had been "breaking attendance records in Houston, Chicago, Columbus, Ga., New Orleans, Memphis and other cities."

Sam was now throwing in his curlicues, as Crain remembers, "whether the song was too high or not." The skinny, pretty manchild with the high cheekbones and the throaty voice had gotten used to grabbing a room and slowly, deliberately, unleashing a flood of emotion. In Fresno, as elsewhere, the whole church fixed on his slight body as men and women began shaking with the spirit, standing and testifying, speaking in tongues. Among them that night was a young woman who went by the name of Dolores Mohawk. She was a singer herself, mostly ballads in the style of Dinah Washington. Earlier in the year, she'd played a three-month engagement with a local band, the Kirk Kirkland Quintet. Henry Kirkland remembers her as a "marvelous singer. She had a beautiful voice; she was a pretty girl; so all that worked hand in hand for her." Dolores knew about playing a crowd; plus, she'd been raised in the Holiness church herself: she was used to seeing Sister Flute cross over. But what the Stirrers' pretty lead singer could do was something else, and she wanted to get closer to it.

After the program, the groups always came forward to shake hands with the congregation. Dolores made a point of talking to Sam, and, with his eye for the ladies, he wouldn't have missed her, either. One thing led to another, and soon the young woman was standing before Crain. She was striking—straight black hair, hazel eyes, what one of Sam's friends would remember as "a whole lot of good-looking woman."

"Mr. Crain?"

"Yes, young lady?"

"I want Sam to stay down here with me."

"Oh, no!" Crain answered. "I can't do nothing like that! He doesn't know you." While the group had its women friends, you didn't just go off with them like that; you didn't let yourself be picked up so blatantly—not in front of Sister Flute and the church elders.

"I'll guarantee you I'll take care of him," the woman said. "Ain't nothing gonna happen to him." "She was a pretty girl," Crain remembers. "If it was me, I'd sure want to go. I put myself in his stead, and I relented." What Crain called that "Texas personality," her quick smile, helped sway him; it turned out Dolores had grown up not sixty miles from Crain's hometown of Trinity. "Now, I'm holding you responsible for Sam's safety," he said sternly. "What *is* your name?"

It was Sunday night. The next day the Stirrers were up in Bakersfield. Then they had the recording sessions in Los Angeles and a date in Oakland on the following Sunday. "I want him there Saturday by two o'clock 'cause we got to rehearse." Dolores was as good as her word. From Oakland, the Stirrers went on to Sacramento, Stockton, and, finally, San Diego, where the California tour ended. The two weeks had been long enough for Sam and Dee Dee (as he'd begun calling her) to fall in love. A month later, the group came back to the coast, and by late October, Sam, twenty-two, and Dolores, just twenty-three, would be married.

Some didn't approve, and nearly everyone was surprised. Johnnie Morisette, Sam's friend and fellow gospel singer, was a bachelor, too, and the men had often partied together. "I always said I wasn't never going to get married, and he always said he wasn't never going to get married. And then one day, when I saw him again, he told me he married!" J. W. Alexander—who was already keeping a protective eye on Sam—remembers speaking with R.B. at one point. "I knew of Dolores, and I knew some of the guys that she'd been running around with. We were at the Dunbar Hotel on Central Avenue, and I says to Robinson: 'You guys, why don't you look out for this young boy?' R.B. says, 'Well, let him get his head bumped!' " That may have been simple jealousy speaking—the young lead drew all these women—but the older men may also have seen that Sam was headed for trouble on the road and needed to learn a lesson early.

Certainly, Dolores came with some baggage. She had been born Dolores Elizabeth Milligan on September 16, 1930, in Lubbock, Texas. Her father didn't stick around long, and Dolores's mother wasn't the stay-at-home type, either, so Dee Dee had mostly been raised by her aunt. When she was a teenager, the extended family had joined the flood of Texas Negroes heading for the coast, and they'd ended up in Fowler, a tiny town just south of Fresno. By the time she'd graduated from high school, Dolores had decided she was Dolores Mohawk. She didn't know her father, and after all, her grandmother had some Cherokee blood in her, so why not? Toward the end of high school, age seventeen, Dolores got pregnant by a local Mexican boyfriend, then married one of her uncle's coworkers at the veterans' hospital up in Oakland. She named the baby boy Nathaniel Brown, Jr., after her new husband. When Brown left—just as Dolores's father had—she changed the boy's name to Joey, just as she'd changed her own to Mohawk, and he ended up being raised mostly by his great-aunt, just as Dee Dee had been. It was a history of busted-up relationships and invented identities. At twenty-three, Dolores was undoubtedly ready to be whisked away, and the gorgeous gospel singer looked like just the man for it.

By all appearances, it was a romantic, impetuous, probably rebellious romance. Certainly, Dolores didn't fit the profile of the Soul Stirrers; neither Crain nor any of the others attended the wedding. Alexander's feeling was that the Cook family never really accepted her: "I think everyone preferred he have one of those Chicago girls." But Sam's brother Charles disagrees. "The first time I met her, Sam was home, and I went to the train station with him to pick her up." The family, as always, was accepting. Sam was grown and had been on the road for a few years; it didn't matter to the Reverend and Mrs. Cook that Dolores had a child or what her past was like. "As long as he was happy," Charles recalls, "they were happy. And I guess he was, for a while."

Joey, five years old at the time, can remember the long train ride out to Chicago. The Soul Stirrers were back home briefly; there was a program at DuSable in the beginning of November. On October 19, Dee and Sam were married under a license issued by the county clerk, Richard J. Daley. They moved, almost immediately, into R. B. Robinson's basement apartment at 6505 South Langley. It was tight—a one-bedroom with a living room and a kitchen—but they were lucky to find anything. In 1953, the population in the center of Bronzeville had grown to an astonishing 100,000 per square mile—three times the citywide average—and the press was featuring stories of colored families living in old storage bins and camping out in half-razed buildings or garages. The Robinsons' place was a nice solid brick building; across the street was the James McCosh Elementary School for Joey.

Among those less than happy about the marriage was Barbara Campbell. Even though she and Sam hadn't married when Linda was born, everyone assumed they were still somehow promised to each other. Dora Robinson recalls Barbara coming over one time. "I can't remember whether Dee Dee saw her or not, but I told Barbara that I didn't really think it was nice for her to do something like that. I asked her how would she feel if she was married and somebody that liked her husband would come over."

Dora Robinson became Dolores's protector and friend. Both women were from California and both had five-year olds. "I knew how she felt being away from home," says R.B's wife. The friendship was important: Dee Dee quickly realized she'd be seeing more of Dora than her husband. The Stirrers toured ceaselessly, and "we didn't carry no wives with us," says Crain emphatically. "We didn't play that! Wasn't no room: six men didn't have but one car." It didn't leave Dee Dee much to do. For a while she sang some gospel in a group along with L. C. Cook's wife, but mostly she raised Joey and waited for Sam to come home. She worried, of course, about her husband: she'd seen the kind of adoration he got on the road. "Sam was young, and the women did like him," Dora Robinson remembers. "He was a man about town. But I always tried to comfort her, if there was any comforting to be done."

The first couple of years went fairly smoothly, if any marriage can run smoothly with that much time apart. Despite her loneliness, Dolores liked Chicago. And for a man who'd been avoiding exactly this responsibility, Sam took to fathering. The young couple saw Sam's brothers and sisters often, and Sam used to take Joey to museums when he was in town (his interest in drawing remained) or to the Stirrers' programs. Sam often acted like a kid himself. His goddaughter, Sammie Tate, can remember sneaking into the kitchen with him to "make breakfast." It resulted in more fun than food, and Sam loved the mess. But there was also a stern side. Once, Joey recalls, he misbehaved at a program. Sam took the boy outside and talked to him. When he did it again ("I was a little mischievous"), Sam strapped him.

The punishment, instead of alienating the boy, convinced him that Sam cared. As a grown-up, Joey would call Cook "the only real father I ever had," and he was Sam's first "real" child, just as 6505 South Langley was his first "real" place. It makes his comment a few years later all the more interesting: "That's what ruined my life," he would say, laughing, "that apartment." It marked the beginning of Sam's adult life, so maybe what it ruined was the childhood he hung on to so strongly. Or maybe he was mixing those early years of the marriage with its later ones, for those were—from all descriptions—stormy and long.

Sam had good reason to be out on the road. "Religious Field Growing Bonanza" is how *Billboard* headlined it at the beginning of 1954. The trade paper was startled to discover that the "heavy box office" of the Herald Attractions package was equal to and sometimes better than Nat King Cole's and Ray Robinson's (better known as Ray Charles). The Stirrers had grossed $78,000 in 1953, thanks in part to massive crowds like the ten thousand who saw them in Columbus, Georgia. By this time, Cook was—in soul singer Jerry Butler's words—"the main cat." Butler was about fifteen when he saw Sam at a program at DuSable High. He and another member of the Northern Jubilee Gospel Singers, Curtis Mayfield, would go on to form the Impressions and collaborate on early gospel-based r&b hits like "For Your Precious Love" and "He Will Break Your Heart." But that afternoon in the DuSable gym, Butler was just another young gospel singer in awe.

"Sam was a very classical kind of singer. And because of that beautiful voice of his and the ability to be as sweet or as funky as he wanted to be, he really didn't have to be overly gymnastic or emotional." The Blind Boys preceded the Soul Stirrers that day, and had brought down the house. They had voices, Butler recalls, that "could just scream and holler and just tear your soul out. . . . I was sitting there thinking, 'How do you top this? How do you get onstage when the Five Blind Boys have just got everybody in the place jumping out of their seats?' " How Sam did it taught Butler a lesson he would carry into his own, definitive soul singing. "He didn't try to step into the space that the Blind Boys had. He moved it slightly to the left and up a notch. You know? And it started off and it swelled and it swelled and it swelled [till] everybody was in tears and jumping and shouting!" Butler was amazed by what he calls "this prodigy turned man."

Sam's coming of age occurred as r&b sales boomed, accounting for eight of the twenty-five best-sellers in 1954. This despite the fact, as *Variety* put it, that "the idiom of the lyrics uses the specialized jargon of the restricted Negro community." Hits like Hank Ballard's "Work with Me, Annie" may have used jargon, but it was easy to interpret—and if the white public had any doubts, the follow-up record, "Annie Had a Baby," made the meaning of "work" explicit. Negro dj Tommy Small was bringing r&b packages to the Apollo, and Alan Freed had moved from Cleveland to New York, where he was doing the same at the Paramount. While Herald Attractions might occasionally outdraw a solo r&b act, these packages dwarfed anything gospel could do. On Christmas weekend 1954, Freed's show at the Academy Theater grossed $125,000—more in one weekend than the Stirrers had earned the entire previous year! One sure sign that there was money in r&b was that white artists had begun covering it. The Crew Cuts did a version of the Cords' "Sha-boom"; Patti Page tried Ruth Brown's "O What a Dream." And in Memphis, an unknown named Elvis Presley covered Arthur "Big Boy" Crudup's "That's Alright Mama," and Sam Phillips released it on his Sun label.

There was also what musicologist Charles Keil has called "the postwar Texas clean-up movement in blues singing." It was led by artists like the crooner Charles Brown, Specialty's own Percy Mayfield, and Ivory Joe Hunter. This jazzier, quieter style was naturally based in Los Angeles, since that's where the Texas migration headed, and it influenced young singers like Jesse Belvin (who wrote the crooning hit "Earth Angel" in 1954) and Ray Charles (who at this time still sounded like Charles Brown's double—all soft-voiced and smooth). Despite his Chicago/Mississippi roots, Sam inclined toward this "cleaner" sound, partly because it fit his voice and partly because the distinctive Texas swing of the Soul Stirrers (and Rebert Harris) was much closer to crooning than it was to Big Boy Crudup. What Sam was doing in gospel in 1954 sounded a lot like the year's #1 r&b hit, "You'll Never Walk Alone": a ballad by the clean-cut former church singer Roy Hamilton.

"Any Day Now," from Sam's next single, is a prime example. Faidest Wagoner, a woman keyboardist, singer, and longtime friend of the Travelers' Kylo Turner, wrote the tune, whose mournful melody was inspired by "The Bells of St. Mary's." It's arranged as almost a solo: the Stirrers humming wordlessly in the background, while Wagoner plays a light, ornamental piano and Sam does all the rest. He attacks the song note by note, milking each word—"morn-or-ornings" and "go-oh-o-ing"—the whole phrased in silky, confident slides. It's the direct gospel equivalent of the emotionally drenched Roy Hamilton style—a tour de force that leaves the Soul Stirrers as little more than a backup group.

In fact, during most of this early 1954 session, Foster is submerged into the chorus, as the Stirrers bypass their trademark double leads to let Sam loose. "In my weak-a-ness-a make-a me-uh so strong" is how Sam phrases one line from "He'll Make a Way," all in the highest end of his range. And he's the sole lead on "Jesus I'll Never Forget," though the number spins forward on Crain's brilliant, swinging arrangement and Farley's foot-tapping bass line: about as close to dance music as gospel got at that time. Sam grooves on the tempo, dodging in and out, biting off some words with clenched-teeth phrasing while gliding over others till the Savior becomes "Jesus-whoa-wo."

The one double lead on the session was with the newest member of the Soul Stirrers. Julius "June" Cheeks stayed with the group less than a year, but he had a profound influence on Sam. Cheeks was one of the hardest gospel shouters of his era, and looked the part: square-shouldered, solidly built, June was all country. According to gospel historian Anthony Heilbut, poverty had forced him to quit school in the second grade, and he'd grown up on a farm in Spartanburg, South Carolina, listening to the Dixie Hummingbirds, the Fairfield Four, and the Soul Stirrers on the radio. He joined the Sensational Nightingales in 1946 and, modeling himself somewhat on the hard-shouting Archie Brownlee, soon became, in Brownlee's own words, "the baddest nigger on the road." In 1954, the 'Gales were on Don Robey's Peacock label, but, for all Cheeks's power and excitement, they weren't making any money. So he'd come over to the Soul Stirrers.

"He did a noble service for me," is how Crain puts it. "He inspired Sam. Old June was a yeller; he'd get Sister Flute or die! He'd tear the house down on you, and he didn't care who you are or where you come from. He'd do everything!" Cheeks told Heilbut about a program in San Francisco. Sam was still in the Stirrers' tradition of standing flat-footed and respectful—what Cheeks called "real pretty." June, caught up in the spirit, shoved him, and he fell offstage. "People thought he was happy. I said, 'Move man,' and the two of us fell into the audience."

The one number the Stirrers cut with June, "All Right Now," gives some idea of how he fit in. Cheeks starts the first verse fairly calmly, Cook tries a little shouting of his own on the second, and then June takes it away on the third with Foster relegated to the background. The tune, little more than a chant, runs an unheard-of three and a half minutes (most singles were closer to two). By the third verse, Cheeks has started to grind his voice. "When I was in trouble," he growls, "I didn't have no God by my side." He gives it all the roughness of a cotton-field shout. Sam's just clinging on with the other men, as Cheeks stretches out into a little preaching, and then repeats "all right now" till it verges on the hypnotic. "Reverend Cheeks," says one of the 'Gales, "was just anointed. . . . He'd give you all that he had. . . . I knew it was the Lord because the things he did you wouldn't do over and over and over of yourself. . . ."

Though the circuit stayed the same, June changed the gospel highway for Sam. The Stirrers had their four programs in Chicago and a date in California that July, and in December they went back to the scene of Sam's apprenticeship to be part of WDIA's Goodwill Revue in Memphis. (The station had grown along with gospel and r&b; it was now a 50,000-watt beacon throughout the South.) Cheeks egged Cook on at every program, and they became the best of friends. June was, in Crain's phrase, "bullish" onstage. "That scoundrel do anything! He and Sam jumped off a stage ten feet high in Washington, D.C.! Sister Flute—" And Crain can just shake his head in wonder.

Cheeks was as country as Sam was urban, as much the clown as Sam was trying to be the sophisticate, but June's outreach had another side, and that affected Sam, too. Behind the antics was a real outrage at how his people were treated. In the fifties, Heilbut reports,

Cheeks and Dorothy Love Coates of the Gospel Harmonettes were the only two gospel stars speaking frequently and forcefully about the lynchings and prejudice in the South. When June shoved his buddy Sam off the stage, it was more than just a way to get Sister Flute. It was also to knock Cook off-center, to put him on notice that he couldn't just stand there all pretty. Things had to change.

While segregation wasn't a factor at the programs—they were in the colored part of town in the colored churches—between shows, trying to find a place to stay or a bite to eat, it was a constant problem. Lou Rawls (at this time with the Chosen Gospel Singers, also on Specialty) remembers that you had to "just deal with it. You don't go in there with a negative attitude because all you're going to get is a negative return. . . . You can circumvent it; say, 'Okay, I don't have to deal with this. I can go on or I can go and stay over at Sister Flukey's house. She's got a room for rent.' "

If you couldn't circumvent, well, you used your wits. Crain recalls a typical example when he was stopped speeding out of Florida on the way to Waycross, Georgia. "Boy," said the cop, "what you driving that fast for?" Crain answered, "Officer, some white boys back there was trying to catch me, and I'm scared! I'm shore glad to see you, 'cause they *will* hurt you down here!" Crain kept laying it on good and thick: "This old car don't run fast enough! I'm gonna tell that man he sold me something don't run. Those old boys about to catch me! Man told me this thing will run!? It won't run!" The cop let him go, and the Soul Stirrers' manager concludes with a laugh: "You can tell them policemen down South anything, but you got to know how to tell it."

The Stirrers passed on this approach to Sam. "In my generation," Crain says, "we didn't demand nothing. We prayed for it." Those who did otherwise—Negroes who forgot their place down South— often just disappeared. "We sang in the old South where they got colored and white, when you couldn't use this and couldn't use that." Still, S.R. was well aware of the coded messages that helped the Stirrers shake churches all across the country. "It reminds you of the way the Christians were treated in Rome. They couldn't express it to

Caesar; they'd get their neck cut off for that. . . . You couldn't say everything you thought, but you sung them."

Back in the nineteenth century, Frederick Douglass had recognized the spiritual "Steal Away" as a hidden challenge for slaves to escape to the North; a hundred years later, the opening to Cook's "Any Day Now" played to a similar interpretation: "One of these mornings, I'm going away."

Maybe religion was an opiate, as political organizers had argued in Bronzeville during Sam's childhood, but the heaven he sang of was as much about real possibilities as pie-in-the-sky. For many Negroes, the "invisible church" was the one organization in position to support the struggle, and its music had always been a major source of solace and strength. First, slavery spirituals had been, as author James Cone phrases it, "the essence of black religion, that is the experience of trying to be free in the midst of a 'powerful lot of tribulation.'" Then, the jubilee style had celebrated hope to supposedly "free" colored people during the disastrous post-Reconstruction period. Now, as the 1954 *Brown* v. *Board of Education* ruling announced the start of a new civil rights era, modern gospel reflected the northern migration and the conscious decision of urban Negroes "to be themselves."

Sam's younger, more impatient generation was typified by the preacher who took over the pulpit at Montgomery's Dexter Avenue Baptist Church in September 1954. "Little Baptist church," as Crain recalls it from a program the Soul Stirrers did there one night. Though never close friends, Sam and Martin Luther King knew each other. Martin's daddy was a minister, too, and like Reverend Cook, used to "walk the benches" to get his congregations. King Jr., however, was a college graduate. He considered his father's bench-walking "the most vaudevillian, primitive aspect of his heritage." While he would become a leader of the folks out on the street, Martin wasn't one of them—not in the sense Sam was. While Martin had been in theological school studying interpretations of the Gospel, Sam had been in little crossroad churches learning how to bring the Spirit into the house.

Despite these differences (which were much the same as those between the outcast Holiness church and the self-defined middle-class Baptists), the two men were working on the same building. And King certainly recognized the importance of gospel music to his movement. The executive director of his Southern Christian Leadership Conference, the Reverend Wyatt Tee Walker, bears witness to the connection: "As a participant for nearly a decade in the nonviolent movement in the South, most of the time in the front lines, this writer is thoroughly convinced that there would have been very little 'movement' without the music of the Black religious tradition."

Chapter 8

"**A**rt was always sticking his one, five, and ten cents in" is how Crain explains the Soul Stirrers' early-1955 decision to record in Chicago. "We didn't want Art Rupe hanging around; we didn't want nobody but us. We wanted to see how good we were. . . ." If the February 16 session is an indication, the Stirrers were plenty good. At Universal Studio (where the Chess brothers that year produced Muddy Waters' "I'm Ready" and "Hoochie Coochie Man," Chuck Berry's Top Ten "Maybelline," and Bo Diddley's ode to himself, "Bo Diddley"), the Stirrers cut four sides, all four of which turned out to be hits. "It's amazing what happens when a group sings together so long" was how Rupe thought of it. "They're just like a basketball team: when they throw a note someone will be there to respond to it. Beautiful, the way they worked. . . ."

Some credit is due the accompaniment, which—along with King's guitar—is the more traditionally "gospel" ensemble of piano, organ, and drums. In fact, both the piano player, Edward Robinson, and the organist, Willie Webb, worked extensively with the queen of gospel, Mahalia. Cook's connection to Webb went back a couple generations. Willie's grandfather had run the Church of Christ (Holiness) main temple in Chicago and had preceded Reverend Cook as pastor down in Chicago Heights. During the war years, Willie had come up with the Roberta Martin Singers and had become one of the city's most popular accompanists. He had also organized the choir for the Reverend Clay Evans's new Fellowship Baptist Church. Sam would join Fellowship that fall, even though it was Baptist instead of Holiness. He was hardly an active member, but he knew Evans from the QC days, and Fellowship was becoming the gospel singers' church: a place to be seen—and to be heard over its regular program on WVON. So a Webb and a Cook were once again co-parishioners, and their collaboration at the recording session had a certain historical symmetry. It's probably just coincidence that the biggest hit from the session reflected this shared background: a condensed history of gospel and a kind of commentary on Sam's career up till then.

"Nearer to Thee" begins with Webb playing a processional organ, and then Cook describes a preacher leading his congregation, a lot as his father had on Shields Avenue or in hundreds of other churches. If that verse calls up Sam's youth, the second brings us to the present, as he states his goal as a gospel singer is to tell a story, to move the congregation, to testify. What links the past and the present is the old hymn "Nearer My God to Thee." On the chorus, Sam wails into a near-pop version of the standard, with a long, sustained yodel toward the end. The song works as personal history—from the Singing Children to the Soul Stirrers—and also as a bridge between Sister Flute's old-time religion and the young girls pushing to the front. As a piece of songwriting, it's Cook's coming of age, as he takes the tradition—in the form of "Nearer My God to Thee"—and restructures it right before your ears.

The session included another Cook song, the gospel dirge of "Be with Me Jesus," led by Foster, and James Cleveland's "One More River." On the latter, the background calls, "One more river to cross," as Sam takes a note out of the mix, bends it, and responds, ". . . before I'll be free from here." The dynamic is older than slavery: the group repeating lines that set up the soloist, who, in turns, builds the tension until the two switch roles, Sam repeating "one more" as the group now takes the lyric. Finally, on Crain's "I'm So Glad," with the organ and piano trading solos behind them, the Stirrers break the line "Got my religion in time" down into individual syllables and drum on each like saints marching lockstep to glory. And at the end, in a lesson learned from June Cheeks (back with the Nightingales by this time), Sam turns the first-person-singular pronoun into "I-uh-I-uh." It's a rasp that would soon be called soul singing. Here, it's a gospel cry.

"I trust that I made a good Session," Crain wrote Rupe two weeks later. "[T]he Songs go over Big with the audiences wherever we appear. . . . 'Nearer to Thee' is a house reaker [sic]." Crain ended the letter by writing "SMILE"; Rupe soon did. "Nearer to Thee" took off: within three months, it had sold more than 23,000 copies and would eventually become Cook's best-selling gospel work, with only "Jesus Gave Me Water" even approaching its popularity. "I like all the numbers you did," Rupe wrote back, "and the group sounds real fine."

It was turning out to be a great year all around for Specialty Records. On top of artists like Lloyd Price and Percy Mayfield, Rupe had added Guitar Slim, whose "The Things That I Used to Do" reached #1 on *Billboard*'s r&b charts. The tune, recorded in New Orleans, had been arranged by the about-to-be-famous Ray Charles. Charles would use a similar small-combo swing style on his own 1955 hit "I Got a Woman," a gospel tune he sang with an Archie Brownlee vocal after changing the lyrics from "I got a Savior." Rupe's "specialty" music had definitely crossed over, and he suddenly had a small business crisis: too much success. He coped by hiring a thirty-seven-year old a&r trainee, Robert "Bumps" Blackwell, who would play a major role in Cook's career.

Blackwell came from Seattle, where he'd had a barbershop, a meat market, and a music school, as well as heading a small-territory band that occasionally employed Ray Charles and a young saxophonist, Quincy Jones. With his slicked-back hair and eager smile, Bumps was a man always looking for the angle, always working on a number of projects at once. Back in August of 1952, when the Stirrers had been appearing at the National Quartet Convention in Los Angeles, he'd been in town, too, presenting his "Harlem Revue" at the Elks' auditorium. In Los Angeles, as he told author Rob Finnis, "the sun was shining, everything was happening and I got to meet some musicians." He returned to rainy Seattle, closed up his businesses, and came south to seek his fortune.

As Rupe remembers it, "He walked into our Sunset Boulevard office looking for a job." An ambitious, clever, talented man, Blackwell prided himself on his university education and his sophistication. "Initially," Rupe says, "he was hired to audition and screen talent and song material for me." A couple of weeks after he joined the label, Bumps listened to an unsolicited tape from a musician in New Orleans. The tape began, "Mr. Art Rupe, you are now going to hear Little Richard and his Upsetters. . . ." Bumps and Rupe liked the sound enough to sign the unknown, but it took them six months or so to get him out of a contract with Don Robey's label.

In the meantime, Rupe assigned Bumps to another r&b project: Jesse Belvin. Belvin, a former choir member at L.A.'s Olivet Baptist Church, had been part of that city's r&b scene since he was seventeen and had cowritten the million-selling "Earth Angel." According to the author of "Louie Louie," Richard Berry, Jesse "was the father of us all, of rock & roll in Los Angeles. We were all trying to sing like Jesse so that we could get the girls like he could." Belvin's vocals, while churchy, had a sexier, more teenage sound than any of Specialty's gospel acts. Bumps led a session in March 1955 where Belvin was backed by a local harmony group, Bumps' brother Charles Blackwell on drums, jazz keyboardist Ernie Freeman, and a guitarist named Cliff White who had just left the middle-of-the-road vocal group the Mills Brothers. The lineup anticipates by a couple of years how Bumps would approach Sam Cooke's pop sound. He emphasized Belvin's balladeer qualities—the slow, squeezed note—with jazzy arrangements that stemmed directly from his small-combo background.

Sam couldn't help but notice what was going on at his own label and across the country. By mid-March of 1955, thirteen of the top thirty pop songs were either r&b or their covers. A couple of Italian–American producers called Hugo and Luigi had fashioned a pale version of Etta James's "Roll With Me, Henry," called it "Dance with Me, H   y," and pushed it to #1, where it stayed for almost six months. Pat Boone pulled off the same coup in July doing Fats Domino's "Ain't That a Shame." And by the end of the year, Elvis had not only appeared on *The Ed Sullivan Show* but had signed with a major label, RCA: a sure sign that the biggies felt this "new" music was no passing trend.

Cook viewed all this from the perspective of one of the country's premier gospel stars. After five years on the circuit, he was not only a major draw but had started to inspire a crowd of imitators. Quartets were rushing to get young leads to try to tap the teenage market. In July, despite a thirty-day streetcar strike, the Herald Attractions package drew more than four thousand to the Shrine auditorium in L.A. Billed as the "first annual Mid-summer Festival of Gospel Music," the package consisted of Sam and the Stirrers, the Travelers, the Caravan Singers with Albertina Walker and James Cleveland, the Gospel Harmonettes with Dorothy Love Coates, and Brother Joe May. Specialty Records decided to tape the program.

Though Rupe ended up feeling the recording had no commercial potential (he wouldn't issue it for twenty years), today it offers an extraordinary opportunity to hear how Sam and his competition worked. The Travelers open the proceedings with a couple of numbers, including their latest single, "Straight Street." It doesn't get the house, but it's a sly, swinging story of moving from Sin to Straight Street, and George McCurn's bouncing bass line sounds like basic listening for all the doo-wop to follow. At one point during their house-wrecker, "Mother Bowed," Kylo Turner's acrobatic lead is obliterated by an ear-piercing, ecstatic screech from the congregation as some church sisters cross all the way over.

The Caravans follow, and Sam's old neighborhood friend Albertina Walker leads the congregation through an achingly slow Alex Bradford tune as James Cleveland hammers the piano, and the crowd shouts encouragement—especially when the group breaks into double-time. Brother Joe May's controlled, operatic "It's a Long, Long Way" ranges from almost a whisper to what sounds like an aria, his notes reverberating in the air. And when Dorothy Love Coates and her Gospel Harmonettes reprise their first Speciality single, "Get Away Jordan," the crowd comes down like thunder on the beat. "I don't know about you," Dot declares in her straight-ahead, roughened voice, "but I been born again!" Nobody had more passion or anger than Dot Coates—her voice blows the mike right out—and soon the Shrine is crying and shouting.

None of these acts were easy to share a program with; the combination seemed to leave nowhere for the Soul Stirrers to go. But when Sam rips off a hoarse-voiced "whoa-a-o" at the start of "I Have a Friend," the church shouts an answer like old buddies trading hellos. The live version of their latest single, "Be with Me Jesus," makes it clear that Sam wrote it as a vehicle for Foster. Cook offers a rough lead that sounds like it's ripping his throat, but it's Paul's resonating hollow of a voice that takes over. Soon, Sam is calling, "Sing it, Paul!" and "Come on, Paul!" and Foster starts to shout, "Yea, Jesus!" again and again, till Sister Flute begins to tremble. By the end, the song is reduced to a chant, Sam tracking Paul's wordless shouts, the group clapping behind, King playing rhythm guitar.

It's the last number, "Nearer to Thee," that is the clincher. The group has extended "Be with Me Jesus" to almost eight minutes; this one they simply won't let go. Sam starts it in the middle of the applause for Paul's performance, hitting and holding a rasped note. There's nothing sweet or light here; the other groups have issued a challenge: this is gospel war. Sam slides through the two verses the congregation would have known from the single and then just keeps going. In the third verse, he gives himself up to God's will; shouts are heard. He's singing hard, railing at the words. When he works on a note, it sounds like a man trying to bend a piece of iron. In the fourth verse, Cook adds what sounds like improvised autobiography: sometimes he likes to be in company, and sometimes he likes to steal off by himself—with singing his one and only consolation. On he goes, the congregation riding with him now. Do you know that bad company will lead a good child astray? The church screams that it does, and when Sam resorts to Mother—as in mother prays for even the bad child—the cries of "Jesus! Jesus!" deafen. By the time Paul roars into the chorus like a bull elephant, the place is gone. It's taken Sam and the Soul Stirrers nearly ten minutes, they've resorted to almost every trick in their arsenal, but they've got Sister Flute. This is

Sam's first home:
2303 7th Street,
Clarksdale, Mississippi.
Note pecan tree out back.
(AUTHOR'S PHOTO)

Typical Church of Christ
(Holiness) church:
Clarksdale, Mississippi.
(AUTHOR'S PHOTO)

3523–3527 Cottage Grove Avenue, 1954: 3527, where the Cooks lived, far right.
(CHICAGO HISTORICAL SOCIETY, PHOTO BY MILDRED MEAD)

Sam's high school picture.
(COLLECTION CHARLES
N. EDMUNDS)

The Cook family, circa 1957.
Sam's brother David
(kneeling); brother-in-law
Eddie Jamison; sister
Agnes; Annie May, and the
Reverend Charles Cook.
(*CHICAGO DEFENDER*)

Soul Stirrers, circa 1951: Sam,
R. B. Robinson, Paul Foster,
S. R. Crain, J. J. Farley.
(COLLECTION S. R. CRAIN)

Soul Stirrers sheet music,
circa 1944. R. H. Harris in back
row center. (COURTESY MRS.
KENNETH MORRIS)

Typical program, circa 1954: Farley, Foster, Cook, Robinson, Crain, and June Cheeks. (COLLECTION S. R. CRAIN)

June Cheeks gets in the house as Sam shouts him on. (COLLECTION S. R. CRAIN)

Sister Flute. (COLLECTION S. R. CRAIN)

The Pilgrim Travelers,
circa 1957: George McCurn,
J. W. Alexander, Lou Rawls,
Jesse Whitaker.
(COLLECTION S. R. CRAIN)

Sam, Dolores Mohawk, Joey Cook.
(COLLECTION S. R. CRAIN)

Bumps Blackwell in the Keen studio; John Siamas
over his right shoulder. (COLLECTION ANDY ALLEN)

Backstage, late fifties.
(*CHICAGO DEFENDER*)

Trying to reach
the nightclub crowd.
(*CHICAGO DEFENDER*)

On the r&b circuit,
with Cliff White.
(COLLECTION
CLIFF WHITE)

Barbara and Sam at the
California Club.
(COLLECTION ANDY ALLEN)

trench warfare of the most brutal kind, and you can hear a stubborn, determined Sam Cook gaining ground inch by bloody inch.

"Art told Bumps to come down and listen so he could learn something about gospel," Alexander recalls. Blackwell, a jazzman, had never seen anything like it. "People were screaming, throwing purses and umbrellas and stick-pins. You were liable to get yourself killed! It was awesome, phenomenal: he was like a black Billy Graham. Shit, the girls were following him around like the pied piper. Girls and young guys, musicians, but the chicks would just be completely gone."

The self-styled university man immediately began figuring angles. "My initial impression was 'This cat should be pop.' . . . That was just too much voice to be in such a limited market." Rupe threw a banquet afterward at the Watkins Hotel, and Blackwell took the opportunity to approach Cook with his idea. "That was our first argument." As Bumps remembers it, "He was afraid of losing his religious market. . . . For some unknown reason, the preachers say if you sing a pop song, you're a person of the world, and you can't be religious. They can be homosexuals; they can drink whiskey; they can do all kind of sinful things, but they can't sing a pop song. I," Bumps concluded, "call it superstition and ignorance."

Of course, Bumps was looking at it from the outside, whereas Sam was right up against it. Two days after the Shrine appearance, over at L.A.'s Wrigley Field, Lionel Hampton was appearing with Big Jay McNeeley, the Penguins, and the Medallions. Brother Joe May, for one, was outraged by what he heard. Saying he'd made a "serious study" of r&b as he clocked his 100,000 miles a year around the country, May concluded the dance stuff was "completely undermining the basis of gospel music." In fact, this so-called rock & roll was just a minor variation of what he and the other acts did at the Shrine: "Nothing more than an offshoot of good gospel song." May warned his fans, "While I do not condemn those who follow R and B's [sic], as a hobby, I do caution against an overindulgence in this fad. . . ."

But May was just another in a long line who failed to stem the trade-off back and forth between the church and the dance hall. The Pilgrim Travelers ended up in hot water that fall when their single

"Troubled in Mind" included r&b star Charles Brown on organ—and a tenor sax! "Certainly," J.W. announced, "we would be the last group in the world to do anything to offend or desecrate the dignity of gospel . . ." and then he tried citing biblical passages that mentioned the use of reed instruments in religious song. With black unemployment at over 10 percent and the gospel programs drawing thousands, religious performers weren't about to switch over. Not yet, anyway. But when they saw *their* music selling tens of thousands of records, they all paid attention—especially Sam Cook with those good looks, that clear voice, and Bumps Blackwell whispering in his ear.

Cook began to focus in on the money end of the music. "Nearer to Thee" had emerged as the biggest hit in the field. Sam didn't fuss about his record royalties or Venice Music owning the publishing, but he brooded on the way the Soul Stirrers had always split the writer's royalties equally. Hadn't he, after all, written the hit? Finally, he took his manager aside. "Crain, I want my money. And you oughta get yours." One look and Crain knew Sam had his mind set. As the other songwriter in the group and the main arranger, Crain understood Sam's point, but the manager didn't want to mess with the way the Stirrers had been doing things since before the Depression.

When Crain finally put the idea to the rest of the men, Foster and Farley fell silent. Crain took it to mean they might agree. R. B. Robinson wasn't so easy. He, after all, had been Sam's landlord. When it had come time to pay the money due to keep a roof over his wife and child, more often than not, Sam wouldn't have it. "If he had fifty dollars and he owed you twenty-five, and he's coming down the road and saw a sweater that cost twenty-five, he'd get that sweater!" Give him more, he'd just spend more. "I want my money!" Robinson said. "I want it like this." And he slapped his hand in front of Cook. R.B. was talking to the kid he'd picked off the street, trained as a QC, brought into the greatest quartet in the world. No, R.B. wasn't changing any Soul Stirrers' policy, thank you.

Sam got up into it, the blood rising. The argument happened to hit as the group was about to get in the car to go on to the next stop. "I'm not going to the program," Sam said, "Not on those terms."

Crain looked on in anguish. The group that needed a "oneness" to make it on the gospel road wasn't going far like this. In the end, Sam gave in and played that string of programs. And in the end, the group agreed that he and Crain would be the only members to have individual artist's contracts with Rupe; they would be signed at renewal time in February. But Crain could see it gnawed at Sam, gnawed at R.B., too. "That wasn't the straw," Crain says, looking back on the eventual breakup. "Sam was going to leave anyway. . . ." But it sure didn't help.

On October 14, 1955, the Soul Stirrers celebrated their twenty-first anniversary with a giant program at the Chicago Coliseum. Hotels as far away as Newark and Oakland took out ads in the souvenir program, as did radio stations, gospel promoters, car dealers, music publishers, and their own Specialty label. They called the classy, gala occasion "the World Series in Gospel Singing," and after its initial success, they took the extravaganza on the road. But in the late summer and early fall of 1955, Bronzeville's main concern was the death of a fourteen-year old from the neighborhood. Everyone knew him as Bobo; his Christian name was Emmett Till.

While visiting his uncle in Mississippi, Till was kidnapped by two white men who accused him of whistling at a woman storeowner. His body was found two days later in a nearby river. His head was crushed and he was weighted down with a 150-pound fan from an old cotton gin.

Bobo might have been just another dead colored kid, except the times had changed. His mother insisted on an open casket "so everybody can see what they did to my boy." A picture of Bobo ran in the *Defender;* it showed a young boy neatly dressed in a black jacket and white shirt—and nothing that could be identified as a face. The funeral parlor reported every tenth mourner fainted at the gruesome sight. Three weeks after the funeral, the two white men accused of the crime were found not guilty.

At Philadelphia's Academy of Music, there had already been a benefit concert to support the NAACP's legal defense fund. Billie Holiday was there, Dinah Washington, the Dominoes, Ruth Brown, Joe Louis and Clara Ward; the event cut across the gospel-versus-r&b battle. By early October, there were mass meetings across the country. Ten thousand people flocked to the Metropolitan Community Church on 41st and Parkway in Chicago. Fifty to sixty-five thousand attended a rally in Detroit; fifteen thousand gathered in New York and heard Thurgood Marshall rail: "You have to wait until a 14-year-old boy gets killed before you get excited. Yet, every day in the deep South our people go through the same thing Emmett Till went through except that they are not killed. And some are killed—their deaths are just not reported."

To many, Till's death was the beginning of the modern civil rights movement. Others dated it to that December 1, when Rosa Parks refused to give up her seat on a segregated Montgomery bus. Whatever began it, the ever-larger gospel packages carried news of the uprising from town to town. J. W. Alexander can remember coming through Montgomery during the bus boycott, as the Negro community led by Dr. King organized three hundred car pools a day. The Herald package shifted its program to a small local church and donated some of the proceeds to the movement. And as the World Series swung through the Midwest, an article noted how Alexander "has electrified audiences everywhere when he fervently asks that prayers be offered both for Miss Autherine Lucy [the first Negro to try to enter the University of Alabama] and the citizenry of Montgomery, Alabama."

Though they might carry the civil rights news, the quartets didn't have the luxury of concentrating on much more than personal business. The Stirrers' guitarist, Bob King, had leukemia. To everyone's amazement, he had managed to struggle out of his hospital bed and play one last program at Newark's Armory on October 16, 1955, but within a week, he had passed. His replacement, Leroy Crume, was a friend of Sam's who'd sung against the QCs at 3838 South State and sat in on acoustic guitar occasionally with the Stirrers. Cook found a soul mate in Crume, a good-looking twenty-year-old with a big, gap-toothed smile and striking gray eyes. Crume describes the various members: "Foster was sort of the chaplain like; Crain was the businessman; J.J., he would help Crain some, and he was the treasurer—took care of the cash; me and Sam, we were just running wild!" As far as Leroy could see, Sam was married in name only. "The road offers a lot of temptations," he says, "and we did yield. Quite a bit. . . ."

Crume remembers he and Sam were the youngest guys on the road, and you can hear this generational split on the first single of 1956, "Wonderful"/"Farther Along." Theodore Frye's "Wonderful" is lightweight pop. Sam grabs the first note and splits it, unravels and reweaves the sound, in a solo effort that is almost all about the singer. There's just barely a song there and hardly a quartet. The piano, drum, and guitar backing builds to a climax where all the elements pound at the same beat: what would come to be known as a rock & roll climax. "Farther Along," in contrast, is a traditional hymn that's been arranged to sound like a country waltz. Back in the late thirties, the Stirrers had been on the radio with the Stamps-Baxter Quartet, the leading publishers of white gospel music, and "Father Along" owes a debt to that influence. Cook falls back on a Harris-like rasp that recalls ancient hard times. It's as if the group had released the past and the future on one record.

If the February 1956 recording session was a generational battle, Cook dominates, writing three out of the four cuts released as singles and relegating the quartet more and more to a background voice. The gem of the session is a Cook tune called "Touch the Hem of His Garment." Its theme is taken from a brief episode in the Book of Matthew. Jesus is walking in a crowd, and a sick woman comes up behind him and touches his robe. Jesus senses she's there, turns, and as she apologizes, assures her that her faith will make her whole. It's the sort of miraculous healing that the Holiness church was built upon.

Cook wrote it as a concise two-verse narrative. In the first, we see the woman pushing through the crowd; in the second, Jesus turns and asks who has touched him. The song hinges on this moment of revelation, and when Sam sings "It was I," he holds the "I" through a clear, sustained yodel that extends the moment, jacking up the tension and underlining how scared and determined the woman must have felt. The instant of identification—"I did it, I!"—works on another level, too. This "I" could only be Sam Cook: no one else turned a note like that; no one else stopped time in quite that way. In the chorus, Cook's trademark *becomes* the song: Sam curlicues, the rest echo. The remarkable thing is that it isn't just a mannerism: the yodel pushes the narrative forward, pulling us into the miracle itself. "Touch the Hem of His Garment" sold over 25,000 copies, burnishing Sam's reputation as one of gospel's great storytellers.

By now, the explanation in gospel circles was that Cook had a miraculous "gift," and Sam liked to play to that. Bumps Blackwell tells the story of driving to the studio for this recording session in a Chrysler Imperial. Crain was at the wheel; Bumps and Sam were in the back, clowning, until Crain turned around and told them to cut it: they needed another song for the session, and it was serious business. "Give me the guitar," said Cook, who had learned to play some from King and Crume. "He starts strumming those little chords, his little pet chords. He starts thumbing the Bible, and he ran across one page and says, 'Oh, this looks pretty good! Wait a minute.' " Bumps asked him to read it aloud, but Sam, apparently deep in the creative process, answered, "No, no, let me get it. . . . If you don't like it, just tell me, good kid. . . . But just listen." And "reading the Bible straight across," Cook came out with a completed version of "Touch the Hem of His Garment." Bumps, normally sensitive to shtick, described the incident as evidence of "a God-endowed gift."

Since the QCs, Sam had worked at his songs, waking at night with ideas. Crain recalls that a lot of times when Cook was behind closed doors with various women—and the group assumed they knew what was going on—they'd hear him singing in there: trying out tunes. While Leroy Crume's recollection of Sam's working habits almost exactly duplicate Bumps' recollection, it's without the seemingly miraculous composing speed. "We'd sit in the room," Crume recalls, "and we'd go over all his new stuff. And we'd go down the road sitting in the car. He had a little four-string ukulele, and we'd practice in the backseat. When we got the material down, then we'd take it to the group."

A song like "Touch the Hem of His Garment" was put through

a long process: from trying it out on individuals, to working it over with Crume and Crain, to performing it at various programs until it finally got recorded. Art Rupe described Sam's songwriting as "well-structured and disciplined" and Sam as "a perfectionist. He would work for hours rehearsing, producing. He gave the impression of being very sure of himself." Sam cultivated the unruffled cool of a man to whom things just came, but some of the confidence—and most of the miracles—grew out of plain hard work and his unquenchable desire to get ahead.

Chapter 9

"**A** Friend I've Been Knowing For Quite A While Asked Me If I Would Consider Recording Some Popular Ballads For One Of The Major Recording Companies If He Could Arrange It. I Told Him Yes."

It is June 1956. The handwriting is Sam Cook's: capitalized, cheerful, a product of Doolittle Elementary School. He is writing Art Rupe. Sam's plan is to cut the pop records "Under Another Name. And I Would Continue To Record And Sing With The Group. I Have My Material Ready And All I Need Is An Okay From You." In his characteristic mixture of innocence and ambition, Sam is announcing he'd like to go pop (jeopardizing the Soul Stirrers' future) on another label (cutting Specialty out) and, at the same time, would like Rupe's permission. It is a particularly charming, deferential threat.

A year had passed since Bumps had first mentioned crossing over. Sam's friend who was arranging all this was Bill Cook, Roy Hamilton's manager, a Newark gospel dj. The two Cooks (not related) had talked before about Sam going pop. But in Crain's view, Sam had been "scared. He didn't want to go out there." Then, in early June of 1956, Roy Hamilton announced that he had chronic pneumonia; it had affected his voice; he was retiring. The *Amsterdam News* described Bill Cook as "speechless," but the manager immediately set to work on Sam. By the end of June, he'd talked the gospel lead into becoming his new ballad singer and a "Major Recording Company" (most likely Atlantic) into backing the deal.

Rupe's response was a swift and absolute no; Sam was under exclusive contract to Specialty. But that didn't mean the idea was all bad, or that Rupe was against it. "[W]e most certainly would be very happy to record you in the Pop field ourselves," Rupe wrote back on July 3, "and we feel that we can offer you considerably more success." The letter ends with Rupe urging Sam to call immediately to discuss the matter.

The opportunity was obvious. The teen population had jumped from 5.6 to 6.8 million in a decade. Rock & roll's popularity was phenomenal. Elvis Presley's current #1 hit, "I Want You, I Need You, I Love You," was his fifth Top Forty entry already that year. Closer to home, Bumps had taken Little Richard into a New Orleans studio in the fall of 1955, and Richard had turned Marion Williams's high-pitched gospel "wooo" and a lot of Professor Alex Bradford's piano into a two-sided monster: "Tutti-Frutti"/"Long Tall Sally." The result didn't sound much like what Sam did, but if Bumps could hit with Little Richard doing Marion Williams . . .

Confident and ambitious as he was, Sam was still moving cautiously. Conventional wisdom said he could do either pop or gospel, not both. As his pastor, Reverend Clay Evans, put it, "You're a pig or a possum; an orange or an apple. Make up your mind on one side or the other." Sam had every reason to believe that if he did cross over, Sister Flute would never accept him back. What would he do, then, if the pop attempt failed? Rupe, concerned about breaking up his premier gospel act, moved slowly, too. It would take him five months to set up a pop session for Sam, and then he went in with the plan to cut him under a different name.

Even as Sam started writing secular material, he headed toward a long-delayed gospel face-off with R. H. Harris. The July 22 program at Atlanta's City Auditorium featured the Stirrers, the sweet-voiced Edna Gallmon Cooke, and the Christland Singers. The last now included Harris, Medlock, Bruster, and Leroy Taylor from the pre-Cook

Soul Stirrers. The Christland Singers were mostly a local Chicago group, but Harris had been lured back out on the gospel road for what promoter Herman Nash billed as the "first battle of song": old versus new, master versus apprentice. It was fitting that it take place in Atlanta, which may have been the ultimate Soul Stirrers town. Over the years, they'd established such an invincible reputation there that they were often booked alone or with small supporting acts: they drew too well to waste the whole Herald Attractions package. "We were almost like the Beatles," Leroy Crume would later recall. "We were so popular there until Nash didn't want us to walk the streets. He says, 'Let the people pay to see you. Don't let them see you for free!' "

The night of the program came, and Harris's group went on first. If the Christland Singers couldn't match the Stirrers' harmonies, Harris's voice was still a thing of wonder, and, certainly among the older members of the audience, it was recognized as the authentic goods. Crain, trying to be objective, admits Harris was still the better singer. "Man, Harris come up there [and sings], 'I'm gonna tell God.' Lord! He just stood there; that's all he said! And they shouted, 'It's all right! Come on, Rebert!' And, man, that bald-headed guy: he baad! And a man come from the back; he walk every bench from the back to the stage and didn't hurt nobody! You think I'm lying? I'll get you fifty thousand witnesses tell you that!"

Backstage, meanwhile, Sam gave off his usual air of assurance—unless you noticed the hand-wringing. Despite the fact that he was in his power as a gospel lead, he was still just twenty-five and singing against a gospel legend. When it came time, the Stirrers were introduced by an Atlanta gospel dj. Here's where the advantage of records paid off. Harris's popularity was based on word of mouth and a few recent recordings, but nothing like the Stirrers' output on Specialty, which the audience heard every day on the air. Now they went crazy as the group hit the stage—and this was without Sam. Coached by Crain, he remained seated until guitarist Crume hit the opening bars of "Wonderful," their current single. Then, Sam rose and, in Crain's words, "the little boy flash that smile: dtttttt!" With that one look of pure pleasure and confidence—as if he welcomed the chance to sing with Old Man Harris—with that, he had them. "He tore Sister Flute up!"

It was his voice, sure, and Foster's, too, as they launched into "Peace in the Valley." But, more than that, it was his personality burning through that clear smile. Cook had a way of presenting himself—churchgoers would have called it a spirit—that simply leveled the house. It went beyond music into the charismatic realm that Holiness preachers played so effectively. While Sam hadn't "won" the battle of song, he'd held his own against an acknowledged master and a better singer.

Even as he triumphed, Sam was talking about using that power elsewhere. Paul Foster remembers a night in Atlanta when Sam was leafing through a magazine. "One day," Sam told his roommate, Foster, "I want to be just like this fellow here," pointing to Harry Belafonte, whose smooth calypso styling and good looks had helped produce 1956's #1 album. Maybe it was holding his own against Harris that let Sam confide a little in Paul. Turning the pages, he went on, " 'Cause I gone just about as far as I can go on this side. I'd like to change over and try some other field."

Cook often tested out ideas on friends, but Foster (who would later become Reverend Foster) didn't much hold with this one. "I think it's better for you to stay where you at. The Lord will provide for us right here."

Sam nodded. "I know that, Paul, but I just want to change over. I want to do something different. . . . And better my condition."

Paul understood Sam's impatience. "We had it hard in some places," Foster recalls. "Sometimes we would ride all night. We'd get there just in time and couldn't even get a room to stay or sleep. . . . Sometimes, we'd get to a place, and there wouldn't be no program. The program would be canceled. Some of the time, we would be near out of money. Or it would rain us out. Lot of times, we would just drive miles and miles and thousand of miles, and we wouldn't have no program."

To the religious Foster, it was a test of faith. To Sam, it was starting to seem like too much. He kept turning it over even as he moved from the triumph in Atlanta to another challenge up North in New York City.

The famous Apollo Theater had staged its first all-gospel program the previous Christmas. A big success, it had highlighted Specialty acts like Brother Joe May, but the Stirrers, in Crain's words, had "shunned" the Apollo. "I wasn't thinking about singing all week for eight hundred dollars!" Not when they could go across the river to Newark and get double that for a fraction of the work. The Apollo's first program had done so well, however, that its owners, the Schiffmans, were now offering larger fees. And the money was only part of it. As Crain put it, "When the Apollo got big, that the biggest thing going." The other gospel groups who had already played there had garnered enormous publicity—made a kind of show-business history—and been seen by most of the major agencies in the city.

Starting August 21, however, the Schiffmans pretended they had nothing to do with such crass desires. "We'd take huge gothic arches and cover them with stained-glass paper so they looked like stained-glass windows. And we'd do all sorts of lighting. . . . The beginning of the show, all of the performers would walk down the aisles with candles. We did a whole thing!" The place seated sixteen hundred; the top acts drew over forty thousand a week under an incredibly demanding four shows a day, six days a week. The one exception was amateur night, when they only had to play three. According to Crume, the Apollo "was the hardest work that we'd ever do."

It also had a famously tough crowd, and, as the date began, Sam and the Stirrers started to realize what it would take to get them. The quartet sang its hits, of course: "Be with Me Jesus," "Nearer to Thee," but the song that had been getting Sister Flute lately was "Wonderful." Those long, manipulated notes drove her right over the edge. Sam sang it that first weekend, and it got the quartet in the house all right, but Sister Flute would still wait, still watch. Instead of stopping the tune where it ended on the record, the group had to go over it and over it, and finally—after Sam had worked each note till it shone—they'd hear Sister Flute's amens.

On Monday morning, after twelve shows like that, Sam discovered he couldn't get out of bed. Crain, horrified, called in a doctor, who diagnosed the flu and prescribed complete bed rest. But they were headlining at the Apollo! The doctor was adamant. So, leaving Sam to be nursed back to health by a devoted female fan, the group went to another room to consider their options. "Crain and them wanted to give up," Paul Foster remembers. "They didn't think I could make it by myself." But Paul insisted he could carry the weight.

That Monday, the Stirrers went on with Foster as their sole lead, but they carefully avoided their big hits: those were all Cook's. Finally, Foster called for one of Sam's numbers. "Uh-uh, Paul," Crume whispered. "Don't do that. Sing your songs, man." Onstage, with the Apollo's crowd waiting, Foster turned to his guitarist. "Look, Crume—is you gonna play it? Or am I gonna have to get somebody else to play for us?" Crume played, the Stirrers sang, and Foster covered Sam's hits in a way, he confessed, "which was surprising to the whole entire congregation." If he didn't have the same subtlety or range, he made up for it in passion. And when he forgot the words (which he was notorious for doing), he just hollered: wawawawawawa—a babble that unbelievers took to be nonsense but Sister Flute heard as the Holy Spirit. Cook returned by the end of the week, but, meanwhile, Foster had shown the group how it was possible to survive without Sam if—when—they had to.

Bill Cook happened to be following the Stirrers at the Apollo, doing an impromptu act on a Lloyd Price/Drifters bill, 10 percent of the proceeds to go toward Roy Hamilton's medical bills. He and Sam took the opportunity to work on secular material: a rewrite of the already pop-sounding "Wonderful" and some original tunes. Cook, meanwhile, continued to test the waters. "If you feel that that's what you want to do," the Reverend Sammy Lewis told him, "you shouldn't even ask nobody. It doesn't stop you from being a Christian. What you're doing out there is making a living: you're not shooting nobody. . . ."

Some of the public, however, was reacting to rock & roll as if it were worse than any bullet. In April of 1956, the head of the North Alabama Citizens' Council told *Newsweek* that rock was "designed to force 'Negro culture' on the South. . . . [T]he basic heavy beat of Negroes appeals to the very base of man, brings out the base in man, brings out the animalism and vulgarity." Negro columnist A. S. "Doc" Young had long since complained about being "assaulted . . . [by] raucous jukebox renditions." And radio stations and record labels, rather than fight this kind of pressure, were rolling over. Boston dj's set up a moral code; in August, Negro dj's met at Small's Paradise in Harlem to do the same; and Associated Booking claimed its new rock & roll package consisted of "specially screened" acts.

"Frankly," Sam would later recall, "the pop field hadn't much attraction for me . . . but the more I thought the more interesting it became. Bumps, of course, had a good deal of influence. He was constantly prodding me. . . ." The prodding was in purely economic terms. "If [the Soul Stirrers] went in and came out with five thousand dollars for an engagement, that was big money," Bumps remembers. "By the time Crain paid all the expenses, paid the room rent, got gas in the car, and fed them, and then they got a couple of dollars to send home, that five thousand dollars went no place." Sam's mind was about made up. "There were a lot of things I wanted to do," he said. "I wanted to do things for my family, and I wanted nice things for my own. Making a living was good enough, but what's wrong with doing better than that?" Nothing, although in late 1956, no gospel star of the first rank had crossed over.

Sam still had to have one more conversation. The Reverend Cook, now sixty, gave his blessings in almost the same words he'd used when Sam had asked to join the Stirrers. "Oh, the church folks raised sand! [But] I told him, 'Listen, before you leave town, them folks got to pay you half of the money that they're gonna give you for that program. You working for money! You're out there making money, boy! That's your living. Don't let anybody tell you nothing about no church song!' " Father and son agreed the supposedly uncrossable border between Saturday night and Sunday morning was mostly talk.

Art Rupe—though still, in his own words, "lukewarm on the subject"—finally agreed to a pop session in New Orleans. While he carefully approved the songs, the musicians, and the arrangements, he left the actual producing to Bumps, who was going to New Orleans anyway: he was getting married there on December 16. The

Stirrers had a big program lined up for December 9 in Houston's City Auditorium: the Blind Boys' sixteenth anniversary. Then they had a second Apollo date lined up for the Christmas season. So, Rupe arranged the pop session for December 12, between the two gigs. It was booked under the name Dale Cook.

The session was at Cosimo Matassa's on Governor Nicholls Street, a tiny place, seventeen by twenty-eight feet, but already legendary as *the* New Orleans studio. This is where Fats Domino cut his hits; "Blue Monday" was climbing the charts as Sam went in to record. It's also where Specialty had scored its biggest pop successes. The secret of Cosimo's wasn't the producer or the studio's "live" sound or the first-take undubbed approach; it was the musicians. As well as that "second-line" rhythm—an easy roll that seemed to grow like some hothouse plant only in New Orleans—Cosimo's house band was famous for quick, killer, head arrangements: both Little Richard's and Lloyd Price's first hits had been studio improvs that Rupe had then polished and marketed.

The leader at Sam's session was Earl Palmer: a magician on the drums, capable of going from street-corner funky to rock-steady. "Palmer started off as a kid dancer, literally dancing in the street for quarters," Cosimo told author Rick Coleman, "so he had a built-in rhythm. I can remember they'd do a take and it would be too long—in those days everybody wanted short records—and they'd say, 'Earl, that was three minutes—can we get one at two-fifty?' And he'd jokingly pretend to be winding up a clock on his ankle and speed it up that much . . . and he did." Warren Myles was on piano, Edgar Blanchard played guitar, and Frank Fields bass. Plus, there was a horn section which was more than likely Lee Allen on tenor sax, and Alvin "Red" Tyler on baritone. It was the New Orleans hit-makers, and, almost to the man, the players Bumps had supervised earlier that year on Little Richard's "Long Tall Sally," "Ready Teddy," "Lucille," and "Good Golly Miss Molly."

For Sam, the musicians weren't asked to create the driving frenzy that had made Richard. Instead, they did ballads: two Cook originals, a tune by the horn player, Red Tyler, and the rewrite of Theodore Frye's "Wonderful." This last, "Lovable," began the session, and it still seems a pretty brassy move. Any notion of fooling the church audience with the Dale Cook subterfuge flies out the window when we hear Sam's distinctive voice (complete with a little gospel growl) doing one of his religious hits over nearly the same arrangement. All that changed was the object of his affections: "He" was wonderful, now "she" is lovable.

After that, Sam cut two originals: "I Don't Want to Cry" and "That's All I Need to Know." Both have the slow beat, the whoops, and some of the infectious charm that would mark Sam's later hits, and both are sung with complete confidence, slowly and seductively. Despite Sam's obvious ability to put over this kind of material, it wasn't what either he or Bumps had in mind. Red Tyler's "Forever" came closer to that, a pleasant if undistinguished mainstream ballad. "We are not interested in Blues at the present time," Bumps would write J. W. Alexander a couple of weeks after the session. "We would like Pop tunes with a blues chord structure which lend themselves to blues back-grounds. . . . In writing the lyrics try to write 'white' for the teen-age purchaser rather than 'race' lyrics. It seems the white girls are buying the records these days." Sam's first single, "Lovable"/"Forever," wasn't r&b that might cross over, but sweet ballads bordering on lounge tunes and aimed right at those white girls.

After the session, Sam flew up to New York to rejoin the Stirrers for their Christmas program at the Apollo. He had Dolores and Joey meet him there. The marriage had, by now, hit bottom. Dolores had moved from R.B.'s to an apartment behind the Kenwood Hotel, and Joey can remember the Cook family pressing her to keep a gun there. After all, given Sam's schedule, she was essentially living alone. An outgoing woman, beautiful, used to being the center of attention, Dee still didn't have much more to do than raise little Joey and wait for one of Sam's visits.

The low point had come one day when Crain got a call from a Chicago police station: Dolores had attempted suicide. "Now, what cause her," says Crain, "you can only—we used to use the word 'surmise.' " He thought it was Sam's independence: "[He] was the only man Dolores had had that actually didn't bow to her. That her beauty didn't bring him to his knees . . . this she couldn't take." Crain recalls her trying to cut her wrists—or threatening to—and ending up in temporary custody. "I don't think it was Dee's fault or Sam's fault. Sam was just that kind of man. I think he was just tired of being married. Usually, when he was with a woman awhile, he didn't want her no more. Just seems like that's the way he acted. Not only her, every woman he had."

Cook tried to do the right thing. During the Apollo run, Sam, Dee, and Joey stayed together in Newark, but there was a sense of finality about it all. Joey, nearly nine, didn't know what was up, but as they walked around town, he spotted a little white cocker spaniel in a pet store and asked if he could have it. Sam went in, bought the dog, and then asked the boy what he wanted to name it. "I don't know. Happy? Sad?" He looked up at his dad. "Why don't you name him Newark," Sam said. "After the town. It'd be something for you to remember."

Onstage, meanwhile, Sam was astonishing: "one of the more exciting things I ever saw," says the Apollo's Bobby Schiffman. "I'd stand in the back sometimes," says Schiffman, admittedly romantic about his time running the theater, "and there'd be a dynamic, young, new performer nobody ever saw before. All of a sudden the electricity would hit. The kid would show some extreme talent, and the audience would flame into applause, and you could see little bits of stardust. . . . I swear you could!" In an extraordinary move, the Apollo extended the program an additional five days through Christmas.

Bobby, who had broached the subject a few months before, began hammering at Sam to go pop. "If the rules are more important to you than the money—and I'm not so sure those rules are written in stone—but if the rules are more important to you than the money, then stay there. If the money is more important to you, come this way. I *guarantee* that with your looks and your talent and your voice, you will be a major superstar in America within a year." Bobby Schiffman's memory is that he then called the William Morris Agency, got in touch with Larry Auerbach, an agent there, and told him, "Larry, there is a kid up here who will set you on fire he is so good! His name is Sam Cook, and he's out of sight!" Auerbach concedes, "It's possible that Bobby did call me, but I didn't know what to do with him without a [hit] record."

"Lovable"/"Forever," released at the end of January, was no hit. After the session, Bill Cook had optimistically written Bumps that "it sounded like you might have captured the thing that we were looking for." Blackwell knew better. The single was a "good introduction," he answered, but "I know we can and will do a better job on our next release—with stronger material." *Billboard* agreed. Its reviewer commended Dale Cook for his "church touches" but concluded "he struggles against pale material and weak backing." Later, Bumps would argue that the single failed because they pretended he was Dale Cook—"We changed his name, but we couldn't change his sound"—and people resented it. Sam believed Rupe undermined the experiment, never pushing his pop stuff. The single eventually sold around fifteen thousand copies: fine for gospel, modest for pop.

"[It] didn't do great," Leroy Crume says, "but it got around. Everybody that we knew knew about it." And that was now the rub. Not only had Sam failed to come up with a hit, but the Dale Cook ruse hadn't worked for a minute. Crume recalls how Sam tried to lie his way through it—"That was my brother"—but when the Stirrers did a gospel TV show not long after the single was released, the announcer even introduced him as Dale. Crume burst out laughing; the others were considerably less amused. Crain and Farley later cabled Art Rupe, pleading with him to stop the rock & roll: "THE ONE ALREADY RELEASED IS HURTING US IN THE SPIRITUAL FIELD AND ANOTHER RELEASE WILL STOP US COMPLETELY SO PLEASE DO NOT RELEASE ANY MORE."

Sam decided to approach J. W. Alexander about his next move. If Crain was a kind of moral center for Sam, he'd come to rely on Alex for business advice. Behind J.W.'s sweet, high-pitched voice and ready laugh, he was, in fellow Traveler Jesse Whitaker's estimation, "really shrewd, man. He'd know what was happening. He'd know how to go about it. . . ." And he had no problem with the idea of pop. Alexander had begun his career in Tulsa, Oklahoma, singing what he calls "doo-raps" with another kid from Carver Junior High. The duet would go out to the Lions or the Rotarians and perform everything from plantation melodies to "folk things," then pass the plate. After high school, he'd gone into the Civilian Conservation Corps and then had pitched in the Negro League for the famous Ethiopian Clowns. They'd barnstormed from Denver to Chicago, until Alex had headed to California to join a gospel quartet. Now he was simultaneously scouting gospel groups for Rupe and crossover talent for Bumps. Over dinner at Newark's Cecil Hotel, Sam outlined the situation.

"Art says the record sold about twenty-five thousand," Cook confided, exaggerating a little, "so they want to record me again. What do you think?"

"Sam," Alexander replied, "I think you can make it. But you can't be an ostrich and stick your head in the sand. You got to be Sam Cook." As Alexander recalls it, "At that particular time, the young black girls didn't have anybody. Johnny Mathis was out, but Johnny Mathis was white, see? There was really nobody. Sonny Till had messed up with the Orioles. There was one kid: Sam Cook. The time was just right."

What Alex also knew but may have been slow in acknowledging—it was, after all, a scary and unlikely notion—was what Bumps was arguing: it wouldn't be just young black girls who would swarm toward Sam. Where "race music" had always been seen as a singles market, in the six months since October 1956, the number of r&b albums being issued had doubled—a sure sign that music was appealing to the richer, white market. *Billboard*, smoothing over centuries of racial history, was calling it "an interesting case of integration of the tastes of the minority into the majority." Some artists like Little Richard were crossing over without (again, *Billboard*'s phrase) "refining" their sound, but the independents were also taking aim at the majors by developing more balladeers like Jesse Belvin and Otis Williams. "The end of the racial identifications with either the pop or r&b idioms is gradually but steadily coming to a halt," the trade journal concluded, envisioning "a great economic boom" not only to Negroes but to everyone in the business. It was a brief, exquisite opening: a passage through music's restrictive covenants.

Sam's Chicago recording session on April 10, 1957, turned out to be his last with the Stirrers. The material gives an idea of the pop direction in which he might have taken the quartet had he stayed with it. As well as Crume on guitar, Willie Webb was back on organ, Evelyn Gay played piano, and Sam's brother, L.C., is credited with drums after the union drummer walked out. In Sam's arrangement, the traditional hymn "Mean Old World" begins with a tripping, doo-wop bass line by Farley and then is paced at a stroll. Sam may have picked this bluesy format and subject matter for personal reasons. According to court documents, he was formally separating from Dee around this time. When he sings how this is a mean world to live in "without a friend, children or even a home," there's a quality of understated sadness that sounds like the real thing. Still, it's that hope of his that comes across as he snaps his fingers and claps in the face of sorrow. The song breaks open after two verses, when Sam hands the lead over to the group and answers them with whoops, curlicues, and even a falsetto way beyond his range—all filled with a kind of pure delight. "This is what we use for our theme song," Crain wrote Rupe after the session, and it's gospel's classic theme: good news in bad times.

Cook had by now perfected the art of putting himself into a song. In "Were You There?"—another traditional number—two men are walking the road to Jerusalem, and one asks the other if he saw the crucifixion. The song hangs on the singer's ability to convince us that the answer is yes. Cook fills the old tune with conversational asides: "Tell me: did they really—did they pierce him in the side that morning?" After years together, the group can toss rhythms across Crain's beautiful, fluting arrangement as if they were all in the same family—never mind whatever squabbles might exist outside the studio. "Whoa," Sam shouts, and they echo, "(oh)." "Sometimes (sometimes) it causes me (I have to) tremble (tremble) tremble (tremble)." To say this is call and response is to understate what's going on here; it's the complicated, single beat of a heart, and the syncopated claps, Crume's jangly guitar, all underscore the testimony: yes, we were there.

The one original number Sam brought into the Chicago studio can be heard as his farewell to the Stirrers. "That's Heaven to Me" signals a new era. While it does mention the Savior once, it's basically a secular definition of the promised land. Heaven is kids playing on the street, a little flower blooming, or even—in Sam's patented style—"the leaves growing out, growing out, growing out on the tree." Over a slow, ascending melody, Cook declares to the gospel world that "it doesn't have to be a miracle"—and yodels his proof. It's still a religious song, deeply so, but from Crume's bluesy guitar intro to Sam's intimate vocal, it's a crossover tune in content as well as in sound. It announces that a man can find his God in the everyday, that he can "dirty" himself with the world and still hold his vision, that he can and maybe ought to find his redemption right here on earth.

A week after the session, on April 21, Sam went into Detroit, where Reverend Franklin was hosting an Easter program at the State Fair Coliseum. Cook had long since lost count of how many programs like this one he'd performed, how many Easters in Detroit with these old friends and teachers, how many times he'd stepped in front of Farley, Crain, and Robinson, heard Crume hit a chord, and begun trading leads with Foster. There was June Cheeks (back with the Sensational Nightingales), urging him on as in the old days, pushing him past his limit. Alex and the Travelers looked on, Dot Coates still mopping her brow from her last run down the aisle. Right out front there, Sister Flute waited for the spirit, moaned for the pretty man to do to her what they both knew he could. Sam gave that low, gospel chuckle and, slipping off his coat, walked down the aisle into the congregation, singing all the way. "You know," Crume recollects, "I didn't know Sam was gone until he was gone. . . . There wasn't a big fight. . . . He just didn't show up."

Chapter

10

L ate in April 1957, Sam sent Bumps a six-tune demo tape of pop songs. "The Only Music I Used Was The Guitar," Sam wrote in the enclosed note, "And I'm Playing That. I Hope You Get A Rough Idea of What The Songs Are Like. . . . There Are Two Which I Definitely Want To Do," Sam went on. "And That Is The First One, 'I'll Come Running Back To You,' And The Last One, 'I Don't Want To Cry.' " Bumps, however, was convinced that Sam's arrangement of Gershwin's "Summertime" was the hit. There was also a number called "You Send Me" that Bumps thought had some potential.

As Blackwell had written Bill Cook, he envisioned Sam as "definitely a modern Morton Downey"—which is to say a modified Irish tenor—and aimed to "bring Sam right to the front—with both teenagers and housewives." Art Rupe was leery: Specialty's music was r&b, not standards from *Porgy and Bess*. The label owner now says he was "amused by [Blackwell's] proclivity for exaggeration, accepted his strong ego, and admired his ability to communicate with our artists . . . I liked him." But by mid-'56, Rupe had written into his deal with Bumps that the a&r man could "personally manage ONLY THOSE I APPROVE." And soon, Rupe was checking to see if Blackwell really was the "university man" he often claimed to be, discovering that

Bumps had taken one class at the University of Washington and some piano lessons.

Still, the man's success with Little Richard was undeniable, and Rupe gave the go-ahead for another pop session with Sam. He even agreed to Bumps' request to record at Radio Recorders instead of with Specialty's usual engineer, Bunny Robyn. The switch to the "classier" studio should have tipped him off, but, despite setting up an arranger and listening to "Summertime" and the other material, Rupe apparently didn't understand what Cook and Blackwell were up to.

Bumps saw "tremendous discrimination in the industry." Negro singers were "not allowed to be balladeers" until they had paid lengthy dues in r&b. But instead of leaving gospel for r&b, Bumps and Sam planned to leapfrog all the way over into mainstream pop, where the white market was, the status, and the big money. Part of this strategy was to bring in guitarist Cliff White.

White, a jazzy player with a soft touch, had toured with the Mills Brothers and been on Bumps' earlier date with Jesse Belvin. Ten years older than Sam, White had gotten interested in music as a child in Dallas. The great bluesman Blind Lemon Jefferson was a friend of White's uncle, and Cliff used to walk Dallas's Deep Elem section carrying the singer's little metal shaker full of pennies. One day, Jefferson left his Gibson guitar over at Cliff's uncle's: "I remember I went and touched it, man, and you know that sound? I was hooked. It couldn't have been no deeper embedded if I'd been a little fish in a brook." White added some classical training when his mother got work in Carmel, California. There Cliff was exposed to the artists at the Hollow Hills Farm retreat, including Marian Anderson and Roland Hayes. So, White's musical reach was large, from Segovia to Blind Lemon Jefferson to jazz guitarist Charlie Christian, whom he calls "the Lord God Almighty."

Before Cook's pop session, Sam showed Cliff how he wanted to do "Summertime." Instead of starting with a minor chord, the way Gershwin wrote it, Cook insisted on an A major, then the jump to F-sharp minor, continuing the vamp throughout. White had never heard of starting a minor song with a major chord—"I have yet to reconcile that"—but the professional musician quickly recognized Cook's ability to see a song whole. The point of what he and Bumps were up to, after all, was to cross over from the colored market. "Summertime" was Gershwin's take on the Delta blues. By rearranging the emphasis, Cook was re-whitening the tune, pulling the Broadway back out from beneath the blues. Masking upon masking, it was as complicated as the racial situation the song circled.

Before going in to record, Sam signed a contract. He was to receive $25 a side to cut eight sides ($10 more than he'd gotten with the Soul Stirrers) and a cent-and-a-half royalty per song (the same as in gospel but he didn't have to divide it). Rupe had Sam add a note that this applied retroactively to the earlier New Orleans session. In fact, the contract was still with "Dale Cook," both the singer and the label owner working on the assumption that Sam would (or at least could) return to the Stirrers. As well as White on lead guitar, the session had arranger René Hall on rhythm guitar and Ted Brinson on bass. Earl Palmer, who had come to L.A. three months earlier, was once again the drummer. Blackwell, as leader, also arranged for Lee Gotch and three other background singers who had worked with jazz bands like Tommy Dorsey's. "With Sam," Bumps states, "being that his voice was so fluid and much different than the other singers—and he sang so far off the melody, which was like a jazz singer—I had to get the melody of the song back in. So, I had the Pied Pipers [as the background singers were called] on the melody. I used them like a string concept."

The June 1, 1957, session began at one-thirty in the afternoon. As Bumps remembers it, Art Rupe was supposed to have gone to Vegas for the day. But as they warmed up on "You Were Made for Me," in walked Rupe. Pappy (as Bumps called his boss) took one listen and "went out there and tore the session apart. Read and raised hell! Wanted to know what those white singers were doing singing behind a black gospel singer. Those 'no-soulful white singers'!"

The young Harold Battiste, fresh from New Orleans, saw the white man in the thick glasses lecturing Bumps and thought, "Wow, this cat's in trouble!" According to both Bumps and Battiste, Rupe wanted to fire the singers on the spot. " 'Now this,' " Battiste remembers him saying, " 'is the way I want you to do it.' He wanted triplets, making it sound more raucous. He wanted the rock & roll, Fats Domino kind of thing: heavier."

Arranger René Hall was worried he'd be blamed. Hall had just worked on "Stardust," a big hit for Billy Ward and his Dominoes. "So, he saw me in there, and he conceived of the idea that I was trying to make Sam into the type of singer that the Dominoes was. He detested that type of music. He had a mental block when it came to pop music." Rupe had okayed a vocal group, "assuming," he remembers, "that René or Bumps would use a typical Negro vocal backing. . . . When I saw and heard the white vocalists I was quite disturbed."

"He didn't curse me or nothin'," says Bumps, but Art made it plain that this was not—and never would be—Specialty's kind of music.

According to Blackwell, Cook's response to Rupe's temper tantrum was instantaneous: "If that's the way you think of me, and that's the way you want me to record, I quit your label!" "There was a hotheadedness to Sam," says his coworker Fred Smith. "He was the kind of person who could show his ass one minute and turn on the charm the next."

When Bumps began to defend Cook, Rupe spun around and shouted, "Okay, Bumps! Then you're fired!" Spinning back around, he spotted Sonny Bono, a young white truck driver who had been hanging around Specialty for months trying to get his songs played. "And you're hired!" Rupe announced, starting a career that would eventually lead to fame with Sonny and Cher.

"After [Art] walked out," says Bumps, "we were standing around looking at one another like we had egg on our face."

Rupe doesn't remember anyone being fired or quitting on the spot, but he admits he was infuriated: "I just sat in the booth sulking in anger because I feel [sic] I had been crossed in the crossover. . . ." Somehow, the stormy session continued, including that song Bumps had liked from the demo tape, "You Send Me."

Cliff White had first heard it at the Specialty rehearsal studio at La Cienega and Sunset. After Sam had taken his little four-string guitar and shown White the unorthodox vamp he wanted to use behind "Summertime," he'd played what to White's ears was hardly a song at all, just some "ice-cream changes." But Sam insisted White keep strumming: "Play it, and you just keep on playing it until I tell you." At first, Cook just scatted: "I know, I know, I know." Then he started singing, "Darling, you-ou-ou send me," and White, listening to the note-bending on "you," thought, well, we got something.

The problem was it just kept repeating. "By now, man, we done eight bars. And I say, how the hell!? Where's the song? To myself, you know. In eight bars, all he said was 'Darling, you send me.' So, I make the turnaround, and he tears out and does the same goddam thing again! Only instead of saying 'You send me,' he says 'You thrill me.' Stop and think, man, what this sounds like! I got eight bars of 'You send me,' then I get eight bars of 'You thrill me.' Okay, then I get to the end, and he does the bridge. Well, that kind of makes sense. It's got a little story in there, you know? 'At first, I thought it was infatuation/ da da da.' That's no sweat. And here he comes with this 'You send me' again! This dude," White concluded, "must be out of his mind."

Today, listening to one of rock & roll's most recognized and most successful songs, it's easy to see why White was nonplussed. Only through the prodding of Harold Battiste, who screened songs for Blackwell, had Cook even bothered to change the second verse to "You thrill me" from the otherwise endlessly repeating title line. The key to the song was the performance. Bumps would comment later, "Sam was a stylist. He was not a singer. . . . Get that straight. . . . The song could be 'Mary Had a Little Lamb,' but when Sam Cook did it, it was 'Ooooo, Mary had a little lamb.' "

White, Blackwell, Hall, Rupe—the veterans were amazed at how, on a standard set of chord changes, with a minimum amount of words, this man created a mood of young love, of "infatuation," which would soon appeal to millions. "I just thought it was pretty," Battiste recalls, "because Sam sang so pretty." It was the timing of the line breaks; how he soared on the word "you," broke it into four syllables, and drew it across the beat; how he pulled the listener into his world from the first note. Cook "had a great sense of timing," says White. "Phenomenal! No great voice, but soulful. And in tune. He was *so* in tune! When Sinatra was in his time, he was another, had that great sense of timing." White, playing behind him, could hear Sam "singing melody and counterpoint at the same time. Carrying a couple of melodies at the same time!"

"You Send Me" may have been more singer than song, but what the veterans were missing was the grace of the melody, the way the bridge stuck in your mind and wouldn't leave, and how the comforting, intimate feel of the tune suited the times. There's an extraordinary combination of reassurance and seduction in the gentle stroll of "You Send Me" that, in retrospect, mirrors the placid surface and strong undercurrents of the late fifties. "The song seemed kind of dumb to me," Bumps remembers, "but I thought, 'Oh well, it doesn't matter, because "Summertime" is gonna be the hit.' " Of course, with Rupe's temper tantrum, it looked like nothing was going to be released anyway.

Rupe began figuring out terms for Blackwell's departure almost immediately. In notes dated three days after the session, he outlines his proposed deal: in return for $1,500 and the masters to four instrumentals Bumps had cut, Blackwell would release Specialty "of all considerations." That meant all the past and future royalties that he had coming. About a week later, Bumps returned to Specialty's office to clean up old business. In an argument that must have picked up at about the same temperature at which it was dropped a week before, Bumps insisted he'd done right by Cook. In fact, Sam and Bumps wanted to renegotiate their contract based on the session.

It was the ultimate insult: the label's founder and his a&r man were accusing each other of having no ears for a hit. "They used to call me that 'half-white, nigger-Jew manager,' " says Bumps, "because I was on top of it!" In the cutthroat small-business world of early rock & roll, when little labels scratched and fought to stay alive against majors like Columbia and RCA, you had to be something like a "nigger-Jew" to make it. That's how Rupe, in his own right, had built his business. Now, neither man would budge.

And then there was the issue of color. "Art Rupe's attitude towards blacks in music," Bumps sneered, "was a monkey on a string. He didn't want blacks and whites to mix." That was patently untrue. Rupe had brought Lil Cumber into his company. But what Rupe was adamant about was the segregation of sound. His first love was "race" music, and his special feeling for gospel was based on the "soul" he thought was even clearer there. It was an eminently liberal attitude through the forties and early fifties—separate but equal. Except now, to men like Sam and Bumps, it began to smack of keeping Negroes in their place. They wanted the equivalent of what had recently been won in the Montgomery bus strike: equal access. In this case, the vehicle was ballad singing in the pop market.

"You think so much of this Sam Cook stuff," said Rupe, "I'd like to make a deal with you." As Blackwell looked him over carefully, he added, "You a gambling man?"

"I don't know," Blackwell answered, although both men, by the very nature of the music business, rolled the dice again and again.

"You think so much of Sam, just forget what you got coming in royalties with Little Richard, and you take Sam. And you can have the masters."

At that moment, Little Richard's "Lucille" had just finished a seven-week run on the charts, peaking at #21. While Specialty was having a terrible time getting Richard back in the studio (there were rumors he wanted to quit rock & roll for the church), Bumps knew what was already in the can awaiting release: "Jenny, Jenny," "Keep a Knockin'," and "Good Golly Miss Molly." He might not have foreseen that all three records would hit the national Top Ten, but given how hot Little Richard was and the quality of the material (all three are now rock & roll classics), Bumps knew he was walking away from big money. (He later estimated something close to $50,000 had been riding on the wager.) But the offer was more than dare; it was an insult, the equivalent of saying Bumps couldn't have cut a hit on his own.

"Okay," Bumps answered. "You got yourself a deal." And left.

Months later, when "You Send Me" hit, Rupe told Harold Battiste, "Bat, we're all wearing black around here. In mourning." But the deal made sense at the time. Specialty had always been run as a mom-and-pop operation; now, the sheer volume of rock & roll made that impossible. "Man," he told Battiste, "we spend all of our lives preparing ourselves to make records; we spend money to get the best engineers. And then we have to take it to some jerk who's a radio announcer, and he sits in judgment as to whether it's good or bad. We ought to make them sons of bitches *pay* to play Specialty records. Because we put the expertise in. And if we don't make the records, they don't have a job!" For Rupe even to consider such a total reversal of reality was a sign that he was growing weary.

Art was in the middle of a divorce from his wife, Lee, who had helped build the label: keeping the books, dealing with dj's, hassling distributors to get their money. J. W. Alexander always felt the divorce contributed to Rupe's hasty decision to let Bumps and Sam go. "An interesting bit of Freudian insight" is Rupe's response. "Frankly," he concludes, "I think I tired of the game. . . . I was about forty. It was time to look for new challenges—which I did."

The release, signed June 17, gave Bumps his instrumentals and Sam's contract—with the understanding that Cook could be called back to cut eight more sides. (Rupe probably figured he could get a few more Soul Stirrers singles.) As for the pop masters, Art wasn't going to fight over "Summertime" and that other nonsense they'd cut. After all, Venice Music still had the publishing; if by some fluke the stuff with the white backup singers did hit, the money would still come to him.

What Art didn't know was that Bumps had an ace up his sleeve. According to court documents, Blackwell had been negotiating with another label since mid-May and had signed on two days after the "You Send Me" session—almost a week before taking the bet with Rupe. "I don't know if Bumps was smart," Rupe would later say, "or being smart." That June day, Blackwell walked out of the Specialty offices with the masters of "Summertime" and "You Send Me" under his arm and headed straight over to Keen Records.

The label had been started four months earlier by John Siamas and Bob Keene. Siamas, a Greek businessman, had made a lot of money manufacturing hydraulic parts for Los Angeles' booming airplane industry. Keene, a clarinet player, had worked with the Artie Shaw band and done some regional TV until, in his words, "the band business kind of fizzled out because it was getting into rock and roll and stuff." In the midst of that fizzle, Siamas approached him out of the blue with the classic line "Man, let's start a record company." Though he didn't know a lot about it, Siamas loved music and wanted to use some of his airplane capital to make pop versions of traditional Greek music. When Keene suggested that might not be a commercial success, Siamas asked did he "know any black guys: rhythm and blues?" "So that," says the clarinetist, "is how Keen Records started."

As Keene understood their oral agreement, he'd act as a&r man, finding and recording artists, and for his services would share an equal part of the profits with Siamas. After renting a little office at 5405 Hollywood Boulevard, the new partners did cut a clarinet album with Keene and then produced a couple of undistinguished rock & roll sessions. Siamas quickly realized his original $5,000 wasn't going to be enough, but Randall Parts, the family business, was enormously successful. Siamas put in another $5,000 and got an additional $10,000 each from his brother, Alex, and his uncle, Andrew Karres: the Greeks, as their employees called them. It was a kind of hobby for the family, says Alex, not a tax shelter but "a sort of side business." Meanwhile, Keene and Siamas had gotten close enough that when Bob got married that May, John acted as best man.

The new partners approached Blackwell with a job offer and what Bumps understood to be an option to buy 5 percent of the company, Rex Productions. Again, it was an oral agreement. "When we looked at Bumps as a producer at Keen records," says fellow employee Fred Smith, "it wasn't r&b; it was specifically this and very dominantly this: he had even the Alabama Blind Boys! He had all the religious groups that were out there available to him. . . ." The gospel field was beginning to be recognized as a major source for r&b singers, and Bumps did bring the Pilgrim Travelers with him to Keen. That summer, they cut some sides with their new tenor, Lou Rawls. (Sam sat in, singing backup on "Motherless Child.")

As Bumps spent all that July and August trying to find the right product to launch the new label, Sam cooled his heels. He was sleeping on a couch in Bumps' apartment, surviving with the help of a little money Crain sent from the road. Far from home, his marriage over, Cook had suddenly gone from gospel star to another wannabe on the fringes of the Los Angeles scene. He signed up for a drama class and spent time reading the trades and watching the news. Back in Chicago, a hundred Negroes out at a picnic in Calumet Park had been attacked; thirty-five were injured as whites roamed a two-mile area in search of victims. In Levittown, Pennsylvania, a rock-throwing mob of five hundred came out when a Negro family announced its intentions to move into the all-white planned city. In May, Martin Luther King, Jr., had helped lead a Washington prayer vigil of more than 35,000 people to mark the third anniversary of the Supreme Court desegregation ruling—a ruling that hadn't seemed to change things much.

Meanwhile, in the pop world, Roy Hamilton had come out of re-tirement and was headlining a package tour of one-nighters through the South that was expected to gross $150,000 in two weeks. So much for Bill Cook's being Sam's manager. Clyde McPhatter was set-ting attendance records at the Howard Theater in Washington, D.C., with a box office of almost $40,000. And LaVern Baker was about to sign a $5,000 deal to appear on *The Ed Sullivan Show*. These were all former gospel singers. Those who'd stayed in the field were doing pretty well, too. In July, Mahalia sang at the Newport Jazz Festival, while reassuring her fans that, unlike others, "Mahalia isn't ready to depart the church that made Mahalia. . . ." Clara Ward announced her "Big Gospel Show," billed as "the first major attempt to sell gos-pel singing in the general market." Everyone was on it—the Blind Boys, the Sensational Nightingales, the Caravans, Dorothy Love Coates, even Sam's own Soul Stirrers. They were touring the nation and Canada, and there was talk of going over to Europe. Sam watched all this from a distance and must have wondered if he'd made the right decision after all.

In the middle of August, Bumps gave up. "When the time come to release, I had stuff recorded on Lou Rawls, Herbie Alpert; oh, a lot of people. And it wasn't nothing there that I felt strong enough to make a record—or for me to call [disk jockeys] . . . to get them to really get on it: to break a company. There was nothing there worth a damn." That included some new cuts with Sam: " 'Desire Me' and some shit," as Bumps put it. "So then I went home, up in my closet, and pulled out these masters of Sam's."

The question is what these tapes were doing in his closet. Bumps had walked off a job over this material, bet thousands of dollars. Had he hidden them in the hopes of proving himself at Keen with new material he alone produced? Had his exit from Specialty been more about leaving Rupe than going with Sam? Or was the truth of the matter that no one—including Bumps and Sam—felt really confident that "Summertime"/"You Send Me" was a hit?

As Bumps tells the story, the Greeks sound the most convinced. "When they put them on the machine, the office went apeshit!" Siamas offered to buy the cuts then and there. "Buy it?" Bumps replied. "I don't even know what I paid for it." Logically, the price was Little Richard's back royalties. "If you paid me what I paid for it, it wouldn't be fair to you. But if I sold it for less than what I paid for it, it ain't fair to me." Bumps would later contend that Siamas had agreed on a price, but Siamas eventually won a court case arguing that the agreement for "You Send Me" was simply Bumps' regular royalties. After all, these were no more than promising cuts by an unproven talent.

However the deal went down, late in August, Bumps transferred the masters into 78s, and soon after, Keen Records released "Summertime"/"You Send Me" by its new artist, now calling himself Sam Cooke. "Sam was superstitious," Bumps recalls. "The name-changing was mine, because it was then uneven numbers"—there were seven letters in "Sam Cook"—"and even numbers was what was important." It also added a touch of show biz and may have signaled the new life Sam was beginning. Cooke signed with Rex Productions on September 7, 1957; he got three and a half cents per record sold, a half-cent improvement on his Specialty contract.

Bumps was still convinced that "Summertime" was the side that would sell, and his first move as Sam's producer and manager was to cut a deal with John Dolphin. Dolphin's Records was the major r&b record store in Los Angeles. Dolphin also had his own label and produced a popular KGFJ r&b show out of the store's front window on

Vernon and Central. His early media monopoly meant he could sign, record, promote, and sell products on artists like Jesse Belvin without ever leaving his desk. Now, Bumps offered him Sam Cooke for a dance date at the Elks Club in return for $100 and airtime on the new single; Dolphin got to keep the profits from the personal appearance. As soon as Dolphin's dj's started playing the record, it was clear that on Central Avenue, anyway, the B-side was the hit. By the time Sam played the dance—only two weeks after his record's release—he was already being billed as Sam "You Send Me" Cooke.

The single started in the r&b market only. "We sold eighty thousand copies in Los Angeles," says Bob Keene, "before it was ever played on a white station." As it broke locally, Keene reminded John Siamas about their plans for a shared corporation, and Siamas immediately started backing away. On August 27, Keene got a letter from his best man saying Bob could buy 25 percent of the company for $5,000. "I came in the next day," Keene recalls, "and all the door locks were changed on the office. . . . Then a couple of guys show up on the doorstep, and they want all the [recording] equipment back."

Keene eventually took Siamas to court, but by the time the case came to trial, the clarinet player was more interested in the progress of his new find: a young Latino singer, Ritchie Valens. After cutting "Come On Let's Go" on the equipment he'd refused to return to Siamas, Keene and his wife decided to call the new label Del-Fi, for the Greek oracle of inspiration. "After all," she told him, "you just got fucked by a Greek."

Thanks in part to Sam's gospel reputation, "You Send Me" now began to break in the national r&b market. In Chicago, Negro dj Richard Stamz ("That son of a bitch Alan Freed ain't started r&b!") and promo man Howard Bendo were sitting around with Eli Toscano, a half-Italian, half-Mexican distributor who co-owned the Cobra label with Bendo. In walked a white guy. "Man, I got the hit record of the day! You all know Sam Cook of the Soul Stirrers?" The three men, veterans of Chicago's music scene, said they knew him all right, and the white guy took out a 78 and put it on the turntable. Bendo and Stamz looked at each other and said, "This *is* a hit!" Stamz was one of the leading dj's on WGES, a major Negro station in Chicago; if he said the record was a hit, it would be. Toscano bought a thousand 78s out of the white guy's trunk for thirty-five cents apiece. With an exclusive in the area, he started selling the 78s for $1. "We laid on that record!" Stamz recalls, and Toscano eventually jacked the price to $1.25 as Cooke, the hometown boy, took off.

Out in St. Louis, disk jockey E. Rodney Jones strolled into Robert's Distributors to take a look at the latest releases. On the manager's desk was a demo pressing on a new label called Keen. What caught Jones's eye was the artist's name. Jones had heard and met Sam when he was with the Stirrers and remembered the impact as unbelievable: "a voice that would capture people." "Hey, man!" Jones told the manager. "This might be the kid was with that gospel group." The man had no idea what Jones was talking about. Gospel? "Do you mind if I hear it?"

As soon as Jones put the demo on, he knew the voice. He persuaded the manager to hand over the only copy he had, and Jones played it on his next KXLW show. "The phones exploded!" People liked "Summertime" all right, but it was the flip side, "You Send Me," that killed them. "It was very repetitious . . ." Jones explains, "but it showed the voice that I had remembered from 'Peace in the Valley.' . . ." Others agreed; the first calls were from Sam's hard-core gospel fans. They got the record the airtime it needed to break r&b.

All this was great, but it wasn't the crossover pop market Sam and Bumps wanted. The only way to get that was to go out on the road and press the flesh. After playing the Elks Club dance, Sam did one of Art Laboe's r&b packages out in Long Beach. Then, Bumps reports, "I took five thousand dollars, and Sam by the hand, and we went around the country on a promotional tour." It proved to be a critical time to head out.

The day after Sam appeared at the Elks Club, Governor Faubus of Arkansas removed his National Guard troops from around Little Rock's Central High, leaving the white mob free to attack the nine Negro children trying to attend. By the time President Eisenhower sent in the 101st Airborne, the damage was done.

Reaction across Negro America was swift and sharply critical, marshaled in part by an unlikely leader. Trumpeter Louis Armstrong was

a revolutionary musician—he'd transformed jazz—but he'd managed
the crossover Sam was now attempting by masking himself as a smiling, handkerchief-waving ambassador of goodwill. Now the mask
dropped. He called a press conference and announced he was cancel-
ing his State Department–sponsored trip to Russia. "It's getting so
bad a colored man hasn't got any country," Satchmo told reporters.
"My people—the Negroes—are not looking for anything—we just
want a square shake. But when I see on television and read about a
crowd in Arkansas spitting and cursing at a little colored girl . . . do
you dig me when I say I have a right to blow my top . . .?" Lena
Horne, Eartha Kitt, and others lined up behind Armstrong. (Kitt
called Ike "a man without a soul.") Just as Cooke was trying to ma-
neuver his way through the racial minefield of crossing over, the rules
were changing. As the head of the Little Rock NAACP put it, "We
are fighting a civil war."

One of Bumps and Sam's first stops was Atlanta, the Soul Stirrers'
old stronghold. In this case, it was Sam who took Bumps by the
hand. As Cooke later told the story: "I ran into B. B. Beamon, a promoter who booked the Soul Stirrers. He booked me into the Magno-
lia dance hall for a one-night stand and paid me a thousand dollars."
Cooke headlined with Shirley and Lee and was billed as "formerly
with" the Stirrers. In his publicity shot, he's obviously playing to his
new market. He's traded in the clean-cut Christian good looks for a
conked pompadour, a thin mustache, and the narrow-lapeled suit of
a hip cat.

That week, *Billboard* highlighted "You Send Me" as a best buy.
"Sales are unusually heavy on all markets," the reviewer wrote, but it
was the Detroit market that Bumps always credited for the crossover.
There, the evening rock & roll jock on WJBK was a young man
named Casey Kasem. Kasem, who would go on to be a nationally
known radio and television personality, recalls that when Bumps arrived to promote "Summertime," "I just told him that the flip side
was the side." Bumps was startled. He knew "You Send Me" had
emerged as the r&b hit, but in the white market? Those days, Kasem
says with some nostalgia, there weren't musical programmers or Top
Forty play lists: "If you wanted to play a record six or eight times a

night you could." When it came to this Sam Cooke single, Kasem wanted to.

"When Sam hit," Bumps later recalled, "we hit so goddam big! And the kids were going apeshit, and we were burning up the airwaves." You could still hear the joy and excitement in Blackwell's voice three decades later. In a week, "You Send Me" jumped to #16 on the charts. It was breaking all over the country: a territorial bestseller in Detroit, L.A., New York, Newark, Philadelphia, St. Louis, and Kansas City. The next week, it was #3, and it entered the r&b charts at #4.

The problem—and Bumps knew it well—was going to be covers. The same way Pat Boone's white-bucks version of "Tutti Frutti" had outsold Little Richard's, there were bound to be those who—smelling the blood in the water—would try to cut a "cleaner" version of "You Send Me." "See, when we put the record out," Bumps recalls, "everybody in the country, all the majors, knew we were a brand-new company . . . so they tried to cover it to put us out of business." Sam's friend and Bumps' former artist Jesse Belvin made a run at it on Modern. Saxophonist Plas Johnson had his combo cover it on Capitol. But the real threat was the white artist Teresa Brewer, who did the tune for Coral. Brewer had had nine Top Forty hits in the last three years and was, in Bumps' words, "a big, big name." Her version of "You Send Me" was nothing if not perky: a little girl's voice coming out of a woman's body. Bumps, besieged, swore there were twelve cover versions: "a fucking nightmare!"

Blackwell had his strategies. A year earlier, he'd had Little Richard record "Long Tall Sally" at such a breakneck speed that "Boone wouldn't be able to get his mouth together to do it!" Sam's note-bending and the intimate quality of his voice produced a similar effect: you could cover it, but you couldn't duplicate it. The vanilla changes lost their meaning when Teresa Brewer plodded through them; she turned the swoop of "You-ou-ou" into the stop-action "You. You. You." In Bumps' words, "Everybody that sang 'You Send Me' were not singing 'You Send Me.' They were singing Sam Cooke."

This time, Bumps' gratitude went to Chicago dj Marty Fey, who dedicated a portion of his prime-time show to defending one of Chicago's native sons. According to Bumps, he "really racked Teresa Brewer for the audacity of trying to cover a great voice like this, and here she was a white singer. . . . Oh, man, when he got through ranking that record, that record came off the air so fast!" (Actually, Brewer's version eventually climbed to number eight, but the important thing was it never eclipsed Sam's.)

"You Send Me" became an astonishing phenomenon. Almost instantaneously, Sam was selling more records a day than he had in a year as a Soul Stirrer. The single eventually racked up a reported 1.7 million copies. Amid competition like Elvis's "Jailhouse Rock" and the Everly Brothers' "Wake Up Little Susie," it went to #1 and stayed on the charts for more than half a year. "I still don't know what happened," Sam would tell a reporter. "Here I am one night singing church songs and thinking that maybe I'll have to get me a side job waiting table or something to get enough bread to make ends meet. Then all of a sudden Sam Cooke is rich—well, that is, having more money than there is in the world to spend. I've heard the stories of Cinderella singers like Elvis Presley . . . but I never expected to be in on one of those big payoffs myself." In a sense he never recovered—certainly he was never the same—but it was false modesty to say it was unexpected. He and Bumps had maneuvered hard to get here, and they now moved quickly to capitalize on the success.

"The thing is," Bumps recalls fondly, "that Jack Giraldi was following me around and William Morris . . . all the top agencies. . . . I was hiding from them. But there was this one guy, named Larry Auerbach. He used to wear a little stingy-brimmed derby hat and his trench coat and a little umbrella. Goddam, every time I looked around, that son of a bitch was right behind me!"

Auerbach had joined the William Morris Agency back in 1945 as an office boy and had worked his way up to where he was running what they called the Recording Department. His main job was to make record deals for middle-of-the-road live acts the agency already handled. The mighty William Morris Agency considered rock & rollers beneath its consideration. "I think nobody else wanted to bother with the garbage I was dealing with," says Auerbach. "I don't think anybody else knew or really cared." But it was becoming impossible to ignore the music. In October 1957, a third of the money in the recording industry was coming in through singles, and the independents accounted for two-thirds of that revenue.

Auerbach admits he didn't know much about the business at the time, but one day, Bernie Lowe at Cameo-Parkway Records told him this "You Send Me" record was going to be a monster. Auerbach tried to find out who handled the Cooke kid and finally reached Bumps somewhere on the road. They set up an appointment in New York. "I'll never forget," says Auerbach: "Six-thirty on a Thursday." When the day arrived, Auerbach waited in his office. Six-thirty came and went; so did seven. At seven-thirty, he started calling around town, finally asking the bartender at Al and Dick's Steak House—a music-business hangout on 54th Street—to connect him with anybody sitting at the bar. Goldy Goldmark, an industry character, picked up, and Auerbach asked him if he'd seen Bumps. "No, but he's sitting in Moe Gale's office." That was bad news. Gale managed acts like Chick Webb and Erskine Hawkins, and Bill Cook was affiliated with the Gale Agency. If Blackwell was talking to Gale, Auerbach was in real danger of losing him.

The agent immediately called Gale's office, but when the secretary answered, Auerbach realized she'd never put him through. On the spur of the moment, he said, "In this terrible dialect, 'This is Timmie Rodgers; I want to talk to Bumps Blackwell.' " Rodgers was a famous Negro comedian of the time, and the agent was put through; when Bumps picked up the phone, he got an earful. "This is Auerbach! Get your ass over here! I'm not gonna wait much longer; it's too important to you. . . ."

When they finally sat down together, Auerbach began his sell. He'd never seen Sam perform, but he'd heard the record, and it had this great "clean" sound. "The trick is," he told Bumps, "—and I think it will give you staying power—is moving him into the non-black market. And we can do a hell of a job there." Auerbach ran through all the nightclubs William Morris serviced, the access it had to television, the other headliners it could put on a bill with Cooke. He told Bumps too many artists were one-hit wonders, and if they wanted to stay up there, they needed a large agency like his. "You'll make bigger dollars at the moment playing one-nighters. But unless you keep coming up with hit records, those one-nighters won't be there next year." Then he offered to do a one-shot with Bumps. Let William Morris prove itself by getting Sam on *The Ed Sullivan Show,* one of the most popular TV programs in the nation. Bumps could see how he and Auerbach got along and go from there.

As Bumps circled the bait, Auerbach sweetened it. "If things work out, I'll get you the Copa in March." Bumps looked at him. Frank Sinatra played the Copa; Sammy Davis, Jr. To Blackwell, it was the definition of class—exactly the jump he and Sam wanted to make. "Shit, man! The Copa to me was up here! I took it. It was a big mistake, but I took it."

Chapter

11

Sam's appearance on Ed Sullivan's show was a disaster—and helped make his career. That Sunday, November 3, 1957, Sullivan, as usual, had a hodgepodge of acts booked ("a really big show!"), and the nice-looking Negro singer was on last. Bumps and Sam were in a state. It was lip-synching, so all Sam had to do was keep up with the record, but, as he paced backstage in his natty suit, he knew it was his career-making introduction to middle America. Finally, the moment arrived. Sullivan announced Sam Cooke and the song that was sweeping the nation; Sam sauntered out, looking cool and collected, smiled to the applause, delivered the opening "Darling, you-ou-ou"—and was cut off. It was live TV; they had run out of time; nothing could be done about it. Sam mouthed the words for a few seconds, not realizing they'd pulled the plug, then walked offstage feeling foolish.

Sociologists often point to Elvis's censored, from-the-waist-up appearance on *The Ed Sullivan Show* the year before as a turning point in modern American pop culture. They mean white America. Across the country, African–Americans who never cared about Elvis can still tell you where they were when Sam Cooke got cut off Ed Sullivan. To the millions of teenagers who were buying "You Send Me" at an astonishing clip, it was torture to get only that first, promising line.

But to many Negroes who knew nothing about Cooke or his music, it looked like plain old prejudice.

Backstage, Bumps and Sam smiled like gentlemen as the Sullivan people apologized, but once they were out of the studio, they felt furious—and powerless. What they didn't know was that Sullivan's phones had already begun ringing. Soon, mail was pouring in from all over the country. The letters ranged from polite requests to get Sam back on to rants about the "pale-faced motherfucker" this and that. Sullivan happened to be especially sensitive to the charge of racism. As early as 1951, he'd been singled out by *Ebony* magazine for his liberal attitude toward bookings. "Recognizing the place of the Negro in television is not generosity," Sullivan had written then. "It is just common sense and good business." Now, how was he supposed to explain to his audience that he'd scheduled Cooke last because he was a rock & roller and a relative unknown, not because of the color of his skin? The solution was simple. Before Bumps and Sam even made it back to the West Coast, Sullivan had called to rebook.

Meanwhile, Cooke was trying to get his personal life in order. He stopped by his former apartment in Chicago and had Dolores sign what amounted to an authorization for divorce. Dee later claimed Sam told her the papers were to help him in a California paternity suit. She could believe it. After all, there was Barbara's child, Linda, and Denise Sommerville in Cleveland. In fact, there was a letter waiting for him at Specialty Records. "Hi Sweet," it began, ". . . I am expecting YOUR baby around the 1st of November." The author, a high school girl, had left her hometown of New Orleans to deliver the child in Washington, D.C. She assured Sam, "You are the only other person I went with in March and if you will count from March to November you will see that it is yours. Between you and I," the letter went on, "the baby will have to be adopted because I cannot take care of it and go to school too, as bad as I hate to do it." It ends, "Look Sweet whenever you get a chance write me back because I still love you very much. . . . By the way I saw you on television and you looked good enough to EAT (smile)." Someone at Specialty filed the letter away with a terse note: "Sam made this school girl pregnant and did not come for this letter."

In fact, Sam kept in touch with the baby girl and her mother. He never picked up the letter because he was in the middle of a knock-down drag-out with Art Rupe. Back in August, just as "You Send Me" was coming out, Bob Keene had come by Specialty. According to Rupe's notes, he had shown Keene the deal with Bumps, which said quite clearly that "songwriter's contracts shall not be affected by this release." Keene, flabbergasted, had immediately called Andy Karres and told him "to reconsider what he's doing—he's throwing a million bucks out the window—Bumps doesn't know what he's talking about—the publishing on 'You Send Me' does not belong to Higuera (the Siamas' publishing company)." What it meant was that Rupe—not Siamas—would pull in the lion's share of the profits from the million-seller. The Greeks had reacted quickly. On September 4, before Sam even signed with Keen Records, they had registered "You Send Me" with the copyright office as having been written by Sam's brother, L. C. Cook.

Rupe called it an "obvious conspiracy," but by the time his Venice Music tried to claim the song, it was too late. Art fired off a registered letter to Bumps. Siamas's lawyer, John Gray, answered by saying Cooke was rescinding his Dale Cook contract and standing by his claim that L.C. composed the song. The next day, Gray wrapped up the package by writing the songwriters' association BMI to assert not only that L.C. was the songwriter (BMI froze royalty payments till the matter was settled), but also that Sam's songwriting contract with Venice had been obtained "by menace, fraud and duress."

Rupe could barely contain himself. He wrote directly to Sam this time. "You know this is a bald-faced lie, and that when you signed . . . you were more anxious to enter into this contract than we were." The "You Send Me" session had been the day after the contract signing. "It doesn't make any sense," Rupe sputtered on, "that you would have recorded four sides for Specialty . . . *after* you signed our contract," if under duress. Rupe ended with a plea to "stop this needless bickering." There's no evidence Sam ever responded. Art had had his chance: when Sam had asked to cut pop, he'd dragged his feet; when the Dale Cook single had finally come out, Rupe hadn't promoted it properly; and when they'd cut this hit record that Rupe now wanted so badly, he'd stormed in and stopped the session, claiming Sam and Bumps didn't know what they were doing. Sam had made enough money for Art Rupe over the last six years, thank you. Now leave it to the lawyers.

The owner of Specialty was a man obsessed, and for obvious reasons: the publishing to "You Send Me" was worth a fortune. He made a note to himself that in early November, a dj on Los Angeles' KDAY had played "You Send Me" and then said, "That was Sam Cook singing a song he wrote." In January, he was in contact with Leo Price, a bandleader from around New Orleans who often supplied Specialty with material. Price's note (opening with "Hi Boss") asserted he, not Sam, had written "You Send Me." Rupe was delighted and wanted Price to take a lie-detector test. And in December of 1958, Rupe was in touch with one Willie Henderson, a Chicago friend of L.C.'s and Sam's, who claimed to have been present "many times when the Cook boys laughed of how they put over this deal with Specialty." The trouble with Henderson was that he was vague about dates and places, had a terrible stutter, and was presently prisoner #22544 in a Chicago jail. Specialty's lawyer decided he wouldn't be much of a witness. It would take nearly two years for the matter to be settled; then a U.S. district court judge ruled that Rupe's Venice Music should get $10,000 from BMI for performance rights on "You Send Me" and retain the other tapes by Sam that were in its vaults. In return, Rupe gave up title to the hit and any future income off it and officially rescinded Sam's songwriting contract. A note in the Specialty files shows that in the end, the battle cost Rupe over $5,000 in legal fees.

Did L. C. Cook write "You Send Me"? Almost certainly not. All the songs L.C. was credited with writing for Sam—"You Were Made for Me," "Win Your Love for Me," "I Don't Want to Cry," and "That's All I Need to Know"—also happened to be the ones recorded at Specialty and, therefore, in dispute. On one tune from that time, "I'll Come Running Back to You," Sam listed a friend, Willie Cook, as the author. Later, when she was his fiancée, he'd give credit to Barbara Campbell for writing "Love You Most of All," "Everybody Likes to Cha Cha Cha," "Only Sixteen," and "Wonderful World"—all published during his dispute with Rupe. But once he got out of his Venice Music songwriting contract, the only Cook on any of his songs' copyrights was Sam. Cliff White, who worked out the chord changes on "You Send Me," says categorically that Sam wrote it. And Leroy Crume remembers Cooke calling him, explaining his contract to Rupe, and offering to put Crume's name on "You Send Me." "I want my effing money though!" Sam told Leroy. "Don't go messing with my money!" To this day, Art Rupe won't forgive or forget. "I admired [Sam] as a unique talent. However, as a human being, I feel he was a tragic figure. He was arrogant, avaricious, and willing to compromise ethical behavior—qualities which possibly contributed to his untimely demise."

Sam would have laughed at the notion of being a tragic figure. As to the charge of avarice, how had Rupe made the money he was now investing in real estate and oil? Hadn't it been off men like June Cheeks, who continued to sing himself to death on the gospel highway? Still, Sam seems to have recognized that "You Send Me" had carried him into a complicated, unfamiliar realm. That November, he put in a call to his mentor S. R. Crain. "You hear my record?" Sam began.

"Yeah! I hear it every minute, Sam! The car can't turn over without my hearing it."

"So," Sam chuckled, "when can you get here?"

"What for?"

"I want you to be my road manager."

Sam promised Crain he'd be sending home $250 a week: more money than he'd ever seen in the religious field. Still, Crain didn't go for the offer immediately. It not only meant leaving his beloved Soul Stirrers, but it raised "all that mess," as S.R. says, of how a decent man should make a living. "In your mind, you don't want no blues. A good gospel singer don't need no blues to tell the truth. But when you get to thinking about your family, and what you want to get them . . ." Crain eventually accepted and, that day, moved from Philadelphia's Chesterfield Hotel to the far ritzier Park-Sheraton. "This," he said to himself, "is living!"

In late November, with "You Send Me" heading for #1, Sam returned to the West Coast to do a string of one-nighters from San Jose to Tacoma, then went into the studio to cut some follow-up material. Over at Specialty, Rupe had dug through Sam's demo tapes and found one of the songs Sam had wanted to release, "I'll Come Running Back to You." Although Art may not have been willing to admit publicly that he hadn't been able to hear Sam's hit, he was too canny a businessman not to try to duplicate it. Bringing in the very team that had infuriated him at the "You Send Me" session—the "no-soulful" white Lee Gotch singers and arranger René Hall—he sweetened the basic tape. To the song's lilting shuffle, he added a guitar intro, a walking bass, and an answering chorus. In the midst of all this production, Sam's vocal (cut, after all, to nothing but his own guitar accompaniment) sounds like a man talking to himself, but that private quality fits the subject perfectly. Rupe released the insistent little tune on November 18, in the midst of his fight with Siamas. On the flip side, he put "Forever"—the Dale Cook tune that had gone nowhere—and took out a two-column ad in *Billboard* proclaiming Specialty #619 "New!" Well, at least one side was, sort of.

The release put Specialty Records in position to follow up one of the year's biggest sellers. That hurt more than just the Greeks' pride. Record distributors were notorious for slow payments. The only proven way of motivating them was to come up with another hit; then the label had the leverage of not shipping them the follow-up unless they came through with payments on the original smash. Keen, a small label, was especially vulnerable, since it had no track record and, despite the Siamas airplane money, had just so much capital to keep the operation going. Their choice to follow "You Send Me" was "Desire Me": some of what Bumps called "the shit" he had in the can from earlier that summer. An absolutely undistinguished pop song, it puts "desire me" in the place of "you send me" and then plays the same variation of background singers and repetition. "You Send Me" may have been simple, but it was Sam's own simple, and he obviously felt the sentiment in a way he didn't with this follow-up.

Luckily, the record had a flip side. While still at Specialty, Sam and Bumps had been playing around with a cover of the Nat King

Cole hit "(I Love You) For Sentimental Reasons." Cole, after all, was one of Sam's prototypes for the cool, crossover balladeer, and his LP *Love's the Thing* had held the #1 position for eight weeks that summer. Cole's version of the song featured a small-combo sound with a smooth, intimate vocal, a jazzy guitar solo, and plenty of Nat's smart, understated piano. Sam's take on the tune is almost purely ornamental. He opens by singing "I love you" fifteen times in a row, then proceeds to decorate almost every phrase that escapes his mouth. This is the polar opposite of "I'll Come Running Back": wildly self-conscious and public. Which isn't to say it fails totally. On the bridge, the white backup singers pull an old Soul Stirrers trick by taking the lead, and Sam answers them, sounding comfortable and in command. Then the tune ends with Cooke repeating "I love you" another twenty-one times before he's faded out. Not to be outdone by Specialty, Keen took a two-page spread in *Billboard* proclaiming theirs "the NEW Sam Cooke hit" and boasting of a 200,000 advance sale.

On December 1, 1958, as he competed against himself on the charts, Sam returned to *The Ed Sullivan Show*. It was a typical mix, opening with the Glenn Miller band playing a medley of their hits, then featuring Buddy Holly and the Crickets in their TV debut singing "That'll Be the Day." The General Mills All-American College Football team followed. Then, after a brief intro, Sullivan ad-libbed, "Sam, here's the time," and Cooke, looking suave and sophisticated, lip-synched "You Send Me." He'd shaved the little mustache, had his hair in a close-cropped near-Afro, and was dressed in an immaculate jacket and bow tie. He had his routine down pat: his long fingers clasped together as if in prayer, and a quick little kiss at the camera to accompany the lyrics, before strolling off like a man in complete control. When he reappeared, later in the show, Sullivan said more. "I did wrong one night here on our stage by young Sam Cooke. From the coast. And I never received so much mail in my life, Sam. But the applause and the audience ran overboard that night; I never did get him on. But he has been on the first part of the show, and here he is singing his new hit record." Sam then did "For Sentimental Reasons."

If Sullivan didn't make the effort to introduce Sam to middle America (as he had earlier with Buddy Holly), no one out there in TV land—certainly no Negro—could mistake this for anything but an apology. It was a triumph—the performance of a professional (all the more impressive because he looked about eighteen)—and he and Bumps couldn't have bought the publicity that Sullivan's introduction generated. Years later, Bumps saw the Ed Sullivan recovery as typical: Sam always seemed to turn a negative into a positive. "That's why I call him the Cinderella Man. . . . Here was a guy who always stepped into a bucket of shit and came out smelling like a rose."

"You Send Me" carried Sam in some great updraft, an invisible rush that lifted everything into a new realm. It was like the Reverend C. P. Jones's Holiness vision, except secular. With people clamoring for his new records, "I'll Come Running Back" reached #18 pop and sold half a million copies; the Keen release, "For Sentimental Reasons," charted one position higher.

For a man who loved *this* world, it was heaven. *Sepia* magazine caught up with him in Chicago. Checked into a fine hotel, Sam posed for pictures "fondling one of a number of spanking new expensively tailored suits." When he went out to sign autographs, he dressed in a Humphrey Bogart trench coat and black fedora. And for his headlining appearance at an all-star rock & roll show at the Civic Opera House, he wore formal clothes complete with a crisp black bow tie. His friends were suitably impressed. "Everybody modeled Sam from Chicago," says Dimples Cochran, then of the Spaniels. "They can lie and say they didn't but they did." It wasn't just the look and the money, either; a lot of the guys who'd grown up on the streets of Bronzeville agreed with Cochran that Sam was "the baddest dude as far as voice-wise and singing and manipulating and using his voice. . . . The man was a jewel from God! And that's my heart talking."

There's a shot of the Cook family assembled outside the Civic for his triumphant return. Everyone from little brother David to Reverend Cook is grinning widely. Only Momma Cook looks a little worried. Or is it puzzled? There was talk of moving the family out to California. "We're already buying in Chicago," Mrs. Cook announced. "Maybe we'll stay six months in one place and six months in the other just so long as Sam is satisfied."

Annie May Cook was right to be worried: the high that came with sudden fame kept turning into alarming lows. After Chicago, Sam dropped by the Brown Derby restaurant in Los Angeles to accept his "You Send Me" gold record and a check for $60,000. (Willie Mays was about to sign a $65,000-a-year contract that made him the fourth-highest-paid ballplayer in the majors.) The public, crazy for more, had put five of Sam's songs in *Billboard*'s Top 100. And the next day, he flew out for an eight-day, $6,000 stand at the Uptown Theater in Philadelphia. "I was paying Dinah Washington twenty-five hundred a week," the Apollo's Bobby Schiffman recalls. "Sarah Vaughan twenty-five hundred a week. Sam Cooke six thousand! What are you, fucking crazy?!" But in Philadelphia, Sam's fame caught up with him.

The city had always been good to the Soul Stirrers; the Ward Singers anniversary each May 30 drew tremendous crowds, and as their lead, Marion Williams, recalls, Sam "was just a beautiful person. . . . The minute he opened his mouth, the young girls and boys would just fall out." Connie Bollings had been one of those young girls: a fair-skinned, well-educated twenty-five-year old with a good job as a secretary over at the Navy Yard. A year earlier, she had had Sam's child, a boy. Cook had been treating her the same as the other mothers of his children: offering some support, visiting when he was in town, staying friendly but not much more. Now he discovered that, as a rock & roll sensation, the rules had changed.

After his first show at the Uptown, a sheriff and his deputies from Philadelphia's municipal court appeared backstage. "Are you Sam Cooke?" Given the last forty minutes of screaming adulation, it was a pretty funny question. It got less funny when they served the papers and arrested him on paternity charges. Crain and a friend of Sam's, a former state senator, hurried to the jail, posted the $500 bond, and managed to keep the whole thing quiet. But there was a hearing set for a few months later, and it was a question of how long the damage control could last.

No rock & roller could afford this kind of incident, not with the music under constant attack. Frank Sinatra was testifying in front of Congress that the teenage music consisted of "sly—lewd—in plain fact, dirty—lyrics." A Negro performer especially had to be careful to mute his or her sexual appeal, and one like Sam—who had the white girls falling out—couldn't be too cautious. On top of that, the incident had taken place in Philly, where Dick Clark was parlaying *American Bandstand*'s ability to break a song to eight million viewers into considerable industry leverage. For the short term, Sam was all right. Even as the arrest went down, the *Philadelphia Tribune* was calling Cooke—with his Ivy League clothes, good looks, and gospel manners—"the dream of tomorrow's entertainer." Two weeks later, he appeared on *Bandstand* and lip-synched both sides of his latest Keen single.

For the long term, Sam's strategy had always been to present himself as more than "just" a rock & roller. "There will always be music with a beat," Sam told an interviewer around this time. "I don't like to call it rock and roll." And asked his influences, he listed Sinatra, Billie Holiday, Harry Belafonte, and Johnny Mathis. In the beginning of 1958, the accepted wisdom was that rock & roll was a brief teenage fad. If you could establish yourself in Sinatra's and Sammy Davis's type of venue, you ended up in Vegas, selling albums to grown-ups: the only viable definition of a long-term, well-paying career for a pop singer. So, after Philadelphia and an appearance on Patti Page's *Big Record* TV show, Cooke played the Club Elegante in Brooklyn, a classy suburban nightclub.

He and Bumps had just put together their first Keen LP. It was almost all ballads and show tunes like "Ol' Man River," "Moonlight in Vermont," and "Danny Boy," all of which Bumps had orchestrated to a fare-thee-well. The result was a syrupy, awful mess. Sam's version of Fats Waller's "Ain't Misbehavin'," for example, begins with an incongruous banjo lick, a bouncy drum heavy on the cymbals, and then Sam singing above it all like a man in top hat and tails—which is exactly the look he was working on over at the Elegante. He was determined to make it in this new world, and after a second appearance on Steve Allen's TV show, he went into the ultimate nightclub, the Copacabana.

The Copa was run by Jules Podell, a short fat man who looked a little like J. Edgar Hoover and spoke with a deze-dem-and-doze accent like a movie gangster. Brassy, always shouting and drinking, he wore an onyx pinkie ring he'd rap sharply on the table for service. During the war, Podell had testified before New York's deputy police commissioner that mobster Frank Costello had an interest in the restaurant Podell ran; most people assumed that was true of the Copa, too, and of the Vegas clubs connected to it. The whole scene had Sam a little intimidated, until he and Bumps went to check out the place. Tony Bennett, in the middle of a string of Top Twenty hits, was headlining. After Bennett's version of "On the Sunny Side of the Street," Sam had leaned over and whispered, "Bumps! That fucker sang that whole song out of tune!"

Blackwell had started chuckling. There they were at the most prestigious nightclub in New York, listening to one of the classiest shows the place could muster, and Sam was right: the singer was out of tune "from git to go." If this was the quality of the acts, Sam was sure he could turn the room on its ear. Plus, William Morris had booked him to open for another client, Jewish comedian Myron Cohen. "I thought I was ahead of the game when they said Myron Cohen," Bumps remembers. "Sam had no competition of no woman up there showing her ass, no legs, no babies. I was afraid of putting my artist onstage with little children, to follow sex. But to follow a comedian? Hell no, man!"

Bumps figured that "anybody with soul, anybody with blood in their veins, when they hear Sam Cooke, they're gonna like it." But he didn't act that way. Instead, Blackwell brought in a choreographer to teach Sam a few soft-shoe moves, hired a costume designer, and concentrated not on the hits but on the schmaltzy ballads off the first Keen album. Sam's friends looked on in horror. "There had been some discussion," guitarist Cliff White recalls, "about Sam didn't know what to do with his hands and all that. They were trying to choreograph some stage presence. For a guy like that, it's like an auto mechanic working on a watch." And J.W. remembers walking in on a rehearsal. "This cat they had called in was making five or ten thousand dollars, and he tell me that Sam looked just like a little doll. . . .

I told him, 'Yeah. That's just what he looks like. A little doll. He sure doesn't look like Sam Cooke!' "

Bumps, however, thought he knew what the middle-aged, middle-class white nightclub audience wanted. He was supported, if not led along, by William Morris, and there's no indication that Sam resisted. After all, the whole point of leaving gospel had been to make it in the American mainstream. If Sam wasn't exactly sure what its rules were, he knew he wanted in; the same way his family had gone from Clarksdale to Chicago, now he'd move on up a little higher.

"That wasn't his act," says White. "His act was to go out there and preach a little bit. That was Sam Cooke. Go out there and horse around with people and relax and talk that jive bullshit and preach them a little sermon. That's what his whole act was: a Baptist preacher's sermon." Still, White—a veteran of years with the Mills Brothers—understood the motivation. "We were looking for Vegas and that kind of thing, you know. Where you're cooling. Get off the road and quit doing them stupid one-nighters. Oh, man, that's a nightmare! Any way you figure, you're eating out of a paper sack most of the time and sleeping in somebody else's bed. All that kind of bullshit."

So, Sam got ready to do a soft-shoe and sing, "I'm putting on my top hat," but he didn't get ready enough. Lou Adler, a young songwriter who'd just been hired at Keen, was shocked by what he saw opening night. "They forgot to get arrangements! They got there, and it was a bigger band than Bumps had told Sam there was gonna be. . . . The agent [Auerbach] I'm sure took it for granted that Bumps was the manager and that Sam would be rehearsed and Sam would have arrangements for the orchestra and that he would have an act. But he had his rhythm arrangements he used on the rock & roll tours, which were basically lead sheets. And they were just scrambling!" Minutes before the curtain opened, René Hall, Cliff White, and Bumps were all on the floor trying to finish writing the horn parts. Adler is convinced that if Sam had "stood up there and just sang, he would have knocked them out. I mean, it's been a while since they heard a beautiful singer like this. And he had a tremendous amount of sex appeal he could get by with."

Till his dying day, Bumps was sure the act wasn't the problem, it was the audience. It turned out Myron Cohen was exactly wrong. The crowd was packed with Borscht Belt fans of his homey ethnic humor. Between jokes, they all sang Yiddish tunes. "Senator Javits and those people," Bumps says, "were rattling the tables. They had little wooden things that looked like all-day suckers, but they were wood. So they could beat on the tables [to] certain rhythmical Jewish songs. They were having a ball!" On top of everything else, it was the first day of Purim, and the Copa was full of what *Variety* called Cohen's "old friends."

Backstage, Sam and his entourage were in culture shock. "We were sitting there," Bumps recalls, "like, 'What the hell is this?' And when Sam gets on the stage, they had their arms folded like, 'Well, what in the hell are *you?*' "

Sam opened with a swing tune, "I'm Blue All Day Monday," then did "Canadian Sunset" off his LP. Although he did sing "You Send Me," he didn't even use it as a finale, following it instead with "Because of You." He tried his soft-shoe, although anyone who knew him well knew the preacher's son couldn't dance a lick. The beginning of the end, Sam would later recall, was when he tried to do "Begin the Beguine" with the big orchestra. "About halfway through, the orchestra was going that way and I was going over this way. I thought we'd never find each other. I got scared and went into the handclapping and shouting bit." Which is to say that, panicking, he fell back on gospel techniques. "Jules Podell told me to cut that stuff out or get out. So I cut it out."

It was the entertainer's worst nightmare: the cold flop sweats. "The audience's reaction," Adler recalls, "was apathetic. . . . There wasn't booing, but . . . moving around. And leaving. I remember not watching a lot."

The review in *Variety* concluded that the "handsome young Negro lad" might be a teen idol, "but he doesn't seem to be ready for the more savvy Copa clientele. . . . In many of his jump numbers, it appears that the orch was drowning him out. His stint seemed overly long and there was a feeling that he had overstayed his welcome." In Los Angeles, columnist A. S. "Doc" Young noted that "Sam Cooke, the 'You Send Me' kid, laid a golden egg at the New York's famed Copacabana. Some smart-aleck Broadwayites had predicted that he would goof."

"Sam knew it," Adler remembers. "He knew it wasn't right. It was sad." Cooke played with the act during the engagement, throwing out some tunes and adding some sing-along, and he began to get a sense of how his style could work here, too. "At the end of three weeks," Sam would recall, "I was a pretty good entertainer but I wasn't a smash." That was said after years of healing. At the time, it felt like a total fiasco. Here he'd had his big break, and he'd blown it. He'd blown it; he'd blown it; he'd blown it. If part of the problem was that the door had never really been open—that he was trying to go too fast too soon—Cooke's stubbornness and pride wouldn't admit that. "His feeling was," says Adler, "that if he ever went back, he knew what to do."

Chapter
12

S am had failed at the Copa. But he still had rock & roll. He'd managed to dodge the career-threatening scandal of Connie Bolling's paternity suit, by paying her $10,000 out of court. While Negro papers like the *Philadelphia Tribune* and the *Los Angeles Sentinel* made it front-page news, the white press had barely noticed. With his charm and talent helping to smooth things over, his latest single was a two-sided hit. The catchy "You Were Made for Me," off the same demo tape and cut from the same cloth as "You Send Me," went to #7 r&b. The flip side, "Lonely Island," was by the author of Nat King Cole's smash "Nature Boy," and Sam sang it in Nat's crooning style over lush strings.

On April 5, 1958—just a couple of weeks after the Copa—Cooke headlined the opening date of Irving Feld's "Biggest Show of Stars." Feld, a Washington druggist and record shop owner, was the king of giant rock & roll tours. He'd put together "a million-dollar package," including Clyde McPhatter, whose "A Lover's Question" had gone Top Ten; the Everly Brothers, who were in the middle of a string of major hits including, that month, "All I Have to Do Is Dream"; the Silhouettes, who had the number-one record with "Get a Job"; and LaVern Baker. There were white teen idols Frankie Avalon and Paul Anka, as well as the Crescendos, Jimmie Reed, and Huey Smith and the Clowns. Finally, Feld included the young Jackie

Wilson (McPhatter's replacement in Billy Ward's Dominoes), who was just notching his first solo hit, "To Be Loved," written by a young, ambitious Detroiter named Berry Gordy, Jr. Jackie's song, like Sam's breakthrough number, was a fairly sophisticated mid-tempo ballad, and this tour began a friendly competition between Wilson and Cooke that lasted throughout their lives.

It's a testament to Sam's popularity that he had top booking on what was billed as "the most formidable array of rhythm and blues and rock 'n roll ever assembled." Press releases noted that the weekly payroll was $40,000, and the stars would be traveling in air-conditioned buses complete with TVs and chefs to "prepare hot sandwiches for the performers as they roll across the countryside." If it sounds like a circus, there was good reason for the hype. Feld was facing direct competition in the form of disk jockey Alan Freed's first road tour. Freed, from his base in New York, had signed on the very hot Jerry Lee Lewis with his current hit, "Breathless," Buddy Holly and the Crickets, Chuck Berry debuting "Sweet Little Sixteen," Frankie Lymon, the Chantels, and Screamin' Jay Hawkins, among others. It was a battle of the giants. The two huge packages totaled about a half-million-dollar commitment, or, as *Billboard* put it, "almost enough to mount two Broadway musicals of the caliber of *My Fair Lady* and *The Music Man*."

The Feld roster of nineteen artists rehearsed in New York for a few days before opening in Norfolk, Virginia, on Saturday night. In order to make his nut, Feld had booked an especially tight schedule, but, unlike some of the kids on the bill, Cooke was used to it: he had the gospel highway behind him. They went from the Deep South to Canada, from San Diego to New Haven. As Phil Everly put it to author Roger White, "We were doing one-nighters and motoring constantly but it was fun all the time. We were young and strong." But his brother Don had a slightly different take. "To be a rock & roll star in the fifties was to be low-class. You were treated terribly, especially in the States. The people that ran the business hated it and made fun of it. You'd go to interviews and, especially being from the South, they would look and check if you had got your socks on."

Segregation was another, constant factor. On Feld's tour the year before, the white acts had been forced to sit out a half-dozen shows in cities like New Orleans and Memphis where Negro and white performers weren't allowed on the same stage. Even when they did play the same bill, the audiences were often segregated, with whites downstairs and the balcony referred to as "nigger heaven." Sam had been asked during a December interview how he felt about playing before segregated audiences. It was, in this era of growing activism, a loaded question. The Negro community had reacted with outrage when, in 1956, Nat King Cole had been beaten up onstage by a member of Birmingham's local KKK. But the outrage had turned into a "cold fury" when Cole announced he would nevertheless continue to play to all-white audiences because that was the way things worked in the South. "We won't say he got what he deserved," the *Amsterdam News* had editorialized, "because we simply can't condone violence." For Sam, used to almost exclusively Negro gospel programs, it had never been an issue. He could honestly say, "I know it is bound to come, but I'll cross that bridge when I come to it." Now, he came to it immediately, opening night in Norfolk, and he appears to have bowed to custom.

The issue, however, wasn't going away. He faced the insults of prejudice daily. Blackwell recalls stopping at a Howard Johnson's on the New Jersey Turnpike not long after the Copa. "They wouldn't come and feed us," he remembers. "Other people would come in, and they were serving them and wasn't serving us. We said, 'Oh well, let them go. They'll have to get us sooner or later.'" This was, after all, the North. As Sam and the other men waited patiently in their booth, someone punched up "You Send Me" on the jukebox. "This fucking waitress won't serve us," says Bumps, "[but] soon as that record starts playing, [she] runs over by the record with her hand on the thing, swooning! Everyone in the place swooning!"

Sam just stared for a minute. Then he said to his friends, "Ain't this a bitch!"

"We got up," Bumps remembers. "I put Sam's coat on. . . . And the people looked at us like, 'Well, who the fuck are you? *We're* listening to this Sam Cooke.'"

On the Feld tour, for all the backstage crap games and practical jokes (Paul Anka putting ice cubes in Don's and Phil's beds), white Southerners like Buddy Holly and the Everlys hung together, while Sam and LaVern Baker and Clyde McPhatter spent time harmonizing gospel tunes backstage. They even told a reporter they wanted to do a religious album together. Behind "The Biggest Show of Stars" was another gospel program in disguise.

The tour's popularity ended up swinging widely depending on where it played. The South was enthusiastic—sixteen thousand fans showed up in Charlotte, North Carolina, in early April—but in Philadelphia, a week later, that dropped to one thousand, and the next day, there were only twelve hundred kids in New Haven's six-thousand-seat arena. It may be too simple to say the variable was purely race, but in different places, the audience expected different things. In New Haven, Frankie Avalon was a "show-stopper," according to *Billboard*, and hailed as "the successor to Elvis Presley." In early May, on the other hand, when the package played the Chicago Opera House, it was old home day for Sam. And in Atlanta, where the Soul Stirrers had been told they were too popular to walk the streets, the paper gushed that "enthusiasm for Sam Cooke is at an all-time high."

His gospel audience was one of the keys to that popularity. An often-published story about Cooke has him appearing at a Soul Stirrers program in Chicago after he'd left gospel and being roundly rejected by the crowd. Supposedly, they shouted, "Get that blues singer down. . . . This is a *Christian* program," and Sam, badly hurt, had left the stage. The story originates with R. H. Harris and fits neatly into his strict Saturday night/Sunday morning distinction. But the evidence is that it never happened.

Bumps remembers just the opposite. In 1958, as they streaked around the East Coast capitalizing on "You Send Me," Blackwell had noticed that the big religious package "The Gospel Train" was in Philadelphia. "Hell," Bumps said one night, "let's go see our folks." "Well, I don't want to," Blackwell remembers Cooke saying, but when Sam finally walked in the place, "he couldn't get down the aisle! People were, 'Sam! Sam!' They were raising hell! So Sam went back and saw the Stirrers, and he went onstage and sang with them. . . . The crowd accepted him, and he tore the house down. And from that day to the day he died," Bumps felt, "he worked as a completed person."

Gospel star Marion Williams recalls how "it hurt my heart" when Sam crossed over but acknowledges that he remained "beloved" in gospel circles. Likewise, the Caravans' Albertina Walker remembers thinking that "for him to walk off and go with the rhythm and blues, rock & roll, whatever you want to call it, it really showed a bad reflection on the gospel singer" but admits that when "he'd jump up there onstage and sing with the group, people loved it! They still loved Sam Cooke." Fellow Stirrer Leroy Crume is the most insistent. "About them booing him? That's a lie! Everybody wanted to hear him sing; I don't care what he was doing. . . . I have never, ever in my life heard anybody boo—and I was there every time Sam stepped on a stage with the Soul Stirrers."

On the Feld tour, Sam dealt with the competition of McPhatter, Baker, and the Everlys just as he had with June Cheeks, Dot Coates, and the Blind Boys. After the shouting was done, after the other acts had run through their hits and sent the teenagers screaming and dancing in the aisles, Sam would stroll out. Standing at center stage, moving little more than his long, articulate hands, he would decimate the crowd. All he had to do was begin "You Send Me" or sing the I-love-yous at the start of "For Sentimental Reasons" and the place would collapse. The years on the gospel road had taught him how to milk a moment, how to build toward it and sustain it just as he sustained a note: bending people's expectation, teasing. Teenagers—come to scream for Frankie Avalon's "De De Dinah"—had never seen anything like it. Sam would just smile that confident smile—dtttt!—and the girls discovered weeping fits they didn't even know they had in them. Night after night, town after town, he'd engineer twenty minutes to half an hour of mayhem just by standing still and letting his voice work the register. The *Atlanta World* had taken to calling him "the sensational swoon singer." To S. R. Crain, watching from the wings, it was just Sam getting Sister Flute.

But many saw this cross-racial appeal as a major threat. Early in the tour, Feld had told his stars to "play down suggestive gestures and material." Despite that, the press described the concerts as having a "powder-keg atmosphere," and, at some, fistfights broke out. When their competition, Alan Freed's tour, reached Boston in May, a white girl did the rock & roll equivalent of crossing over, rushing to the edge of the stage and grabbing at the crotch of one of the Negro singers. The Boston cops couldn't handle that; they cleared the auditorium, and Freed was indicted for inciting a riot. He had to cancel the end of the tour and quit (or was fired) from his radio show in New York. The industry recoiled. Dick Clark postponed his own package tour, and an r&b "Cavalcade" lasted all of a week before folding. Promoters of Feld's tour were quoted as saying. "You could flip a coin as to whether we're making money."

While some in the business took the opportunity to announce that rock & roll was over, Sam finished the tour and went back to Los Angeles to cut some new singles. The June 6 session sheet at Radio Recorders was signed by Keen's new employee, Lou Adler. Adler was a streetwise, intense Jewish kid from the Mexican section of Los Angeles. His dark good looks were so close to high school buddy Herb Alpert's that the songwriting partners were jokingly referred to as twins. Lou was the word man, quick with a line, and Herbie the musician, always fooling with his trumpet. Bumps had spotted their talent, and he was eventually proved right. Both would go on to have their own labels and make fortunes in the music business: Lou producing the Mamas and the Papas, Herbie with the Tijuana Brass. Now, Adler supervised a session that, along with Cliff White and arranger René Hall on guitars, featured Keen's regular rhythm section: Bumps' brother, Charles Blackwell, on drums, and Adolphus Alsbrook on bass. Blackwell had gigged with many of the famous big bands: Lionel Hampton's, Stan Kenton's, Count Basie's. Alsbrook was a solid player with a nice direct approach and a deep knowledge of music. His one problem was that he suffered from a kind of sleeping sickness, so he wasn't much use on the road—periodically falling offstage—but in a session you just waited till he woke up, and there he'd be, right on the beat.

The first single from the three-hour session, "Stealing Kisses"/"All of My Life," was released late in July but never made it to the charts.

Given Sam's popularity at the time, that was evidence of true dreck. The formulaic sound could have easily come out of the new, clean-cut, mass-produced chart-toppers of the time: Paul Anka, Frankie Avalon, Fabian. Except Sam's version didn't sell. Gospel-pure as he might photograph, Cooke's music had to have some gospel grit to get over. The follow-up single did much better. "Win Your Love for Me" was, once again, credited to L. C. Cook. It's a deceptively simple tune cut to a sparse arrangement. Alsbrook's stand-up bass is way forward, providing the deep water in which the rest of the parts swim. A bongo (probably Jack Constanza) accentuates the Latin rhythm. The gospel element here isn't so much in the vocal—although Sam runs a few changes up and down a "whoa"—but in the feel of the melody. Trying to win the little girl's love sounds both pessimistic and, when the chorus repeats itself in a minor key, doomed. It's that dark side that seems to inspire Sam: a secular variation on gospel trials and tribulations. "Win Your Love" eventually went to #4 r&b (charting for over four months) and reached #22 on the pop charts.

Sam was single-focus when it came to making records, but he did have some other things on his mind during this session. A month earlier, Dolores had filed an affidavit with the superior court in Los Angeles; she claimed not to have known that the papers she'd signed back in November had waived her right to contest Sam's divorce. In fact, she swore she hadn't even known the divorce was proceeding until early May. Dolores testified she had always "trusted and relied upon her husband," that she was unemployed and "in need of medical care," and that Sam's grounds for divorce—extreme cruelty—were made up. In mid-June, the court gave Dee a chance to claim alimony and a share of the communal property, including a 1958 Cadillac convertible, a house in Los Angeles Sam was in the process of buying, bank accounts, and record royalties. To Bumps, it was Connie Bollings all over again. The solution was the same, too: fork out another ten grand. Unlike with Bollings, however, Sam stayed friends with Dee, and he kept in touch with her and Joey. Along with the ten grand, Sam bought Dolores her own convertible and got Joey a bicycle. The cocker spaniel, Newark, learned to ride around Fresno on the handlebars.

Sam, meanwhile, was living the bachelor's life at the Knicker-
bocker Hotel, where he roomed with Lou Adler. "During that time,"
Adler recalls, "at nine or ten o'clock we'd go eat. In the evening.
Then we'd go to the California Club, Santa Barbara and Western.
Then we'd either stop by the 5–4 Ballroom, or we'd go to another
club. At six, we were at an after-hours place. Just go the whole night!
We did it at least a month—we did that straight!" Besides the pure
partying, Sam was also absorbing the city's r&b scene, from the blues
of Johnny "Guitar" Watson to the dance tunes of Little Willie John's
crack band, the Upsetters. He and Adler were forever working on
songs; he wrote with J.W.; he tried things out on Crain. As "Stealing
Kisses" had just proved, Cooke couldn't make it without strong material: Sam understood that while his voice and personality could
carry him through almost any song, he had to have something he felt
and cared about in order to let loose.

The sound he was after wasn't that different from Little Willie
John's. John was a great, often underestimated singer. In fact, the arrangement for "Win Your Love for Me" owes a debt to John's moody
1956 hit "Fever." And, tit for tat, "Talk to Me, Talk to Me"—John's
#20 pop song in April of 1958—has some of the laid-back vocal dis-
play of "You Send Me." "I want to sell records to white and colored,"
John told journalist A. S. "Doc" Young, "and the only way I can is
to give them something they want." Which was not, in his opinion,
selling out. In fact, John, a sweet-faced, young-looking Negro who
eventually went to prison for knifing a man, loses his temper a little
when discussing the music: "Rock 'n roll is not rhythm and blues.
Every time I think about that claim, I get mad! Count Basie had
been playing rock & roll from 1937 to 1958. White people are just
waking up to it. Anything we have they change anyway because we
let them do it. It's ours; it belongs to us."

John sounds more militant than his music, but like Sam, he was
trying to feel his way through a complicated situation. As the President of the United States advised Negro leaders that the way to get
their rights was through "patience and forbearance backed up by profound education" (and Martin King, choosing his words carefully,
said he was "puzzled" by this analysis), Negroes across the country

were trying to figure out what came next after the televised spectacle in Little Rock. If music like Nat King Cole's was one end of the pop spectrum—patient to the point of compliance—and Little Richard's the other, then Sam, Willie John, and artists like Jesse Belvin (just signed with RCA) were searching for a synthesis.

That was for the singles. Sam and Bumps were still aiming the albums at the nightclubs. According to Lou Adler's liner notes, their second Keen LP, *Sam Cooke Encore*, was created "to record permanently some of these memorable performances which have excited hundreds of thousands of patrons of the after-dinner circuit." Tell that to the listless crowds from the Copa. This time, Sam tried everything from "Accentuate the Positive" to "Along the Navajo Trail." Though he strains to make sense of the numbers, the quality of innocence and surprise in his voice just doesn't fit. It makes "I Cover the Waterfront" sound as if he's never been near the docks. On the other hand, that same quality makes "When I Fall in Love" slightly more successful. "When I give my heart," Sam sings, "it will be completely," and he sounds naive enough to convince us he really hasn't, yet. The twenty-seven-year-old from Bronzeville was certainly experienced, but the best he can convey here is a kind of wistfulness and regret. For numbers that called for a worldly quality, he didn't seem to have either the instrument or the skill.

Late in August, he took this new material into Chicago's Black Orchid. An intimate, classy club in his hometown, it seemed an ideal spot to keep working on Sam's "act." *Variety*, however, panned his twelve-tune, thirty-minute set, saying he lacked "sincerity. . . . As they play now, pipes are a bit too mechanical to really rouse tablers." It must have confused Cooke: those pipes were the same that had turned out hundreds of churches and climaxed rock & roll packages. While he couldn't manage to fill the Black Orchid opening night, Sam did renew some old acquaintances, most notably with Barbara Campbell. How Barbara had been supporting herself and their daughter, Linda, is unclear, but friends allow as how it was a lot harder row to hoe than Sam had faced—and had more to do with the streets of Bronzeville than it did the bright lights of the Copacabana. Crain remembers Sam giving her money from time to time, but when she reappeared, Bumps lumped her in with the rest of Sam's paternity suits. "I was the one who went to see [Dolores] in Fresno, and I was the one who went to Philadelphia to see the other little girl [Connie Bollings]. And then the only one I didn't have to pay off was Barbara because he married her."

There was almost certainly more to it than that. Sam talked to Lou Adler about the relationship; Lou remembers that Linda was a big factor. Sam wanted a family. And he was a man who consciously and deliberately brought his past with him. One of the things he became known for, as he toured the rock & roll circuit, was keeping in touch with the guy on the street. More often than not, he'd stay in the Negro hotels—the upscale ghetto hotels—even when he could have moved downtown. He made a point of visiting with old friends like Leroy Hoskins and Louis Tate; he turned to J. W. Alexander as an adviser and brought Crain onto the pop payroll. Barbara, his childhood sweetheart, was a part of that past. Faced with the complexities of establishing a career and the failure of his marriage to Dolores, he turned to someone he knew. As he sang in "When I Fall in Love," "My first love will be my last."

The magazines dated their secret engagement to that fall of 1958, about the time the divorce with Dolores was worked out. That also meshes with the musical evidence. Sam's next single, "Love You Most of All," was recorded in September; instead of L.C., the writer was listed as Barbara Campbell. And by October, when Sam was back in Los Angeles for a few days, he was proudly introducing his new fiancée to columnist Gertrude Gibson. "Gert," he said as Barbara snuggled against him, "I love this girl, and I want you to see that she meets people and the two of you get to know each other." Gibson eventually brought Barbara into her social club, the Regalettes.

Word was that Sam planned to marry after he fulfilled his fall dates: an October 22 appearance on *Dick Clark's Saturday Night Show,* followed by a string of one-nighters through the South. Clark's show was scheduled to broadcast live from the Southeastern Fair in Atlanta. It wasn't until Sam flew into town that Clark's producer informed him that this was the first integrated show ever at the fairgrounds. Teenagers had begun lining up for tickets for five days;

at the same time, the producer had started getting threatening letters and phone calls telling them "the KKK was gonna fix our asses." It was serious enough that he'd called the local police and the National Guard; he'd also bought a gun. As Clark tells the story in his *Rock, Roll & Remember*, he met Sam at a motel before the show. Sam listened as the producer explained the situation and how no one could guarantee anything. Sam answered quickly: "I'm going on." The producer explained some more: a lot of the National Guard were also members of the KKK, so they weren't liable to be the best security. "I gotta go on," Sam repeated. "That's all there is to it." At that point, Clark says, he interrupted, "That's it. Sam is with us so we do the show."

Dick Clark calls it "one of the few ballsy things I ever did." That may be, but it was Sam who had to stand up onstage and sing. The night of the show, the angry owners of the stadium told Clark's crew to set up in the colored men's room. And then a half hour before showtime, there was a bomb threat. The six-thousand-seat grandstand was sold out, and thousands of other teenagers wandered the fairgrounds or strained to get a view. Danny and the Juniors opened, singing their year-old hit "At the Hop" while sitting on a slowly spinning Ferris wheel. After Clark did some plugging, Conway Twitty, a white Mississippian, thrilled the teens with his #1 song "It's Only Make Believe," sounding more like Elvis than Elvis. Backstage, men in Confederate Army hats watched the proceedings. Now it was time for Sam to sing.

Dressed in a gray suit and tie, snapping his fingers, he performed "Win Your Love for Me" with what *Billboard* would later call "an aura of good showmanship." It was the epitome of cool, and when the show was over, it seemed like just another Dick Clark appearance. But Sam had crossed a line. There were things he'd do for the sake of his career—at the Copa or on the Feld tour; now he was learning what he wouldn't do. If he gave in to Jim Crow, he could lose not only his self-esteem, but what he was coming to recognize as his core audience. "When the whites are through with Sammy Davis, Jr.," is how Sam used to put it to Lou Adler, "he won't have anywhere to play. I'll always be able to go back to my people 'cause I'm never gonna stop singing to them. No matter how big I get, I'm still gonna do my dates down South. Still gonna do those kind of shows. I'm not gonna leave my base."

It had been a year now since "You Send Me" had swept Cooke up, and he'd come a long way from his and Bumps' initial plan to leapfrog r&b for the white market. Around this time, he began to let his hair go natural; enough of the artificial, straight-as-a-white-man's processing. It shocked his contemporaries. Jerry Butler, for one, had never seen anyone from his background take this kind of pride in his blackness. It set Butler and a lot of other young singers and a host of Cooke's teenage fans to thinking.

After the Clark show, Sam headed out to play to his "base" on a six-week tour through the South. This was a much smaller, less-well-funded tour than Feld's, with even longer drives between gigs. "I remember one time," says Cliff White, who had become Cooke's main guitarist and bandleader, "we had a gig in Atlanta and the next gig is Denver, Colorado! And they gave us a day to make it! I thought these dudes must have got drunk and just threw at the map with some darts!" It was a nocturnal existence, as exhausting as it was exhilarating, and—one way or another—the pace took its toll. "We had talked about it," White recalls. "About traveling and the percentages and how the odds keep getting narrower the longer you're out there."

On this trip, they'd been out a couple weeks when they pulled into St. Louis the night of November 10. The date was with Sam's old gospel rivals the Travelers, by now also trying to make it as a pop act on Keen. The show started at nine, the band warmed up the crowd for an hour, and then the Travelers came on with their young lead, Lou Rawls. They played a forty-minute set, Sam closed, and by midnight, another show was over, though the partying had just begun. The older veterans, Crain and Alexander, pushed on to arrange the next booking and get some sleep. But Cooke wouldn't leave. "Yeah, well, that was par for the course," says White. He and Rawls hung around St. Louis with Sam and some girls till nearly three in the morning. Then the three men piled into Cooke's brand-new yellow 1958 El Dorado convertible. Sam sat in front next to his driver, Eddie Cunningham, and Rawls and White got in back.

The next engagement was three hundred miles south in Greenville, Mississippi, down below Memphis, back in the Delta country where Sam had been born. The main road in between, Highway 61—memorialized in countless blues songs—was wide open, flat and straight. Making connections between one-nighters, the band was always running late, always hauling ass through the night, but Cunningham "knew the roads like a truck driver." So, trusting in Eddie, the three entertainers immediately dozed off. As the car sped through the winter dark, Sam was in front, Lou Rawls behind him, and Cliff behind the driver. "Eddie was doing about a hundred and forty," is how White puts it—or, in Crain's words, "Everything that Cadillac could get, Eddie was getting it." Soon they were just across the river from Memphis, near the little town of Marion, Arkansas, at almost the exact spot where blues singer Bessie Smith had had her fatal car accident twenty-one years before.

When White woke, "it seemed to me that Eddie had pulled out. I don't know; when you wake up, all kinds of funny things in this drowsiness. . . . Eddie's out here and he's going about two hundred miles an hour! And it seems to me that I remember another big truck coming."

Eddie pulled back into his lane, only to find it blocked by another truck—a farm truck whose driver had stopped to check his load of soybeans. With nothing to gauge by along the straight two-lane but the unlit Southern night and the sound of the wind, it was hard to tell what was moving and what wasn't. "When I raised up and looked, here's this big thing . . . and he's trying to make it in whatever that little hole is before this other thing gets there. . . . The first thing that popped into my mind," White continues, "was that we were going to hit that truck and be under there, and I grabbed Lou and pulled him down. When we came down and impacted, Lou hit the back of the seat, and I went down behind Eddie. That's probably part of what sandwiched Eddie in there."

The yellow convertible, going full-bore, plowed into and actually under the parked soybean truck, shearing the top right off the El Dorado, windshield and all, and leaving little more than a tangled iron knot. "Yeah, we hit that truck in the name of Jesus, man!" When

White came to, Sam and Lou were nowhere to be seen, and he didn't learn about their condition till later. But Cunningham was still in the car, jammed against the driver's seat by the steering wheel. The edge of the wheel had gone through his stomach right to the spine. "I remember on the way out, Eddie is sitting there, and he's saying, 'Goddammit! Shit! Goddammit! Shit!' He got hung up on that, and he said that forever."

Chapter 13

E ddie Cunningham died in surgery two hours after the accident. Cooke, Rawls, and White were all rushed to the hospital. Rawls, sitting behind Cooke, had struck the convertible's steel overhead bar. When he was admitted to intensive care, there were no vital signs. White had broken his collarbone and some ribs, and the guitarist's fingers were mashed. Cooke, riding in the death seat, sound asleep, had somehow slid beneath the dash and, miraculously, had only a cut on his left arm and some glass slivers in his face and eye. (The first news reports said he'd been killed; Adler, back in the Keen offices, remembers going into shock before the correction came through.)

As soon as he could, Sam called Crain at the next engagement. Although there hadn't been any news coverage yet, when Crain got to the West Memphis hospital, a crowd had already formed. "Anything happened to [Sam], man, it would get out!"—especially in the South, where the colored population had, by necessity, established a web of underground communication. And the news wasn't simply that Cooke had been in an accident; he'd been taken to Crittenden Memorial Hospital in West Memphis, Arkansas. Any Negro knew what that meant, knew the place was segregated and knew Sam Cooke wasn't going to get the right kind of care, wasn't going to be safe until he was out of there. Conditions like these had fueled the rumors about Bessie Smith, that she'd died because she'd been refused adequate treatment after *her* Highway 61 crash. Even before Crain arrived, a black nurse and friend of Cliff White's had arranged to send an ambulance from Memorial Hospital in Memphis.

Crain went to the hospital's back door, found Cliff "where they got the dirty towels; that's the way they do it down South," and announced he'd come to collect his men. The white hospital workers stopped him right there. "Well, boy, I can't be responsible for you." Crain said as how that was all right—"I'm taking mine!"—got Cliff and Sam, and moved them to Memphis. "Next thing," White says, "I woke up and there was that little fat girl, Squeaky, puttering around the joint, trying to tell me to get back in bed."

Meanwhile, Rawls, because he was a veteran, had gone straight to the navy hospital in Memphis. There he stayed in a coma for five and a half days. "Had they taken me to a public hospital," Rawls believes, "I probably wouldn't have lived. . . ." The accident helped break up the Travelers, who'd already had some close misses on the highway.

Sam, on the other hand, came out of his four-day stay in the hospital more determined than ever. As an immediate sign that this wasn't going to scare him off, he hired a new driver: his brother Charles. Then, as soon as he was well enough, Sam moved to Memphis's Lorraine Motel, where he began the process of taking control of his future. Alexander had been bending Sam's ear for a while now about music publishing. Letting someone else publish your songs was giving away half the proceeds. John Dolphin (the same who ran Dolphin's Records and had helped break "You Send Me") had recognized this early on and used to poke fun at Alexander even back in the Specialty days. "Hard as it is," Dolphin would say, waving one of his big black cigars, "you give Art Rupe everything?" Alex had listened. While "Loving John" Dolphin had a notorious reputation—adding his name as author to songs, trading masters, not paying artists their royalties— he was still a colored man who had ended up with part of the action that normally went to the likes of Rupe and Siamas. Sure, he'd been shot that past February by a songwriter furious at not being paid, but Alexander had still admired Dolphin enough to sing at his funeral.

Since then, Alex had been trying to pass on Dolphin's message to Sam, but the singer had always hedged. "I don't know. . . . Bumps says they're gonna give me twenty percent of Keen." J. W. had heard that one before. "Man," he repeated, "you oughta have your own company! Hell, I got one. I ain't got nothing going, but I got a company: KAGS Music. That's *my* company!" The Sunday before the accident, Sam had said how he planned to record the first song registered to KAGS: a ballad Alex had written called "Little Things You Do." Then the accident, in Alex's words, "cut the conversation short." Now, the first morning of his recuperation at the Lorraine, Sam called. "Alex? What you doing?"

Truth be told, Alexander wasn't doing much. His lead singer was lying in a coma, and his quartet was disappearing around him. Although many people thought of him as Sam's manager because he was always around, advising, the two men had no formal agreement.

"So," Sam began over breakfast, "tell me about this publishing company. Who-all's in it?"

"I'm in it," Alex answered, laughing. "Why don't you all have one?"

"Well," Cooke replied, "what about us being partners?" And they shook on it.

Maybe the car crash had persuaded him to act—maybe it was what had happened at the Dick Clark broadcast or the reality of putting together a career now that the rush of "You Send Me" was over. But Sam had been heading this direction since at least gospel days; pre-gospel, if you traced it back to the Reverend Cook's independence and his mother's Mound Bayou self-reliance. Where Alex and Crain had dreamed about getting their own business in their own hands (both were at first listed with Sam as copartners in KAGS), it was Sam's generation that was coming into position to make those dreams true. Almost no singer of that era owned his own publishing, much less a Negro r&b artist, and it would prove the difference between Sam Cooke and a legion of others who had just as many hits but ended up penniless.

Even as Sam returned to Los Angeles to recover, a new single, "Love You Most of All," began charting. Lyrically, it's pretty lightweight, but it's one of the most engaging melodies Cooke ever wrote. Jumping in with no introduction to announce, "You're my girl," the song mostly just amplifies on that, but there's a beautiful moment in the bridge where the couple is walking down the street, looking so good that all the brothers go "Whoo-ee!" The tune's only two minutes long, but once heard, it refuses to let go.

That's partly due to the loping, irresistible beat, but a major factor is Sam's vocal. Now and then he uses a trace of gospel ad-libbing, like when he tosses in an "I believe." Mostly, it's a very precisely enunciated, syllable-by-syllable echoed lead. Given the way Sam worked at this point, it was more than likely not overdubbed, but was done with a second man carefully hitting each phrase and beat at the same time. The rough harmonizing, the slight variance between the two voices, sounds like church music. Which is to say, it sounds like what would later be called soul. The song (credited to Barbara Campbell, although Leroy Crume says Sam was working on it when he was still a Soul Stirrer) reached #26 on *Billboard*'s pop charts and stayed on the r&b charts for almost four months, making it to #12.

By now, the Siamases took Sam's success somewhat for granted. Keen may be the only record label whose first release became a #1 million-seller; from idle chitchat and a couple of rejected masters, the company had immediately skyrocketed. John Siamas used to joke how "You Send Me" had hit so fast that Keen's promotion department consisted of answering the phone. The downside of that was that Keen had no need to learn promotion. No one had any idea, as one employee put it, "how to put the screws to the distributors. . . . They had hundreds of thousands of dollars in back payment!" Alex Siamas remembers lots of records being returned as defective, "even though they'd had them playing in jukeboxes. They [distributors] could take advantage of you."

Still, with records like "Love You Most of All," the hobby had turned into a prosperous business. While Bumps scouted for other artists, the Greeks sank some of their first profits into a building at 8715 West 3rd Street. An old movie sound studio, the place had offices front and back and a big cavernous space in the middle. The label's engineer, Deano Lappas, rewired it for two-track, mono, with a control booth in front and a business office in back. It didn't have the greatest technology and wasn't that large (Bumps still had to take his musicians elsewhere when he wanted to cut big band stuff), but it was more than adequate—and all theirs.

Now, with time off after the accident, Sam took advantage of the facilities. Bumps usually produced Cooke's sessions (with John Siamas looking on), but they were Sam's show. "He was a very gentle, creative person," says Herb Alpert. "Sam used to come in with a loose-leaf folder of lyrics. On sight, the lyrics just looked like . . . eh! You didn't really get a tremendous feeling from the words on the page. But then you asked him to pick up the guitar and play the song; it turned into a magical experience. . . . I'd look over his shoulder and say, 'Is that the same song you just showed me?!' "

Sam and Cliff would usually work out the basic chord progression, then, once the tune was set, Sam would take it to arranger René Hall. "We had that type of thing," Hall recalls, "where I set up my tape recorders, and he'd sing the tune, and then he'd sing all these little ideas that he had, and I'd put that on a separate tape and voice it orchestrally." Many times, Hall's job was less arranger than translator. "Practically all the arrangements we did were Sam's ideas. He preconceived his arrangements before we got into the studio. He'd come up to my office, we'd sit down, and he'd tell me exactly what he wanted the girls to sing or what he wanted the voices to do. What he wanted the horns to play. Even down to what he wanted the bass to play sometimes! So, he knew, note for note, exactly what his orchestration would sound like before he even went into the studio."

At recording time, the band would be given their charts and would then run down the tunes a couple of times to get the feel, penciling in any changes. Between White and Hall, drummers like Palmer and Blackwell, and experienced bassmen Alsbrook and Bill Hadnott, it didn't take long to get the drift. Then they'd begin to tinker with it. This was before the era of singers singing to tracks, before rhythm sections wore headphones. The musicians played with each other and to the vocalist, and many of the people involved swear the quality of the music came from this direct contact. A lot of times, Sam would sit on a high stool and sing to the guys during rehearsal.

Although he wasn't a trained musician, Cooke had done enough arranging with the Stirrers and then with Bumps to understand the process. Lou Adler credits Sam with teaching him how to communicate to musicians. "He would do it a lot by movement. 'Don't play that; play that! . . .' Or 'Go there; don't go there,' instead of saying jump a key or something." Cooke might imitate the percussion part he wanted or hum the string section. Then, when he had it about how he liked it, he'd step into the three-sided vocalist booth and do a run-through. What came out on tape would be a live, simultaneous take with Sam, the rhythm section, the orchestra, and backup singers moving through the tune together.

"He was able to just close his eyes," Alpert recalls with amazement, "sing from his toes, and let the notes fall where they may. He was of the moment. And every take had some nuances and variations that were just invented on the spot. . . . I had this feeling of someone who was willing to take risks. . . ."

This was Sam's glory, and he knew it. Herbie, classically trained, spent a lot of time figuring out the intonation and structure of songs. But Sam impressed him (as he had Cliff at first meeting) by putting together music that shouldn't have worked but did. Both Adler and Alpert remember a time John Siamas took Sam aside and suggested the singer put in some yodels on a song: after the first phrase would be a good place, and then there was room for two more at the bridge, and end the tune with a few more. Sam had just looked at the man for a moment, "a little startled," in Alpert's phrase, "that the guy even suggested that he should just manufacture." Then he very nicely explained to Siamas, "Man, you can't just throw in a whoa-whoa whenever you want. You have to feel it."

Sam worked on at least three different kinds of music during his time off the road in early 1959. His first job—what kept his career alive—was to make hit singles. While "Love You Most of All" was still on the pop charts, he began playing with other things. "Everybody Likes to Cha Cha Cha" came from culture-watching, one of Sam's favorite pastimes. While in Los Angeles, he spent hours talking about music, seeing what was a hit, keeping track of trends. In early 1959, there was a nationwide cha-cha craze, big enough for Conway Twitty to notice it even at his Deep South dance dates. Closer to home, Mambo Maxie ran a weekly cha-cha night over at one of Sam's hangouts, the California Club. "Everybody Likes to Cha Cha Cha" both commented on and cashed in on the fad.

It seems Sam takes his girl to the hop, every song has a cha-cha beat, and he has to teach her how to do it. Never mind that Sam was about to celebrate his twenty-eighth birthday or that even as a teenager he hadn't gone to hops; the real giggle for anyone in the know was that Cooke had two left feet. Which was probably the song's true inspiration: Sam had just reversed the roles of who taught whom the steps. It's no major artistic statement—Lou Adler always thought if Sam could put this number over, he could have a hit with anything—but it showed Sam with his finger right on the culture's pulse.

At the same time, Sam began to work on a more "serious" project: an album of Billie Holiday tunes. For this attempt to break into the nightclub market, Bumps brought in some heavyweights. Gerald Wilson, one of the most talented West Coast bandleaders and arrangers of the day, had played trumpet on the road with Lady Day in 1950. Saxophonist Benny Carter had been in Fletcher Henderson's orchestra in the thirties and gone on to play sax with everyone from Miles Davis to Louis Armstrong. Carter had done arrangements for some of Holiday's famous sessions with Teddy Wilson's orchestra. Bumps' horn section included William "Buddy" Collette, Plas Johnson, and Bill Green: a who's who of the West Coast bebop scene. Third Street wasn't large enough for this: they moved over to the new Sound Enterprises on Sunset and Western for four sessions in late January and early February 1959.

"Even when I was singing exclusively in church," Sam told Benny Carter, "I was listening to all the pop singers, and Billie Holiday moved me the most." There was something about the melancholy in her voice that got to him, and the tribute album is filled with it, from the dark cover shot of a pensive Cooke standing in what looks like an alley to the choice of songs: Duke Ellington's haunting "Solitude," Harold Arlen's "I've Got a Right to Sing the Blues," and "God Bless the Child." In January of 1959, Billie Holiday was fading fast, becoming—in the midst of her torment—more and more of a legend. That spring, she'd be arrested for sniffing heroin in her bed at New York's Metropolitan Hospital; by July, she'd be dead.

The *Tribute* LP tells as much about what Sam can't do as what he can. Cooke's version of "God Bless the Child" opens with a harp swirl and choral voices and ends on the same cloying note: in between, the sound of world-weariness that makes Billie's version is totally absent. He's able to put some real feeling in the note-bending, melancholy "Lover Girl," but the sophistication of "Let's Call the Whole Thing Off" and the desperation of "Solitude" are beyond him. It seems ludicrous that a tune like "Love You Most of All" could be more energetically defiant than "T'Ain't Nobody's Bizness (If I Do)," but with Sam it was. *Tribute* ends up presenting overwhelming evidence that while he was sincerely moved by jazz singing, Cooke did his best pop work when recording his own songs.

Finally, while he was cutting his jazz LP and working on singles, he was also trying to return to gospel. Or, to be more exact, he was trying to sing spirituals. On March 3, 1959, Sam went into Rex's studios with Cliff and Earl Palmer and Red Callender on bass. First they cut his own "That's Heaven to Me," which Rupe had never released on Specialty. Then they did "I Thank God," a sappy inspirational tune. "Deep River" and "Steal Away," two traditional spirituals, completed the session. All four cuts were orchestrated by Hall for four violins, two cellos, and a harp and are paced excruciatingly slowly.

To hear Sam on these cuts is to realize how raucous and demanding the Soul Stirrers' music was. Whether Alexander (who was part of this project) and Cooke ever verbalized it or not, what they'd removed here in order to sanitize gospel was all the anger and the passion. It was hard going: the four-song session took from eight in the evening till four the next morning. Then, before he got a chance to do any more work on the spiritual album, "Cha Cha" hit the charts, and it was time to go back on the road. Cooke had no way of knowing that this March 3 spiritual session would be his last for Keen.

Before starting his tour, Sam drove up to visit Dolores Mohawk and little Joey. Dee had been down in Los Angeles, auditioning as a singer-dancer with Nat King Cole, but nothing had come of it, and she'd soon moved back to Fresno. From Bumps' description of her at the time, Mohawk had changed. He remembers her as an "exotic dancer . . . [who'd] get down to a little bitty thing and do the snake hips." More than that, he found her "wild, crazy! She drank, and she'd be unmanageable. . . . She was very jealous, very pretty." Crain, too, noticed Dee was different and speculated that the marriage breakup had hurt her pretty badly. Joey (ten at the time) remembers that when Sam came to visit, it looked like the whole neighborhood turned out. "We had people up on top of telephone poles, on top of trees, roofs! You would swear the President had come to town or something. . . . It was like wall-to-wall eyeballs!"

After the visit, Dolores was "despondent," according to her great-aunt. Saturday night, March 21—after getting off her job as a cocktail waitress in Fresno's Chinatown—she stayed out drinking till about twelve-thirty at night. When she left the bar on G Street, some of the other customers offered to drive her home, but she refused. Instead, she got into the 1958 Oldsmobile convertible Sam had given her and careened through Fresno's quiet streets. She ran a man in a motor scooter off the road. Then, going between sixty-five and seventy, she lost control, glanced off a parked car, jumped the curb, and—still accelerating—bounced off a cedar tree and into the corner of a house at 2331 Kirk Avenue, not far from where she lived. Thrown across the width of the car, Dolores hit her head against the handle of the passenger door and fractured her skull. She died in a local hospital.

Sam was on tour in Miami when he got the call. "He took the death badly," says Bumps, but you had to know him to see that. "He didn't break down and go to crying," Crain remembers. "I never seen Sam cry in my life. Never." He just drew into himself, told the family he'd take care of the funeral expenses, and booked a flight to Fresno.

Dolores's family, already upset by the talk that Dee's accident had been intentional, were shocked by the scene Sam caused at the funeral home. "We were just totally mobbed," Joey remembers. "People were coming to the car, and they would have their little pens and saying, 'Would you sign my autograph?' " When the procession wound its way out to the small town of Fowler for the burial, people followed Sam's Cadillac the whole way.

Afterward, Sam spent some time talking to Joey, calling him "son" and mentioning the possibility of sending the boy to a private academy. But Dee's aunt and uncle—who had raised her and would now raise Joey—had seen enough. Active members of the West Fresno Church of Christ, all they had to do was look out the window at the mob to see what had happened to Sam since his gospel days. It was their obligation to give Joey a good, Christian upbringing; the fame and glitter of rock & roll could only get in the way of that. For the rest of his life, Sam spoke of Dolores fondly and, occasionally, with a touch of guilt that he might somehow have prevented what happened. But her family not only squelched the idea of Joey going to an academy, they made a point of keeping Sam and the boy separated. Dolores's funeral was the last time they ever met.

Two weeks after the funeral, Sam opened at the Apollo. "God in His infinite wisdom saw fit to let me stay around a bit longer," he told the press, "but I think I'm a wiser person as a result of my brush with death." He was referring to his own car accident and, privately, perhaps to Dolores's.

The Apollo was a sort of comeback for Sam. He had a new single out and wanted to reestablish himself as a draw. Plus, while Sam had been recuperating, rock & roll had theoretically died. A plane carrying Ritchie Valens, Buddy Holly, and the Big Bopper had crashed on February 1; Jerry Lee Lewis's career was in tatters after he'd committed bigamy with his fourteen-year-old cousin; and Elvis was in the army. Breathy, quiet songs dominated the pop charts: "To Know Him Is to Love Him," the Skyliners' "Since I Don't Have You," the Fleetwoods' "Come Softly to Me." Critics would later call this period "the lull in rock," but that was based on a definition that limited rock & roll to rebellious dance music sung by young white men. If that had died, then Sam and his friends Jackie Wilson, Ray Charles,

James Brown, Dee Clark, Darlene Love, and the Shirelles danced on its grave.

Certainly, the Apollo audience didn't sense any lull. Starting April 10, Sam headlined a week-long engagement with Sally Blair, a dark-skinned redhead more famous for her come-hither pout than her voice. Schiffman remembers that by twelve-thirty on the first day of the run, the theater was "jammed to the walls. . . . Sam Cooke was a major hero." According to the *Amsterdam News*, Sam "ran the audience wild when he 'taught' curvaceous Sally Blair how to Cha Cha." Backstage was awash with celebrities, conmen, industry types, and lots of women, although one witness recalls Sam and Sally "kind of shared the star's dressing room." The nightly parties were memorable, filled with all kinds of people, dancing to the latest records or listening to Sam as he tried out a new song on his guitar.

In early June 1959, Keen released "Only Sixteen" from the sessions Sam had done after his accident. According to Lou Rawls, Sam wrote the song at Rawls's parents' apartment at 3011 LaSalle in Chicago. "I think it was Marian, my stepsister, her birthday was coming up; she was turning sixteen. . . . He would just sit there and be strumming . . . and then he would start singing it. He had it in his head!" It sounds like Sam's old composition trick: the miraculous conception. Whether Sam wrote it for Marian, another sixteen-year-old, or no one in particular, "Only Sixteen" is a song of underage desire that, in other hands, borders on the obscene. (Listen to Dr. Hook's Top Ten cover from 1976.) While it's supposedly about innocent heartbreak, you can't help jumping to what these two sixteen-year-olds were too young to know.

Blackwell once again used bland, white backup singers, but in this case they only served to set off Sam's rich vocal. By the end of the song, they're asking the questions—why did he give in?—like a great, white fifties jury, and Sam is answering as innocently as he can. The lyrics (credited to Barbara Campbell; Rupe's case over "You Send Me" was winding down in the courts) argue that nothing really bad was going on: after all, he's a mere "lad"—a reassuringly old-fashioned word. Sam makes the songwriting sound easy, but all you have to do is listen to the flip side, Alexander's "Let's Go Steady Again," to realize how hard it is to write something so convincingly adolescent without it being either tiresome or cloying. The solid beat and catchy guitar twang help, and the fresh quality of Sam's voice—the same that undercut the Billie Holiday material—works perfectly here. But the style is only part of it; it's the song—not the singing—that has been covered again and again over the years.

The record climbed into the charts with "Cha Cha" still popular in r&b and eventually reached #28 on the Top Forty. Again, this single broke pop first, but Sam went on to promote it with an extensive r&b tour arranged by Dick Alen over at Universal Attractions. Sam's William Morris agent, Larry Auerbach, was the first to admit, "We weren't equipped, really, to secure dates in what was then termed the black market." Or as Auerbach's assistant Paul Cantor puts it, "We really didn't know what to do to keep a Sam Cooke working. . . ." Alen, on the other hand, knew the "chitlin circuit": Universal handled Jackie Wilson, Chuck Berry, Ray Charles, and Fats Domino, among others. Alen went with "black promoters to mainly black cities . . . a black theater in a black neighborhood where a certain amount of white kids who felt adventurous would go. . . ." It was basically the circuit Sam would ride for the next five years.

On this tour, Cooke co-headlined with Jackie Wilson, who had just come off his second pop hit, "Lonely Teardrops," and was pushing his third, "That's Why (I Love You So)." Sam and Jackie were always carrying on about who should be the headliner. It was a friendly competition: there's a rare film clip of Jackie bumping Sam offstage while he's lip-synching on a local TV show: the two men are all mock anger and banter. As the tour opened, 3,500 disk jockeys had just honored Wilson, along with Clyde McPhatter, for having the most records played on the air. To back this up, Wilson was an incredibly personable, acrobatic performer: a great mover known for his splits and spins. "He'd be on the floor," Alen recalls, "he'd be up and down. He's be taking his shirt off."

It was a seemingly impossible act to follow. Like June Cheeks in gospel, Wilson got to Cooke, made him move and abandon his teen-croon voice to shout a little, even laugh that gospel laugh. In the end, Sam still presented the cool, collected figure with the boyish face, but night after night, he'd urge the band—and Cliff as conductor—to come down a little harder. Then Sam would let loose that clear stream of sound: washing away the memories of the previous acts and hypnotizing everyone with his unpredictable rises and trills and falls. Blues guitarist Lonnie Brooks (known at the time as Guitar Junior) saw Cooke for the first time on this tour. "Oh man!" Brooks recalls. "That cat was just incredible! He could easily make a man cry, the way he could sing. He'd get it from the gut. I would sit there, and I couldn't take my eyes off the guy. A little bit of a guy like that had so much voice! It's just something I'll *never* forget."

In Charlotte, North Carolina, the package played to a crowd of nine thousand; seven thousand fans came out in Dallas. In Atlanta, they filled Hernandon Stadium at $2 a head. There Brooks saw Sam apply his Sister Flute techniques to an r&b audience. "He'd sing so hard till women starts to faint and fall out! Get the ambulance to come get them!. . . Everybody, the whole place, wanted him!" After the concert, Sam couldn't even get to his crowded dressing room but ducked into a waiting limousine instead. "A couple of women saw him in there," Brooks remembers, "and, boy, they ran trying to grab him. So he jumped out the other side—I was getting in the cab— and he jumped in the cab with me."

Trailing this kind of wild adulation, the Cooke/Wilson package arrived at the Norfolk Arena on June 12. Sam had been here a year earlier on the Feld tour and seen the policy of segregated seating: whites center and right, blacks to the left. Then, he'd let it pass. Now, both he and the times had changed.

That spring of 1959, the white South was sending notice that despite gains in Montgomery and Little Rock, this was still its turf. In late April, Mack Charles Parker, a Negro accused of raping a white woman, had been dragged out of his cell in Poplarville, Mississippi. His body had been found nine days later with two bullet holes in it. While the Mississippi NAACP, led by field secretary Medgar Evers, organized meetings across the country, the state's governor, J. P. Coleman, rubbed the nation's nose in it by publicly declaring he thought Parker was guilty.

The same week as Cooke's Norfolk concert, an all-male, all-white jury recommended a light sentence for four whites found guilty of raping a nineteen-year-old Negro coed at Florida A&M. In Birmingham, the Reverend Fred Shuttlesworth, using all his restraint, declared that the punishment "does not make southern justice seem perfect. . . ." Meanwhile, an arm-waving, sweaty Governor Faubus of Arkansas announced in front of the Mississippi Bar Association that "if the South's cause is lost, it would be a good thing if the Russians do destroy us."

And it wasn't just the South. By early summer, the headline on page one of the *Amsterdam News* would read, "NEGRO REVOLT." Harlem community groups were organizing against inferior schools, stores that didn't buy from Negro salesmen, and landlords who were gouging high rents for tenement rooms with subhuman conditions. "The apparently unplanned but well coordinated series of 'revolts,' " the paper declared, "left Harlem in the most hostile and serious mood it had been in since the early thirties. . . ."

Sam wasn't hostile, but he was certainly serious. This time when the package arrived in Norfolk, Sam told the management of the Arena that unless the seating was totally integrated, he was prepared to walk. It wasn't the way the good old boys were used to being addressed by colored entertainers, but Sam was adamant—polite but adamant—and, as the headliner for a show that cost the promoters thousands of dollars, he knew he had the power.

The way Frank Guida, local record store owner and later record producer, remembers it, everyone pretended it was no big deal. Before the opening number, Sam appeared before the audience and, in his usual smooth manner, calmly informed them that this show would *not* be segregated. There were no incidents among the audience (more Negro than white) and no publicity, but Sam was way out in front on this one. Guida, who continued to live and work in Richmond, watched other acts go on playing to segregated seating. "He was the only one with the real guts to do it." Sam's audience, especially the Negro part, never forgot.

Chapter

14

ollowing the Jackie Wilson tour, in June 1959, Sam appeared at the Casino in Washington, D.C.: his first nightclub date in a year and a half. He was still determined to have chitlin *and* glitter, and *Variety* decided that while "his initial entry into supper clubs fizzled . . . he's ready now. . . ." By the end of the month, the "You Send Me" fight with Art Rupe was settled: Sam could now write under his own name and put the songs in his own publishing company. His career seemed ready to take another leap; the question was whether he could get there with Keen—and he was starting to wonder about Bumps, too.

According to Crain, Bumps had promised Sam he owned at least part of his songs. "Yeah, good kid," Blackwell told him one night at the Park Sheraton in New York, "you been asking if there's any publishing: you got publishing!" But the Greeks denied it, and Bumps was having trouble even getting his own record royalties. By August, when Sam came back from a two-week engagement at the Bellvue Casino in Montreal, a meeting was in order. John Siamas had just given Alexander his first statement for "Little Things You Do." "They must have owed me thirty-five hundred dollars or something," J.W. recalls, "and he wanted to give me a check for a thousand dollars." Alex wouldn't accept partial payment.

When the partners in KAGS Music—Sam, J.W., and S.R.—went

into Siamas's office, Sam decided to push it a step further and asked for an advance. Siamas turned him down. "Truthfully," says Alexander, "I thought that they were stupid. Yeah! They were stupid; that's the whole thing. If they didn't have the money, with an artist like Sam Cooke, they could have gotten it from the distributors. . . . They were all amateurs in the business." Cooke stood up, told Siamas, "You got an unhappy boy here!" and walked out of the meeting.

At first, Sam may have just wanted his money, but as the summer turned into fall, he started pushing to get free—and not just from Keen but from Blackwell, too. It was a combination of things. "After the Copa," Lou Adler feels, "he was very down on Bumps. Because it's one thing to make a mistake and say Bumps shouldn't have done this, you shouldn't have done that. But if you put yourself up onstage: that was one thing he couldn't take." Then there was Bumps' not coming through on the publishing and his tendency to jump from one project to the next instead of concentrating on being Cooke's manager. Sam wanted a major label; he wanted another chance at the high-class gigs; he wanted other options besides the one-nighter trail.

One evening, Sam drove over to Bumps' place, and the two men headed up the freeway to a little restaurant they both knew in Santa Barbara. Blackwell, Cooke often acknowledged, had been the key man in the switch over to pop. At the beginning, Sam had lived with Bumps, sleeping on his living-room couch, waiting for their shared plans to work out, and Bumps had helped on everything from picking material to sweet-talking the jocks. Now, Blackwell knew what was coming. "I expected," as he put it, "some kind of shit." In the quiet restaurant, with Sam's new sports car out in the parking lot, the singer began by telling his manager not to get upset.

"Don't say nothing. Listen to me out. I don't want you to jump and do like you see other people do: jump at me on the words. Listen to everything I got to say, and then see what you got to say. Bumps," Sam said, taking a breath, "the doors out there are hard to get through. And you and I, we're gonna have problems getting through them. I can get through those doors if you let me go. And, listen to me, no sooner than I get through them, then I'll come back and get you."

Privately, Bumps blamed the Greeks for filling Sam with the notion that "in the South, distributors wouldn't deal with me as a black." But Sam was a pragmatist, and he'd become convinced he needed a white manager to get through those doors. Bumps didn't for a minute believe that Sam would really come back for him—"I just figured it was a nice way to bow out"—but both remained gentlemen. They shook hands, and that was that.

Sam hated having to let anyone go or leave anyone behind, and even as he was breaking these old ties, he got ready to formalize others. The wedding with Barbara had been put off since his car accident, nearly a year ago. Now he set a date, assuring his fiancée that this time his obligations wouldn't get in the way. First, he did a week at the Apollo with singer Barbara McNair and comedian Redd Foxx; then another at Detroit's Flame Show Bar. The Flame was one in a series of key Negro r&b clubs that dotted the country. Like the Peacock in Atlanta and the 5–4 in Los Angeles, it was a place to dress up, have a drink, and spend your money on a good time. For Sam, it offered a chance to blend his hits and his nightclub standards in more relaxed, extended versions; "preach a little," as Crain would put it.

Lou Adler had seen Sam live before, but never in this setting. "He would turn it into a church, in the sense that he had women screaming. I mean, he had an Elvis Presley quality. . . . That frantic female response that Presley got, Sam got it all the time. . . . They'd be screaming at him, reaching for him!. . . They came out of their seats." The intensity that Art Rupe had seen in the young gospel singer ten years before had, if anything, increased.

The day after the Flame show date ended, Sam caught an early flight to Chicago. Barbara Campbell met him at the airport. The two had been sharing a place in Los Angeles at 2704 West 43rd Street in the middle-class, tree-lined Leimert Park area, experiencing a "joy," according to one report, "they couldn't share with the world, not just yet." Now, Sam and Barbara drove from the airport through Chicago's South Side to within a few blocks of where the two had attended Doolittle Elementary. Waiting at Barbara's grandmother's, in a room full of flowers, was the Cook family as well as Barbara's two sisters and some friends. It wasn't a big wedding—Sam's father performed the ceremony; S. R. Crain was the best man—but a certain amount of controlled publicity was guaranteed by inviting a reporter and photographer from the national magazine *Sepia.* The subsequent story didn't mention their eight-year-old daughter, Linda; in fact, the *Chicago Defender* described the ceremony as the fufillment of "a whirlwind courtship." Instead, the press focused on the blue mink stole and the circle of diamonds Sam gave his wife.

The couple honeymooned in Chicago, "revisiting their old haunts, seeing old friends again." The city's Negro population had doubled in the last decade. Bronzeville's business district had shifted south from 47th to 63rd, and Sam and Barbara's old neighborhood was in the process of being reduced to empty lots filled with rubble, many of which would wait another thirty years without seeing the "renewal" that had been promised. The signs of a growing restlessness were everywhere—from the new, harder-looking gangs that roamed the streets to the growth of the Nation of Islam led by the Honorable Elijah Muhammad. It reminded the newlyweds of where they'd been and how far they'd come. Sam never lost touch with Bronzeville—he made a point of visiting with the old-timers and just hanging out on the street—but, as one friend put it, Sam always felt if his label owner had a house with a swimming pool, why couldn't he? In Barbara, he'd married someone who shared his ambition for the good things in life.

A week after getting married, Sam filed a complaint against the Greeks. While Alex Siamas remembers Sam's leaving as "a pleasant separation: no hard feelings one way or the other," court documents tell a different story. On October 19, Rex Productions was issued a summons, based on over $30,000 due Cooke in back royalties. The day after the summons, the Los Angeles County sheriff came in and attached everything at Keen's recording studio, from the Olivetti adding machine to the grand piano. John Siamas, meanwhile, was hurriedly trying to cash in on his unhappy star, issuing an LP, *Hit*

Kit, that included the extraordinary string of seven Top Forty singles Sam had made in the last two years.

The November 9 *Billboard* reported "the hottest rumor around the trade" was that RCA Victor a&r men Hugo and Luigi had made Cooke "a fabulous offer," complete with a $100,000 guarantee. The offer had come about after Sam had spilled some of his unhappiness to Larry Auerbach; from there, the grapevine had taken over. Auerbach knew a young white PR man, Jess Rand. Rand was a personable, talkative chain-smoker who wore his hair in a Tony Curtis pomp and appeared to have the connections—through his work with Sammy Davis, Jr., and the vocal group the Lettermen—to get Sam into Vegas, television, even the movies. When they got together, Sam "began to tell me what he didn't like about Keen Records," Jess remembers. "He wanted me to go in and straighten out his records and get an audit. . . ." Rand's accountant found some discrepancies in Keen's books ("You always will as long as the record audit says, 'Miscellaneous: Promotion and others' ") and then started shopping for a new label. "The word went out so fast around the business," says Rand, "it was ridiculous. . . . Three companies were hitting on me for Sam, in this order: RCA, Atlantic through Ahmet Ertegun, and Capitol Records through Nick Venet."

Atlantic's Jerry Wexler (the great producer who cut hits for everyone from LaVern Baker to Aretha Franklin) has called Cooke "the best singer that ever lived, bar none. I mean *nobody* can touch Sam Cooke. . . . Modulation, shading, dynamics, progression, emotion, every essential quality—he had it all." But Atlantic wanted Sam's publishing, and that was the one nonnegotiable. Sam was now thoroughly convinced of the value of KAGS. According to Rand, Sam had other doubts about Atlantic. He'd seen what had happened to his friend Clyde McPhatter, and he told Jess, "I don't care what the man promises or suggests, he'll steal it back some way."

Capitol Records had Nat King Cole: a good indication that the label could deliver what Sam wanted. On the other hand, Cooke worried that Cole occupied Capitol's one "Negro" slot.

RCA was a huge corporation that had always treated records as just a come-on to get consumers to buy its audio equipment: "a calling card with a dog on it," as Jess Rand put it. But Elvis had convinced Victor that rock & roll made money—lots of money. And though, as Rand says, it appeared that the only black on the label was the color of its records, RCA did have Sam's friend Jesse Belvin and his old role model Harry Belafonte.

On December 9, Sam became legally free of Keen. Atlantic was eliminated from the competition, and Capitol failed to match RCA's offer. So, on January 6, 1960, Sam signed with Victor, and, a week or so later, went up to meet the independent producers who would handle his recordings.

Hugo and Luigi were middle-aged Italian-American cousins. Hugo Peretti was forty, the musician of the two: a trumpet player who'd worked in Broadway pit bands. Luigi Creatore, three years younger, was a short-story writer and published novelist. They'd made their reputation in the age of covers, using white shouter Georgia Gibbs to produce such note-for-note replicas of r&b tunes that LaVern Baker had gone to Congress to have Gibbs's 1955 version of "Tweedle Dee" declared illegal. Later, the two young, ambitious a&r men had gone on to form their own label, Roulette, with the notorious Morris Levy, whose businesses the FBI called "a source of ready cash for the Genovese LCN [La Cosa Nostra] Family and its leaders." The same time "You Send Me" was raging through the charts, Hugo and Luigi had struck gold for Levy with "Honeycomb" and followed it with ten other Top Forty hits by the sweet-voiced Jimmie Rodgers.

In 1959, when RCA announced it was looking for more "teenage attractions" like the incredibly successful Elvis Presley, the cousins were an obvious source. "We made our conditions," says Creatore, "and it involved a million dollars—which was unheard-of then . . . and we'd be independent producers: they paid Hugo and Luigi Productions, and we gave them so many records a year." For the first nine months, the deal looked like a dead loser. After the freewheeling style of Roulette, Hugo and Luigi couldn't adjust to RCA with its college-educated, radio-dumb promotion men. But the cousins refused to appear worried. They made a point of announcing to the press that they had started practicing yoga in a section of the sixth floor Victor had given them: Luigi was very good at standing on his head, while Hugo fancied the lion pose, sitting on his haunches with his tongue hanging out. So much for RCA's corporate image.

Their first breakthrough was Della Reese, who reached #2 in October of 1959 with "Don't You Know." As she hit, Hugo and Luigi were following the rumor that Sam Cooke was unhappy at Keen. Cooke was not only a proven commodity, but he had that clean-cut Ivy League appearance and a record of "tasteful" hits that would reassure RCA. Now Sam went in to meet the cousins, whom Jess Rand describes as "the Leopold and Loeb of the record business. . . . Magnificent scammers!"

"He came up alone," Luigi recalls. "He just walked in. So we started talking . . . and Hugo started going over some songs on the piano." Sam, charming and apparently as relaxed as always, watched his new producers closely. While he had to respect the cousins' recording experience, he'd gotten used to his freedom at Keen. Plus, he was accustomed to working with a Negro producer, arranger, bandleader, and manager. Now Sam stood alone on the sixth floor of a famously white institution facing two Italian-American producers who were even then handing him an incredibly pale pop tune.

"Here," Hugo said from the piano, "sing a little of this," and ran through the melody of what they'd decided would be his first single for RCA, something called "Teenage Sonata." Sam read the words, but when he began to sing, his voice cracked. He explained he had a slight cold and started again. Again, it cracked.

"Shit," said Luigi, "they sent us the wrong guy!"

That broke the ice. After the laughter, Sam mentioned that he'd been working on a tune. "Oh, what's that?" asked Hugo. Sam sang the first four bars of a song that began with just grunting: "Uh-ah! Uh-ah!" "Okay," said Peretti, the musical side of the duo, "let's do that." The producers and their new singer were dancing around each other, Sam protesting he hadn't finished it, Hugo and Luigi saying again that it sounded real promising. Everyone seemed convinced he was being charming. "From then on," says Creatore, "we got along as buddies. I really thought of him as my friend."

If the results of the first session are any indication, the new friends still had a way to go. The three and a half hours in RCA's Studio A on January 25, 1960, were a mess. First they tried to cut "Teenage Sonata." A formulaic pledge song, it came with a big, sweeping string section and a melody that fell somewhere between the Platters hit "The Great Pretender" and no melody at all. While Sam sings credibly enough, his patented buildup had nowhere to go: he repeated "my, my, my" as in the gospel days, only to slide off in what almost sounds like embarrassment at the punch line: "lips." That first night, working with a big orchestra conducted by Glenn Osser, Sam couldn't get it at all. Finally, they decided to spend the rest of the session on the tune Sam had written.

Without the benefit of René Hall and Bumps, Sam had to reinvent his method of musical communication. "In the rehearsal," Luigi remembers, "Sam would sing, and the background—the accompaniment—would come out of him. Because if he began singing, you'd get the mood from him; you'd get the rhythm, the mood, the feel of the song." But this first session, Cooke had to convince the new producers that he knew what he wanted—and that it worked.

He'd been writing the grunting tune since the Jackie Wilson tour that last June. Charles Cook, the replacement chauffeur for Eddie Cunningham, had been driving Sam and Jackie between gigs in Georgia. There, against the endless red-dirt fields, they'd seen a dozen coal-black men dressed in eye-stunning pure white uniforms. It was a picture that passed for pretty until they'd gotten close enough to see the mounted guards nearby, double-barreled shotguns across their laps. Then they'd realized the black men were chained, ankle to ankle. The prisoners were singing, Charles recalls, "and asking for cigarettes. We'd go to the nearest store, buy up a lot of cigarettes, and bring them by. With the permission of the guards, you know." Sam heard the sound of the men working—the call-and-response as the gang answered the lead, chanting in time to the long day's work—and started writing, there and then. After all, this was underneath all blues and gospel—as old as slavery, as old as the advent of black-skinned people on the continent. "It was his idea," Charles remembers, but all three men in the car helped with the song: struck not only by the scene outside the window but by the very fact that it *was* outside—that the three of them somehow managed to be driving through Georgia in a new car, free to make the next gig, to write a song about chain gangs, while their brothers were locked together under the Georgia sun.

Sam couldn't just explain to these RCA musicians that he needed that chain gang sound; it didn't translate up here. The one member of his old team who was there, Cliff White, remembers that "he wanted a good, solid sound," a real thunk. They did a couple of takes, but Sam wasn't happy. Then they started trying various studio tricks, including putting a wallet on the snare skins to give it a heavier sound. That playback didn't satisfy him either. Hugo and Luigi, sitting in the booth, watched Cooke ask the drummer to try the tom-toms, now the bass, now the bass muffled, and must have wondered where the hell this was going. He did have a track record of making hits, but still . . .

Finally, after fooling around with a dozen different ideas, Cooke asked the drummer to stand and hit his leather stool once. Yeah, that was more like it! A real whack with a kind of sticky resonance to it. But they weren't done yet. Sam knew percussion was the key to the song. He had the backbeat with the leather stool, but he wanted the actual sound of metal: the ring as the men shuffled across the fields and link struck link. White recalls they tried the obvious—real chain—but it didn't record right: some kind of overtones that ruined the mix. By now, expensive studio time was ticking away. There Sam stood, in the middle of downtown Manhattan, in one of RCA's finest recording studios—the same place the company used for its famous Red Label classical recordings—with the best studio musicians the producers could find, trying to get the aural equivalent of a bunch of colored prisoners shuffling across a red-dirt field somewhere in Georgia.

He called for another setup. Could they move around the mikes some? Maybe that would get it. As they were shifting things, somebody dropped one of the microphones against the bottom of the stand. "That's it!" Sam, jubilant, set up a take with one percussionist pounding on his stool while another knocked on the base of a mike stand with a piece of hollow metal. The backup singers grunted on the downbeat, two guitars worked on Cooke's familiar, dry rhythm sound, and Sam himself soared above the arrangement, as Hugo and Luigi looked on.

" 'Chain Gang' was written by Sam," says Cliff, "sung by Sam, and generally, you might say, produced by Sam. Because in the end, it came out like what he wanted to happen." One of the striking things about the finished product is that it *isn't* a protest song. It has all the makings of one. In fact, objectively, it would seem impossible for a black man to sing about such a scene without confronting, explicitly, the generations of pain it evokes. But what Sam made, instead, is a middle-of-the-road dance tune. For one thing, the rhythm is up and lively. For another, the vocal is, for the most part, suave and almost offhand, as if Cooke were just going on about another Saturday night at the hop. Instead of a hard gospel chorus, there are professional white singers.

It's a strange arrangement, seemingly at odds with itself and the subject matter, but Cooke was constructing a song and a sound to walk the line between social commentary and finger-snapping. Given the temper of the times—the attitude of not just the record-buying public but the major label he'd just signed with—there was no way he was going to record a secular equivalent of "Were You There When They Crucified My Lord?" Instead, he masked the message, using sound effects as you might in a novelty song, pulling in a bit of his gospel background for the bass singer's "Don't you know?" and arriving at a chain gang that played one way in suburbia and quite another on the South Side.

By the time the session was over, at eleven-thirty at night, they'd done some fifteen takes of Sam's tune, not to mention the tries at "Teenage Sonata." Luigi, looking back, says they knew "Chain Gang" was a hit. It's odd, then, that RCA wouldn't release it for another six months. No, as far as the label was concerned, the session hadn't produced anything good enough to be a first single. So, three days later, they went back into the same studio, still with Glenn Osser conducting, and tried again. They redid "Teenage Sonata" in four takes and cut a few other potential singles as well. Jess Rand remembers being so horrified by the cheesy material, especially "Teenage Sonata," that he suggested to Sam, outside the studio between takes, that they find a lawyer and get out of the whole deal.

"No," Cooke answered. "I ain't gonna do nothing to that tune. I'll never do it live. Let it die, and then you go in and say, 'See, you can't produce Sam Cooke. We'll do whatever material we want.' "

In early February 1960, with "Teen Angel" the #1 song, RCA took out a full-page ad announcing "Teenage Sonata" backed by "You Were the Only Girl." *Billboard* dutifully spotlighted the record as a "winner of the week." After all, if Annette Funicello was selling, why wouldn't this? The record was in the r&b charts two weeks; it never made Top Forty. Maybe Bumps, who had moved over to Mercury Records by now, had the simplest explanation for the failure of "Teenage Sonata": "It was shit."

Chapter 15

I n the summer of 1960, Sam would offer his feelings on the growing civil rights movement in the opening lines of a syndicated
piece he wrote for columnist Dorothy Kilgallen. "I'll never forget
the day when I was unable to fulfill a one-night singing engagement
in Georgia because I wouldn't sit in a Jim Crow bus and because no
white taxicab driver would take me from the airport to the city—and
Negro cabdrivers were not permitted to bring their cabs into the airport. . . . I have always detested people," he goes on, "of any color, religion or nationality who have lacked courage to stand up and be
counted."

J. W. Alexander talks almost matter-of-factly about traveling
through the South with Sam. "Once we were in Charlotte, North
Carolina, and the young white girls got up to dance. Sam was singing. And the police come and draw their clubs at them, and they sat
down. And once we were in Greensboro, North Carolina, and this
young white boy got up and he was dancing. And they chased him.
It was funny. This kid was in good condition, and they chased him
all over. . . ." As Alexander continues his list, the matter-of-factness
starts to drop away. "And one other time, in Louisville, Kentucky,
kids got up and they started dancing. The cops said they were going
to shut the show down. And the kids were going to riot. So then
they came to me and wanted me to put him back on. So, I demanded

that they change their attitude. . . . I would put him back on, but certainly I wouldn't put him back on if they maintained that type of attitude. . . . They were all isolated incidents," Alex adds. "Nothing organized."

On February 1, 1960, four Negro freshmen at A&T College in Greensboro, North Carolina, decided, almost on a dare, to go down to the local Woolworth's and sit at the whites-only counter till they got served. Similar demonstrations had taken place over the previous three years, but now the idea caught on. The next day, twenty others joined the original four. By the second weekend, there were demonstrations—dubbed "sit-ins"—in half a dozen North Carolina towns. And by the end of February, thirty-one cities in eight Southern states had gotten involved. In every case, this brushfire of protest was sparked by students. Older, wiser heads continually advised caution and were repeatedly ignored. While Baptist churches in various cities eventually helped with transportation and preachers acted as go-betweens, the sit-in movement took off outside the established Negro organizations. This wasn't the Soul Stirrers' generation running out of patience; it wasn't even Sam's; these were teenagers, the generation of rock & roll fans.

Four days after the first sit-in, Jackie Wilson, Little Willie John, Arthur Prysock, and Jesse Belvin were playing in Little Rock, Arkansas. It was a segregated Friday-night dance: the first audience Negro, the second crowd white. According to newspaper reports at the time, there was supposed to be a white band there, but they never showed up. Wilson played the first half of the gig but refused to go on for the white crowd. An ugly shouting scene followed, made uglier because Little Rock was still reeling from its school desegregation case. (One of the students who'd integrated the local white high school would have his home bombed just a few nights after the dance.) Cornered late on a Friday night in a city full of hate—with a rowdy white crowd waiting to be entertained—the r&b stars nevertheless refused to go on and were finally ordered out of town at gunpoint. Prysock in his white Lincoln Continental, Wilson in his 1960 Cadillac, and Belvin in his '59 Caddy headed South to their next gig in Dallas.

Wilson and Prysock had just passed Hope, Arkansas, when they started getting their first flats. While they'd been arguing in the dance hall, someone had slashed their tires. Belvin wasn't so lucky: five miles south of Hope, on Highway 67, his car went out into the passing lane, going eighty-five, and hit another vehicle head on. Belvin, his wife, and the driver were all killed. No one ever proved that Jesse's tires had been cut, but the accident was a sign of the times. The rock & roll road was dangerous enough all on its own; add sudden national attention to a civil rights movement, and the singers became actors in a larger drama.

According to Jess Rand, Sam was back in Los Angeles for Belvin's funeral, but, overcome, turned around on the way there. Cooke must have felt haunted: his own car accident, Dee's, and now his old friend's, all within a year and a half. Plus, Sam didn't want to bring Barbara into a church jammed with 3,500 people: she was three months pregnant. They had already leaked the news to the press, adding that they were "hoping for a boy." The couple now had a nice house and, with the RCA deal, some money in the bank, and Sam was exploring ways to get off the road. Rand had gotten him an act-ing part, his first, in a half-hour TV movie called *The Patsy*. It starred Rand's old client, Sammy Davis, Jr., and was broadcast over CBS's prestigious *General Electric Theater*, hosted by actor Ronald Reagan. Sam's part in the military drama was small—too tiny even to be mentioned in New York's *Amsterdam News*—but it was a start and seemed to prove that Rand had the connections Sam wanted.

His next business move combined his growing racial awareness and his ambition to expand his career. "It wasn't meant to be a rec-ord company at first," J. W. Alexander recalls; it was just a produc-tion company to go along with the music publishing, KAGS. But Sam was beginning to want a financial base stronger than the success of his next single. He understood that the industry saw artists as dis-posable: "pains in the asses," as Roulette's Mo Levy put it. There were examples of Negroes owning labels—John Dolphin and Dootsie Williams in L.A., Berry Gordy and his still hitless Tamla/Motown in Detroit—but *no* rock & roller of any color owned his or her own label.

As Sam was considering the possibility, Art Rupe, in Leroy

Crume's words, had "lost all interest" in the Soul Stirrers. Vee Jay immediately offered them a sizable advance. Sam told Leroy Crume he couldn't match it: "I'm just getting started with you guys—no way I could come up with that kind of cash!" But then he flashed that smile of his. "I can't beat it—not in cash—but in the long run, I can do better." He ticked off the advantages: Sam was a proven songwriter in the gospel field, and the Stirrers would get first stab at his material; he now had connections in the mainstream record industry that could help the group; plus, there was always the possibility that sometime in the future he might cut a record with them. The Stirrers went for it. "Sam didn't pay nobody," is how his old friend Sam Moore describes it. "He didn't pay; he would charm you out of it."

He decided to call his new label SAR, standing for Sam, Alex, and Roy. He teased J.W.—"Alex, you keep coming up with these ideas!"—but it was Sam who went into a Chicago studio and produced the first Stirrers single, "Wade in the Water"/"He Cares." It did pretty well in late 1959, plus, he got the group on a New York TV show of the time, *Rate the Record:* an unheard-of development for a religious quartet. Cooke had launched his label with one of the premier gospel acts in the nation—and with almost no capital outlay.

SAR was Sam's idea of the civil rights movement put into practice and a big step toward controlling his own product. But he had picked a difficult time to begin. In November of 1959, a government subcommittee started a payola investigation into "pay to play" bribery in popular music. Alan Freed, who had never quite recovered from the rock & roll "riot" up in Boston, was one of the first to fall. He was forced off TV late in November, and a couple of weeks later he was hauled before the New York attorney general to explain why the two mortgages on his Connecticut home were owned by Hugo and Luigi's old partner, Morris Levy. Freed's reaction to all this was telling: "I know a bunch of ASCAP publishers who will be glad I'm off the air."

The dj and many others believed that the payola scandal, though disguised as a moral crusade, was really about reestablishing a monopoly. In the forties, when the older, stodgier songwriters' and music publishers' association, ASCAP, wouldn't touch "minority" music, a competitor, BMI, had emerged. Rock & roll had turned it into a gold mine, and now ASCAP was petitioning the Federal Communications Commission to block BMI, accusing its rival of using its $10 million distribution budget as a "collective payola fund."

In Chicago, the investigation had forced veteran r&b jock Al Benson to open his books: he was getting $855 a month from nine different distributors and labels. Art Rupe's old rival Don Robey, down for $50 a month for his Peacock label, was outraged. "If they want to clean something up," Robey said, "they should go into the Top Forty end of it. They're after the horse's tail when they should be after the head." On the West Coast, r&b star Johnny Otis was even more pointed. Otis was convinced the payola investigation was, at bottom, a reaction against the racial aspects of rock & roll. "Teenagers, black, white, Mexican, and Oriental had something in common . . . they all loved rock & roll music. . . . It was *theirs* . . . it was unique . . . it was exciting. Democracy, one of the important things taught (but not necessarily practiced) in our schoolrooms, was manifesting itself in the ballrooms. A spontaneous integration occurred. Rock & roll audiences became integrated."

That the investigation wasn't an across-the-board cleanup became burningly clear when Dick Clark, despite numerous tie-ins with Philadelphia labels, came away from the government hearings free and clear. RCA quickly signed a consent agreement, admitting no guilt and promising not to do it again. It was the music industry's equivalent of McCarthyism, and the "moral" atmosphere naturally affected the kind of music that got played and recorded.

Sam's first RCA LP, *Cooke's Tour*, couldn't have been safer. A concept album that offered a musical journey around the world, it featured antique vehicles like "South of the Border," "Galway Bay,'" and "Arrivederci, Roma." As a fifteen-piece string section, augmented by three guitars, a flute, and a harp, saws away, Sam plods through what sounds more like Cooke's tour of acceptable singing techniques—from a Nat King Cole's copy of "Bali H'ai" to a deadly Harry Belafonte tribute on "Jamaica Farewell."

Meanwhile, instead of releasing "Chain Gang," RCA put out a second single, "You Understand Me"/"I Belong to Your Heart," that sank faster and with even fewer ripples than "Teenage Sonata." Sam, used to a hit every three months or so, now hadn't put anything on the Top Forty since "Only Sixteen," nine months earlier.

Hugo and Luigi had Sam cut another middle-of-the-road album just three weeks after the first, this one called *Hits of the Fifties*. One indication of rock & roll's forced retrenchment was the music's first wave of nostalgia. Mo Levy's Roulette had started to put out golden oldie LPs; on the West Coast, Art Laboe's Original Sounds was doing the same; and on the charts, classics like "In the Still of the Nite" and "Earth Angel" were reappearing. So, wouldn't the teens love Sam Cooke's versions of "Unchained Melody," "Cry," "Venus"? "You just called in your strings and things and made the arrangements, and he sang," Luigi admits. "It was not inspired, and as a result, it didn't go anyplace. . . . It was a job at that point, for him, too. He sang well, but so what?" That's exactly how it sounds. In retrospect, Luigi blames RCA for the choice of material, but the producers certainly went along with it. For that matter, so did Sam.

Of all the unlikely saviors, Sam's turned out to be John Siamas. Siamas remembered how Art Rupe had come up with the million-selling "I'll Come Running Back to You" after Sam had split from Specialty, so he had his engineer dig into the Keen vaults. Deano Lappas came up with a tune called "Wonderful World." It dated back to 1958, when Lou Adler and Herbie Alpert had begun collaborating on a song about the difference between the head and the heart. "I don't know a good book from another," is how Adler remembers the lyrics, "but I don't have to read a book to be a lover." And the chorus was something like "All I know is that I love you so." During the time Lou and Sam had roomed together, they'd tossed the song back and forth, Sam playing the few chords he knew on the guitar and messing with both lyrics and melody. Cooke fiddled with it as he did with all his material: trying it out on various people, announcing this was his latest hit, showing off to women by claiming he'd written the tune right there, for them. It took shape over a long time and a lot of partying.

"Then what happened," says Adler, "is we were in the back of Keen Records on 3rd Street, and he decided he wanted to cut some things, but we couldn't get the normal drummer that we used. We were cutting them more or less as demos, because Bumps wasn't there. . . . We got a drummer that was fifteen or sixteen years old and was a nephew of one of the other musicians. . . ." The session on March 2, 1959, could hardly have been more bare-bones. As Adolphus Alsbrook laid down a rumba bass line, the teenage drummer tracked along, and Cliff White picked a pretty, high guitar line. Behind Sam, hitting the last, rhymed word in each line, is Lou Rawls; Deano Lappas remembers him standing about a foot and a half behind Sam, singing into the same mike.

"Wonderful World" is a deceptively well-made two minutes of song. The melody hangs through the lyric about the facts and figures we're supposed to understand but can't—the universal boredom of school—then turns to announce what real knowledge is. He loves her and, if she loves him (the tune slips to a single-line resolution), what a wonderful world it will be. Sam puts it in a relaxed, unself-conscious groove, a lot like "I'll Come Running Back to You."

There wasn't much to do to the track—the levels had been set at recording—and Lappas just made sure it was clean. Keen released it in April 1960 with the album cut "Along the Navajo Trail" on the flip. (*Billboard*, showing taste a lot like RCA's, decided it was this B-side that was going to draw "spins a plenty.") Within a month, "Wonderful World" would reach the pop charts and stay there almost three months, eventually climbing to #12. It hit *Billboard*'s r&b charts later than the pop, but when it did, it shot to the #2 position. If RCA had been paying attention, it might have seen "Wonderful World" as a forceful argument that Cooke did his best work left virtually alone in the studio to find the sound he heard in his head.

As Sam began another week at the Apollo in May, the still mushrooming sit-ins had spread to sixty-eight cities in thirteen states. Former President Truman clucked from Missouri that "the Negro should behave himself. . . . If anyone came into my store and sat down, I'd throw him out." But Harlem's *Amsterdam News* pointed out that the protests were having "a devastating effect not only on the white economic world. . . . but also in reactionary slow-moving Negro leadership circles."

Not far from the Apollo, Sidney Poitier, Harry Belafonte, Nat King Cole, Diahann Carroll, and Mahalia Jackson took part in a benefit to help defend Martin Luther King on tax charges that threatened to jail him. Sam wasn't on the bill, nor were any other rock & rollers. But what the "slow-moving Negro leadership" didn't get the organizers around the sit-ins did. While the benefit for King was unfolding, Jackie Wilson, reggae/r&b singer Johnny Nash, and Dizzy Gillespie were at a Boston University rally to raise scholarship money for the kids expelled from college for protesting. The split in the movement was like the split in the music: the difference between Mahalia Jackson and Jackie Wilson.

Some of Sam's family still wondered if he shouldn't have stayed on Mahalia's side. By the time Cooke arrived at Chicago's Tivoli Theater in the middle of May, it was clear that "Wonderful World" was a hit. (As further proof of Cooke's songwriting ability, he'd given his old neighborhood friends, the Flamingos, an up-tempo number called "Nobody Loves Me Like You." The song was now heading for #30 on the pop charts.) But as he settled in for a week in his hometown, Sam's mother was still worried about him. "They really was deep into religion," observes guitarist Lonnie Brooks, who had begun playing behind brother L.C. and was put up by the Cooks for about six months. "They used to tell me all the time, 'Y'all out there playing that ol' devil music, you should be playing for God!' " From what Brooks could see, even as Sam was packing them in at the Tivoli, his parents "would rather for him to have been with the Soul Stirrers. . . . He would give his mother nice gifts, but they didn't really appreciate it too much: him giving them anything. He would just do it anyway."

With all this pulling at him—his family, his career, the escalating civil rights struggle—it must have been a relief, a few weeks after the Chicago run, to take Barbara (six months pregnant) on his first tour outside the continental United States. The Caribbean was a growing r&b market: Fats Domino, Clyde McPhatter, and Little

Richard, among others, had already made the trip. Still, Sam was surprised by his reception. When they arrive at Jamaica's Kingston airport, customs waved the whole entourage through. "Oh, don't worry about it," said the officer in his lilting accent. "It's the man from the Wonderful World!" Outside, as people recognized him, the crowd began making spontaneous music: banging on tin cans, Coke bottles, garbage-can lids and shouting, "Hello Sam Cooke! Hey Sam Cooke! Hello mon!" Sam waved from his car as they slowly crept along the two-laner, the green sugarcane fields in the distance, the stray dogs barking at all the excitement. The sea of black faces just grew— "Sing us a song, mon!"—until Sam finally agreed, stepping out of his car and singing under the strange, sharp-leaved palm trees.

Cooke was delighted with the tour, by the foreignness of it and the oddly familiar feel of being in a world where everyone was his color. He laughed with the others when Cliff White gave a guy $20 for a bottle of the local rum and got ninety-seven Jamaican dollars in change. "Goddam! This is a place I want to stay! I'm gonna get every twenty dollars I can find and change it." And after one of the stops during the ten-day tour—"Surinam or something," says White—a delighted crowd threw dirt all over Sam, then surged in and started rolling him on the ground. Cooke came up fighting, teeth bared, fists cocked, till someone finally explained to him that this was the local version of a standing ovation. Or as Crain puts it, "That was their worship of Sam." According to *Variety*, Cooke "broke all records" on the trip, and his sweet-voiced style would influence Caribbean stars like Johnny Nash and Jimmy Cliff.

When Sam got back to Los Angeles, the city was hosting the Democratic Convention, where John Kennedy was nominated for President. The social problems JFK would face were mirrored in the continuing attacks on r&b. The city of Birmingham banned rock & roll altogether. At a Jackie Wilson concert in New Orleans, when a cop asked costar Larry Williams not to climb off the stage, a shoving match followed, and soon most of the audience of five thousand had joined in, throwing bottles and fighting the police.

But if the music was seen as dangerous, RCA had finally figured out that having Sam Cooke release ultrasafe material was a bust. At last, in late July, the label released "Chain Gang," six months after Cooke had cut it. The record immediately took off, shooting to #2 in both pop and r&b. Soon the whole country seemed to be grunting along with the chain gang. The record was, in its own way, as crucial to Sam as "You Send Me" had been. It reestablished him not only as a chart-topper, selling more than half a million copies, but also as a songwriter and producer who could fashion his own hits.

Sam's dry spell had helped drive home how tenuous a rock & roll career was. In the guest piece he wrote for Dorothy Kilgallen that summer, he acknowledged he'd made "a fantastic amount of money" in the last three years, but he also considered himself "realist enough to know that . . . few readers of this column would recognize the titles of most of my hits." Rock & roll, Sam theorized, was filled with one-shot wonders because "they did not understand that show business was a business." So, Sam had devoted "as much time to the practical business end as to the 'show' end. . . ." He'd sunk his early profits into building up a club act. Now he had a publishing company "showing handsome profits" and his own record label. "If in the future, I can't find anyone who will pay me to sing, I'll still be in a position to get paid when others sing."

By this time, J.W. had rented a tiny ten-by-fifteen-foot office at 6425 Hollywood Boulevard. There were two desks: Sam's, which was almost always empty, and J.W.'s, which had room for two phones and a bookkeeping machine. On the door, it said "KAGS Music Corp./ SAR Records Inc." (They'd also added an ASCAP publishing company, which they decided to call Malloy. "It was an old established type of name," Alex recalls with a laugh. "Irish! There were certain prejudices at this time, so I had to use all the subterfuge I could.")

SAR was turning out to be a direct outgrowth of Sam's gospel roots. As well as the two Stirrers singles in 1959, Sam and Alex had persuaded the former Pilgrim Travelers lead Kylo Turner to try two of their pop compositions. Now, Cooke added Johnnie Morisette, the gospel singer he'd first met outside the Twilight Cafe in Mobile. Johnnie had ended up cutting a couple of singles for Art Rupe under the name Johnny Two-Voice—for his trick of switching from his low register to a high, eerie falsetto. But Johnnie's the first to admit his main interest at the time was pimping. Little Richard was pretty, he says, but "I had long motherfuckin' hair and my nails was longer than his. I had diamond rings!" In Sam's complicated social world—where he could slide from talking business at William Morris to singing harmony with old gospel friends—Johnnie was street: always up for a party, bringing out a side of Sam many of his straighter friends never saw.

Driving along in Cooke's car one day, Sam talked Johnnie into trying "Never," a Cooke/Alexander tune written for Kylo Turner. Sam set it to a cha-cha beat, led by a snare drum that sounds straight off the parade grounds, and used strings as a rhythm section—the way Bumps used to. The B-side was another Cooke/Alexander composition, "In My Heart." Morisette was impressed by the full string section—"He did everything first-class"—and by how prepared Sam was; "He had that assurance," says Johnnie, "because he did his homework." Morisette's cocky vocal quickly turns into a gospel growl a lot like Wilson Pickett's, and he ends the tune with a full, sanctified laugh.

The single, released in early August, became, in Johnnie's words, "a turntable hit. I never got no money," but the record shows what Sam had in mind for SAR. Here, on his own label, with full artistic control, he could explore his funkier (which is also to say his more gospel-influenced) side. While he left most of SAR's business up to Alex, Sam wrote the material, laid out arrangements, even cut demos so SAR artists could model their vocals exactly on his. The label would prove to be his training ground for new talent and his test tube for new sounds.

Cooke's main interest, however, remained his own career. As he wrote in the Kilgallen column, "I burn with the ambition to achieve the kind of show business stature that Harry Belafonte and Nat King Cole have achieved." When Sam had a preliminary conference with Hugo and Luigi in New York, the atmosphere, while still friendly, had changed.

Cooke was adamant about what the success of "Chain Gang" meant. "I want to sing for my people," he told the producers. "So," Luigi recalls thinking, " 'sing for my people.' What did that mean?"

The two cousins quickly concluded it meant "good stuff." Given their track record with Cooke, they were in no position to force their taste on him. Though they still had plenty of input, from then on, Hugo and Luigi began to leave more of the production decisions up to Sam. If he wanted to spend time hunting around for the sound of a chain gang, it was, they now realized, time well spent. For this new *Swing Low* LP, he'd do the usual middle-of-the-road cover songs, but there'd be some Sam Cooke originals, too. They'd even try a version of "Pray," the Johnny Taylor gospel number that Sam had cut with the Stirrers before leaving Specialty.

The planning got interrupted when Barbara went into labor. With a recording date set and needing to finalize the numbers, Hugo and Luigi sent a new arranger, Sammy Lowe, to the West Coast. "Both Sams paced the hospital corridor," the producers write in their liner notes to the LP, "until Mrs. Cooke presented Sam with a fine baby girl. . . ." So, it wasn't the son they'd been hoping for—or twins, as Barbara had half suspected—but a second daughter. They named her Tracey Samie: the first name, Cooke told the press, pulled out of a hat by "the girls at RCA." That same day, Sam went into United Recording and helped the Soul Stirrers on four cuts for their next single on SAR; the next day they cut four more; and within three days of Tracey's birth, he was back in New York, recording the tracks for the *Swing Low* LP.

Hugo and Luigi had brought in a hipper band, including jazz greats Milt Hinton on bass and Hank Jones on piano. The title song, "Swing Low," refashions the old spiritual in the shape of "Chain Gang:" it even begins with an "Ooo-baa!" percussive chorus. When the arrangement falls away to leave a simple finger-snapping background for the verses, Sam's voice grows sweet. Still, it isn't the Soul Stirrers: by the time the horns kick in for a big finish, the emphasis is definitely on the swing, not the chariot. The original, "You Belong to Me," on the other hand, is the best thing to come out of the album sessions. It lists what Sam will give his woman, including his love, his hands to work for her, and, Cooke's ultimate gift, his voice. The melody sounds a little like the still-unwritten "Blowin' in the

Wind"—which is to say, it borrows a folk tune—and Sam sings it well, in a mellow voice with a slight yodel.

In September 1960, with "Chain Gang" tearing up the charts, Sam headlined his first big, integrated rock & roll package in two years. The bill included teen idols Bobby Rydell, Duane Eddy, and Dion and the Belmonts, and it proved a chance for Sam to rework his live act. The common practice at the time was to use the house musicians in each town. Now, Sam decided that along with Cliff on guitar, he wanted to carry his own drummer. It wasn't only that he cared how the band sounded—though the perfectionist in him most certainly did—but also that he knew it would make his set stand out from the others. Sam hired Albert "June" Gardner, a sweet-faced, creamy-complexioned man with big ears who wore a mustache and a hip little lower-lip beard. He had come up through the New Orleans apprentice system, and though he wasn't as versatile as Earl Palmer or as innovatively wild as other great New Orleans drummers like Hungry Williams, he had a driving rock-steady beat.

June joined Sam and Cliff White in Richmond, Virginia, and at first found the gig a little intimidating. White was a big man, and, as a bandleader, he used his size to make sure he got exactly the sound he wanted. The lover of Segovia had, after all, also hung out in the Dallas joints with Blind Lemon Jefferson. "We'd come into town, and we'd have rehearsal, and one of Cliff's famous lines was: 'If you don't play my music right, I'm gonna snatch your arm out and beat you with the bloody end!' " June quickly learned to keep the rhythm the way Cliff wanted it.

Sam was, if anything, more demanding, and his temper was real, not White's good-natured bluff. Sometimes they'd come offstage and Sam would say, "Cliff. June. Come over here. That beat seemed it was off by a fraction."

"No, Sam," Cliff would begin. "You did—"

And before he could get any further, Sam would go off: "Aw, bullshit! Fucker, don't tell me!"

Then, as Gardner remembers it, the storm would disappear as quickly as it had come up. Sam would order drinks all around and,

"Wssssh! Meeting over with." While Sam demanded respect, he always treated his musicians the same way: sharing dressing rooms and making sure to introduce them onstage.

Some of June's fondest memories are of the times when Sam would turn to Cliff in the middle of a performance and say, "Tell them fuckers to lay out!" Then the other players—bass and horns and whatever else the local band might have provided—would stop playing. And Sam would sing with just Cliff and June behind him: his own personal band. "We killed them," June remembers, "with just guitar and drums!"

Chapter 16

I n the endless haze of one-nighters that Sam played in the early sixties, some dates stood out. One day, for example, the band found
itself at an amusement park near Brandywine, Maryland, "way the
hell and gone out in the country," Cliff White recalls. It was the sort
of gig Sam booked himself to fill the empty dates during a tour.
Someone had set up a little stage, five or six feet off the dusty
ground, and as Sam started up the stairs, a local guy leaned forward.
"Get on up there and sing, motherfucker. Don't be grinning at me."

Sam just smiled: "Hey, baby, everything's okay. I'll do my best."
But as the band kicked off the first number, Cliff looked out and saw
that Charles, always his brother's protector, had gotten into it with
the guy. "They're really dancing! They got to waltzing around the
place at about forty miles an hour! They're making as much of a
show down there as we are on the stage. I'm playing," says Cliff,
"and the next thing I know, Sam's gone. He's out there, man, got the
biggest dude in the joint. Cat's so big, Sam's holding him by the col-
lar, got to jump up in the air to hit the man!" Cliff tore off the stage
to join in. "Oh, Lord, this cat's got my job and everything out there!
Figuring to get it killed."

Charles was down on the ground with someone kicking him so
hard in the face that Cliff's first thought was they'd kicked his eye
out. "And here we are out here in this Brandywine . . . and man,

ain't no doctor, no nothing! And these strange dudes, and they're hot about their women. 'I don't want your women, man! I just want to get out of town!' "

Crain came rushing out, as White began throwing people around, and the guitarist shouted, "Just get the money, and let's get the hell out of here!" They fought their way to the cars and got Charles to a hospital. Cliff had ripped a $300 suit and busted his guitar. "And the funny thing was, Sam didn't get a scratch nowhere! And he was right in the middle."

The road was like that. Crain can remember going in to get their money from a promoter, only to find the man sitting with a shotgun across his desk and explaining he didn't have the box office. Even in classier venues, like Harlem's Rockland Palace, where Sam played that fall of 1960, it got wild. Five thousand people packed into the club (more than double its legal capacity), clapping and singing along to "Chain Gang." "The rhythm is so hypnotic," a visiting French music critic observed, "everyone dances—I honestly wonder how, it's so squeezed. But everyone dances." The song went on and on, Sam extending it to fifteen minutes, playing with the melody as he'd learned to do in his gospel days, giving the crowd what the recorded version could only hint at. When Hank Ballard and the Midnighters followed, they tried to top Cooke, doing twenty minutes of nothing but their hit "The Twist." Ballard was known for raunchy material—"Work with Me, Annie"—and now, as the set built to its close, all the Midnighters stripped to their underwear. The crowd went wild, and security had to be called in; but when the Midnighters were hustled backstage, the audience howled for more. With the room teetering on the verge of a mob scene, Sam was called back out and somehow managed to restore calm. "I can recognize," wrote the awestruck critic, "the hand of a master!"

At the beginning of October, Cooke interrupted the road life just long enough to cut his next single. He'd already laid down a moody ballad, "Love Me," for the B-side. Now he went back in the studio to redo a tune he'd tried six months earlier. Cooke had been known, even in his gospel days, as a man who sang more about joy than sorrow, so "Sad Mood" was something of a departure. There's an aching quality to his voice as he talks about how his baby's left him, and the simple arrangement of Milt Hinton on bass and Ernie Hayes on a trickly piano fits perfectly. If the male chorus is a bit much (especially when it does an exact imitation of the "Uh! Ah!" from "Chain Gang"), "Sad Mood" still has one of Sam's most delicate melodies. He had told Hugo and Luigi he wanted to sing for his people; this was a deeper, more melancholy, more three-dimensional sound.

Sam followed his long tour out East with another batch of one-nighters on the West Coast and then went home to L.A. to get to know his new daughter. Kennedy had won the presidency, sweeping Harlem three to one over Nixon, and many Negroes had high expectations for change. As the civil rights movement swung in the direction of the student activists, the Drifters' "Save the Last Dance for Me" became the nation's #1 song; its message—when the party's over, don't forget who's taking you home—could have served as a warning to the President-elect. A week after his election, New Orleans exploded into mob rule as a thousand whites tried to stop some six-year-olds from entering an all-white elementary school. In Atlanta, after considerable persuasion by a group of students, Martin Luther King, Jr., had agreed to take part in his first sit-in and had been arrested. Joining in the protest was Clyde McPhatter, a lifetime member of the NAACP. He told a youth convention that summer that there were no greater heroes than those "willing to risk verbal abuse, physical assault, expulsion from school and imprisonment in Dixie dungeons."

Sam spent his time off taking Barbara to local clubs, something they both loved to do. The California Club over on Santa Barbara was one of their regular hangouts: the manager, Andy Allen, was an old friend, and the club served good ribs. During that holiday season, Sam heard a little singer from Texas, Patience Valentine, and he was soon in the studio helping her cut an upbeat number he'd written, "Dance and Let Your Hair Down." But the other discovery Sam made at the California Club was even more important for SAR.

One evening, he ran into Zelda Sands, whom he'd first met during his run at the Copa. Zelda was the sort of woman men whistled at: a brunette with a tremendous figure and a tick-tock walk who dressed in bright, attention-getting clothes. But she was also a tough, savvy businesswoman who had worked at the giant Hill and Range publishing company and at Decca Records. "Chief Longhair," Sam greeted her, using a nickname from back East. "Did you ever get married to that boyfriend of yours?" When Zelda said no, Sam grinned and said that was good. The teasing went on until Cooke asked, innocently enough, how her Christmas had been. At that, Zelda broke down. After almost two months in Los Angeles, she was living alone in a motel room with no phone, no friends to speak of, and her money just about gone.

Sam hated to see people cry. He kept trying to press $50 into her hand. Then he got a better idea. How would Zelda like to work for his record company? They could use someone to call the distributors, arrange for publicity, all the stuff Sam was a little vague about and Alex didn't really have time to do. "Just name a price," Sam said, and then added, "Make it as low as possible. . . . We don't have enough to pay with." That evening, Zelda became SAR's first full-time employee—at $80 a week. Soon, Z-Z (as Sam took to calling her) was rearranging the files, phoning the jocks, and heckling the distributors; she became the business end of SAR Records.

By now, SAR was Sam's vehicle for actively recruiting gospel singers to go pop. Some resented it. Clarence Fountain of the Blind Boys tells the story of Cooke pulling out a great wad of greenbacks and announcing, "This is my god now!" But for every one who felt that way, there were plenty who saw Sam as a model of independence and SAR as a sign of a Negro finally getting his own. His costar at the Apollo that February was one of these.

According to the *Los Angeles Sentinel*, her name was "Oreatha Franklin," an understandable misspelling given Aretha's lack of exposure. The girl who would become the Queen of Soul was eighteen and had spent most of her life in the shadow of her father, the Reverend C. L. Franklin. Reverend Franklin was now one of the nation's best-known Negro preachers. More than seventy-five of his sermons were issued on record, and his church (where Sam and the QCs had lingered early on) was a stopover for every major gospel act in the country. Aretha had picked up her piano chording from James Cleve-

land and her vocal style—the throaty leaps and swoop:
Clara Ward, but it was Cooke who had captured her

She'd been thirteen when Sam's "Nearer to Thee"
the churches. According to Crain, Sam and Aretha ha
back "when they was still little children." Aretha was a round-faced
young girl who liked to cook and eat and have a good time, and she
thought Sam was "just beautiful: a sort of person who stood out
among *many* people." When Sam went pop, he'd tried to talk her
into joining him on duets, but the Reverend Franklin forbade it: "I
didn't want her to start out *too* young." Instead, beginning in 1957,
she'd toured with her father, the Davis Sisters, and a three-foot singing midget, Little Sammy Bryant, following the gospel highway
from Los Angeles to Philadelphia.

By early 1961, however, Aretha had signed a pop contract with
Columbia Records (based on demo recordings paid for by her father)
and was now making her first appearance at the Apollo. She was understandably nervous. Used to sitting behind a piano or standing still
in front of her father's choir, she had no idea how to move. Those first
few days of the run, she looked, in June Gardner's words, "like she'd
be falling over logs." Sam took her aside. He'd gone through this
same transition, trying to go from gospel to pop, uncertain about
how much and how to act onstage. "Now, baby. This is the way. This
would help," he coached her. "With Sam," Aretha has said, "it was
out-and-out admiration. . . . If he didn't capture everybody in a room,
they didn't have nothing going on. And sweetie, he wore a whole lot
of ladies down when he got married. He wore me down. Ooooh, I
loved him. I just loved him. That man could mess up a whole room-
ful of women!"

The other young act on the Apollo bill was Little Anthony and the
Imperials. The sweet harmony group out of Brooklyn had had major
hits with "Tears on My Pillow" and "Shimmy, Shimmy Ko-Ko-Bop."
Now, at the Apollo, Anthony was working on a song where he fell
to his knees and then, as he told author Ted Fox, "I went to my gospel roots and my emotion went into the audience, and it totally blew
the Apollo down." The Imperials called it simply "I'm Alright"; the
trouble was it had almost no lyrics except the title. One day during

the week's run, the owner of the Apollo took Anthony aside and said, "I got you some words. I want you to go down and practice with Sam. He's gonna put some words to it." In the basement of the theater, Cooke pulled out a little piece of paper and started jotting down lyrics: "When my baby holds me in her arms, I'm alright—I'm alright." Sam was taking gospel and—as he himself had done, as he'd influenced Aretha to do—was transferring it directly into pop. Where Little Anthony would later regret it—"We opened up a can of worms"—in fact, it had long since been opened.

This Apollo run, then, was a study in how gospel was taking over r&b. While Anthony dropped to his knees and Aretha tried hard not to stumble, Sam was busy selling his new single, "That's It—I Quit—I'm Moving On." A brassy, danceable number, it featured a rapid-fire, almost patter verse that Sam contrasted with the title line, which he sang with a full break between each phrase. It was a long way from "Sad Mood" or the sound Cooke was getting on SAR, but, for his live performance, Sam goosed up the tune, making sure June came down extra hard on the chorus breaks, turning it into a piece of soul theater. Debonairly dressed, banking his gospel fire in a way that drove his audiences wild, Cooke was by now as big a draw as the r&b circuit had.

On April Fools', after touring the South with Aretha, Sam brought his act back to New York, where he spent a week devastating a club called the Town Hill in Brooklyn. "It was just his presence," explains Jerry Brandt, a young white waiter at the club, "and his voice. And his phrasing and his music. And his body and his soul and his eyes and his vicious laugh!" Brandt would go on to be Sam's agent at William Morris, but at the time, he was just a kid infatuated with rock & roll and used to thinking of Sam Cooke in terms of his singles or his gentlemanly appearances on TV.

The Town Hill was an eye-opener. "They throwed them panties," S. R. Crain remembers. "That's just the way they do over there in Town Hill. Sam would catch them and just keep right on singing. And lay them down there. If he catched them for this lady and lay them down, smiling, then here come another! . . ." Afterward, the women would line up six deep to get into the dressing room, where

S.R. or Charles would be keeping watch. "Look like he ain't singing to nobody but me," one would say, "so I'd just like to tell him."

"Well," Crain would answer with that big smile that lit up his face, "a lot of men tell me that, too, child."

In the midst of all this, Sam continued to yearn for gospel music. During the Town Hill engagement, he announced to the *L.A. Sentinel* that he was planning to make his next LP "a deluxe limited edition of all-time favorite hymns and gospel songs with backing by a famous choir." The project sounds like the last, aborted spirituals session at Keen, and it, too, never came to pass. Instead, Sam "turned" gospel singers to the possibilities of rock & roll.

In mid-April 1961, he went into the studio to cut Johnny Taylor for SAR. In 1953, Taylor had replaced Sam as lead for the QCs. Four years later, he replaced Sam again, this time with the Stirrers. Cooke, says Taylor, "came and got me at 47th and Greenwood in Chicago," said he was leaving the quartet, and advised Taylor to take his place. "I trusted his judgment—and he was right." Johnny could "do" Sam Cooke the way Sam had done R. H. Harris. Now, in his first SAR session, Johnny was following Sam again. He cut two pop songs, including "Whole Lotta Woman," a funky tribute to how much female it takes to satisfy the singer's soul. Taylor wouldn't shake Cooke's shadow until his mid-sixties hits like "Who's Making Love," and even then he called his publishing company TAGS in honor of Cooke's KAGS. "We all loved him," says Taylor. "He was a beacon."

At the same session, Sam brought by a duet called the Sims Twins. The day he heard Bobby and Kenneth Sims on a gospel program, Cooke asked them to meet him at the California Club to see if they wanted to sing background on his new single. As they were talking, say the Sims, "he asked us did we want to know how we sound on a record. And we did." At the Taylor session, Sam ran down two songs for them. "Don't Fight It—Feel It" is a variation on an old seduction line: don't fight the feeling, baby, go with the music. Sam's inspiration for the second number, "Soothe Me," was, according to Lou Rawls, a comedy routine done by either Redd Foxx or Slappy White. It was a takeoff on a TV commercial, except the comic was talking about liquor, and the line that tickled Sam was "I drink this gin 'cause it's really smoo-ooth!" "Smooth," repeated over and over as Rawls and Cooke drove around L.A., turned into "soo-oothe"—and the song's hook was born. Sam was planning to cut it himself the next day, but he let the Simses hear themselves do it.

While Kenneth and Bobby start "Soothe Me" with a pretty good imitation of Sam's yodel, their voices soon turn rougher than anything Sam had yet tried on RCA. The tune moves along as a loping and joyous modified mamba and owes an enormous debt to Earl Palmer's goofy, offbeat drumming. At the end of each verse, Sam had the Simses put in the trick he'd been honing in live performances of "That's It": a stop/start that kicks the tune into the chorus with extra energy. Sam knew a smash when he heard it. Within a week, the Simses got a call from Cooke. "You cats hot!"

"Hot about what?"

"I put that song out," said Sam. "You cats burning up New Orleans."

The twins were amazed: "What song?"

The next day, Sam had the Simses and the same core musicians into RCA's studio. The difference was additional strings, horns, and the material, "Cupid," which, at first listen, sounds as far from "Soothe Me" as black from white. Back in New York, Hugo and Luigi had talked to Sam about writing a song for, in Alex's words, "this little girl on a show with Perry Como. . . . She didn't do anything but just look up at Perry Como in the most wistful-type manner." Cooke had put together a cute thing called "Cupid" and made a demo of it. Then they'd gone into Hugo and Luigi's office, but before they got the demo out of Alex's briefcase, the producers had them listen to the girl sing some other tunes. "Sam looked at me," Alex recalls, laughing, "and I said, 'Oh man!' We weren't gonna give her our song. I said to Luigi, 'This one's for Sam!'" The snag had been that Sam had another tour of the West Indies scheduled for mid-April, and if they wanted to cut it before, it would have to happen in Los Angeles. That suited Sam just fine, but Hugo was terrified of flying. Finally, Luigi agreed to come out alone.

This was Sam's first chance since his days at Keen to cut in L.A. with René Hall and the old gang of musicians. Creatore remembers making a point of getting all dressed up to meet the West Coast crew. Otherwise, he figured, there was liable to be some hard feeling: "You come in from out of town, and you're the enemy." So he'd slicked back his hair, put on his white shirt with the cufflinks, and worn a thin tie with a neat knot. "How are you? I'm Luigi. You're so-and-so; I've heard about you." Hall had a string section assembled, the whole bit, and the producer carefully worked the room. The only one missing was Sam.

Then the phone rang. "Luigi? Yeah, it's Sam. Look, I'm sorry, but I can't make the session. Something came up. Sorry you had to fly all the way out here."

"Oh," said Luigi, trying to keep his cool. "What are we going to do now? We got all these musicians." The band was looking at Luigi with a peculiar expression.

Then Sam stuck his head in the door, and everybody cracked up. As RCA's young engineer Al Schmitt recalls it, Cooke had gotten there early and, seeing Luigi hadn't arrived, slipped out to a pay phone. If it was all in good fun, it also managed to make clear whose turf this West Coast studio was—and wasn't.

Luigi's philosophy was "If you got the right song, and you got the right arrangement, and you got the right feeling in the studio, then you're a midwife. The baby is gonna come! . . . By the same token, if there's a breech, you gotta go in and fix it." Sam delivered "Cupid" after seven takes. René had a beautiful arrangement, opening with a French horn and adding a swirl of strings by the second verse. Earl Palmer clocked out a gentle cha-cha beat, and the whole rolled along in a groove with the Simses chorusing behind. Sam, as Al Schmitt recalls, almost always messed around a little with the arrangements. He'd press the guitarist into trying a different rhythm—"a little more in the pocket for the tune"—or ask the strings to cut out at the beginning. In this case, Sam added the novelty touch of making the sound of a loosed arrow—"ZZZZhhhttt!"—when the lyric called for it. It filled a hole with a sound that was bound to buzz the young radio listener.

For a tune originally meant as a sweet nothing, Sam sings "Cupid" with a surprising, understated intensity. It's almost shocking to hear his gospel growl on the last word in "hear me when I cry." But substitute the name of Jesus for Cupid, and you begin to see how Cooke got into the number. He is, after all, calling on a god's intervention. That it's a little pink baby instead of the Savior of the Holiness Church disappears by the end, where Sam riffs off murmuring how Cupid should help him—he's calling! It's a straight gospel plea.

Sam and Barbara left right after the session for his return engagement in the West Indies: again promoted by Steven Hill, again a sellout, with his shows in Jamaica, Montego Bay, and Trinidad bringing in more than $45,000 in advances. The culture shock was less this time around—more like a vacation—and, as it turned out, Barbara became pregnant again. The only cloud on the horizon was a political one: as Sam toured the islands, President Kennedy authorized a fourteen-hundred-man invasion of Cuba at the Bay of Pigs. The army of CIA-trained Cuban-American exiles was soundly defeated, and the politically aware Jamaicans may well have found some humor in Sam's latest hit, "That's It—I Quit—I'm Movin' On."

Back home, Cooke's next tour of one-nighters coincided with a new wave of violence in the civil rights movement. On May 4, the first busload of Freedom Riders left Washington to test the laws against segregated travel. Twenty-one-year-old John Lewis, trying to enter the whites-only waiting room in Rock Hill, South Carolina, cited his rights; the young hoods blocking his way replied, "Shit on that," and then beat him up. Ten days later, when one bus had reached Anniston, Alabama, a mob of angry whites shot out its tires and set it afire. The next day, in Birmingham, the police allowed a crowd of Klansmen with baseball bats and chains to beat on the Freedom Riders for fifteen minutes before they intervened. Attorney General Robert Kennedy requested a "cooling-off" period, but the Freedom Riders pushed into Mississippi, and the Confederacy was in an uproar.

Singer Jerry Butler, in the middle of a string of hits for Vee Jay, remembers Sam heading out to join student protests—quietly, without any fanfare. According to drummer June Gardner, "the civil rights guys would all come around Sam. . . . Everyone was aware of what was going on." In fact, Butler sees the soul singers as being "at the vanguard of the movement. . . . Young people like us, we were at A&T in Greensboro and Johnson: that whole corridor of black schools that starts at Baltimore. . . . The entertainers would go in with the kids," Butler continues, "because we knew better than anybody that it wasn't about money. It was about color. 'Cause we had the money!"

In those days, Butler adds, you could gauge the level of awareness by which direction the entertainers faced. At first, Negro singers playing mixed venues down South had to face the white audience. Then they'd tried playing to both: Butler remembers a whole concert spent singing to a wall, because he didn't want to offend either half of his audience. Finally, after talking it over with people like Sam and Jackie Wilson, Butler recalls their mutual decision: "Look, man: here are *our* people, who we got to turn our back on in order to sing to *those* people, because *they* don't want to sit with *our* people. . . . We're going to sing to our people! And if they want to see our faces, they'll bring their asses around to the other side!"

The other variation, as Johnnie Morisette recalls it, was concerts like the one in Amarillo, Texas, where "they wanted all whites to come in and no blacks. They didn't want no black in there!" The audience, which was going to be drawn largely from the nearby army base, refused to go along. "We love Sam Cooke," Johnnie remembers the white soldiers saying, "but we ain't coming in this show. 'Cause a lot of these guys on the base with us are our friends." And Cooke helped lead the boycott. "Sam was in the dressing room talking to the kids. I was in the car, ready to go—all ready to get away from that. But he was the type of dude . . . he had money and that made him have power, and he had prestige. I got out of there!"

Even as Sam grew more militant, he was still "singing to the wall" with some of his music—especially on the albums. In New York, he cut an LP called *My Kind of Blues* that was really *their* kind, from Irving Berlin's "The Song Is Ended" to "Nobody Knows You When You're Down and Out" to the well-sung but dispassionate "Since I Met You Baby."

Still, as Sam flew into Detroit to do a week at the Flame Show Bar, his influence was everywhere. The #1 r&b song that summer of 1961 was Ben E. King's "Stand by Me," a note-for-note plundering of a Cooke/Alexander arrangement of "Stand by Me, Father," done by Johnny Taylor and the Soul Stirrers two years earlier. "Cupid," mean-

while, had entered the r&b charts and would eventually reach
#20—#17 pop—his most successful single since "Chain Gang."

RCA suddenly discovered they had a star. Luigi recalls the day one
of the label's execs stopped him in the elevator and said, "You know,
we ought to have a lunch for Sam Cooke." Creatore, the industry operator, was horrified. "Don't do a lunch! We're doing fine. Let's not
get the whole thing—"

The naive exec interrupted, "But we have to do something. Do
you know he's selling second to Presley?"

Creatore fairly shouted, "I know that! I make the records! You
think I don't know what happens?"

Jess Rand jumped at the opening and began renegotiating a deal
that would bring Cooke a $30,000 bonus and a higher guarantee.
Rand also wrote an hour-long TV show called "Sam Cooke Phenomenon" that his friend Michael St. Angelo, produced on *PM East,*
hosted by Mike Wallace. Hugo and Luigi appeared, as did Rand, and
Cooke sang a dozen numbers. *Cash Box* called it "an unusual honor,"
but despite this success, he kept looking elsewhere. Thirty, with two
children at home and a third on the way, Sam told a reporter that
summer, "I want to sing, until I have enough money to invest in
something else. . . . When I get a little older, I'd like to leave the
singing to the younger fellows."

Those included his latest find for SAR, the Womack Brothers. Sam
had first heard them back in Cleveland when little Cecil was still
standing on fruit crates to reach the mike; now, Cecil was the only
brother who hadn't graduated high school. After Roscoe Robinson of
the Five Blind Boys recommended them, Sam quickly set up a session.
Poppa Womack only let it get that far because he figured Cooke, Alexander, and Crain would keep his children on the gospel track. But almost immediately, Sam started asking the boys about crossing over.
After the boys cut a Roscoe Robinson tune called "Somewhere There's
a God," Sam told Curtis Womack that for some reason it "pictured to
him in his heart" his first wife, Dolores. "Rerun the track," Sam said,
"and let me do it." His version was exactly the same, except he
changed it to "Somewhere There's a Girl." It would take a little while,
but Sam was grooming the Womacks to come over his way.

Meanwhile, he needed to keep making hits. In mid-August, Sam returned to the RCA studios in New York. (Even with "Cupid's" success, he hadn't convinced the label that he should be recording regularly in Los Angeles.) The first thing he did at the session was a nightclub version of the old blues tune "Frankie and Johnny." He was back to the string sound with an orchestra conducted by Stan Applebaum. "Feel It," on the other hand, was from the Sims Twins' session that had produced "Soothe Me." While Sam didn't shout quite the way he let the Simses, he jumped on the tune, only to discover even this taste of hard gospel had its consequences.

Not long after RCA released "Feel It," the manager of the Music Mart in Baltimore told *Billboard*, "The teeners like the rhythm and the beat, but the parents listen to the words, and they won't have the record in the house." The words in question come in the second verse: Sam tells his girl that when they're dancing close, and he starts to tease, if she feels like giving a squeeze, well, she shouldn't fight it. He then repeats "feel it" seven times, underlining it with a heavy bass drum. While he never says what "it" is that she should squeeze, he isn't singing with his innocent "Only Sixteen" voice. The *Billboard* article came complete with the sort of headline Sam's clean-cut, Ivy League image had been trying so hard to avoid: "Parents Rap Cooke Single." The record made it to #62, but after four straight Top Forty hits over the last year, that had to be a bit of a disappointment.

"Feel It," however, was just Sam's response to a changing market. He knew that a tune like "Cupid" was starting to appear a little tame—not to Ricky Nelson fans, maybe, but to the people buying Ray Charles's newest, "Unchain My Heart." He could see the change at his performances. Cooke headlined a show late in August at Chicago's Regal Theater. The "Recording All-Stars" show included the Drifters, their old lead singer Ben E. King, and the Olympics, among others. According to Purvis Spann, a Chicago dj who helped manage the Regal, the package was put together based on the fact that Cooke drew a more adult audience.

"If I put Sam Cooke on, kids wasn't going to break the door down to get to him," Spann observes. "I'd have to put maybe two groups on that would draw me the little teenager." To the young r&b crowd,

Cooke's desire to go nightclub was becoming obvious. At the same time, although Regal manager Herb Hopkins announced that booking agents would be reviewing the package to see about possible Las Vegas engagements, there was no avoiding the fact that Sam's older fans were overwhelmingly Negro: not exactly Vegas's idea of an audience. A major star, Sam was still in danger of being caught betwixt and between.

It wasn't that he *couldn't* produce a harder, more danceable hit: he was in the midst of proving that with the Sims Twins. On September 9, *Cash Box* noted that "Soothe Me" was hitting nationally, and Sam and Alex took out their first small ad, opposite a full-page one for Lou Rawls's debut single on Capitol. "Soothe Me" went to #25 r&b and hung in that area for a month or so. Then, instead of dropping off, as Sam's "Feel It" did, it started back up. At the end of its second month, it went to #13 r&b—then #4—and then it suddenly appeared on the pop charts, too.

Some of the credit for this long chart life has to go to Zelda Sands. Energetic and tough, she was dedicated to Sam: the only male in the business, she says, who ever helped her career. SAR's natural advantage, as Zelda puts it, was that Cooke "was like worshiped and adored among black people." Alexander, ever the businessman, adds that the industry figured Sam might record on SAR someday: a strong reason to treat the label well. But while that helped get the record into the radio stations, SAR had to do what every other independent did to get its stuff played. "You signed off for how many dollars you were going to pay, first," says Zelda. She worked the dj's and stayed on the distributors. At one point, Sam said to her, "Z-Z, I spoke to a couple of the guys, and they told me when you called to promote the record, you know, you used 'fuck' and all that. Is that true?" Zelda had never sworn in front of Sam; now she admitted, tentatively, that, yes, sometimes it was necessary to use a little profanity for the sake of the label. Sam fell out laughing. "Go, girl! Go!" "Soothe Me" stayed on the r&b charts for nearly six months, as well as making it to #42 on the pops, and Sam let Zelda redecorate the office in her favorite colors: orange and black.

Chapter 17

O n October 19, 1961, the Los Angeles County sheriff went to the offices of John Siamas's Rex Productions and took possession of seven cartons of tape recordings. Sam had won his royalties case against the Greeks to the tune of $11,000, and the two parties had agreed to a deal. Siamas would have a sheriff's sale of all Cooke's master recordings—everything from "You Send Me" to "Wonderful World"— and use the proceeds to settle. Plus, Sam and Alex were allowed to bid. Since the first $11,000 in proceeds went to them, they could get Sam's old hits for nothing and then resell them.

It was a clever little two-step, although when their lawyer, Sam Reisman, saw the seven dusty cartons, he was horrified. "Let's get our money," he told Alex, "and get the hell out of here!" But Cooke and Alexander had an idea what these boxes might be worth to the right people. If J.W. needed any further proof, Lew Chudd—owner of Fats Domino and Ricky Nelson's Imperial label—had sent a lawyer there to bid against him.

What had been an inside deal turned into an auction. However, once the price climbed to $13,000, Chudd's representative figured Alexander couldn't be using his own money—he must have RCA behind him—and dropped out. As Alex notes with a chuckle, he ended up buying all Cooke's past recordings on Keen for what amounted to a couple thousand dollars. Of course, the premise behind all this was that they could then turn around and sell the masters. The natural buyer was RCA: if they owned the Keen material, they could, for example, put out a greatest-hits LP. Or exploit the stuff however they wanted in combination with Sam's new recordings.

The trouble was that Alex couldn't get them interested. As far as RCA—and most of the industry—was concerned, rock & roll was about your latest hit. Who wanted a singer's old records when they had a contract for all his new ones? Alex and Sam played it very cool. First, they put a small piece in *Cash Box* late in November; it noted that KAGS had bought the masters, including some unreleased sessions. It also announced they'd be coming out on SAR. Then they sat back and waited.

While Alex fished for RCA, Sam went house-hunting. Barbara was due in the middle of December, and Leimert Place was too small. They found a house at 2048 Ames Street, up in the hills behind Hollywood in the Los Feliz area. It had a view out over the city, a marble bar inlaid with silver dollars, and a big swimming pool right by the driveway. Sam had a private rehearsal room built with full-length mirrors, and the previous owner, the Hollywood sound engineer Glen Glenn, had packed the place with audio equipment. According to Jess Rand, the house was sweetening in the new RCA contract he'd negotiated. Whether it was spelled out or not, it was certainly a direct result of Sam's string of hit records—and a star's home, at last. Not long after they closed, Barbara gave birth to the son they'd been hoping for; they named him Vincent.

Sam had blocked out a little time around the birth. He used some of it to go into the studio and cut a tune that, like "Cha Cha," commented on the dance craze of the moment. A year earlier, Chubby Checker had taken Hank Ballard's r&b tune "The Twist" and crossed it over to #1 pop. Now, to the amazement of the trade, adults had discovered the teen dance, and Checker was back on the charts with four singles and four LPs. Everybody was trying to cash in: Alan Freed had opened a Twist Room on New York's East Side, and Della Reese went so far as to produce a twist version of the gospel hit "99 and a Half Won't Do" for Hugo and Luigi. Sam was at home one morning watching the *Today* show on TV and noticed clips of New

York City's Peppermint Lounge filled with socialites swiveling their hips and grinning. "That gave me the idea," he later told a reporter. "I switched the set off, sat down, and wrote 'Twistin' the Night Away.'"

Instead of making a novelty record that just capitalized on the fad, Sam took advantage of being able to cut at home. He brought in René Hall's regulars and worked on "Twistin'"—and that cut alone—for a full three-hour session. The song opens with Earl Palmer doing the tune's signature rhythm: a four-beat roll that kicks the tune into gear. The horn section blows soul accents, and then Red Callender settles into a bass groove that's all about moving your hips. Eddie Beal's piano noodles behind, and the whole is sizzling before they've even reached the chorus. Then any doubt you're at a party disappears as a crowd starts clapping away at the downbeat. Cooke, meanwhile, rides the rhythm effortlessly, and while he doesn't go into any gospel pyrotechnics, his voice is rough with warmth and confidence: the sound of a man who knows a good time when he sees one.

Sam once told an interviewer that the key to his string of hits was "observation." Not his voice—not the melody or the beat—but observation. "Twistin'" is written from the point of view of an almost objective outsider. Over here, we have a man in evening clothes—hard to tell how *he* got into the party. His partner is some chick in slacks. Then there's the guy in blue jeans; he's dancing with someone Sam calls "an older queen." (If he isn't talking homosexual, it's a mighty odd choice of words, but he slides the observation into the mix, avoiding any chance of the sort of outcry he got with "Feel It.") Between verses of this inventory, the musicians shout out dances of the time: watusi, fly, and, of course, the twist. The fact that Sam could barely do any of them (had to be taught to twist by J.W. once it was time to sing the song on the road) didn't faze him in the slightest. This wasn't about Sam Cooke, except as a kind of reporter and guide to what was going down.

By the time RCA released "Twistin'," and *Cash Box* hailed the "sparkling, self-penned hand-clapper" as a pick of the week, Sam had already set out to duplicate it for SAR. He rented a studio at United Recording and had René assemble the same band. Then he wrote a tune for Johnny Morisette called "Meet Me at the Twistin' Place." To Morisette's ears, it sounded like the old spiritual "Meet Me at the Old Camp Ground" with a new beat. Johnny pulled out all his tricks: there's a spoken intro wondering where he could go to have a good time, then a heavy bass and Palmer kicking the drum while the chorus just keeps repeating "over at the twistin' place." Soon, everyone in the room is chiming in, and Johnny "Two-Voice" has jumped into his falsetto range for a gospel lick or two. As he fades out of the song, he goofs on the gospel tradition of a heavenly roll call ("I'll see my mother there!") by shouting who'll be at the Twisting Place: Caledonia, Della, Uncle Remus. SAR had Morisette's record out and an ad in *Cash Box* by the end of the month. It soon climbed to #18 r&b, #63 pop.

Meantime, Alex and Sam were upping the ante in their strategy to get RCA to buy Sam's old Keen masters. They took two unreleased tracks, "Just for You"/"Made for Me," and put out a single—or, more precisely, about five copies of a single. Then, Alex recollects with a laugh, he paid some promotion men to carry it to a few select radio stations. As 1962 began, *Cash Box* ran a small item that Disc Distributors was "riding high with Sam Cooke's 'Made for Me.'"

It was only a few mornings later, as Alexander was sitting eating breakfast, that RCA's West Coast promotions person came up to him, and she was burning mad. "J.W.! I busted my butt, trying to do everything for Sam and you—"

Alexander, nodding and grinning like it was all in good fun, said, "We ain't got no problem. Tell Bob Yorke [RCA executive] to give me a call; I'll kill it."

The prospect of other Sam Cooke songs competing against their own was too much for RCA: it bought the Keen masters from KAGS for the same $13,000 Alex and Sam had paid. They had managed to recoup what Keen owed them in back royalties—and then double it. Plus, they had the satisfaction of teaching RCA a lesson. That they didn't get any more for the back catalog, however, indicates that even Sam and Alex underestimated what these songs were really worth.

"Twistin' the Night Away" was another major success for Cooke, climbing to #9 pop and becoming the #1 r&b record. Now, RCA wanted him to make an album to go with it, and Sam got the label to agree to record it in Los Angeles with the same crew. Luigi flew out for four days in February. With René Hall leading, they cut some pure nods to the craze—remakes they called "Twistin' in the Kitchen with Dinah," "Twistin' in the Old Town Tonight," and "Camptown Twist." Most of these were head arrangements: Earl Palmer and Cliff White knew Sam well enough to wing it, as did the two saxes—Plas Johnson and Jewell Grant—and they managed to give these old melodies new life. Sam also did a few originals, including "A Whole Lotta Woman," cut earlier by Johnny Taylor for SAR, and "Movin' and A'Groovin'," cowritten with Lou Rawls. On the latter, Cooke finally comes clean: it seems his girl only wants to dance, and, in order to keep her, he has to learn. Which is a lot more likely than the Reverend's son teaching the world how to twist.

Nearly all the pop material Sam had recorded up until now had had a subtle sexuality. He'd used his pretty-boy voice to croon the girls his way. On the twist LP, he lets loose a tougher side he hadn't shown since gospel days. Bassman Ray Pohlman, for one, thought part of it was working with a live band Sam trusted. "We're playing against each other. It's like a stage play: everybody does their bit, does their line. When there's a singer, you play to support the singer. And he sings to you! It's call-and-response. That's gospel."

Sam added his version of the Sims Twins' hit "Soothe Me" (*still* on the r&b charts at the time), letting his voice go rough as Rawls eggs him on in the background. Last, Cooke included a song that really does sound like his kind of blues—unlike the earlier, East Coast album. "Somebody Have Mercy" is full of tried-and-true lines— "going down to the bus station with a suitcase in my hand"—that can be traced all the way back to Blind Lemon Jefferson. Sam sets them to a soul horn riff, and there's even a harmonica solo in the break; the whole thing wails with memories of Clarksdale and cotton. Sam had spent four years making middle-of-the-road albums in order to break the LP charts, but it was this dance album that ended up being the first to succeed since the "You Send Me" LP.

Far from fading away, rock & roll was expanding. In the first part of 1962, the record business had generated more than half a billion dollars, and RCA's earnings were a record-breaking $14 million: up nearly 25 percent from the end of 1961. Given these flush times and his track record, Sam finally persuaded his label to let him record regularly in L.A. Now he let loose.

On April 26, he cut both sides of what would turn out to be one of his most important singles. It was nine at night when Cliff began the first tune with a twangy Latin intro echoed by a ten-piece string section. Then Sam—the observer again—starts to describe another party, and he's got all the details right. The Cokes are in the icebox, the popcorn's on the table, and the dj's playing requests: "Soul Twist" (by r&b saxophonist King Curtis) and Barbara George's "I Know." A verse into the tune, Cooke has managed to evoke a generic, nonthreatening, middle-American teen dance. But by the time the chorus has been repeated a few times, with everyone in the room joining in—J.W., Lou Rawls, the musicians—the party sounds like it's moved somewhere across the tracks, far from the rec room.

That's impossible, of course—it's either a Negro party or a white one—except that rock & roll was now proving that contradiction a reality. Millions of white teenagers were dancing to Sam's music and beginning to adopt some of Bronzeville's mannerisms and attitudes. Later covers of "Having a Party" would be rave-ups, unconditional dance jams like the version by the New Jersey bar band Southside Johnny and the Asbury Jukes. Sam doesn't read it that way. There's a bittersweet feel both to the melody and to his vocal, as the lyrics call up an American teen dream even as the voice places us outside it, looking in. No wonder they had to do thirteen takes before Sam was satisfied; beneath the surface of the simple little pop tune lay a whole nation of contradictions.

By the time they got set to cut the B-side, it was getting late, although, as Cliff White recalls, no one was feeling much pain. Sam had brought in "a couple of jugs, you know? And these guys got full of that yocky-dock, man! And by the time they got around to doing this song, I think that was one of the things that gave it its flavor. . . ."

The passionate plea of "Bring It On Home to Me" was outside Sam's established pop range, and he'd actually tried to give the tune

Sam with
Jess Rand.
(COLLECTION
JESS RAND)

On the set of
The Patsy, with
Sammy Davis, Jr.,
and unidentified.
(COLLECTION
ANDY ALLEN)

Sam, George McCurn, René Hall, J.W., Lou Rawls. (PHOTO CLIFF WHITE)

Lou Rawls, Sam Cooke,
and friend, on the street.
(PHOTO CLIFF WHITE)

At the office.
(COLLECTION JESS RAND)

The RCA star.
(AUTHOR'S
COLLECTION)

Backstage, Cincinnati, fall 1960: unidentified; S.R.; Cliff; unidentified; Sam; unidentified; June Gardner; Linda Cooke; unidentified; Tracey Cooke; Barbara.
(COLLECTION S. R. CRAIN)

Relaxing at home, circa 1961. (COLLECTION ANDY ALLEN)

Aretha Franklin and Sam on
tour in Atlanta, spring 1961.
(PHOTO CLIFF WHITE)

Sam at a pop session with the
Soul Stirrers, January 1964:
Leroy Crume, guitar; Foster;
Sam; unidentified; Crain; Farley.
(PHOTO CLIFF WHITE)

"I got a big ego!"
Pre-Copa, June 1964.
(AUTHOR'S COLLECTION)

At Comiskey Park show,
August 1964.
(*CHICAGO DEFENDER*)

The Hacienda Motel, the night after the shooting. (*SEPIA* MAGAZINE)

Lisa Boyer. (COLLECTION
ANDY ALLEN)

Bertha Franklin.
(COLLECTION ANDY ALLEN)

The funeral in L.A. (*CHICAGO DEFENDER*)

At Forest Lawn. (AUTHOR'S PHOTO)

away to his buddy Dee Clark. Clark had made his rep as a shouting
Little Richard sound-alike, but when Cooke had offered him "Bring
It On Home" one night backstage in Atlanta, Dee had turned it
down—maybe because he'd just had his biggest hit ever with the
milder pop tune "Raindrops." So now Sam cut it himself with his
slightly tipsy band.

"Home" opens with Ernie Freeman playing a bluesy piano, then
the drums strike up a high-hat beat, and Sam enters harmonizing on
an urgent vocal. The lyrics are a plea for forgiveness, which for
Cooke—perpetually smiling, apparently unwilling to talk about his
problems—was a stretch. His fans weren't used to Mr. Cool admitting that though he laughed when she left, he'd only hurt himself.
Not since Soul Stirrers days had Sam arranged a call-and-response
structure this powerful, and he hadn't sounded this committed since
sharing leads with Paul Foster. The whole drunken room may have
been singing, but it's Sam and Lou who are locked into each other,
trading "yeas" as in the good old days. Sam wasn't "The Man Who
Invented Soul," as RCA titled a posthumous album; he would have
been the first to point out that no one person invented what he'd
grown up with. But "Bring It On Home to Me" is one of the defin-
ing examples of what was about to be identified as "soul" music. And
the basis of the sound laid down in RCA's Studio 1 that midnight is
easy to identify: it's Sam Cooke and Lou Rawls singing directly to
Sister Flute.

The more soulful, powerful sound of Sam's new single was partly
in response to his competition: James Brown was riding "Night
Train," his biggest hit so far, and in early May, Ray Charles's "I Can't
Stop Loving You" reportedly sold more than a million records in
three weeks. But these successes, in turn, reflected a change on the
street.

The day after and not far from where Sam cut "Having a Party"/
"Bring It On Home to Me," two white officers of the Los Angeles
Police Department stopped a car and questioned the two Negroes inside. Both were Black Muslims. When one raised his arm to "motion
the officers not to search without a warrant," the cop hit him with a
flashlight, and when that brought another man out of the nearby

mosque, the cops shot him dead. They then began a random search, tearing coats, ripping pants up the back, and shouting "nigger" this and "nigger" that.

The *Los Angeles Sentinel* described it as a "police Muslim riot." When a young leader of the Nation of Islam flew out from New York, his words were considerably tougher. The police "want only killed and shot Muslim members," Malcolm X told the press conference at the Oasis Club on South Main. In a cold precise voice, he defended his religion, arguing that Muslims weren't anti-integration: "The white man is. He's mad because we told him to keep what he had and we'll make it on our own."

For most of L.A.'s Negro community, this kind of police brutality was nothing new; certainly, Sam knew it. Johnnie Morisette recalls the night, around this time, when he and Cooke were out driving. The cops "just walked up and started with any black during those days. You didn't have to be doing nothing. We were out on 68th and Central, and these two county sheriffs came up. White. And called us some old foolish name—'Shithead!' I never will forget that. And Sam was gonna fight the police! They found out he was Sam and they let us alone." The harassments, the constant pull-overs and questionings, were commonplace. What was different about the "police Muslim riot" was the degree of open resistance shown by men like Malcolm X. Cooke was keenly interested. You could hear it in his music, even before he got to know Malcolm.

"Having a Party"/"Bring It On Home to Me" quickly turned into a two-sided smash. First, "Party" hit the pop charts, rising to #17 and charting through the summer of 1962; then "Home" climbed even higher, to #13, and stayed over a month. Both took off in r&b: "Home" to #2 and "Party" going to #4 with the single keeping Sam on the r&b charts for four and a half months. He had the magic touch now, and it made him even more insistent that his gospel acts cross over and reap some of the benefits. "That's the move," he kept telling the young Womack brothers. "That's the right move!" Laughing, Sam told the boys to think about his big house on Ames Street and the driveway full of cars the next time they recorded: "That'll make you sing real hard!" Finally, it worked. Poppa Womack's sons came home to Cleveland one day and announced they were going to sing pop. "I ain't never seen him cry before," Curtis Womack remembers, "but he was then."

They cut a single "in about two hours," according to Bobby Womack, "with just a guitar and a piano." It was exactly the same two tunes as SAR #123, except this time they called themselves the Valentinos—and they sang "Somewhere There Is a God" Sam's way, calling it "Somewhere There's a Girl." For the traditional "Couldn't Hear Nobody Pray," they kept the rocking arrangement, Alex put a little more emphasis on the beat, and Zelda's lyrics transformed it into "Lookin' for a Love." It would reach #8 on the r&b charts, as well as breaking into the Top 100 pop.

In early July, Sam took some of his profits from all this success and bought into a "real" business: a brewery run by one Herbert C. Cook (no relation). Sam was made president of the renamed Cooke's Beer, Inc., and the plan was to use him in all the advertising. "Westcoasters," wrote a *Sentinel* reporter, "are admiring Sam's business acumen. . . ." The problem was, as Alex puts it, "they were a bunch of crooks. . . . Not Mafia-related or anything, but con men." A month after Sam got involved, the Baltimore headquarters of Cooke's Beer was the scene of a numbers raid. Eight cops turned the place upside down in a search so thorough they made the employees take off their shoes and socks. "They treated us like dirt," Herbert Cook told the papers, and he vowed to file a complaint. But Sam had had enough. If this was going legit, he'd stick to the record business.

Sam loved money, loved the feel of a roll in his pocket, loved unpeeling a bill and shrugging off the thank-yous when he gave it away. On Johnnie Morisette's birthday, Cooke shook him out of a sound sleep to surprise him with the key to a red-and-gold 1961 Cadillac. "He gave my wife more furs than he gave his own!" says Crain. And Cooke was especially generous to his old gospel friends. "The first five-hundred-dollar bill I ever had," June Cheeks told author Anthony Heilbut, "Sam gave it to me." Cheeks was one of many; to Cliff White, it seemed like Cooke was helping every gospel act on the road.

On the other hand, he could afford to. Sam was on a roll now, with SAR doing great, his own two-sided hit, and plans for his first European tour in the fall. Then, just as he seemed to be firing on all cylinders, the word went out that he was dying.

The first published notice may have been in Gertrude Gibson's *Los Angeles Sentinel* column of August 2, 1962, where she mentions the "false rumor . . . of an incurable disease." By the middle of that month, it had spread nationwide. Washington's Negro paper, the *Afro*, was flooded with calls that ranged from "Is Sam Cooke dying?" to "I just heard Sam Cooke is dead." The paper denied the rumors, but it did no good. Soon calls were coming in every ten minutes. Finally, the paper got in touch with Sam's agency. Jerry Brandt—the kid who had been waiting table at the Town Hill in Brooklyn—had worked his way up to where he and Roz Ross were handling rock & roll for William Morris.

"Hi, Jerry," the reporter began. "This is Chuck Stone of the *Washington Afro* and I'm calling you about—"

"No, Sam Cooke's not sick, he's not dying, and everything is fine with him." Brandt laughed off the story but was clearly tired of the calls. "He's got leukemia like I've got leukemia. He'll be around collecting his money for the next 10 years."

Sam was back in Los Angeles when the story broke, and while he and Barbara took in their usual round of clubs and parties, he made a point of being seen and photographed in good health. But the leukemia rumor kept expanding: now Sam was dying and had left his eyes to Ray Charles. There was nothing to do but keep denying it; still, it gave Cooke the creeps. In the Clarksdale of Sam's infancy, there were whispers that pacts with the devil—strange midnight transactions—gave people unearthly artistic power. This was like some modern version of that payback.

Late in August, as "Having a Party" dropped off the Top Forty, Sam went into RCA's L.A. studios to cut another single. "Nothing Can Change This Love," a lush, slow blues, used every instrument in the twenty-two-piece orchestra. Sam's voice, by this time, sounds permanently roughened from the years of live shows, and it adds a touch of experience to the vocals: something he couldn't deliver for his Billie Holiday covers four years before. Eddie Beal drips some slow piano, Cliff takes a little guitar solo, but mostly it's Sam promising adult-sounding fidelity over a bank of strings. The song would spend two months on the pop charts, reaching #12—and do even better r&b: #2 and on the charts for three months. For the flip side, he chose "Somebody Have Mercy," the bluesy workout he'd cut for the "Twistin' " LP. It went to #3 r&b, but it was ill-timed. In the opening line, Sam plaintively asks somebody to tell him what's wrong with him. To much of Negro America, it read as a clue; the answer, of course, was leukemia.

Late that summer, he did a seventeen-day tour with Little Eva (whose "Loco-motion" had gone to #1). As they traveled the Deep South, lynch mobs were surrounding SNCC offices in Greenwood, Mississippi, movement supporters' homes were being shot at, and, in ten days in August, five rural Negro churches were burned down. President Kennedy called the actions "outrageous": his strongest statement to date.

Sam passed through this violence an increasingly popular and prominent figure. In mid-September, RCA released a greatest-hits LP. If the label's executives had had any doubt about their purchase of Keen's back catalog, this record dispelled them. With everything from "You Send Me" to "Bring It On Home to Me," the yellow album with Sam's smiling face on the cover reached #22—his second LP in a row to break the Top 100—and it stayed on the charts for an extraordinary run of nine months. Then, in early October, Sam left behind this strange mix of fame, violence, and premonitions of death for a short tour of England.

His co-headliner was Little Richard, already curiously intertwined in Cooke's career. It had been Richard's success at Specialty that had given Bumps the chance to try to cut pop with Sam. And back in 1957, in the same *Los Angeles Sentinel* column where Gertrude Gibson had announced that "You Send Me" looked like "a solid hit," she'd also noted that Little Richard had come into her office carrying a Bible and "not only looks different and talks different but acts different. . . ." For the next five years, Little Richard had taken the shout he'd appropriated from Marion Williams back into the gospel field. It was as if Sam and Richard had passed each other going opposite directions. Now, British promoter Don Arden had brought them back together for what was billed as a British rock & roll tour. Richard, however, assumed he'd be singing spirituals; he brought along sixteen-year-old organist Billy Preston, a gospel prodigy, as an accompanist.

As author Charles White describes the first date, October 8, 1962, in Doncaster, England, Richard came out "in a long religious-type robe to the sobbing organ of Billy Preston, and began to sing religious songs 'Peace in the Valley' and 'I Believe.' " The crowd was disappointed, and the promoter panicked. When Sam, delayed by fog, arrived for the second show, the promoter took him aside and begged him to talk some sense into Richard. Alex interrupted, "Look, if I know this guy right, he's a competitor. Don't need anyone else to say anything to him. Sam'll just go out there and he'll kill that audience. Richard'll come out and take care of himself." Cooke closed the first half of the show with a wild, extended "Twistin'." Little Richard came on after intermission in an all-white, gospel-looking suit. The promoter held his breath. Then Richard tore into "Long Tall Sally" and never looked back. In Brighton, they had to hold the bus an hour as the crowd pressed to get at the stars. In Mansfield, Richard danced on the piano during "Lucille," then fell to the floor as if dead, only to rise again singing "Tutti Frutti."

The two stars got along famously, and the tour sped by. "So fast," Sam told a British reporter, "I don't get a chance to see as much of England as I want to. . . . I can see myself going back home and people asking, 'What's London like?' And I'll have to say, 'I don't know—we didn't stop long enough!' " Despite the pace of one-nighters, Sam and his band kept a fine eye for social detail. The British thing, as Cliff White puts it, "is more class than the business of color," like the night there was a big dinner, and the stars were invited, but the band members weren't. Sam and the others immediately recognized it as the equivalent of "whites only" and decided, in Crain's words, that "class distinction is worse than segregation. . . . [The British] got these stations and nobody trespasses down or up."

They all ended up feeling a little out of place, a little lonely. Some of the guys managed to meet women, but not often. At their first hotel, they'd had some guests up to the suite, and, in Alex's words, "we were challenged so we moved out." Night after night, they found themselves with full pockets and no one to party with. Sam began working on a song about it.

In West Liverpool, Cooke played a date with ex-vaudevillian Sophie Tucker. There he heard a regional hit, "Love Me Do," by a local band called the Beatles. They were huge Little Richard fans and persuaded their hero to do a couple of extra dates with them at the end of the tour. (Richard eventually called Art Rupe from Liverpool to try to get him to sign the kids—saying they could imitate anybody—but cover artists had never interested Rupe.)

Toward the end of the tour, news came from America that President Kennedy had demanded the Russians remove their missiles from Cuba or face the possibility of an atomic strike. In his first fourteen months in office, Kennedy had avoided taking the lead on the civil rights issue, but he'd added $9 billion to a defense budget that was already half of everything the nation spent. Now, as the crisis deepened, all U.S. military commands went on full alert for the first time since the Korean War. "Little Richard went and prayed for about twelve hours!" June Gardner remembers, laughing, but at the time, Sam and the rest of them felt a long, long way from home.

Sam returned to the States in time to catch the end of the Womacks' run at the Apollo. Earlier in the summer, the group had complained they weren't getting good enough gigs, despite their hit "Looking for a Love." So, Sam had given them a little cash, told them to get themselves a car, and had set up an East Coast theater tour. Curtis remembers "gospel-rockin' " the Apollo, using the hang time in the middle of "Looking for a Love" to come forward, in June Cheeks style, and get the house. Bobby, on the other hand, would later tell *Black Music* magazine, "First thing that happened after we checked in the Cecil Hotel . . . we ran into this white chick. Now dad had always warned us about white women, but we were feeling pretty big, being in New York. . . ." By the end of the run, "we hadn't eaten in three days and were so sick from the clap we could hardly sing."

The crowd probably didn't notice, given the headliner that week, the outrageously talented James Brown. James and Sam had always been, in Johnny Morisette's words, "more or less butting heads." Now, Cooke got a chance to watch Brown's explosive, stripped-down display of soul, driven by an incredibly tight horn section and punctuated by James's moans, screams, shrieks, and smears. If Cooke's live show was a variation on the Baptist preacher, Brown's was based on the supplicant. "Try me!" he'd yell and drop to his knees to beg. Against the advice of almost everyone, Brown had pooled his own money and decided to record that week's show on an album to be called *Live at the Apollo.* It would eventually reach #2, staying on the charts for more than a year and a quarter, and to many it became the definitive live soul recording. As Sam watched from the wings, he couldn't have known how phenomenally influential and successful James's album would be—but he knew a challenge when he heard one.

Two weeks later, it was Sam's turn at the Apollo. He'd already made a major addition to his live act: a driving backup band called the Upsetters. They'd come out of Houston with Little Richard and established themselves, in Richard's words, as "the rockinest group on the road at the time." Well-dressed, sharply choreographed, the Upsetters had their own crowd-pleasing act, but they excelled as a backup band with an especially tight horn section led by Grady Gaines on tenor. By this point, as the Upsetters' manager, Henry Nash, puts it, Sam had a "basic format" that he varied depending on the crowd. "If the audience was swaying with him, he would just drop hits on you. And then you could tell when he was fishing—when he was searching, seeking. . . ."

At the Apollo that November, with the Upsetters pushing up the level of performance, Sam invited women out of the audience to twist with him or sat on the edge of the stage as he wailed through "Bring It On Home to Me." It was more polished, if no less calculated, than Brown's act, and featured many more pop hits. (Brown's break in that market, "Pappa's Got a Brand New Bag," was still three years away.) It was also adjustable; a week after the Apollo, Sam took a modified version of this sophisticated soul onto *The Tonight Show with Johnny Carson.*

In England, Sam had watched Little Richard devour a crowd. He'd written a song based on Richard's catchphrase "Well alright!" He had begun touring with Richard's old backup band, and now Sam went into the studio to recut one of Richard's hits. Back in 1956, Bumps Blackwell and Art Rupe had arranged "Send Me Some Lovin'" as a slow grind with Richard's own banged piano, a vocal that seemed to echo Red Tyler's sax, and a simple horn figure repeating in the background. The song had gone to #3 r&b, based largely on Richard's grunts, moans, and falsetto shrieks; it sounds like a man humping his way to heaven.

Sam's version is considerably lighter. Arranger Harold Ott supplies strings instead of horns, and Ray Johnson's piano is jazzier than Richard's. A white chorus opens, singing the title phrase in bland, angelic voices, and Sam answers them with a lazy hum. As he glides through the number, Cooke riffs off the chorus, using it as a gentle reminder of the old hit. Little Richard—like James Brown—could shout anybody under the table. Here, Cooke makes an argument that he, in contrast, could smooth you into submission. It's no less a grind— only a tad slower and a whole lot creamier.

Everyone in the studio could hear it was a hit, and Sam smiled that smile, as Jess Rand's wife used to say, "like a Christmas tree." The single would go to #13 pop and become Sam's sixth straight to reach r&b's Top Four. As 1962 ended, Cooke could look back on a year filled with triumphs. So, why was he so restless?

Chapter

18

"He was a happy dude," says Johnnie Morisette—and that was the impression a lot of people had of Sam. Life seemed to pop off his fingertips, and they swarmed to be around his easy, reassuring charm. Then, toward the end of 1962, Johnnie says, "They put that jacket on him. That's when he started changing. . . . They said he had leukemia; the public, over the radios. He was dying of leukemia. He started drinking a lot more. Because people were always asking. They used to ask me, ask different people in the band. . . ." J.W., for one, was getting angry about it. After telling the papers Sam was in perfect health, that the lyrics on "Somebody Have Mercy" were pure coincidence, that Sam was not willing his eyes to Ray Charles, he called the rumor "one of the meanest and lowest canards I've witnessed during many years in show business and public life."

But the restlessness was more than that. Cooke had always wanted to be bigger—the biggest—but somehow he'd never managed to get over to the public what he was capable of doing. At the beginning of December, he announced he was signing a one-year contract as an a&r man with Scepter Records. All he ever actually did with the label was produce a couple of album cuts for the Shirelles, but his former William Morris agent Paul Cantor had come over to Scepter, according to the label's owner, Florence Greenberg, "because he expected to manage Sam Cooke." Cooke's association with Scepter should have been a signal—to Jess Rand and CA—that he was, once again, "not a happy boy."

Before the end of the year, Sam recorded another middle-of-the-road album called *Mr. Soul*. With Harold Ott arranging and René Hall conducting a large string section, the LP fell somewhere between Ray Charles's *Modern Sounds in Country and Western Music* and its main competition on the previous year's LP charts, the sound track from *West Side Story*. Although on cuts like the confident "Cry Me a River" and Charles Brown's "Driftin' Blues," he was as cool as Ernie Freeman's piano playing, as hip as the former bop player Red Callender's bass, the LP was mostly good taste with only occasional flashes of feeling.

Still, few questioned Sam's right to the *Mr. Soul* title. In Detroit, Berry Gordy was smoothing out church harmonies while accenting the beat, a lot as Sam had. It brought Motown crossover hits like the Miracles' "You Really Got a Hold on Me," which author Smokey Robinson says was inspired by "Bring It On Home to Me." Motown worked seemingly endless variations on the pattern with a final goal—like Cooke's—of taking it to the nightclubs. The young Otis Redding, on the other hand, appeared to want to *be* Sam. Otis had been a sixteen-year old down in Georgia when "You Send Me" hit. Now, his first single, "These Arms of Mine," tried to merge the sounds of Little Richard and Sam. Redding adored Cooke's style, his independence, and his songwriting. During his too brief career, Otis would cover five Cooke-related tunes, including "Cupid" and "Chain Gang."

Before Christmas, Sam managed to squeeze in a SAR session with Johnnie Morisette doing a version of Albert King's "Don't Throw Your Love on Me So Strong." "Sam loved blues singers," Johnnie recalls: Wynonnie Harris, B. B. King, Charles Brown. This tune has Two-Voice full of deep chuckles and shouts, wailing for Johnny "Guitar" Watson to "take it in the alley!" But Sam's restlessness needed something more than the blues, something other. After Morisette had headlined a Christmas party at L.A.'s Nitelife, Sam flew East. He called his agent and friend Jerry Brandt at William Morris. "You ever been to a gospel show, Jerry?" Brandt hadn't.

"You're going New Year's Eve." "Holy shit!" Brandt remembers responding, "Why you doin' gospel?"

It was a perfectly reasonable question. Here was a man who'd long since left the gospel highway with its crummy sound systems and its bologna sandwiches. Brandt didn't know Sam had been talking with Leroy Crume about cutting with the Stirrers—or that he'd been dropping in on programs around the country—or that he'd produced an R. H. Harris session for SAR. While Cooke loved the money and the excitement and the special treatment that came with rock & roll, there was a part of him that always missed gospel, a part of him that thought no theater in the world could ever compare with a packed church on a good night. Sure, it was something to have the little girls scream at "Send Me Some Lovin'," but Sam had heard Sister Flute fall flat out—and not just because he was cute, but because his voice helped bring the Living Spirit down onto the earth.

His appearance that New Year's Eve in Newark wasn't a drop-in. He was an announced special guest on an all-star package that included the Dixie Hummingbirds, the Swanee Quintet, the Caravan Singers, and, of course, the Soul Stirrers. When Brandt arrived with his wife, they found themselves the only white people in the place. Outside were ambulances; inside, roaming the aisles, nurses in white uniforms.

"All of a sudden," the William Morris man recalls, "the show begins, the Soul Stirrers go on, and they bring out Sam. And the house comes down! And he's singing a duet with this lead singer of the Soul Stirrers which becomes who's better than who: who's the king here. And they exchange lines like you never seen in your life; each one trying to top the other one! It's hitting this pitch, and Sam is taking off, and I look around, and I see, right next to me almost, this woman stands up, gives a big shake, and goes out! Lands on the floor, stretcher comes, put her on it, take her out. I say to my wife, 'I think she just came.' She thinks it's God that's in her soul, but this chick just had an orgasm that popped!"

There it was. Brandt—devout rock & roller, the kid who'd watched the panties fly at Town Hill—saw sex. Sister Flute—forgiving Cooke as his voice poured through "Touch the Hem of His

Garment" and "Nearer to Thee"—felt the Spirit. And in the middle stood Sam, about to turn thirty-two, doing what he did best and wondering where it possibly fit in. "Hey man," Sam used to say to Jess Rand, "there's a lot you don't know about me." It was more complicated than a divided soul. It was shades of white and shades of black. Three weeks after cutting a syrupy ballad album, he was turning the church out wailing a gospel lead. Ten days later, his restless drive to show the public what he could do took him into the Harlem Square Club in Miami to cut a live recording of his soul act.

Sam had some precedents—Ray Charles had cut "In Person" back in 1959; Jackie Wilson had recorded his show at the Copa—but not many. At this time, January 1963, James Brown's King label still hadn't released *Live at the Apollo*, but Sam had seen it being cut and could smell the time was right. By the end of the year, a live single by twelve-year-old Little Stevie Wonder, "Fingertips—Pt 2," would top the pop charts, and Trini Lopez's live version of "If I Had a Hammer" would go Top Ten, as well.

It was Sam's idea to use the Harlem Square Club in North Miami. "It was like, just a big dance hall," Luigi recalls, set in the midst of the ghetto, and Sam knew the management well enough to arrange for the session. It was Saturday night, date night, and soon the room was filled to its two-thousand-seat capacity. Sam's intention wasn't to do anything special: just his regular show, adjusted a little, as June Gardner recalls, "according to the audience." In an open shirt, with a smile for the crowd and a sharp, commanding look for the band, Sam waded out through Miami's good-timers as the announcer introduced him as "Mr. Soul."

"Okay, Cliff," he signaled his bandleader, and the group (which included the King Curtis Band) cut into a slightly raggedy vamp. Cooke pulls it together by repeating, "Don't fight the feeling." The tune was his least successful single in years, and he gives it prominence here as if to say, "Hey, fuckers! All my records are hits; you just missed this one." But more important, as he rides June's high-hat beat, "Feel It" becomes the perfect intro for the soul sermon he's going to preach that evening.

Reverend Cooke begins his service by reading the lesson: "Make you groove right when you feel the feelin'!" Does the congregation understand? "Oh yea!" Are they sure? "Oh yea!" Fine; then let us proceed to examine what "groove right" means through a number "designed to make you feel good." "Chain Gang" expands on the text, taking it back into a shared history of men in chains walking red fields. Sam's voice is slightly hoarse—a voice used to shouting— and he turns it loose on the last word of "sun going down," till it corkscrews through the crowd. Again, he has them singing back to him and lets loose his low, gospel chuckle as if to acknowledge who's in control here. The live version of "Cupid," that "very nice, little song," pulls King Curtis's sax farther forward. The short, seemingly tossed-off gospel fade-out from the record gets underlined with soul horns and worked into the body of the tune. All Sam really has to do is scat a bit, a rough version of his yodel—"ya ya ya"—to move the crowd in the direction of the main subject of the sermon: love.

"Fellows—I want to tell you," he preaches during "It's Alright," "—when someone comes and tells you what your girlfriend has done or your wife has done, I want you to remember one thing," and the deliverance is all in the way his rough voice rises to the ceiling. Without a break, he slides into "I Love You (For Sentimental Reasons)" and gets the couples swaying and singing together on the bridge. Now that the crowd's deep in the groove, Sam and the band bring them to the act itself—or as close as they can get in a club. "Twistin' " is driven by horn punches and Curtis's gut-bucket sax solo, and before it ends, in a flurry of gunshots from June's drums, the crowd has its handkerchiefs out and waving in the overheated room.

The form is straight gospel: the little bits of advice between numbers, the handkerchiefs, the chorded segues from tune to tune so the mood continues to build. But the content is secular: that "good loving" which, years later, Marvin Gaye would call "something like sanctified." Raw-voiced, interspersing his gospel laugh, repeating and bending phrases, Cooke does a version of "Somebody Have Mercy" that calls up the healing power of sex, maybe even love. "I don't know what it is," he calls to the crowd, "but I feel good!" And then in a brief aside, as the band cooks behind him, he takes a swipe at that blue thing that's been following him around: "I ain't got leuke-mia! That ain't it!"

Now this other spirit—this body-driven but holy spirit—is in the room. If Sam knows the difference between this and what happens to Sister Flute, he's bleeding the borders. "S-s-s-something starts to move down inside me," he announces, duplicating the Holiness stut-ter he's heard from a hundred preachers in a thousand meetings. It's time to testify, and he does it with his first and still biggest hit. At the Harlem Square Club, on a Saturday night five years after it changed his life, "You Send Me" gets turned back into a gospel moan—almost tuneless—taking the listeners back to before words. Sam ends the tension (he still isn't singing, really; he's holding the crowd in the air between songs) with a holy chuckle and a sustained a-a-a-ah that sounds uncannily like Blind Boy Clarence Fountain.

"Bring It On Home to Me" is the release, the equivalent of what a New Orleans band does on the way back from the burying ground. The congregation/crowd takes Lou Rawls's part and calls "yeas" back at Sam till it becomes almost too much to bear, and he starts a gospel shout, heading out into the unknown—then catches himself. "I bet-ter leave that alone."

Finally, there's the promise that "Nothing Can Change This Love," the vision of hope and heaven that closes the service, where Sam ar-gues love lasts whether or not she brings it on home. "I don't wanna quit," Sam calls to the crowd—as James Brown called to the crowd, as Paul Foster and Claude Jeter and Dorothy Love Coates would call to the crowd when the spirit had them—"but looks like I got to go!" And he finishes with the moral of the whole sermon, the evening's lesson: "No matter where you're at, remember I told you: to keep on having that party!"

Luigi remembers it as a "wild night—just teeming with excite-ment," and while it was certainly that, it was also—as June Gardner recalls—just another in a long string. That's what Sam Cooke did: he preached. He picked up a crowd and moved it any way he wanted. Jerry Brandt, trying to sum the man up, calls what he had "sex ap-peal that women loved and men did not resent." It was that, and it was something more than that, because there was something more than sex in the room. Within ten days, using almost identical techniques, Sam had sent over a gospel congregation in Newark and a Saturday-night date crowd in Miami. One group went home with the advice to remember Jesus; the other to keep the party going. Sam was smart enough to wonder what the difference was—and what it meant if there was no difference.

RCA didn't wonder and didn't care. It kept the Harlem Square session in the can, because it wasn't, in Luigi's words, "what the label thought a record was." RCA was much more comfortable with the sound of the *Mr. Soul* LP and politely but firmly turned thumbs down on anything as . . . well, as obviously "soulful" as the Harlem Square.

Sam understood. He might not agree, but he understood. In fact, Zelda had just helped persuade him to set up a tamer, classier sister label for SAR. Zelda liked the gospel-derived r&b, but she and Sam understood the real money was across the way, "where I wanted to sit with my beaded gowns," as she put it, "where I could bring my parents. . . ." In England, Alex and Sam had decided to call the new label Derby: British, you know—classy. The first thing they put out on it was Johnny Taylor's version of "Dance What You Wanna." Then they assembled a five-piece group to do an album of jazzy instrumentals featuring the kid organist that Little Richard had brought over to England: Billy Preston. His association over there with the Beatles would later mark his career, but in early 1963, he was an itinerant keyboardist with a strong gospel background. For Derby, Preston covered "Bring It On Home," "Win Your Love," and Ray Charles's "Born to Lose," among others. Then, in late February, with the Harlem Square LP frozen, Preston was brought back into the studio to help on a Sam Cooke album in much the same style.

Sam called the new LP *Night Beat*, because of its 2 A.M. sound. Gone are the strings and horns. Gone, too, is Harold Ott—or any other outside arranger. It was around this time Sam had a public confrontation with his producers. Luigi told Sam they wanted to rerecord some tunes in New York. As drummer Earl Palmer and the other West Coast regulars looked on, Sam got that hard edge to his voice: the one you didn't hear all that often. "As long as I live, René Hall is going to write my music. . . . Because his arrangements are what got me here—and I expect that's what will keep me here." Palmer and the others were impressed by Sam's standing up to the Man and were naturally delighted he wanted to steer the work their way. René Hall, pleased by the compliment, understood that it was primarily a power struggle: Sam, after all, had invited Ott in and would continue to try other arrangers. "It wasn't actually a confrontation," says Hall. "It was Sam being the artist, and they allowed him to have his way because, after all, he was the biggest thing they had."

Night Beat is as close as Cooke ever got to cutting the LP of bluesy standards that he'd been trying to make his whole career. Hall had put together a small combo around two keyboardists—Preston on organ and pianist Ray Johnson—and Sam went for the intimate sound. Again, he covers a Charles Brown blues, but this time Sam opens with nothing but bass and drum, with Johnson adding some nice piano in a hesitant, New Orleans hitch time. He turns the spiritual "Nobody Knows the Trouble I've Seen" into a restrained blues with White adding a flamenco rhythm guitar, and Cooke cuts his own "Lost and Lookin' " with a simple bass figure, the tap of a drum, the singer squeezing the word "cry" till it drips.

If these sides aren't as "live" as the unreleased Harlem Square session, they still sound pretty spontaneous. The jazzy remake of Howlin' Wolf's "Little Red Rooster" was done in two takes. Sam doesn't try to match the Wolf's bellow of sexual power; instead, he stays in the groove and shouts encouragement as Preston and Johnson exchange solos and the great session drummer Hal Blaine stokes the beat. No wonder many thought Sam's shout of "Take it, Ray!" meant Ray Charles was the piano player; it has the feel of one of Charles's laid-back, late-night jams. While many have hailed *Night Beat* as Sam's finest album, it doesn't bear comparison to his great rock & roll singles, which are on another, higher level of condensed enthusiasm and intensity. And listen to the secularized remake of "Mean Old World" next to Sam's ecstatic, harmony-propelled Soul Stirrers version, and the *Night Beat* version all but disappears.

The afternoon of the last *Night Beat* session, Sam went over to United Studios to shepherd his latest discovery through an original ballad. While in England, Sam had announced that Pat Boone was going to do "When a Boy Falls in Love," but neither Boone nor others who tried could make the song work. Now, Alex had found a young singer called Mel Carter. Carter had sung gospel with the Robert Anderson Singers back in Chicago, where he'd been "in awe" of Sam and the Stirrers. When Sam turned pop, Mel had collected all the 45s and played them again and again. The problem was that Carter's main interest was jazz, and he hated "When a Boy Falls in Love."

"Sam sung it for me and showed me the phrasing," says Carter. "I thought it was very, very difficult, because it was very lyrical. A lot of words!" Sam would offer advice and encouragement: "I know you want to take liberties and swoon here or something like that, but we have to keep the song right."

"I was like a child," Carter recalls, "listening to a father, a mentor. I was twenty-one . . . he was a star, you know? . . . It was like instructive criticism, helpful hints. Like a big brother." Sam would sing a phrase, Mel would try to duplicate it. "It took a long time," Carter recalls, "because I was in the habit of singing behind the beat, and this song you cannot sing behind the beat." But when they finally got a version that successfully blended a cha-cha rhythm and the minor-chord chorus, Sam smelled that his Derby label had its first pop hit. "Melvin," Cooke told him, "you got the best pair of pipes in the world. But don't let anybody ask me who my favorite singer is," he added, laughing, " 'cause I'll tell them me!"

Sam was moving at a furious rate now. Three days after finishing *Night Beat* and cutting with Mel Carter, he went in to make a new single. The tune was the one he'd begun writing in England. Like Chuck Berry's "Back in the U.S.A." from 1959, "Another Saturday Night" is a song about homesickness and culture shock. Sam had structured it as yet another party song, except this time it was a lack-of-party song. Over Plas Johnson's sax solo, Sam does a little boasting. "Man, if I was back home I'd be swingin'," and then, pausing for emphasis, "*two* chicks on my arm!" It sounds like Sam—if he could meet them, he could "get 'em"—except, here, the boasts are all hollow: he isn't back home. We're into a variation on the dozens:

self-mocking, high-spirited, sham despair. Yet another Cooke original with a Latin beat, and the tune is driven—from the opening drumroll to the last, satisfying shot—by Hal Blaine, the rhythm master who appeared on many of Phil Spector's greatest hits and the Beach Boys' surfing songs.

Sam's restlessness pursued him through the spring 1963 tour, as did the leukemia rumor, now six months old. He went out with most of Scepter's artists—the Shirelles, Dionne Warwick—joined by, among others, the Womack Brothers. June Gardner recalls that Sam took Warwick—a young former gospel singer—under his wing much as he had Aretha. Warwick's "Don't Make Me Over" was just charting, but some audiences booed the pop tune as not rock & roll enough. Warwick was in tears, but Sam would assure her that rock & roll was bigger than just the beat. It was the battle he'd fought and won with "You Send Me," and she'd win it, too.

The other youngster on the tour was an unknown, intense guitarist from Seattle named James Hendrix. Little more than a gofer at first, he stayed mostly to himself, endlessly practicing his guitar. At one point on the road, when Harry Womack lost some money, he blamed the solitary kid and got his revenge by throwing Jimmy's ax out the bus window. It would be years till Hendrix got famous for his playing (and his own version of guitar destruction), but some of his training was right here—with the likes of Cooke and King Curtis, masters of the teased climax. "I'd have learnt more," he later told a reporter, "if they'd let Sam finish his act. But they were always on their feet and cheering at the end and I never heard him do the last bit."

It was on this tour that Sam's brother Charles was knifed. A stagehand at the Howard Theater in Washington, D.C., wouldn't let some people in—"some real important people" is how Curtis Womack remembers it—and soon Charles was punching him out. The stagehand, Curtis recalls, "was just rocking and reeling: didn't look like he was doing anything. But he was pushing that knife into Charles's stomach while Charles was beating him like that." When Sam rushed out to see what was happening, the stagehand looked a lot the worse for wear, until Sam noticed a red stain spreading across Charles's front. "My brother's bleeding!" The damage to his intestines took ten hours of surgery to repair. Afterward, Sam insisted his unconscious brother get a private room. The next day, when Charles awoke, groggy, with his stomach hurting, he was surrounded by pregnant women. All sorts of biological impossibilities ran through his head, till the nurse told him Sam had raised so much hell that they'd gotten Charles something like privacy—in the maternity ward.

It was also during this tour that Sam made a career-changing decision. Instead of going into Philadelphia's Uptown Theater, the usual venue, the package had signed on for a ten-day run at the State. The State had recently been reconditioned and was being run by a partnership of Doug Henderson and Allen Klein. Henderson was better known as Jocko, one of the highest-paid Negro dj's in the country. Klein was a music business accountant looking to meet new acts. One day at the State Theater, he took Jocko aside. "Doug, I want him so bad!" Henderson was happy to help: "Sam, I'd like to introduce you to the greatest guy in the world—who can do more for you than anybody else in the world!"

To someone with Sam's ambitions—and his continuing unhappiness with his career—this was worth checking out. Born in Newark, the son of a kosher butcher, Klein had been placed with two of his sisters in the Hebrew Office and Sheltering Home after his mother died, then raised by his grandparents. Allen was, in his own words, "a very poor student" who took four and a half years to graduate next to last in his class from high school. But after enlisting in the service, he discovered he had an aptitude for figures and sped through Upsala College. In the late fifties, he got a job with an accounting firm. "I was clerking and they represented the music publishers, and I saw what their audits uncovered. I thought, well, my God, if you can find that for the music publishers, look what you can find for the artists. And," he added "I have the ability to think like a thief."

Record companies were notorious for short-changing their artists, and Klein worked hard to ferret out the money owed. In 1962, at a friend's wedding, Klein approached singer Bobby Darin, whose hits "Splish Splash" and "Mack the Knife" were on the Atco label. "I can find you money," Klein opened, "you never knew you had." "Money for what?" Darin asked. "For nothing." Klein proceeded to audit the record label's books and come up with a six-figure discrepancy. Darin eventually switched over to Capitol Records where his deal made him the highest-paid pop singer around. "I was a bounty hunter," says Klein. "I hung up my shingle and I hustled: to the dismay and anger of a lot of people."

Moves like this had given Klein—a glib dark-haired man who concentrated with feverish intensity on a column of figures—his reputation as a genius: a slightly scary, tough-guy genius at that. Allen gave you the clear impression that he could get you there; plus, he was a charmer. And Sam, the great seducer, was susceptible. He was convinced RCA was short-changing him; hadn't Art Rupe and John Siamas tried to do the same? "Send Me Some Lovin' " was out at the time, but it was bigger than any one record. In Crain's words, "they was missing us out our money."

The way Klein would later tell it, "When I met Sam, he didn't have a dime, and was heavily in debt due to mismanagement, loose spending, and an excessive entourage of hanger-on [sic] he was carrying." Sam's manager, Jess Rand, vigorously disagrees, but Sam's rep at William Morris, Jerry Brandt, says most of it was true. "Every artist of his generation was broke. Nothing unique to the man. In other words, except for Presley, everyone was scrambling. . . . It wasn't the time of the artist." Sam didn't tour eight to ten months a year because he wanted to. "I mean, you have a house, the kids, and you're making a thousand dollars a night," Brandt goes on, "but you got five, ten people on the road to pay; you got hotels. I mean, you don't make money. And royalties weren't paid well in those days. . . . They cheated your ass off!"

Sam wanted out from under. He wanted off the road, and he wanted the kind of security that six years of hit records hadn't brought him. Allen, for his part, was mesmerized. "I sat for a whole week and listened to I don't know how many shows a day." Looking back, he remembers it was like "a crush." Klein made his usual offer to go through the books for free. If he found something, then he and the artist would make a deal. Though Crain and Brandt and others around him had their doubts, Sam was won over. He left the ten-day run in

Philadelphia with a handshake and the promise that the man could get him money for nothing. "I started out as an accountant," Klein has said, "and using that. It's like everyone needs milk. You become a milkman. Everybody needs milk and I'm also selling eggs. And that's how it happened."

The eggs Klein was selling were his talents as a manager.

Chapter
19

By early 1963, the center of the civil rights struggle had shifted to SNCC's tiny but influential voter registration drive in the Deep South. The organization had the audacity to bring poor, uneducated Negroes to city hall and have them take the citizenship exams necessary to vote. Late in February, SNCC secretary Jimmy Travis was shot in the head by three white men as he was driving away from a meeting in Greenwood, Mississippi, and by March, the SNCC offices had been burned. The comedian Dick Gregory helped draw the press to the situation—taunting the police and addressing rallies—and Harry Belafonte contributed to the first big SNCC fund-raiser at Carnegie Hall. "There is hardly one major entertainer," Clyde McPhatter told the Negro paper in Norfolk, "who hasn't at some time felt the sting of prejudice or the prick of jimcrow. And there is not one who wouldn't give his all to erase these things from the face of the globe." The same article cited Cooke as one of those who had canceled performances rather than play to segregated crowds.

In the beginning of April, Dr. Martin Luther King launched the Birmingham movement with a manifesto declaring that "the patience of an oppressed people cannot endure forever" and calling on the people to "make a moral witness to give our community a chance to survive." The trouble was, King couldn't get much response, partly—as his biographer Taylor Branch puts it in *Parting the*

Waters—because of his image at the time "as a reluctant and losing crusader." Sam, meanwhile, was expanding his idea of how to fight discrimination economically. He announced that his publishing companies were going to resurrect oldies by great Negro songwriters like Fats Waller. "It amazes me to see music written by mediocres [sic] and neophytes being given top ratings . . . while scores of fine songs by competent Negro writers must go begging. . . ." More and more, Sam's experience told him to follow the money. While he supported this business about being a moral witness, it was a long way from that to a paycheck.

For a month, King tried to get Birmingham to march, but the only people who rose from their church pews to volunteer were kids, and King was understandably reluctant to put them in danger. Finally, the evening before the May 2 march, it got beyond anyone's control. "Tall Paul," a local rock & roll dj, started broadcasting a "jived-up announcement" about the big party at Kelly Ingram Park, and, according to Branch, "nearly every Negro kid in Birmingham knew what he meant." The following day, fifty teenagers led the march out of the Sixteenth Baptist Church, were arrested by Bull Connor's police, and then were followed by nearly a thousand more. The next day, there were another thousand kids, and when Connor turned fire hoses and police dogs on them, the pictures that flashed across the nation sickened people of conscience from the ghetto to the White House. While evening services rallied the troops (choirs singing straight gospel like "Ninety-nine and a Half Won't Do"), King announced gleefully that it was the "first time in the history of our struggle that we have been able literally to fill the jails." The "we" in this case was teenage demonstrators: rock & roll fans.

During the uprising, Sam was headlining a package tour with Jerry Butler, Dee Clark, the Crystals, the Drifters, Solomon Burke, Little Esther, Dionne Warwick, and the Upsetters, among others. Sam's popularity was enormous. When his package came into Pittsburgh, the promoter held back advertising because he didn't want "the obviously superior Sam Cooke show to hurt the gate" of a *less* popular Motown revue that included Mary Wells, the Miracles, Marvin Gaye, Martha and the Vandellas, and the Supremes.

Sam used that drawing power. Butler remembers a show on this tour where the audience was supposed to be kept segregated by a rope down the middle of the theater. The local fire department came backstage and—their Southern accents strained into politeness—said, "Mr. Cooke, we'd appreciate it if you wouldn't jump down into the audience, 'cause we're not sure we can control the crowd if you do." By then, says Butler, "we were all feeling our oats and well into the militancy kind of thing." So Sam said, "They can't tell me how to sing!" and, midway through the show, jumped off the stage. Security knew it was coming, caught him, and threw him back, and Sam was furious—for a day. Then he and Butler got to laughing so hard about it they couldn't stop. "Man," Cooke told his friend, "they *threw* my ass back up onstage!" But the kids had seen, and the kids paid attention.

Allen Klein would later say he felt Cooke stayed on this "chitlin circuit" because of the "rejection and frustration" stemming from his first Copa appearance. "Sam just withdrew." Klein points to the British tour as Sam's first evidence in years that he could play to a white crowd, but the situation was a good deal more complicated than that. Klein was right that Sam still wanted to capture the white club crowd. Why, for example, was his label mate Paul Anka celebrating his twenty-first birthday by doing two weeks at the Vegas Sands, when Sam, thirty-two, with just as many hits, was still playing the same venues down South? On the other hand, Cooke *was* reaching white teenagers, both live and through records. Noting that Cooke's package tour was in Atlanta when Birmingham exploded, Taylor Branch writes that these "stars of soul music and blues stood with King as exemplars of the mysterious Negro church—nearly all of them had been gospel singers—but they were still ahead of him in crossing over to a mass white audience. They unlocked the shared feelings, if not the understanding, that he [King] longed to reach."

On June 11, 1963, President Kennedy gave his first major civil rights speech on national television. It was the midpoint of a ten-week period that would see nearly fifteen thousand people arrested in civil rights demonstrations in 186 cities. "The heart of the question," the President said, "is whether all Americans are to be afforded equal rights and equal opportunities. . . ." That night, in Jackson, Mississippi, NAACP leader Medgar Evers was shot in the back and killed as he walked up the driveway to his home.

Sam was back in Los Angeles, cutting a follow-up to "Another Saturday Night," the #1 r&b record in the country. The evening after recording an overarranged version of "Cool Train," Sam went out to party with Barbara. It was one of the things the two did together. By now, Sam had what he called "an understanding" with his wife. When the young Curtis Womack asked his hero what that meant exactly, Sam told him, "She has a boyfriend, you know. She knows I'm out. Love outweighs that." There was something in Sam's laugh that didn't convince Curtis: a hint of anger, of the "understanding" running into a double standard.

Sam's assistant, Zelda Sands, knew about the arrangement, too. She was over at the house a lot to swim at the pool and play with the kids, and the two women talked. There was the time in Atlantic City Sam had met this woman at a party. When Barbara wanted to go back to the hotel, he told her something like "Okay. Go back then." Even that might have been all right—might have been—except he hadn't come home. As soon as Barbara had split town, murder in her eye, she'd called Zelda and told her the whole story, adding, "I'd liked to have taken a gun and shot him." And Zelda had been at the Ames Street house one night for dinner when Barbara had simply gotten up and announced, "Okay. I have some plans," and walked out, leaving Zelda sitting there with Sam, the two little girls, the baby, Vincent—and nothing much to say.

The easy way to look at it, the view from outside the marriage, was that Barbara stayed with Sam only for the good life he could provide: the house and the cars. But it was more complex than that. For all their differences, they'd come a long way together and went a long way back. They shared the memory of the life they'd left behind, and it made the hard-earned luxuries all the more luxurious. Maybe Sam's marriage with Barbara wasn't a traditional one, but he'd told Zelda, "I won't ever leave that woman," and he'd meant it. They had reached, if not a peace, then a kind of uneasy truce. Barbara "coped with a lot," is how Zelda saw it, "was at her man's side if she could be, learned to keep her mouth shut about a lot. She suffered greatly, but she handled everything. She handled it. Some way or another." And Sam handled it, too. "Sam," said one friend, "never talked about his personal things to people. He kept that pretty much to himself." His brother Charles had never seen him cry, and Zelda remembers him as "a happy individual—very happy—always smiling."

That Sunday night in June, Sam had just given Barbara a pair of mink stoles, and she had a new high-fashion wig. There was no holding them back. A new place, Small's Paradise West, was opening on L.A.'s nightclub row, featuring a nonstop show by jazz organist Earl Grant. The five-hundred-seat club was sold out. Alex was there, so was Lil Cumber (Sam's former booking agent at Herald Attractions), and a cross section of the Negro elite: hotelmen, realtors, actresses, and models. At one table, a local PR woman was downing vodka gimlet after vodka gimlet, but, according to gossip columnist Gertrude Gibson, nobody partied harder than the Cookes.

The next day, while Barbara stayed home to look after the kids, Sam got himself down to the SAR offices, where they were preparing to cut an LP with Mel Carter. Sam and Alex were standing by the front desk when the phone rang. Zelda answered and said it was Barbara's twin, Beverly; she didn't sound good. Sam took the phone, listened a moment, said, "I'll come on," and hung up. Before Zelda or J.W. could ask, he said, "Vincent just fell in the pool." And then he ran like a mad man.

As they pieced together the story later, Barbara had been at home with the three kids when Vincent, eighteen months old, had somehow managed to crawl off, unattended. The pool was in the front yard, right off a little porch area. It was usually covered but had been left open after a weekend of swimming. According to one report, it was "several minutes before the accident was discovered." Then Barbara, fully clothed, had jumped into the water and brought the body out. By the time Sam got to the house, the ambulance had arrived. He ran into the back and, pushing the attendants aside, grabbed the baby and tried mouth-to-mouth. It was too late.

"I remember," Zelda says, "he came back from the morgue, went into the bedroom, and just didn't want to be around people. Which

was so unusual," she adds. Somewhere in that house at 2048 Ames—
the big house he'd been dreaming about since before he joined the
Stirrers, the one he'd worked so hard to get—Barbara sat with her
twin sister and J.W. and Zelda and the other close friends that had
hurried over, and they cried and talked and prayed for understanding,
prayed for forgiveness. And as they helped each other through it the
way they'd always been taught to—by banding together, by finding
comfort in human contact, by having church—Sam sat alone in his
bedroom and changed.

On the same day Medgar Evers was laid to rest at Arlington National Cemetery, his body having been viewed by 25,000 people, the
Cookes had a brief graveside service at Forest Lawn. When they
opened the casket, Sam bent down and straightened Vincent's tie,
talking to him all the time, until they finally had to help him away.
And then as everybody left, Sam stopped and grabbed Jess Rand and
pulled him back to where the boy was buried. Near the grave was a
large rock. Sam leaned up against it, silent, while the other mourners
got into their limousines and began to pull away. Then Sam, "with
the strangest face," turned to Jess and said, "I know my daddy's a
minister. But I know, if I ever get up there to meet that Man, He
better give me some *good* reason why this happened to my boy."

The change in Cooke was sudden and permanent. Sam would come
over to the Rands' house and hold their young son, just looking at
him. He became, Jess concludes, "a very different person." "After the
baby," as Lou Adler puts it, "he was not as quick with a laugh. But
also," he adds, "those were very turbulent times." "I think he
brooded," Alexander reports. "Of course. Drank more than he had
previously." Earl Palmer also noticed Sam was "starting to drink
more than I'd ever seen him. . . . [There was] a distinct change in his
personality. He was very much grief-stricken."

As he tried to figure out how such a thing could have happened
and why, Sam would talk with J.W., his old gospel ally, about the
"will of God." Not about hell and damnation—Cooke had seen too
many fake preachers for that, sat through too many overpious
sermons—but how, "if it hadn't happened that way, it would have

happened some other way," just trying to figure it out. "In many ways," Palmer reports, "he blamed himself. Like most parents would." He wondered aloud if there wasn't something he could have done or prevented; he second-guessed himself—and would go on doing it the rest of his life. Once with Margaret Cranhaw, Crain's sister, he went back over the incident. "If we were going to have a pool," Cooke told Cranhaw, "we should have had it so the kids—" He paused. "Other kids could have got drowned, too. Could have been playing around with my kid and crawled under there."

And finally, as he blamed God and blamed himself, he also blamed Barbara. He couldn't help it. He didn't talk about it much, because he didn't want those feelings. But they were inevitable. And once he began to brood about it, it was like death itself, impossible to forget or forgive or overcome. "That was around at the time," Lou Adler admits. "That question came up. Not that she had [done anything wrong], but the doubt." "The kid was right out front," says engineer/ producer Al Schmitt. "I don't think she saw him fall in, but just leaving any kid that age . . . by a swimming pool doesn't make much sense. . . . I think that was basically the end of their relationship. They still lived together, but . . ." There is no evidence that Sam ever accused Barbara, yet many in his circle of friends could feel it in the air: that unavoidable if, if, if. He talked a little about it to his friend Bill Mercer, known on KGFJ in Los Angeles as Rosko. "Oh my God, if she had just closed the door. If she had done this." It had become impossible to separate the marriage from the death, as it was impossible to walk into the house without first seeing the swimming pool.

At the end of all the analysis, Cooke apparently let it be. Not that he got over Vincent's drowning—and not that the marriage ever really recovered—but he realized he couldn't keep worrying it. There was nothing to be done. Sometime during the next year, in Texas, he saw Cranhaw's little nephew walking around and said, "You know, my son would have been—" and then he interrupted himself. "Why do I keep bringing that up? Just make me miserable. No point talking about that." And Cranhaw could only agree: "No, I don't want to hear it, either, baby." But from then on, as she, too, puts it, he was "a different kind of Sam Cooke." He told Jess Rand he wanted to stay busy. " 'Get me on the road, man!' That's all he wanted to do: get out of town."

Sam made himself go to the Mel Carter album session the day after the funeral. And, as he had with "When a Boy Falls in Love," he helped the younger singer through standards like "When I Fall in Love" and "Hold Me." The afternoon session, complete with a big string section, went along fine until they got to a folk tune they'd planned for the date: a soft nursery rhyme called "The Riddle Song." It begins, "I gave my love a cherry that had no stone," and goes on to ask a series of riddles known to millions of kids: how can you have a chicken with no bones, a ring with no end, a baby with no crying. Sam showed Mel how he wanted him to sing the answer to the last. "A baby when it's sleeping," he sang and softly lifted his voice, "there's no crying." Sid Sharp, concertmaster at the session, looked up and saw tears pouring down Cooke's face. Years later, Alex, the old pro, would discount it; "Sam could get in moods to sing a song," he says. But Sharp remembers it vividly. "I can hear it," he says of this man who never showed his sorrows—the man with the smile. "You could hear his voice break. He definitely was crying."

Chapter 20

am wouldn't cut any new material for six months after Vincent's death. RCA released "Cool Train" with the two-year-old "Frankie and Johnny." And the public drove the latter to #4 r&b, #14 pop.

At the same time, a folk trio out of Greenwich Village was riding the charts with a song called "Blowin' in the Wind" that caught and held Sam's attention. Peter, Paul & Mary were a long way from rock & roll (which they disliked and mocked), but it wasn't the group or the folk poetry of Bob Dylan's lyrics that struck Cooke. It was the fact that a tune could address civil rights *and* go to #2 on the pop charts. His business sense told him there was potential here. His pride made him wonder why the protest songs were being written by white kids in Greenwich Village. And, in the midst of the changes brought on by his son's death, he began to consider possibilities.

Sam headlined Chicago's Regal at the beginning of August. As always when he was in town, Sam hung out with family and old friends. "He was the same Sam that we knowed when he was in the Soul Stirrers," Sammy Lewis recalls. "He had that same friendly, outgoing personality. . . . Even now, sometime, we'd be walking down 61st, out of the Evans Hotel, he'd meet somebody of a minor consequence: he never forgot him. He'd call him by first name. 'Hey, Jim!' Or 'Hi, Jack!' " Cottage Grove and the old neighborhood was a leveled wreck by then, but he saw people who'd known him (and Barbara) from way back, touched base with his old gospel buddies, got to spend some time with his family. They had a "going-away" party for him at the end of the week. A bunch of the old Junior Destroyers, his brothers and sisters and their families, all came down to the Blueflame Lounge and clowned around. Sam shrugged off the condolences he got: better not to talk about it. He posed for silly pictures, talked nice to the older people, kissed babies, and remembered old times.

Allen Klein, meanwhile, was turning up just what he'd expected in the bowels of RCA. While Luigi claims, "They weren't cheating him," Allen had found nearly $150,000 in past-due royalties. That was big money, but it was just the "milk": now Sam bought the eggs. Though they never signed a formal contract, Klein became Cooke's manager.

It was in many ways a replay of his split from Bumps years before. As he'd traded up to Jess Rand for the connections, so he now felt Klein had the contacts and the ambition to push a career break-through. At L.A.'s Brown Derby restaurant, as Jess looked up to see the gold record for "You Send Me" hanging on the wall, Sam tried to explain. "This is business, baby. This is business. The man said he could do this for me and do that for me. . . . You know the only thing that really bothers me about this whole thing?" he added. "I don't want to lose you as a friend."

They were almost exactly the same words he'd used with Bumps, and here, too, Sam managed to stay close to Jess. "It broke my heart," Rand says today, but "Sam was one of the most unique people. Sam was just nice."

While Klein negotiated with RCA, Sam stayed in Los Angeles. Late in August, the dj organization NARA came to town, and Sam agreed both to perform at its convention (a rarity, since he almost never sang in his hometown) and to throw a party at his house. Columnist Gertrude Gibson reported that the "'manse buzzed with a multitude of show folks. . . . Guests began to loosen up and swing from the gaily colored umbrella tables in the patio to the exquisitely furnished music room. Celebrities were all over the place." There, beside the pool, two months after Vincent's death, Cooke put on his smile. "Sam had the capacity of saying, 'Nice to meet you,'" former SAR employee Fred Smith and his wife recall, ". . . and making you think he really *was* pleased to meet you. A riveting of the attention. Which is a great gift. Whether it was real, him as a person, doesn't matter."

A week after the party, Sam signed a new deal with RCA. The package that Klein had worked out was unique. He not only got Cooke a four-year $450,000 advance, but he created a company called Tracey (named for Sam's daughter) that assumed all the conditions of Cooke's RCA contract. Tracey furnished Sam's services; RCA paid the new corporation for the records; then Sam took his money out of Tracey. "It was some kind of a tax thing," Alexander says. "Allen figured out how to get more money out of the deal." When Alex registered Tracey that October in Nevada, the papers listed Sam as president, Alex as vice president, and Allen as secretary, but Tracey was solely owned by Allen Klein. In Allen's words, "He got the money, but it was not in his name, but it was in his control. . . . It was a pretty clever idea!"

That Sam would set up a business to manufacture his records and not own a piece of it strikes many who knew him as highly unlikely. (The Rolling Stones would later have concerns about a similiar tax protection Klein set up in connection with their business.) "We had a simple understanding," says Klein. "You won't touch my money, and I won't touch yours. And we can leave each other anytime we want." The cover of *Cash Box* has Sam smiling broadly as he inks a new contract with RCA: a "continuance," as the caption puts it, of the "highly successful relationship." A label vice president looks on with approval, and above them a portrait of Verdi glares out over the Byzantine workings of the music industry.

RCA, with no new material from Cooke, put out two cuts from *Night Beat* as his fall single. At the same time young Marvin Gaye's reworked Pentecostal call-to-arms "Can I Get a Witness" was breaking, Sam was represented by the jazzy, slightly old-fashioned "Little Red Rooster." It's a testimony to the public's hunger for his product (and the workout groove supplied by Billy Preston's organ) that the record went to #7 r&b and #11 on the pop charts. The RCA deal done, Sam toured behind the single on a double bill with soulful Bobby "Blue" Bland.

On Sunday, September 15, 1963, Birmingham's 16th Street Church was bombed: fifteen people were injured, four Negro schoolgirls were killed. Protests across the country were immediate and immense. In New Orleans, at a memorial service for the children, police beat the president of the Shreveport NAACP. When Cooke, Bland, Dion, and Little Willie John played that city's New Orleans Municipal Auditorium on Thursday, September 26, the local Negro paper took the occasion to mention that, among rock & roll fans, anyway, integration seemed to work: "white girls and Negro girls, white boys and Negro boys seated side by side and together whooping it up."

But five days after Cooke's concert, ten thousand people marched on the New Orleans city hall chanting "Freedom!" and accusing Mayor Shiro of not living up to his promises of integration. That night, the mayor appeared on TV to say he was "unimpressed" by the demonstration and felt Negro ministers "should devote their time to making useful citizens of 'their people.' "

Sam, still touring the area, pulled into Shreveport early on the morning of October 8. As usual, most of the package stayed at the Negro hotel, the Royal, on Marlin Street, but Cooke had asked Crain to book four rooms at Shreveport's Holiday Inn, and S.R. had gotten a telegram back confirming the reservations. They arrived at around six in the morning, Charles driving a Maserati that Sam had recently picked up secondhand from singer Eddie Fisher. The car was in fine condition except it had a short somewhere in the electrical system that made the horn go off when you took a sharp turn. So, as Charles pulled into the Holiday Inn driveway, there was a quick beep, and then Sam went to register.

The motel clerk took one look at Mr. Cooke and said the rooms weren't ready. "Look," Sam replied, "I wired. Why *aren't* the rooms ready?" The only answer was they wouldn't be ready till twelve o'clock. At that, Sam went off. "Well, man, what am I supposed to do? Sit around in your lobby till noon?"

After a few choice words for the clerk, Sam decided to leave: he was tired, and it wasn't worth arguing with the man. He told Barbara and the others, they put their bags back in the car, and the group drove back down to the Royal Hotel to get some sleep. The Maserati's horn went off briefly again when Charles pulled out. They had barely unloaded at the Royal when five squad cars came squealing up and arrested Sam, Barbara, Charles, and S.R.

The headline in the *New York Times* read, "Negro Band Leader Held in Shreveport." The paper reported that Sam and his associates were arrested for disturbing the peace "after they tried to register at a white motel." The police description was that Sam "repeatedly blew the horn, yelled and woke guests . . ." although, in Cliff's words, "From the parking lot through the front of the hotel to the lobby, there was hardly a disturbance."

Never mind why they were there, the inside of a Southern jail was no place any of them wanted to be—especially with all this talk about Northern agitators. Sam explained who he was, but none of the white cops seemed very impressed. The patrolman on duty duly noted their names and ages. When he got to Crain, he said, "You with this show, boy?" S.R., fiercely proud, stood clutching his tour briefcase. "Yeah, I'm with them." Okay, then he was under arrest, too, for attempting to stay at a white motel. Crain—somewhere between angry and ingratiating—remembers mentioning how, actually, it was a red motel. The cop didn't laugh. "Throw that grip over here, and you go around there."

Crain asked him not to throw the grip; his money was in there. With that, the officer decided to have a little fun with the old Negro. "How much money you got in there?" he said, smiling.

"I guess I got about, uh, fifteen thousand dollars."

The cop just laughed and signaled to have the case opened. In it lay Sam's share of the profit from a couple of weeks of touring. The cops were bug-eyed. After a series of calls, they let the group off, Crain paying the bond from his briefcase full of $100 and $500 bills. Because of what was happening in Birmingham, the national press jumped on the incident, and it helped make Sam's reputation as a civil rights crusader. Meanwhile, the important work he'd been doing all along—in the music and at his shows—went largely unnoticed.

Sam and Barbara returned to Los Angeles long enough for Sam to stick his head into the SAR offices and check how the latest singles by Johnny Taylor, the Valentinos, and Mel Carter were doing. Then he flew to New York for what had become his annual week at the Apollo. His last appearance had set a new attendance record; this time, he was headlining with Motown's Mary Wells, working on her eighth Top Forty hit. Sam's picture was all over the city; he and the band were in an ad for L&M cigarettes and getting some teasing for it from the likes of Cassius Clay, who was also staying at the Hotel Teresa. Clay was in town to plug a record he'd cut, "I Am the Greatest," and to appear on Jack Paar's show to hype his upcoming title fight against Sonny Liston. Nobody, recalls fight fan Curtis Womack, thought he had a chance of winning; he looked too young and pretty for one thing. Womack remembers Clay hanging around the hotel, always on the prowl for the girls that found their way to Cooke. The only celebrities that impressed the boxer, according to his friend the photographer Howard Bingham, were r&b stars. Clay "loved Fats Domino, Little Richard, Jackie Wilson, Sam Cooke . . . all those guys. . . . It's like he's still a kid, looking up, and they're the ones on the pedestal."

The opening show at the Apollo was at twelve-thirty; Bobby Schiffman arrived to find lines around the block. Soon the theater was jammed to the walls, and Schiffman remembers thinking gleefully, "This is going to be the biggest week in the history of this theater! We are going to plow people in here every day to capacity!" At two o'clock, news reached New York that President Kennedy had been shot in Dallas. Frank Schiffman announced it from the Apollo stage, and the crowd was stunned. Some shouted, several women got hysterical. Like the rest of America, Harlem stayed home and watched television that weekend. Sam canceled his shows and flew back to Los Angeles. There you could drive down Western Avenue's nightclub row for six or eight blocks without seeing another car. The *Los Angeles Sentinel* reported that the "tan population" hadn't wept so unashamedly since Medgar Evers died.

But not all the "tans" felt that way. Clay's friend and adviser Malcolm X would soon be disciplined by his fellow Muslims, ostensibly for commenting that Kennedy's death was "chickens coming

home to roost." Sam and Malcolm were friends by now; Alex remembers the Muslim leader coming down to New York's Warwick Hotel
to see Cooke, and Jess Rand recalls a dinner at a seafood restaurant
in Harlem. Malcolm "absolutely shined me off," says Rand, till the
white man finally asked, "Do you really hate me that much?" "No,"
Malcolm replied, "I don't hate you as you. I hate you—what the
Caucasian people stand for in this country."

Now, the week of Kennedy's death, Malcolm wrote an open letter to
Jackie Robinson: ". . . you Negro leaders whose bread and butter de-
pend on your ability to make your white boss think you have all these
Negroes 'under control,' better be thankful that I wasn't in Mississippi
after Medgar Evers was murdered, nor in Birmingham after the murder
of those four innocent little Negro girls." It surprised some of his
friends that Sam had begun to hang out with people who talked this
way. Two weeks after Kennedy's assassination, Clay and Cooke appeared
together on the nationally televised *Jerry Lewis Show.* Afterward, Clay
invited him down to Miami for the Liston fight at the end of February;
Malcolm would be there, too. Sam accepted happily.

Before that, however, Sam went into the studio to cut his first single manufactured by Tracey Limited. He had two songs ready, "Good
News" and "Good Times," not nearly so similar as the titles sound.
"Ain't That Good News" (as Sam would later call it) was cut in three
takes using a big eleven-piece band. The bright, up-tempo number
starts with Sharkey Hall's quick drumming and a jangled banjo (nod
to the current folk craze?). With negligible lyrics (it seems baby's
coming home; that's the good news), the song is a calculated blend
of nightclub and soul workout.

Though Sam spent the rest of the three-hour session trying to cut
the other number, he couldn't get it to work. So, the next evening,
before working on some album material, he scheduled a special session and brought in a smaller group. "Good Times" begins with Sam
la-ta-da-ing against his own overdubbed voice, as Sharkey and bass
Ray Pohlman set up a nice, lazy groove. The song quotes from Shirley and Lee's 1956 hit "Let the Good Times Roll," but where they
called on us to "roll all night long" for the sake of the party, Sam
wants us to stay till it "soothes our soul"—and then, dropping into

the minor key, adds with a touch of sadness how that might just take all night. "Good Times" is as bittersweet and as questioning as "Good News" is brassy and bright. One of the debts Marvin Gaye's music owed to Sam's was the introspective groove; Cooke had done it on "Soothe Me" and on "Bring It On Home to Me," and he does it again here. Though the end product sounds effortless, it took Sam twenty-five takes to get a sound that's both thoughtful, even meditative, and danceable. The record is an emotional balancing act: the voice of experience singing that he feels good and then adding that he's not sure when (if?) he ever will again.

Sam was now determined to spend less time on the road. He wanted to finally make good on his promise to concentrate on the business end of his career, and he also had a new project in mind that combined his ideas on civil rights and music.

The project centered around Harold Battiste. Battiste had been at that first Dale Cook session in New Orleans. He'd helped transcribe "You Send Me" over at Specialty, and for a while after Bumps left he'd worked as Art Rupe's a&r man. After arranging and playing on a number of New Orleans indy hits, Battiste—a man of considerable pride and energy—got tired of the setup whereby outside, mostly white-owned labels profited off the crack local musicians. In 1961, he decided to try to organize the Crescent City's music scene and formed the All for One (A.F.O.) Executives: a corporation of the best of New Orleans musicians. Battiste brought together saxophonist Red Tyler (the same who'd written "Forever" for Dale Cook), Chuck Badie on bass, John Boudreaux on drums, and Melvin Lastie on cornet.

The theory behind the A.F.O., as he told author John Broven, was that instead of getting a flat fee, "musicians who play on the session should own the session." Battiste knew full well how much the A.F.O. threatened the music industry. Far beyond black-owned companies like SAR or Detroit's Motown, this was the equivalent of automobile workers claiming to own the cars that came off their assembly lines. For a brief time, it worked. At the end of 1961, the A.F.O. had a giant #3 hit with Barbara George's "I Know" (one of the songs Sam called for in "Having a Party"). Then the A.F.O.'s distribution deal fell apart, and other local musicians began to resent its musical monopoly. By the fall of 1963, they arrived in Los Angeles, having essentially been run out of New Orleans.

If anything, California proved tougher, and they were on the verge of giving up altogether when Battiste and Lastie happened to drop by the SAR offices on a day Zelda needed somebody to write lead sheets. The working relationship soon grew. Sam, a longtime admirer of the band, knew the A.F.O. could help both his music and his label. "I hate to see you guys break up," he told Tyler. "I'm going to have each of you guys on a hundred-dollar retainer a week." It saved the group, but Battiste hadn't come West just to be part of a studio band again. He had an idea.

"I wanted to set up something in southeast or South-Central Los Angeles to facilitate a lot of the black talent. I developed a thing—we called it the Soul Stations. The concept was a series of small offices in the black community that would allow the talent in the community to have a place to come and present themselves, present their material, in an atmosphere where they felt nonthreatened." As a kid, Sam had seen all the groups that had come out of Bronzeville; he knew the deep well of singers in gospel; but, even more, the Soul Stations appealed to his growing sense of pride. As Battiste remembers it, the whole project was based on a single question about black music: "Man, if this is really ours, why don't we own it?"

Sam decided to bankroll not just the band, but Battiste's concept. The A.F.O. found a little storefront on Vermont and 37th, near USC, and Sam paid the rent as well as buying some inexpensive recording equipment. He called it Soul Station #1: the first in a series. It was little more than an audition studio at first, but it held the germs of larger concepts. "I remember, vividly, sitting at the house [on Ames Street]," Battiste recounts, "and we got to talking about the racial things. . . . We were talking almost in the realm of the Black Muslim kind of thing. About trying to find solutions for the tremendous problems our people were having. Sam was really concerned about that."

Cassius and Malcolm were having their influence, but Sam's concern also came from his own background of pride and independence. More and more, his friends saw him reading books on black and African history; Cliff White in his unassuming way turned him on to

W.E.B. Du Bois and Booker T. Washington. "Sam," says Cliff, "was deep, deep into that business."

Battiste's concept also meshed with Sam's anger at the injustices of the music industry. White can remember Cooke walking in on some of the early Hugo and Luigi sessions and stopping in his tracks to ask. "Well, you mean to tell me out of all the musicians in this city, there are only two black musicians who can play?"—then refusing to record till they changed the band. Curtis Womack recalls a knock-down, drag-out Sam had with some union guys at the Apollo. "Nigger, we gonna squash you like a roach!" they yelled, and Sam responded in a rage, "All they got is a charter. They're taking people's money!" According to Curtis, Sam was talking about forming a black equivalent with performers like James Brown and Ray Charles: something like R. H. Harris's Quartet Union.

Now, the A.F.O. became Sam's recording band. First he brought them in to fill out the "Good News" LP. On songs like his remake of the country tune "Tennessee Waltz," their dance-smart soul horns, Badie's heavy bass line, and the second-line drumming added an edge to Cooke's modified supper-club sound. The same holds true for Sam's remake of Johnnie Morisette's "Twisting Place" (with changed lyrics, a slowed beat, and a new title, "Meet Me at Mary's Place"). The "Good News" session also got an enormous boost from its backup singers, the Soul Stirrers. Sam gloried in their familiar harmonies. Then, blurring distinctions further, he brought the A.F.O. over to the Stirrers' session, where they cut "Oh, Mary Don't You Weep" and "Lookin' Back" for SAR.

Sam finished up the *Ain't That Good News* LP with a ballad session that included Earl Palmer and a big string section. On tunes like Battiste's "Falling in Love" and Irving Berlin's "Sittin' in the Sun," he doesn't try to jazz up the melody or even "interpret" in any discernible way. Instead, his voice aches over the heartbreak as René Hall's string arrangement swells in perfect accompaniment. He sounds like a man released—and that's particularly clear in the one Cooke original done that night, a tune he'd been telling his friends "scared him."

"Blowin' in the Wind" had continued to bother Sam. "Geez," he told Alex, "a white boy writing a song like that?" It was a challenge to Sam—as a black man and as a songwriter—and he began working on an answer. Crain can remember him humming the tune on the road through Louisiana and Texas before he finally got back to Los Angeles and finished it. "If you ever listen to a Soul Stirrer song," says the old manager of the group, "you'd recognize it." Of course, if you ever heard "Blowin' in the Wind," you'd recognize it, too. Or Sam's earlier hit, "Nothing Can Change This Love." Or any number of old country blues. Part of what's extraordinary about the song— which Sam called "A Change Is Gonna Come"—is how it combines forms and, in the process, combines meanings.

"Change" opens in a wash of strings with a French horn calling, then Palmer finds an easy beat, and Sam comes in testifying—his voice up high in its range and urgent. He was born by the river in a little tent. If that sounds like gospel—born again in some tent-revival baptism—when he adds that he's been running ever since, we're into the blues. Badie's heartbeat of a bass line gives an under-tone of sadness as Sam hits the chorus for the first time: a change is gonna come. Next, he borrows a line from "Ol' Man River"—afraid of living, scared of dying—and, in one phrase, the Reverend's son passes out of the realm of gospel, announcing that he doesn't know what's up there "beyond the sky." Still, a change is gonna come.

These first two verses, general enough to be from some old spiri-tual, call up the whole scarred history of his people. Then Sam brings us to the present. He goes downtown to the movies and gets told he can't hang around. "This was him talking about these kids going to the sit-ins," says Alex, and many have taken this song to be a musical equivalent of Dr. King's philosophy. Up to this point, it might be, but if you look at "Change" as a sermon, the song's bridge is where we head toward the lesson. In Dr. King's speeches, it was often the "moral curve of the universe" that guaranteed God would eventually bring freedom to His people. But Cooke's already declared he doesn't know what's up there, and in the bridge, when he goes and asks his brother for help, he gets knocked back to his knees. It's a brutally re-alistic observation of what had gone down during the past summer of 1963. Nevertheless, "Change" ends with a statement of faith:

there've been times, Sam admits, he didn't think he could make it; now he thinks he can. A change is gonna come. What sort of faith— what kind of change? We aren't given that, only the rising ache of his voice over the final sweep of sound.

After Sam's death, many of his friends concluded that he'd been scared of "Change" because it was an omen of his own passing. But it's equally possible that he was scared by the song's emotional and artistic leap. "A Change Is Gonna Come" is Sam Cooke taking the chance of commenting on current events—a risk all his hardheaded careerism argued against. When Battiste heard it, it seemed like the culmination of all their talk about race: "one way to express how he was feeling about what he needed to do." While "Change" can be taken as pure observation—as general as some ancient slave chant—it can also read as the story of one man's life: the tent by Clarksdale's Sunflower River, the sorrow too personal to name. It may have scared Sam because the Ivy League crooner, the sexy soul man, had chosen to reveal himself.

Finally, what pushes it beyond a song like Dylan's "Blowin' in the Wind" is how it tries to unite its audience. "Change" crosses musical barriers, combining gospel, blues, the nightclub ballad, and the pro- test song. It wants to be speaking at the same time to Sister Flute, to the drunk on the corner, to the white ladies in their gowns and the kids at the sit-ins. It implies they all have something in common. All the divisions come together here—in his voice—and it carries us over. No wonder the song scared him.

Chapter 21

E arly in February 1964, Sam sang "Change" and his new single, "Good News," on *The Tonight Show*. Two days later, the Beatles went on *Ed Sullivan*, where 73 million Americans heard them sing their #1 song "I Want to Hold Your Hand." The music industry was in for a dramatic shift. From 1955 to 1963, the number of Top Ten pop hits by black artists had increased by 50 percent, and an entire teenage generation, both in the United States and in England, had absorbed the sound. But now, as Paul McCartney brought a repackaged, "mop-top" version of Little Richard back to the States, the net result was to drive r&b off the charts. By the end of 1964, nearly a third of the best-selling records would be British—and the Top Ten would have the lowest percentage of hits by black artists since 1956.

One result was that the pop market became even more polarized. If you liked Paul Anka's nightclub act, you couldn't stand the British blues of groups like the Animals. Sam refused to be limited. He had always seen himself reaching everyone, and as Beatlemania arrived, he was busy retooling his nightclub career. That February, with "Good News" in the Top Twenty, Sam told a New York reporter that his most important immediate goal was getting back into the Copa. His first appearance there had been "a personal failure"; his lack of TV and nightclub exposure stemmed from that; the six years since he'd been "perfecting his act so he [could] come back to New York and kill them. . . ." From Allen Klein's perspective, "Sam had bad memories of the Copa, and he was scared to go back. But I took him there to see Nat Cole and he saw things were different from what he remembered."

As J.W. tells the story, he and Sam were upstairs in the Copa's bar; the stage floor was down a flight. "Everyone was drinking and popping and the chicks were shaking their butts, you know?" Sam took in the scene: admittedly a long way from the Flame Bar, but at least it was rock & roll playing. "Sam," Alex said, "these are the same people who are going to be downstairs. You can give them the same music. You don't have to change." The two business partners then went into the nightclub. In Sam's memory, this was the room of the cold sweats—where the huge crowd had sat still and unmoved waiting for the colored boy to give way to Myron Cohen. Sam was amazed to see it again. "You mean this place ain't no bigger than this?! Book me! I'll stand it on its goddam ear!"

According to Alex, William Morris had been constantly telling Sam he wasn't ready for the Copa; they kept offering alternatives like appearing with Sophie Tucker at Basin Street. Alex thought it was insulting, and he had a point: Cooke hadn't had a white nightclub engagement since 1959. But to this day, Jerry Brandt of William Morris feels otherwise. "Everybody gets their time—in time. Except with Klein, it was like, 'I'll save you five years.' And, my opinion, getting Sam Cooke to take that philosophy and endorse it in the end shortens your life. Because you're trying to do a quick fix, when time will take care of it. . . . You can't jump-start it."

Brandt's analysis sounds a lot like the New York City version of selling your soul to the devil. Klein "got him by the greed! Greed is a great passion. He brought him a big check—but [Sam] signed away his life. The audit was a ruse. Then he got him a guarantee; then he got him front money; everything, soup to nuts. . . ." What Brandt saw as hasty and ill-timed Cooke believed was long overdue. "Man," he told the press with a slow grin, "I got a big ego. I want to get them all. I think I got something to tell them."

Sam flew back to Los Angeles after seeing the Copa and issued a press release that he was quitting the one-nighter field. There would be selective touring—two months of the year instead of eight—but not the kind of barnstorming he'd been doing. "My future lies more in creating music and records . . ." Sam went on. "Records are the main thing that keep you alive." Cooke understood (and the British acts confirmed) that the means of reaching the audience had changed. In Sam's gospel days, records promoted the more lucrative live appearances; that was now reversed. As he told a *Billboard* reporter, he would "rather be the creative producer in the control room than be the worn-out singer in the bistro light." The shift meant fewer live r&b shows, but Sam hadn't forgotten what he called his base. As Klein and his new agent, Buddy Howe over at General Artists, handled the nightclub end, Cooke was also visiting Battiste's Soul Station and staying in touch with the street. "When Sam really wanted to hear some good music," says the Upsetters' Henry Nash, "Sam would come off the stage and go to a nice—not necessarily a nice—he would always go to some of the funkiest joints . . . to hear some down-home rhythm and blues." If anything, Sam's sense of black pride and power was growing.

At the end of February, Sam flew to Miami to see Cassius Clay fight for the heavyweight championship: a match that every expert in the nation seemed to have already handed to Sonny Liston. Cooke sat at ringside between Alexander and Klein—Malcolm and his lawyer were next to Alex—and the whole row cheered on the brash young challenger as he danced around the giant Liston, jabbing and taunting him at the same time, till the champ failed to come out for the seventh round. Ecstatic, Clay leaped in the air, and, in the mob scene that followed, the new champ interrupted an interview to hug Cooke and shout that Sam was "the world's greatest rock & roll singer." And Cooke told the *L.A. Sentinel*, "Once he got by the first round I just settled back and watched him work. Cassius Clay is one of the greatest entertainers and showmen I have ever seen. And he's a great example for our youth."

The last was a slap in the face. The establishment press—black *and* white—had constantly portrayed Clay as an egotistical, uppity loudmouth. The announcement that the new champion was a follower of Islam made the soon-to-be Muhammad Ali one of the most controversial men in America. Black sportswriter A. S. Young described the repercussions: "Negroes are being divided into 'race relations' schisms. Caucasians are being embarrassed. Friends are falling out with each other." Dr. Martin Luther King declared that Cassius had become "the champion of racial segregation—and that is what we are fighting." For Cooke to announce in this atmosphere that Ali was a model for youth was a public act of independence and pride.

A few days after the fight, Sam took Ali into a Columbia Records studio in New York. Cooke had whipped up a rock & roll version of "Hail, Hail, the Gang's All Here" for the champ and was now producing it with the help of arranger Horace Ott. The session was mostly a lark: Ali in awe of the rock & roll star, Sam delighted by the champ's way of improvising rhymes and playing with the press.

When Sam came back from the Clay fight, he called his friend dj Bill Mercer (Rosko) and told him about the Muslim connection. The whole idea, Mercer recalls, was "extreme. Very extreme! . . . You almost whispered it." At the same time, it drew Sam. "We didn't say we were going to join but we were fascinated. . . . Social circumstances drive the individual to that. Because you look for someone to give you strength: to support your feelings and make you realize that, no, you're not crazy! This is really wrong. This is oppression."

Rosko's conversations with Sam covered some of the same territory as the dj's trademark soul raps. "He and I both understood and discussed the fact that we were subjects of colonialism. . . . We looked at the whites ruling this country, the ruling class of this country, as cousins to the British. . . . The colonialists would make the subjects uncomfortable, they would revolt, okay? . . . We felt all that coming." Invariably, the conversation would include business and how Sam, with Klein's help, was trying to get control of his. "[Sam] didn't trust [Klein], but he was using him for the moment, just as Allen was using him. . . ."

While Klein had helped singers with their finances before, Cooke was the first act he managed and became his calling card in the industry. Earlier in the year, with Beatlemania taking off, Klein had gone to London. In a meeting with Beatles' manager Brian Epstein, he discussed Cooke as a possible double bill for the group's next tour.

According to author Phillip Norman, Klein suggested he should be handling the Beatles' finances instead of Epstein. "No," Klein recalls, "it was a little too early. A little later, yes." Klein did make a deal with the Dave Clark Five, however, and within a year and a half, he had a big piece of the British invasion—from Herman's Hermits to Donovan to the Rolling Stones. And he would eventually woo over three-quarters of the Beatles. Klein recalls that when he first met John Lennon, the Beatle hired him, saying, "If you can understand Sam Cooke's music, you can understand mine."

Even as the black pride movement was growing, the British invasion was destroying a lot of r&b careers. SAR hadn't had a hit in almost eight months. One day, the Womacks were running a bunch of new songs by Sam when he stopped them. "Where'd that come from?" The song was "It's All Over Now," and it had come from the pens of Bobby and Solomon Womack. Sam smelled a hit, brought the Womacks into the studio, and began to play with the number. "He put me and Bob together on the end," Curtis recalls, "that double . . . and he wanted more of that real country picking guitar on top that Cecil was doing against Bob's rhythm. And he wanted that bass line that Harry was carrying. He kept getting that in—that groove—till it was real tight." The result sounds like some funky, backroads oom-pah band, as the Womacks' high harmonies and laid-back instrumental rattle along together.

In June of 1964, the Womacks' single broke into the Top 100, pop and r&b, but it was almost immediately covered by the Rolling Stones who were in Chicago for their first, largely unnoticed, American tour. The Stones' "It's All Over Now" rose up the charts as the Womacks' version dropped off. According to at least one critic, the single represented "the start of the Stones as, above all, an irresistible compulsion to dance." It also represented a scenario Sam knew all too well from the days of Pat Boone, where the white cover outsells the superior black original.

Sam was finally getting the freedom he needed to fight back. Hugo and Luigi's five-year contract had come to an end, and Sam's new producer, his former engineer Al Schmitt, gave him a lot of leeway. "Recording Sam," he says, "was like fishing in a rain barrel. He was so easy." There was less and less difference now between Sam's singles and SAR's. The A.F.O. Executives (with Bobby and Cecil Womack) played at a Johnny Taylor session that spring, and then Sam brought essentially the same group in to cut his next single.

"Yeah Man," written during his British tour, sounds like the follow-up to "Twistin'." Sam had been thinking of calling it "Do You Like All the Dances?"—a more accurate title, since the song is mostly Sam shouting dance steps with the chorus, including Johnnie Morisette, answering, "Yeah, man!" The horn section pulls off a riff that later figured prominently behind Otis Redding's "Fa-Fa-Fa-Fa-Fa (Sad Song)." And, in fact, "Yeah Man" would later be lifted whole by Otis and Arthur Conley for Conley's #2 hit in 1967, "Sweet Soul Music." It was so blatant that Conley finally had to concede songwriting credit to Cooke.

When he appeared on *American Bandstand* early that April, Sam's usual confidence was in full bloom. "I've been in the business now for about six years," he told Dick Clark, "and I haven't had a song that wasn't a hit. So, I was on the charts, I think, from the time I charted until now." Not quite accurate, Sam's point was still valid: while other acts had come and gone, Cooke now had songs both in Clark's "Memory Lane" feature and among the current hits. Asked for his secret of success, Sam didn't credit his voice or gospel styling but his songwriting: "I think the secret is really observation. If you observe what's going on—try to figure out how people are thinking and determine the times of your day—I think you can always write something that people understand."

It was a surprisingly serious answer stuck in the middle of *Bandstand*'s usual pop chatter. Sam looked old as he delivered it: his face had filled out, his eyes were puffy. In his Afro and his jacket and tie, he was a senior statesman next to the bad-complexioned teenagers in the studio audience. He explained that he wasn't touring much anymore, he was mostly working with other young singers. And when Clark asked him what the greatest thing was that could happen to him, Sam answered more like a businessman than a teen idol. "The greatest thing that could happen to me . . . ? If all the singers I'm connected with had hits."

He didn't mean just rock & roll singles, either. His last four albums had been successful, and the *Ain't That Good News* LP, shipped in April, was headed to #34: a sign both that younger fans were beginning to buy the long-playing format and that his career strategy was finally working. What's more, Derby had its first successful pop album with Mel Carter, and Sam had high hopes it would take Carter's career into the supper-club market.

By now, the business ends of KAGS and SAR were both being run out of Klein's office in New York's Time/Life Building. One day, Mel called Zelda from a promotional tour in the East worried that Klein, Klein's lawyer, and J.W. were going to get a piece of Carter's management. While he considered himself something of a Sam Cooke protégé, Carter really wanted a career like Johnny Mathis's. Maybe, he now said over the phone, Zelda ought to manage him? After all, Mathis had a woman manager.

Zelda went to Sam with the idea: "Since I run everything anyway, and I'm mother to all the kids . . . how about me being partners with you [in managing SAR's artists]?" Zelda had now been with the label almost four years, so the promotion made some sense, but Zelda recalls Allen giving her an ultimatum: work at SAR/Derby or manage Carter—not both. Furious, convinced that "Klein was trying to take control of everything at the label," Zelda finally had it out with Sam one day on the corner of Wilcox and Hollywood Boulevard. "I want to show you," said the brunette, her eyes blazing. "I'll put Mel where you should have been! You stick with that son of a bitch Klein, and you'll see how far you get! I'll show you how it should be done. Just give [Mel] back to me."

Sam was exactly where he hated to be: caught between friendship and business. It was Barbara who finally suggested that he should "give [Zelda] something. Because she's been good to you, and she should—at her age—have something of her own." Sam let Zelda take Mel to another label; less than a year later, Mel had a Top Ten hit on Imperial, "Hold Me, Thrill Me, Kiss Me."

Zelda's departure was the beginning of a purge at SAR/Derby. Klein had examined the label's books. He found a retained deficit of about $2,000. Late in May, Sam's old friend Johnnie Morisette was dropped with no warning. Alex met with him and some of the label's other artists and "just gave us our release. Said we's big enough to go for ourselves. . . . We had done—sssst!—broke off." Though Sam named Battiste as SAR's new a&r man, the label's family of former gospel singers was breaking up. If Cooke believed he'd hired Klein only to manage his career—not his other businesses—it wasn't working out that way.

But Klein had come through on the Copa gig, and Sam was too busy focusing on that to pay much attention to anything else. Instead of putting out the dance tune "Yeah Man" as his next single, he released the supper-club soul of "Tennessee Waltz." Then he began pulling together his act. He had his band: Cliff, June, Bobby Womack on second guitar, and now he added bass player Harper Cosby. The question was what they'd do—and how.

Klein and arranger René Hall had, in Hall's words, "a BIG blowout." The arranger had a Broadway background, working with Billy Rose, among others, and he insisted Sam had to have "an act." At one meeting, the young Jewish accountant—in a turtleneck, his hair slicked back, his face turning red—started shouting at the older, urbane Negro. "You can't tell me about—"

"Look," Hall said, "I'm only here because of my expertise in show production."

"You make records!" Klein shot back, "You—"

"I'm making records now. I was on Broadway," Hall answered. "I know New York show business—and what you're talking about will *not* work! New York will not accept an artist going up there performing records."

Klein says the disagreement never happened, but in Hall's Version, it was Klein, once again, versus Cooke's old circle. Allen had little or no experience in putting together an act, but he was the future. René's advice, on the other hand, was the kind Sam had deliberately surrounded himself with since he'd turned pop: the wisdom of an older generation of Negroes who had plotted a careful course through the world of white entertainment. Cooke and the rest decided to go up to the Catskills the weekend before the Copa opening to see what worked and what didn't. Sam's group of advisers included his former agent Jerry Brandt. "It was past friends," says Brandt to explain his presence. "I mean, we were bonded."

Everyone seemed to agree that Sam had failed his first time at the Copa because, in Brandt's shorthand, "he tried to be a white man." Sam agreed that this time he'd concentrate on what he did best and not try to outguess the audience. Then, at the first show in the Catskills, before a crowd of mostly white males in town for a firemen's convention, Sam "goes out there and does Frank Sinatra! . . . This is after weeks of discussing. And the room walks out." Brandt thought Sam reverted out of pure terror. He was used to white audiences—or at least mixed audiences—but that was in rock & roll: people who knew and loved the records. Now, on alien ground, it was like some recurrent nightmare: the flop sweats, the foolish grin, the orchestra churning away without him.

Between shows, the advisers gathered and, along with Sam, performed radical surgery. They threw out some songs, added others, and punched up the horn section and the rhythm in general. The next show was better—much better—and they kept working on it. Earlier, Jess Rand had pulled in Sammy Davis's arranger and conductor, Morty Stevens. "You need a big band arrangement," Rand had advised. "You're gonna get white musicians here. You're gonna be doing different-type songs." Cooke, remembering the scramble with Bumps, had agreed, but now he had René redo most of the charts. Soon they had reached a compromise: the dynamics were more like what he'd been doing on the road, though with tamer material. By the time the group moved into New York, Sam had a nightclub act that he knew worked.

The pressure was still terrific. Sam's brother Charles noticed he was going through most of a fifth of Chivas Regal in a night. And Schmitt confirms that Sam always seemed to have a drink in his hand—though he never appeared drunk. Up at the Warwick Hotel, he was spending late evenings at the bar, where he smoked a lot of menthol cigarettes. One night, he talked over his strategy with a reporter.

First he told the bartender he was going to cool it that night; he'd just have a Bloody Mary. Then he started trying to explain the upcoming gig, and even his grammar sounds twisted by the foreignness of the Copa. "I want to envelop another area of entertainment," he began, "which I haven't exploited to its fullest capacity." Did he mean he was getting too old to rock & roll? "I figure these young people have grown up. Now they're clubgoers. I want to mix the old material with the new—a very careful blend of songs which I'm working on." That sure didn't sound like Mr. Soul. Did he resent these British kids coming over and getting all the hits? Sam took another long sip from his Bloody Mary. "Resent it? No. . . . I like the Beatles." He wondered aloud if he shouldn't do a solo cover of one of their songs; they were "clever. They sell emotion." But the point wasn't hit-making—not now. The point was the Copa, a monkey that had been on his back since before the Beatles were even a band. That's why he was up late; that's what had him worried; that's why the bartender had to switch off the lights before he'd leave. As he headed for bed, Sam muttered one last comment. Never mind the Copa or the Beatles, "real gospel music has *got* to make a comeback. . . ."

Nine days before Sam was due to step onto the Copa stage, a 20 × 100-foot sign was installed in Times Square. It read, "Who's the Biggest Cook in Town?" To make sure the message could be read day and night, it was surrounded by twenty thousand watts of light. A few days later, the press was invited to cover "the erection of the tallest figure of an entertainment personality in the Times Square area." The sign had been changed to read, "Sam's the Biggest Cooke in Town," and a 45-foot, 1,500-pound photograph of the singer, arms outstretched, was being hauled into place. Despite the fact that Sam's huge head was still on the ground by the time the publicity stunt ended, the story ran in everything from the *New York Times* to the *Amsterdam News* to *Cash Box*. The last noted that Sam's manager, Allen Klein, had paid for the $10,000 sign to keep a promise he'd made "six years ago" at Sam's first Copa appearance: "I'll make you the biggest man in New York." It was great publicity even if Klein and Cooke hadn't even met in 1958.

But Sam was too intent on the Copa to notice much else. Backstage opening night, Al Schmitt remembers, "He was nervous as hell ... pacing a little bit, rubbing his hands together." As tap dancer and Borscht Belt comic Lee Allen warmed up the seven-hundred-seat room, people kept dropping by to reassure Cooke: Muhammad Ali, various record execs, other singers. Out front was all the RCA brass, and Hugo and Luigi had gotten themselves front-row seats. Sammy Davis, Jr., out East for the run of the musical *Golden Boy*, had agreed to introduce Sam. As that ended, Schmitt told him not to worry: "Everything's going to be great. Just get out and do your thing." Sam stood in the wings in tight black tapered pants, a black-and-white-checked Continental jacket—short, the way they were wearing them that year—and a white silk shirt he'd designed himself. Then the big Copa band went into a horn intro, and Sam came on.

Cliff's familiar rhythm guitar fell in behind him, as he opened with "The Best Things in Life Are Free": a sophisticated bounce meant to assure everyone that, yes, this was going to be nightclub stuff and "fun." He followed it with a jazzy version of "Grandfather's Clock," a song he'd been working on for years. The crowd clapped along, but there was something wrong: the up arrangement and the sentimental lyrics had nothing in common. For a moment, he felt the panic coming back. "If I don't get you in the first five tunes," Sam used to say, "forget it."

He calmed himself with "Bill Bailey," familiar nightclub fare, thanks to Bobby Darin's version. Sam's opened with little more than Harper Cosby's strolling bass, June's snare, and a rhythm guitar. He sang it cool—all finger snaps and smiles—and, as he told the story, he walked across the Copa's stage and pointed to the crowd, drawing them in. At the socko ending, with the whole band chiming in, Cooke did one of his nightclub tricks: pointing up to the sky on one beat, then out to the side on the next, finally biting his lower lip, grinning, and bowing slowly to the last shot of drums. The crowd loved it. He was in.

On the Depression-era "Nobody Knows You When You're Down and Out," he let his voice get grainy and hinted at his Bronzeville past, before pulling back with a laugh. "We're just going to have a little fun tonight," he assured the crowd and launched into "Frankie and Johnny," the first song at all associated with him. The crowd clapped its recognition, and he pushed a little, finding the room to interject asides into the story line, rolling off some soul horns toward the end before bringing it back down.

Compared to what he did at the Harlem Square Club or any other black venue, this was tame; compared to what usually happened at the Copa—to what he himself had done last time here—this was a soul revue. Sitting up on a high stool, he scatted his way into a modified version of his love sermon. Instead of the bluesy "It's Alright," he quieted the crowd with "Try a Little Tenderness" (later covered by Otis Redding). At the Flame Bar or the score of other black clubs he'd played, he'd tell the crowd, "Fellows, when someone comes to tell you what your girlfriend or your wife's done—" and then offer up "For Sentimental Reasons." Here, the same song was preceded by the same message but in white-speak: "All us gentlemen have a tendency to sort of neglect the ladies." And then he slipped in "You Send Me" as part of the hits melody, instead of the gospel moan it had become in his soul act.

The crowd at the Copa didn't join in on his cover of "If I Had a Hammer," but this time around, Sam was prepared. Assuring them that this was one of those hootenannies (laughing at himself for even using the word), he charmed everybody into clapping and singing. Again, for a moment the sheer drive of his voice and the arrangement pushed the song toward gospel, but Cooke pulled it back. He was carefully keeping the emotion bite-sized, consumable. "Once he got out on stage," Schmitt remembers, "he was so relaxed. He was teaching people how to dance. He'd get people from the audience—the twist was in—and he was showing people how to dance." Actually, even in its second, adult incarnation, the twist was long out. But the crowd was still delighted by Sam's mugging. "Twistin' " was only the second original hit he'd done all night, and it barely hinted at r&b. Still, he took off his jacket and tie, let the white silk shirt open to the neck, and worked until his dark skin gleamed. There were little bits of "Chain Gang" and the latest single, "Good Times," mixed in, and then it was time for the orchestrated finale.

Sam got the crowd clapping again: "Help me feel it! Do you feel it?" Then seeing he'd about reached his limit, he broke off a gospel laugh and let the band groove a moment before calling it quits. "I got to get out of here." As he ran backstage, he let the applause build just so, then strolled back out, a bow, more applause, and sat on the stool for the first encore. Again, he offered some diluted gospel: a finger-snapping version of "Amen." It was a song of reassuring, moderate integration; the crowd knew it from Sidney Poitier's Oscar-winning film of that year, *Lilies of the Field*. Sam followed with a soft, bongo-led "This Little Light of Mine" that took what was left of the song's original Christian proselytizing and made it a love-light instead. Then it was into "Blowin' in the Wind."

Crain, the old gospel warrior, was watching from the wings. He could see Sam going for Sister Flute; well, not Sister Flute—she wasn't at the Copa—but going for the house. " 'Having a Party,' 'Bring It On Home to Me,' 'Twistin' the Night Away,' and all like that, them was house-turners other places besides the Copa," says Crain. "Places like the Copa, he did it with 'Blowin' in the Wind.' "

It was the very beginning of Freedom Summer. The Deep South was starting to fill with white, mostly college-age volunteers hoping, in the words of organizer Bob Moses, "to open up Mississippi to the country." Warnings that this would be like going into combat were already proving true. Three days before Sam opened at the Copa, civil rights workers James Chaney, Michael Schwerner, and Andrew Goodman had disappeared on a country road outside of Philadelphia, Mississippi. Though their bodies wouldn't be found for two months, no one in the Movement or the black community had any doubt what had happened.

For Sam to sing Dylan's song in this atmosphere was an act both of protest and reassurance. The reassuring part was that he paced it so fast you couldn't—his voice couldn't—dwell on the lyrics, and the standard big-band rave-up at the end seemed to bring the whole issue to a happy conclusion. Still, the very fact of the performance reminded the crowd who he was—and who they were. It wasn't "A Change Is Gonna Come," but it was the one song he'd insisted be done at the Copa, never mind all the calculations.

Again, he ran offstage to eye the crowd's reaction. They kept applauding, and he came out one last time. "Tennessee Waltz" left them happy and humming. Thank you and good night. "After the first show," Alexander recalls, "when we got in the dressing room, to me it was like having an orgasm." Sam was still all tensed up, his hands balled like a fighter's. "Hey, old buddy, you can lighten up now." Sam grinned at Alex, and then the mob scene began: friends and family, industry people, strangers, all pushed in to congratulate him. The Copa's owner, Jules Podell, said he'd done good and, in his mobster accent, told him to keep the open-shirt thing; he liked dat. And the critics raved.

The *New York Times*, never a big fan of what it called "the leather-lunged set," concluded that "Mr. Cooke's talent stands the test. It may surprise, but he has dignity, humility and feeling to go with a strong voice." *Variety*, recalling his first Copa gig, said he'd returned as "a solid headliner. . . . He gives highly intense renditions to all of his material that stands it apart from the usual run of rock 'n' roll singers." *Billboard* called it a "swinging song affair that has appeal for the adult expense account trade as well as his teenage disk fans."

And the Negro community was equally enthusiastic. This time around, the Copa audience was about 30 percent black, a situation Crain had encouraged by helping to book two or three tables a night for uptown social clubs. The *Amsterdam News* announced that Cooke simply had "the best voice in the smart supper clubs." While he drove the females crazy, the paper observed, even the men "clapped, stamped their feet and added their applause to the deafening, thunderous cheers. . . ."

Sam was exhilarated. "I want to go to Las Vegas," he told a backstage reporter. "I feel I'm ready. I plan to appear along the club circuit and in concerts. Someday," he went on, "I'd like to do a Broadway play. . . ." It was all possible now. Out in the world of rock & roll, Beatlemania was permanently altering the musical landscape: their *A Hard Day's Night* LP sold a million copies in four days that July. But Sam was off in another direction. On the last night of his stand, Jules Podell took Cooke aside and presented him with Copa cufflinks—the ultimate sign of approval—and then RCA recorded the show for a live album. *Sam Cooke at the Copa* would stay on the LP charts more than a year. To observers from Otis Redding to Berry Gordy, Cooke had shown the way to translate soul into the sophisticated, higher-paying markets. Once again, Sam had crossed over.

Chapter
22

Sam flew back to California determined to capitalize on his triumph. A Christmas season booking was arranged for Miami's classy Deauville Hotel. And he set to work proving his talents could stretch from there to gospel—and everywhere in between.

On July 20, he did a SAR session with the Soul Stirrers, in town as part of the big "Gospel Train" program. On "Lead Me to Calvary," the last of the four tunes they cut that day, Sam called out to the group's guitarist, "Crume! Let me sing your part. I feel like singing." So Crume traded places in the studio, and Sam slipped back into the harmonies he loved. "He missed it," Crume recalls. "Anytime we came around and he was there I'd say, 'Do a couple tunes.' "

By now, the Stirrers understood Sam wasn't ever really coming back. In the garage at Ames Street where Sam did his woodshedding, he told Crume that he'd finally gotten his call from Vegas—and he planned to go in on *his* terms. No Vegas lounge band for him. "If they want me, they going to have to take my fucking band!" Sam told Crume. "They been with me ever since. I don't get rid of my guys."

"Oh yeah," Crume grinned. "You're on your way now."

At the end of July 1964, Cooke played the Club Harlem in Atlantic City: a thousand-seat room with a big oval bar that featured a full production—comics, showgirls, and a thirteen-piece orchestra. It was the East Coast equivalent of Vegas, complete with 6:00 A.M. breakfast shows on the weekend, except the audience was 95 percent black. Sam did three shows a night: a quick thirty-five minutes with encores. The crowd ate him up, singing along and even pounding the table with little wooden mallets the club provided (shades of Myron Cohen). After Atlantic City, Sam headed for New York to put together a new single meant to "get everyone."

But the stretch seemed to be getting harder almost daily. Harlem was recovering from a major riot. A white policeman had shot a fifteen-year-old black boy; the subsequent mayhem, according to one reporter, "looked more appropriate for Saigon. . . ." And after touring the area, Martin Luther King declared Northern cities "potentially more explosive" than the South. Even as President Johnson's civil rights bill passed, the idea of integration was beginning to erode. The Great Migration that had carried the Cooks to Chicago had dead-ended in rotten housing, worthless education, and apparently unshakable poverty. SNCC would soon vote to become an all-black organization; the eulogies for the slain civil rights workers Chaney, Goodman, and Schwerner rang with cries for vengeance; and Malcolm X was telling black students, "You'll get your freedom by letting your enemy know you'll do anything to get your freedom. . . ." Producer Al Schmitt's wife, Joan, remembers coming to see Sam at the Copa and having this romantic image of Harlem based on old movies and songs. "You gotta promise me you'll take me," she'd said to Sam in her slight Southern accent. "Woman, I wouldn't go to Harlem right now with Muhammad Ali. You think I'm going with a white chick? You *are* crazy!"

Sam deliberately disregarded all this at the singles session in New York. Instead, with Hugo and Luigi gone, with a guarantee of artistic control, he worked on strikingly un-black, middle-of-the-road songs to solidify his nightclub appeal. His new A-side ended up being a shaggy-dog story called "He's a Cousin of Mine." It featured a ragtime backup straight from some New Orleans tourist trap: "Frankie and Johnny" in even whiter whiteface. Then, two weeks later in Los Angeles, he cut a b-side that was among his most soulful.

For the first time ever, Sam decided to record with his road band:

June on drums, Harper on bass, Cliff and Bobby on guitars. The Sims Twins had tried Cooke's "That's Where It's At" two years before; now Sam did the tune as an echo of "Bring It On Home to Me": the same call-and-response vocal, the same lazy groove (kept a little tauter by June's steady drumming), the same rough and passionate vocal. The song has the sound of languid, late-night lovemaking—the held horn notes, Cosby's sloping bass, and, lyrically, Cooke pinpoints true pleasure as that split second when you both know it's time to go, and she says, "Stay. One minute more." Sam chuckles at the sheer beauty and foolishness of it all, and when he calls out that he can feel his heart beating and time passing, he sounds like a man trying to live every last moment. But as a bridge between his different audiences, the single was a failure. The soul audience rejected "Cousin of Mine" altogether, and "Where It's At" barely broke r&b's Top 100. On the pop charts, "Cousin" did reach #31, but it charted for only four weeks, the shortest run for a Cooke single in years.

Sam had said that a successful songwriter had to "try to figure the times of your day"; now, those times were splitting him a number of different ways. His friend Muhammad Ali, having denounced Malcolm X in May, had become even closer to the leader of the Nation of Islam, Elijah Muhammad. Ali had gotten married August 14, in Gary, Indiana, and Sam happened to be in Chicago the next day for a show. He stopped by to congratulate the groom and his new bride. Sonji, though not a believer, had agreed to follow her husband's religion: she dressed in the long robes, didn't wear makeup, followed the diet. Sam had been reading up not just on the religion but on black history in general and was fascinated. "He was striving for something," Harold Battiste says, "an ideal in his home that he seemed to be real frustrated about not being able to achieve. . . . He had an ideal for a family, but Barbara did not really—" And Battiste's voice drops off. Of course, Sam did not really, either.

The next night, Sam went from Islam to soul. Miller Beer and Chicago radio station WVON were sponsoring a gigantic free concert called the "Blues Revue." It featured some twenty acts—the best in the business—and, by the seven-fifteen showtime, all sixty thousand seats in the White Sox's Comisky Park were full. As the evening went on, it turned into a one-night history of black popular music. Muddy Waters bellowed his transformed Delta blues, Chuck Berry duck-walked through his formative rock & roll, and teenage Stevie Wonder offered inklings of a new, complex funk to come. The integrated crowd loved it all; just when they thought they'd heard the best, another star would come on: Marvin Gaye doing "You're a Wonderful One" or the Marvelettes with "Beachwood 4-5789."

It was Sam's job to try to close the show. By that time, what with the excitement and the beer, minor fights were breaking out in different places in the bleachers. Sam, completely surrounded by security men, walked out dressed in an open white shirt. "As far as just raw talent," says WVON's Purvis Spann, "man, he had it! The crispness of his voice, the pronouncement of his lyrics. I'd range Sam Cooke with the best that ever did it." As he worked the huge arena (by far the biggest crowd of his life), a sheen of sweat spread over him, and his white shirt opened to the waist. He waded into the nearby seats, sent his voice way up toward the outfield lights, and seemed to lift the entire stadium till it floated above his bruised hometown. Within a year or two, integrated audiences like this would be rare—the mid-sixties rioting made sure of that—but for a night, anyway, Sam really did seem to be reaching everyone.

The other side of this coin showed during his appearance a month later on national TV. His old session man Ray Pohlman was musical director for a new rock & roll show called *Shindig*. Originally produced in England, where it had a dark, moody look, the show scared "the suits from New York," as Pohlman recalls. They quickly made plans to do something much brighter, much more like *American Bandstand*. The premier, with the Righteous Brothers, the Everly Brothers, and Bobby Sherman, was squeaky-clean; there wasn't a shadow—or a person of color—until Sam came out.

He did two numbers from his Copa act. "Tennessee Waltz" came complete with jazzy arm gestures and hey-yea! hand claps. When he returned at the close of the show, he sang "Blowin' in the Wind" quietly and without a smile. It's still a nightclub version, but he refuses to let all meaning drain from the song. During the last verse, he mimes how many times a man must look up, then takes the mike and heads toward the almost-all-white teenage audience. As they rise, clapping, all we can see is Sam's back. The one black girl in the place tries to dance along, but there's no beat to the song, just urgency, so everyone ends up standing around Cooke, listening to the protest lyrics, smiling shyly, wondering what to do. It's a strange, revealing tableau; as if the show, the music it claimed to represent, and Sam were all facing the same dilemma. Yes, you can reach everybody—you can be all things to all people—but where exactly does that leave you?

Sam spent most of the rest of the fall in Los Angeles. SAR was quiet without Zelda: the single the Womacks cut in September was the first pop session in five months. And no new talent was turning up at the Soul Station. In fact, there was enough downtime for Battiste to moonlight a little for his old friend and co-a&r man from Specialty days Sonny Bono. It seems he and his girlfriend, Cherilyn, wanted to do duets. Early in October, the two of them parlayed their demos into a record contract and eventual fame as Sonny and Cher. "So the biggest thing that came out of the Soul Station," says Battiste, laughing a little grimly, "turned out not to be for the black community after all." Sam, meanwhile, was focused on his own career. As the *Live at the Copa* LP was shipped, he flew East to do a screen test for Twentieth Century–Fox, with allegedly impressive results. Then, in November, he went to work on his fourth single of the year.

That month a TV special, *The T.A.M.I. Show,* was shot at the Santa Monica Auditorium. The ultimate confrontation between Brit and soul music, it featured the blur of James Brown's legs versus the pout of Mick Jagger's lips. Brown's music was about to rise to a new level of rhythmic invention with the startling "Papa's Got a Brand New Bag," and Sam's next session took a similar approach to the British invasion: dance the invaders to death.

"Shake" opens with Sam shouting the title and being answered (like two gospel men trading leads) by Earl Palmer's powerful, controlled drumming. That turns out to *be* the chorus, and the verses are little more than variations on the theme. Sam calls out to move your body, make it "loose and light," use it like a whip, but always the song comes back to the beat, to Palmer's heavy tom-toms. Sam and the band went over it sixteen times—refining the groove till it was reined-in mayhem. Then they made the sequel. On "It's Got the Whole World Shakin'," Sam treats rhythm like an addictive substance. Somehow, it's gotten into the very air we breathe; it's made the band shout out the title; it's smeared the horns all over everything; it's got the whole world shaking. Sam's workout is nowhere near as frantic as James Brown's (you can almost hear Cooke calculating how this slower, controlled dance number could be adapted to the nightclubs), but it's got the same message: all power to the beat.

Having laid down these statements of pride, Sam then ended the session in compromise. It had been nearly ten months since he'd cut "A Change Is Gonna Come" as an album track. In July, he'd donated it to a SCLC fund-raising LP called *The Stars Salute Dr. Martin Luther King.* Now he wanted to release it as a single, but singles were supposed to clock in at around two and a half minutes; "Change" had been a little over three. Couldn't he cut a verse—perhaps that one about being told not to hang around downtown? Yes, fuckers: if it meant more people would get a chance to hear the song, he could cut the verse. The new single, "Shake"/"Change," would close 1964 with Sam's strongest statement yet of what was going on: the ecstatic dance number as demanding in its own way as the gorgeous ballad. Another two-sided hit, it ended up #7/#31 pop, and #2/#9 on the r&b chart, where it stayed three months.

Sam wasn't doing the grind of one-nighters anymore, but he still wanted to reach his "base." At the end of November, he did five nights at the Royal Peacock in Atlanta. It was a perfect venue for Cooke: Atlanta had been his town since the Soul Stirrer days; the Peacock was a large enough r&b room to guarantee good income but small enough for him to get over; and he didn't have to work all that hard—an eleven-o'clock and one-o'clock show each night with strong supporting acts. The Thanksgiving week performances, says Grady Gaines of the Upsetters, "went over great as you could ask of any show. It was packed—every day, every show, every night." At the end of the run, before flying back to Los Angeles, Cooke threw a big party and, as June recalls, "got everybody down with some money besides your salary, because this was the kind of guy he was." The band had almost a month off, paid, before opening at the Deauville in Miami. "Let's go home," Sam told June, "and get them children ready for Christmas."

Normally, the extended Cook family gathered for the holiday, in either Chicago or Los Angeles. This year, Charles Cook's wife, Phyllis, recalls, was different: "strange." In October, her children had received a package from Barbara, who then called to ask, "Did the kids get the gifts?"

"Well, yes," Phyllis had answered, "but why did you send them?"

"Well, some things just don't always work the way you want them to," Barbara replied, "and I wanted to get these gifts to you now." Barbara sounded very nervous, very high-strung: an uncomfortable conversation. And there were more during the fall and early winter: what Phyllis describes as "I-may-not-talk-to-you-again-but-I-want-to-say-these-things-to-you-now kind of phone calls." Phyllis was convinced Barbara and Sam were on the verge of divorce.

At the same time, Sam called Crain to say he wanted his road manager to fly out to New York with him. "The main thing was he was going to get his money out," says Crain. "I don't know how much. . . ." S.R. was a little perplexed: "I knew he had found out something, because all at once he said he was going to take his stuff in New York out of Allen Klein's hands." Steven Hill, Sam's promoter for his Caribbean tours, had an appointment to see Cooke in New York. Hill, who would later manage Marvin Gaye, was coming to town to discuss a world tour that would include South America and Australia. Klein says there was no money in New York—it was all in California—but that Sam was planning to fly out to appear at Allen's former orphanage in Newark.

Back in Los Angeles, Cooke made an appearance at the *Ebony* magazine Fashion Fair in L.A. and sat in on a Johnny Taylor session for SAR. Delighted with the cuts, Sam grabbed Alex: "Let's take Johnny and make him drunk!" They headed to the California Club, where they partied till the wee hours. The next day, he called in sick with a cold and then did the same Wednesday, though he was well enough to drop by mambo night at the California Club. That Thursday, feeling better, Sam had lunch with his old agent Jess Rand.

When the two came back from lunch, Rand recalls, Cooke talked about his plans. "He couldn't understand the company [Tracey]. . . . And then he was finding out that a lot of the ads—the billboard and everything—that Allen was telling him was going to be paid by the record company were being paid by him. . . ." Sam asked Jess to close his office door, and he said, "I want your dad to get me the best damn New York lawyer you can find." Cooke wanted out of his ties to Klein. He had talked to some of Allen's former clients, and it all was beginning to sound fishy. A few weeks earlier, he'd mentioned something similar to Bumps Blackwell—first asking Bumps to get involved in SAR/Derby and then telling him, "Allen Klein was no fucking good, was a liar, and was trying to cheat him." He was going to "dump Klein."

Klein vehemently denies Cooke and he were having any difficulties, only conceding that Sam might have said such things to keep old acquaintances "on the hook." Whatever his plan, it would wait till after Christmas. Sam had come by Jess's place without much cash (the money from the Atlanta shows was still in a briefcase back at Ames Street, according to Alex). Now he decided he wanted to do some shopping, and he went down to the Union Savings Bank, right below Rand's office, and took out $5,000 from a safety deposit box he kept there. According to Barbara, he rushed in and out of the Ames Street house later that day, maybe to drop off packages, but by early evening, he was over at René Hall's studio, working on some material for the Miami show. When they finished, Sam invited René to join him for dinner with Al and Joan Schmitt. Fine, Hall said; he'd just transcribe the tapes they'd made and meet him later. Cooke left in a happy mood, according to René, "very upbeat."

He arrived for his dinner with the Schmitts a little late, but that was standard with him. Martoni's Italian restaurant was a music-business hangout. In its dark interior, over first-class food, dj's, artists, and promo men cut deals or just kept track of the industry. The Schmitts were waiting at the bar in the long front room. When Sam came in, Joan thought he looked tired; she figured it was from just coming off the road. They sat and had a drink till their table was ready. Sam was drinking martinis, according to Al, and was "juicing pretty good."

They talked about the next album. "Sam and I were going to do a blues album—blues things, [Billie Holiday] kind of stuff," says Schmitt, and Sam was excited about it, about giving another try to the sort of material he'd worked on for so long. He invited the couple to come barbecue at his house that weekend and go over some other ideas for the record.

As Al remembers it, they were sitting at the bar about ten feet from the entrance to the restaurant's back room when a guy by the name of Jim Benci came up. Benci, a luggage salesman, also did some p.r. work for Liberty Records. "That guy," says Schmitt, "had the reputation for being around the record business and—not procuring or getting hookers for people—but for kind of: 'You want something? Oh, I know somebody.' He didn't make his living doing that; he just had access, I guess, to a lot of models and hookers." This evening, Benci appeared at the bar with a Eurasian woman in her early twenties, with long black hair and a round, attractive face. "In Hollywood, pretty girls are a dime a dozen," Joan Schmitt remembers thinking. "She wasn't a drop-dead beauty, but she was pretty. . . . She certainly didn't look like a hooker, but she also wasn't Miss Wholesome All-American looking—somewhere in between."

Sam exchanged pleasantries with Benci and the woman, and then their table was ready. As Sam stood to pay for the drinks, he flashed a wad. Al teased Sam about showing so much cash; Joan remembers it as being "several thousand dollars." The three friends went into the back dining room with their drinks and chatted as they waited for the food. Schmitt said he had to go see some local acts after dinner, did Sam want to come along? Yes, but he was tired. He'd catch the early act around eleven but probably miss the late one. After Sam had had his appetizer, he excused himself to go back to the bar briefly. When the main course came, Al went to see where he'd gone and came back reporting, "Aww, he's talking to some chick out there. He'll be back after a while."

But by the time the Schmitts had finished, Sam still hadn't returned. It wasn't that odd for Cooke; he knew everybody and was always getting caught up in conversations. It was around ten forty-five when the Schmitts headed out to catch their show. As they passed Sam in the bar, he was sitting in one of the booths with the woman Benci had brought by earlier.

Joan Schmitt's clear recollection is that despite Benci's introduction, the two looked like they knew each other. "When I saw them together [in the booth], I thought the girl was a friend. Because they were sitting side by side, and she had her hand on his arm, and she was kind of leaning, almost whispering to him—talking in an intimate way, smiling—and he was smiling. The picture in my mind at the moment was, 'Oh, this is somebody he knows.' "

Al went over and said they had to run; he couldn't miss this act. "Listen," Sam said, "I'm gonna stick around here for a while. I'll meet you later." They agreed to meet over at PJ's, another bar, after the show: around one.

When René Hall finished his transcribing and came by to meet Sam, around twelve-thirty, "the regular woman that he used to see over at Martoni's was there . . . the woman I knew he would sit up and drink with . . ." but the bartender told Hall that Cooke had just left for PJ's. "Hell," René thought to himself, "I ain't going over there," and he headed home.

Around the same time, down in south L.A., J.W. was giving up, too. Sam had called him earlier in the day and said they'd hook up at the California Club. Alexander had been waiting since nine; now, he told the owner, Mambo Maxie, "If Sam comes through, tell him I'll see him at the office tomorrow. I'm gonna get a Christmas tree and put it up for my baby."

Around one in the morning, the Schmitts arrived at PJ's and waited another half hour, but Sam never showed there, either, so they went home. A few hours later, Al was awakened by a call from his friend Lester Sill.

"Did you hear what happened?"

"What?"

"Sam got shot."

"Oh, my God! What hospital is he in?"

"He's not in a hospital. He's dead."

Chapter 23

After that first call, the Schmitts' phone kept ringing—RCA execs, friends, then calls from Germany, England—all asking if it was true. "I can remember," says Joan, "Al and I—after the initial shock—just sort of being immobilized. Not even being able to get up, just laying in bed, holding each other, crying." As they went over what they'd heard of the circumstances of the death—the motel on Figueroa Street; Sam, naked, breaking down the manager's door— neither could believe it. Al blurted out, "Sam Cooke wouldn't be caught dead in Watts!"—and then they both realized how that sounded.

J. W. Alexander was also asleep. When his wife woke him, he turned on the radio to confirm the news. "I was just hurt so. And trying to think rationally. I said, 'Get the baby together and let's go out to the [Cookes'] house.' "

Barbara called René Hall early that morning. "No," he explained to her, that wasn't right: "I just left Sam." Barbara gave him a minute to wake up and then told him again: "Sam's dead."

Johnnie Morisette hadn't slept that night. Around four in the morning, he was up and restless at his girlfriend's place. She kept asking him if he wanted something to eat, some coffee. Finally, he walked into the kitchen, where the radio was on low. "I think it was KGFJ was playing the music, and all of a sudden the music just stopped. And they put on a gospel record. And that was rare. And I said, oh shit! . . . It was some new disk jockey on KGFJ, and he said, 'Ladies and gentlemen, singer Sam Cooke has just been shot and killed.' . . . I thought him and Barbara had got into it. I didn't know what the hell had happened. I don't know [what I did]. I went off into something."

An hour or so later, the phone woke Zelda Sands. It was disk jockey Larry McCormick telling her to get over to Barbara's. "I don't even remember after that. The next few days, I don't even know. My friends tell me about it."

Lou Adler was the same way. "I actually blanked; I don't recall anything about the time. . . . I went away for a week, disappeared for a week. I didn't talk to anybody. I cried all week; I cried a lot. It's one of the only times I ever cried in my life."

"I didn't cry," Harold Battiste recalls. "I never—that wasn't available to me. . . . I just was confused, and I was angry, really angry, at what I was hearing. Because it was sounding like Sam was out cavorting around with a prostitute. My perception of Sam and what I know his soul was—whatever the circumstances was—I *know* that was not Sam!"

Around nine in the morning, Atlanta time, the Soul Stirrers were pulling out of that city and heading to North Carolina for their next program. Leroy Crume had spoken to Sam the day before; Cooke had promised to send on a car because their van had caught fire. They'd waited and waited that morning, but gotten no call, so Crume—ticked off at Cooke—had left town. Driving along, they heard the radio announce, "Sam Cooke has been shot and killed in Los Angeles." Crume, driving, flipped channels for more information. Three different times Sam's old group heard the news, and still nobody said a word. Finally, the longest-standing member, bass singer and manager J. J. Farley, broke the silence. "Well, at least he's not dead." "What do you mean, he's not dead?" Crume answered. "He said 'shot and killed'!" Farley insisted: "But he's not dead." "What do you mean, J.J.?" Finally, another member spoke in a soft voice from the back of the van: "Jesse, Sam is dead." Then there was only the sound of the radio.

And in Chicago, S. R. Crain was also awakened by an early-morning call. It was Sam's father, Reverend Cook. "Oh, Poppa!" is how Crain responded to the news, "You shouldn't say that. Man lyin' and playin' like that!" Charley Cook told him to turn his radio on; turn his television on. "And I heard it on everything in the house," S. R. recalls. "I was in awe of it. . . . It came on me so fast, I just couldn't believe it." Crain's next call was from Allen Klein in New York. Would S.R. go out to Los Angeles to take care of things, since he knew the family and all? Klein would send a ticket.

Crain caught the next plane, then went directly from the airport to the Ames Street house. Barbara's twin, Beverly, was there, and the kids were being managed by the nanny. Barbara wasn't making much sense. "I guess," says S.R., "she was just too excited. . . . Death is a thing that excites you anyway."

"Well, Crain," she said, "let's go see him. 'Cause he's at the motel."

But when the two of them drove out to Figueroa, Sam's body wasn't there; the police had picked it up around four that morning. The motel was roped off. "I saw Sam's car parked out there: his red Ferrari," Crain recalls. "I found a bottle of whiskey in his Ferrari. It was open, but it was all in there almost. I looked at it. This was strange to me, too. Sam don't put no whiskey all over his car."

Neither Crain nor Barbara looked at the scene of the crime, and Crain has regretted it since. "All we had to do—Barbara and I—if I'd have been thinking—but I was in such a hurry to go see where Sam was—I should have went to the sheriff's office, gotten me a policeman, gotten me permission from downtown, handed him one or two big bills: that I could go with him and search both of those places. I could have shoved some money around and done it."

Instead, they drove home. When they got there, Crain asked again where Sam was. Barbara, described in newspaper reports of the time as "heavily sedated," said she didn't know. "You what!?" Crain called the police, who said the body was in the morgue. An autopsy had been performed around ten that morning. The God-fearing Texan was outraged. "Why put him in the morgue?! That's where you put people who ain't got nowhere to go! You wouldn't put a man like

Sam Cooke in the morgue! Why would you do that?" Because no one had called for the body. Barbara told Crain to make the arrangements, and S.R. brought in People's Funeral Home: the city's most prestigious black undertakers.

The next few hours were chaos at Ames Street. People kept coming by—friends, relations, the curious—and the phone wouldn't stop ringing. Though the story had broken too late for the morning papers, it was all over radio and TV. They were broadcasting the police version: that Sam had kidnapped Lisa Boyer, had tried to rape her, and had been killed by Bertha Franklin, the motel manager. The emphasis was on the sleazy aspects: how Sam had arrived, half naked, at Franklin's office, kicked the door down, and wrestled with the fifty-five-year-old black woman before being shot. The first police statements described Lisa—also known as Elisha—Boyer as being a prostitute and having an extensive record. (The police would later say she had no record, explaining that they'd confused Boyer with another Asian, Lisa Lee.) In call after call at Ames Street, people expressed their condolences and then insisted Sam couldn't have died that way. All Crain could say was he didn't know any more than what everyone else had heard.

Producer Al Schmitt's wife, Joan, was as disbelieving as any of Sam's friends. "As the story started being pieced together, I was feeling very angry. How could this happen? How could this man have been shot by accident?" She didn't believe Sam had knowingly left Martoni's with a hooker—or that he would frequent a cheap motel in Watts—or that he would kick down a door to attack a middle-aged Negro woman. Unlike many of Cooke's other acquaintances, Schmitt could investigate. A reporter for a San Fernando Valley paper, the *Valley Times Today*, Joan used her press pass to get into the 77th Precinct the afternoon after Sam's death.

A white woman with a slight Southern accent, she asked what had happened. "What do you mean, what happened? A guy was in a motel with a hooker, and he got shot. That happens all the time down here."

Schmitt, sitting in a room full of white policemen, tried again. "You don't know who this is?"

"No."

"Sam Cooke."

"Who's Sam Cooke?"

Finally, she mentioned "You Send Me," and the officers remembered that one. But their attitude, as Schmitt recalls, was "So what? Big deal. Another nigger shot in Watts on a Saturday night."

As she sat in the precinct looking over the grisly pictures of the death scene—the motel manager's office sprayed with blood, Sam's naked body slumped against the wall—the phones started ringing. Schmitt remembers calls from London, Canada, and Paris, as the press got on the story. The 77th Precinct began to realize that its routine case might not be.

Sam's fans—especially the young black ones—had reacted immediately. While Schmitt sat at the station and Crain made the necessary arrangements, an informal service had already begun out at the Hacienda Motel. As soon as the news hit, teenagers began arriving and, according to the *Los Angeles Sentinel*, "demonstrating against the slaying . . . singing many songs the popular singer had recorded." They kept it up most of Friday night: Watts come out to praise and defend one of its own in the only way available to it—on the streets.

The next morning, Saturday, the news hit the papers. For the Negro press, it was page-one, headline news. The *New York Times* announced the death of the "Negro singing star" on page 34.

By now, the Ames Street house had filled with people. Allen Klein had flown out, Jess Rand came by, Cliff White. Crain had called his sister, Margaret Cranhaw, to come down and look after things. When she arrived that morning, Barbara was so sedated she seemed barely to know where she was. "She look just like herself. Only thing, every once in a while she stop talking. And tears would run out of [her] eyes. . . ."

At the Hacienda Motel, the mourning/protest continued for a second day. As more and more people began to question the facts of Sam's death, a formal coroner's inquest was announced for the 16th. Klein issued a statement:

"Cooke's death as reported is impossible. Sam was known to have carried large sums of money at all times and it is evident that someone is trying to cover up the true reason for the tragedy. Sam was a happily married man with deep religious convictions, who was not a violent person, and the statements given out as to why he was killed are entirely inconsistent with the type of person he was."

The next day, Sunday, the crowds began arriving outside People's Funeral Home shortly after noon. Somewhere between five thousand and six thousand came through or were still massed outside waiting by 11:00 P.M. when viewing hours ended. Double lines of weeping teenagers, elderly gospel fans, young mothers with their dressed-up babies would form again early Monday and Tuesday. "Many, even the men, cry openly and unashamedly," said a People's employee, "and none seems to believe the story behind the killing." It was an extraordinary display; the *Chicago Defender* went back almost forty years to the funeral of matinee idol Rudolph Valentino for a comparison.

Meanwhile, at the Ames Street house, Crain got a call from the Reverend Cook. "I wish y'all would bring my son to Chicago and let them funeralize him here." Sam's mother had been ill and hardly got around at all anymore. "You sure right, Poppa! I'll be glad to do what I can." But Barbara's first, quick answer was no, she wasn't taking her husband's body halfway back across the country to subject herself to two funerals. Crain told Reverend Cook he'd call back. That evening, after dinner, he reasoned with her: "Princess, how in the world you think I can raise my head up if I don't carry that boy to see his momma and his daddy?" Barbara agreed, and Charles Cook started making arrangements.

Meanwhile, the *Chicago Defender* had jumped on the questions surrounding Cooke's death. One of their photographers, Cleo Lyles, had grown up with Sam, and he raised specific doubts. "Kicking a door down just doesn't sound like Sam. He might have met her, but he was never the type of guy who would fight. I believe Sam was framed. It just doesn't sound like Sam—unless something drastic happened to him." The page-one headline over the story read, "Why Was Sam Cooke Slain?" In a follow-up article, Barbara's mother told the paper, "I'll always believe that Sam was framed, for he did not have to do those things. He loved my daughter." And Sam's old gos-

pel friend the Reverend Sammy Lewis pointed out that Cooke
wouldn't have gone with a hooker—women were all over him—and
insisted that Lisa Boyer's background be checked. "I stake my life
that she wasn't kidnapped. The only way you get kidnapped is by
gun or knifepoint. And you just don't take time to go to a crowded
motel and register. . . . And why would that motel manager, Mrs.
Franklin, call Sam a prowler when she registered him? . . . It was
probably a setup between the woman and the motel manager. Poor
Sam," Lewis added. "I hope there will be a grand jury investigation
to bring out the truth."

The white press gave it considerably less play. Sam's old friend
Dorothy Kilgallen, however, used the death as the lead for her
nationally syndicated entertainment column that Tuesday, December 15. "Although the story made headlines, it's really far bigger
than the news dispatches revealed; several pertinent and sensational
angles were suppressed by someone, so it probably will remain another of those Los Angeles 'mystery cases.'"

The same day Kilgallen's article appeared, the *Chicago Defender*
called the 77th Precinct and spoke with the sergeant in charge of the
investigation. "There are no indications that there was any foul
play . . ." he told the paper. "[Bertha Franklin] didn't know Sam
Cooke from me. She was only defending herself. . . . What would
anyone have done if a partially nude man came busting through
the door?" The sergeant added that Franklin had passed a lie detector test.

Lisa Boyer, on the other hand, had temporarily disappeared. The
manager of her apartment building had asked her to leave, TV cameras had recorded her departure, and the *L.A. Sentinel* reported the
police were now trying to find her. They apparently succeeded, because by the next day, Boyer had taken her own lie detector test and,
according to the LAPD, passed it.

On Wednesday, at 1:00 P.M., the coroner's inquest began in L.A.'s
Hall of Justice. The first witness before the seven-person jury was
Barbara Cooke. As she proceeded to the stand with a broad-brimmed
hat pulled low over her eyes, photographers rushed forward. The deputy coroner asked her no more than to state her name and address

and to identify the remains. She did so and returned to her seat next to Crain and directly behind Bertha Franklin.

The medical examiner was then called to testify that the cause of Sam's death had been a .22 caliber bullet that had entered his body near his left armpit, gone through both lungs, and pierced his heart. There were also small scratches on his left cheek and forehead and a two-inch lump on his head. The blow to his head hadn't fractured his skull, and his brain wasn't damaged, but the coroner testified it might have left Sam unconscious. His blood contained 0.14 percent drinking alcohol, enough that "it might affect his judgment." There was no evidence of narcotics, and there were no further questions.

Policeman Wallace Cook (no relation) then testified that he'd been first on the scene, discovered the body, and heard Bertha Franklin's explanation that Sam had broken down the door, searched the apartment, and then begun wrestling with her. She'd shot him with her .22 pistol, and when he'd "continued to struggle," she'd hit him over the head with a stick. The representative of the D.A.'s office had the officer identify Franklin's bloodstained turquoise dress from the night of the murder, her gun, and the stick. When the district attorney's office finished, the coroner turned to a man misidentified as Mr. Macheck, Barbara Cook's attorney. Marty Machat was an attorney who had worked with Allen Klein for a while and done some work for Sam's KAGS publishing as far back as August of 1963. He'd flown out, according to Alex, "to help us try to find out what the hell went down." Machat asked Officer Cook about the layout of the motel manager's office and if people who registered there would normally enter the room. The coroner interrupted to say Officer Cook wouldn't know that. Well, how would a person register? Again, the coroner interrupted to say that would come out later. The question was withdrawn, and Officer Cook was dismissed.

The next witness was Lisa Boyer. She was dressed in a conservative black-and-white-check dress, with a scarf tied closely around her straight black hair, and a pair of dark sunglasses that completely obscured her eyes. She gave her address as 7110 Hollywood Boulevard, a motel, and announced she didn't have a lawyer but was ready to testify. Boyer described meeting Sam at a "Hollywood dinner party" and the two going on to PJ's. She then told how Sam had refused to take her home, speeding south on the freeway instead and murmuring how pretty she was, as she'd pleaded with him to turn around. When she got to the part where Sam had taken her by the arm at the Hacienda Motel and "dragged me into that room," the two hundred people crowded into the courtroom began yelling "No, no!" till the coroner had to stop the proceedings. "There will be no demonstration or no outbursts. If there are, these people will be eliminated from hearing the inquest. . . ."

When order had been restored, Boyer went on to describe how Sam had pinned her to the bed and ripped her dress, how she'd escaped—with her own and, mistakenly, Sam's clothes—and then called the cops. "I had no idea that someone had shot Mr. Cooke." The D.A.'s office then put into evidence a piece of paper with Sam's name and two of his telephone numbers on it. Boyer testified that he'd given it to her the night they'd met and that she'd subsequently been fingerprinted and taken a lie detector test, and the D.A.'s office announced it had no further questions. Nor did the coroner. "May I—" Machat began. "You may be excused, Miss Boyer. May this witness leave the inquest?" the coroner asked the assistant D.A. Lisa left without being cross-examined.

Bertha Franklin was next. In a white sweater with a string of pearls and dark glasses, the motel manager proved to be a straightforward, not-very-well-spoken witness. She told about Sam's breaking into her office, searching the place, then grabbing her by both wrists before she broke free and shot him. The D.A. entered into the record the motel registration Sam had signed. When "Mr. Macheck" rose to ask a question at the end, the coroner again interrupted and explained that Franklin had no attorney present; the D.A. could ask questions; Machat could consult with the D.A. Then Franklin was excused. An hour had gone by, and a ten-minute recess was called.

The next witness was a renter at the motel that night who'd been awakened by the sound of a car pulling up. He'd seen Cooke and Boyer heading toward their room after registering and Boyer offering "a little bit of resistance." No, he hadn't heard any gunshots; yes, he had seen Cooke before. The coroner didn't ask where or when, and

neither the D.A. nor Machat cross-examined. Evelyn Card, the owner
of the motel, testified next, and then one of the policemen in charge
of the investigation, who said neither Franklin nor Boyer had crim-
inal records and both had passed lie detector tests. He then played
the police tapes of Boyer's and the motel owner's calls for help.
Machat did get a chance to cross-examine this witness. He asked
what position Sam had been in when the bullet was fired; the investigator said there was no way of telling. He asked if anyone had testified that Sam had asked for his clothes; the answer was no. Was
anything else missing? The family and Alex said there was a credit
card carrier that should have been there, as well as the wallet and
Sam's driver's license; they weren't found. Machat said that was all,
but the coroner and the D.A.'s office wanted to establish that there
was no evidence of robbery. True, Lisa had not been searched when
she was brought into the station that night. But her purse had been
checked, and neither Sam's credit cards and license nor any extra
money had been found.

If the jury had any questions, including whether Cooke had been
ripped off (friends would later also mention an expensive ring he
wore), they didn't say anything. The inquest, barely two hours long,
was concluded. The jury deliberated fifteen minutes, then ruled
Cooke's death was justifiable homicide; Bertha Franklin had shot Sam
"in protection of life and property." Looking back on it, the foreman
of the jury recalled it as an open-and-shut case. It never occurred to
them to question the police version.

After the inquest, Sam's body was flown out to Chicago, where
Charles Cook had the local undertakers give another try at making
Sam look peaceful; brother L.C. redid the hair himself. The corpse
was then placed in a $5,000 bronze-decorated casket with a beige in-
terior and a glass top. A crowd had begun to surround A. R. Leek's
funeral home; the *Defender* did some on-the-street interviews. "I
think he got too big for his own good," said one sixteen-year-old girl.
A fan and collector of his records figured, "If he had been home with
his family, this would never have happened." And a dj thought he
was a great talent but conceded that if the story of his death was
true, "he got what he had coming."

The scandal and Sam's fame brought more than six thousand people out to the wake that afternoon. Traffic was blocked off a half mile in every direction around Cottage Grove. Although thirty police cars and fifty patrolmen were assigned to maintain order, the streets soon filled with wailing, crying fans, and additional cops had to be called. When it became clear that some people weren't going to get in, the crowd pressed forward and the big plate-glass windows in front of Leek's cracked under the pressure. "There are just too many of them!" the funeral director shouted, and as S. R. Crain remembers it, "They like to tear that town down!"

By the time the funeral ceremony was set to begin at eight that night, the temperature had dropped to three above zero. "Bitter, bitter, bitter," says Crain and then adds in his down-to-earth way, "The colder it is, that's the more people you have in Chicago. . . . See, that's the more furs they can wear." Three thousand people jammed into the Tabernacle Baptist Church; another seven thousand waited outside in the cold. "A few white people were seen among the mourners," a reporter noted, "and a few celebrities, but basically the crowd was formed by the little people off the street. . . ." As the Chicago police shouted through bullhorns and tried to keep the overflow of mourners away from the church, the crowd shoved, pushed, and slugged their way toward the entrance. The cops had to open a path for the coffin, and although a section of the church had been roped off for the family, it took the elder Cooks and other relatives a good forty minutes to get to their front-row pews.

Willie Webb—the Chicago gospel mainstay who'd played on Sam's big hit "Nearer to Thee"—opened the service with "Precious Lord." After a series of Chicago's leading preachers spoke and led prayers, the Reverend Clay Evans, Sam's last pastor, gave the eulogy. He remembers the service as "Colossal! Out of sight! The crowd: that was beyond a congregation. . . . A lot of people were there for many different reasons: some out of curiosity, some out of sympathy. . . . There was a certain amazement. How could this happen?" Comedian and civil rights activist Dick Gregory attended, as did singers Dee Clark and Major Lance, and a number of gospel groups, including the Highway QCs and the Staples Singers. Muhammad Ali appeared with one of the Honorable Elijah Muhammad's sons. Though he wouldn't speak to reporters at the funeral, Ali was visibly moved and later angrily told a radio audience: "I don't like the way he was shot. I don't like the way it was investigated. If Cooke had been Frank Sinatra, the Beatles, or Ricky Nelson, the FBI would be investigating yet and that woman [Mrs. Franklin] would have been sent to prison."

The *Los Angeles Sentinel*'s Thursday edition reported that Sam's "associates" had seen him and Lisa Boyer dating "during the past four years." The article asserted that the LAPD admitted not knowing about the earlier acquaintanceship till after Lisa Boyer had been released. Associates also said that Sam had been at the Hacienda Motel before and knew Bertha Franklin. Franklin, the paper revealed, had been accused of shooting at a motel guest in an earlier incident that had grown out of an argument. The same issue quoted J. W. Alexander as having told police that some things were not being "brought out" about the death. The evening after the inquest, Alexander, Machat, and Klein were at the Beverley Hills Hotel—where the latter two were staying—and "Here comes Lisa Boyer!" Alex recalls. She was one of two women strolling out on a man's arm. Machat advised them to say nothing; by this time, Klein had hired a private detective to look into the case.

Dorothy Kilgallen published a follow-up article on Thursday, December 17. Kilgallen had become nationally known as more than a simple gossip columnist. She had obtained and published portions of the Warren Commission's report on JFK's assassination before it was officially released, and in late 1964 she was working with conspiracy theorist Mark Lane. Now she treated Sam's shooting with the same skepticism. "Adding to the mystery," she wrote, were the facts that Sam hadn't been "drinking excessively or taking narcotics," he had signed in under his own name, he had been "beaten with a broomstick," his card case and license were missing, and no one at the motel had heard screams or the door being kicked in. As a well-known white journalist, Kilgallen added mainstream legitimacy to the rumors that were sweeping through the black press.

Sam's body was flown back to Los Angeles Friday morning, a week after the singer had been killed. It lay in state at People's until Saturday at two, when the second and final funeral rites took place. It started raining early that morning, and, in a city used to perpetual sun, many saw it as a sign. With a week to prepare, with the local radio stations playing Sam's hits and giving out the address of the Mount Sinai Baptist Church, an enormous crowd had formed. One reporter noted "long lines of convertible Cadillacs, Rivieras, and Thunderbirds, ladies in more mink and men in more silk than the Internal Revenue allows, teen-aged fans in bobbysocks and fancy flowered silk stockings stuffed into cold, wet, and uncomfortable pointed toe shoes with spiked heels. . . ." Again, there were fistfights, elbowing, shouting. Hustlers sold Sam's records, publicity shots, even nickle photographs of Sam in his coffin in Chicago.

By two o'clock, five thousand people had surrounded the church and the traffic was backed up in every direction. "We had to park several blocks away," recalls Joan Schmitt. As she and her husband walked in the drizzle through the black neighborhood, they heard Sam's voice coming out of radios and record players, looping in and out of so many songs at the same time that finally all you could hear was the quality of the voice itself.

The crowd, meanwhile, kept growing. "The nearest thing to madness I ever saw," Jess Rand recalls. And Zelda Sands remembers it as "infested . . . a sea of people." The crush delayed the family's arrival forty-five minutes. When Barbara finally did pull up with the children, the crowd pushed in till she could barely get out of the car. "I looked up and Barbara, his wife, wasn't riding in one of the funeral cars," René Hall remembers with a laugh. "She was riding in her Rolls-Royce: Sam's Rolls-Royce. And I looked in there, and she had their banker with them." More startling to many was the earlier appearance of twenty-year-old Bobby Womack wearing what Sam's intimates recognized as the dead man's clothes. Rosko, an honorary pallbearer, remembers a ripple going through the crowd. "Dig that shit!" muttered the Travelers' bassman, George McCurn. It seemed more than tasteless; there was something crazy about the kid arriving that way.

The service began with Billy Preston playing an organ prelude; then there was a choral rendition of "Yield Not to Temptation." Before Lou Rawls could begin a slow, growling version of "Just a Closer Walk with Thee," there was a ruckus. Speakers had been set up outside on the street so the overflow crowd could hear the service, but someone was trying to get in. It was Sam's former secretary and assistant, Zelda. "Some reverend is standing there," Zelda recalls, "saying, 'Sorry. Nobody else can go in.' And I just flung! I had a fist: I was screaming; I was kicking!" She ended up punching her way into the church. "If there's ever humor at funerals," René Hall says, it was this incident with Zelda: "Every time things would get real solemn and quiet, she'd push back these guards and force the door open and they'd snatch her back."

Columnist Gertrude Gibson read a eulogy that reviewed Sam's life and ended with a poem: "Life is a game . . . God decreed we must play./And before we know it . . . we are called away." Bobby "Blue" Bland sang, as Johnny Morisette, drunk and despairing, jumped from his pew and yelled, "Sam! Sam! I'm sorry, Sam!"

"It wasn't uplifting," is how Lou Adler puts it. "I've been to other black funerals where they make you forget about the fact the guy died, you know? There was definite sadness. There were a lot of people breaking down . . . screaming . . . 'You can't take Sam!' "

Dr. A. B. Charles, Mount Sinai's pastor, delivered the final eulogy. "Sam Cooke has lived his life. He has made his contribution. If he had not died when he did, Sam Cooke would still have to die sometime."

The final performer was supposed to have been Bessie Griffen of the Gospel Pearls, but she'd collapsed, unable to go on. Now, as the crowd sat quietly in the pews, a whisper began working its way from the back of the church forward. "Brother Ray's here! Brother Ray's here! Brother Ray's here!" Slowly, the congregation swung around, and there was Ray Charles being led down the center aisle. He paused to put his hands on Sam's glass-enclosed casket. When he turned back to the crowd, tears pouring down his cheeks, he asked what they wanted him to do. "Sing, Ray! Sing, brother!" J. W. Alexander held the microphone as Charles, unprepared, seated himself at the piano. "Sam, baby," said the blind singer, "this is for you." And then he sang a slow version of the old spiritual "Angels Watching

Over Me." Thirty years later, witnesses still cry when they talk about it. Charles rocked back and forth on the piano stool, his voice cracking and hanging on the notes, as the huge crowd that surrounded the church stilled. Even Alexander, trying to take care of business, found the mike shaking in his hand and the tears falling.

When the service was over, around four o'clock, the crowd poured back onto the streets, Cooke's voice still drifting up from the surrounding buildings. Then the funeral cortege slowly made its way to Forest Lawn, where the body was finally laid to rest under a small bronze marker that read:

SAM COOKE

I Love You

1930–1964

Until the Day Break,

And The Shadows Flee Away.

Having the wrong birth year on the marker somehow fits an ending where nothing seemed quite right. After the inquest, despite many protests, the city D.A. upheld the 77th Precinct's investigation and refused to file a complaint. Klein and Alexander hired a private investigator for a "sweeping probe." On the front page of its Christmas Eve edition, The *Los Angeles Sentinel* ran an article headed "Nation Seeks Answers." Its switchboard had been flooded with people asking what had become of Sam's money, credit cards, license; why did the angle of the bullet go from the left armpit down to the right, as if he'd been shot from above; why had Franklin had the motel owner, Evelyn Card, call the police instead of doing it herself; "Was Cooke dead when Miss Boyer phoned police she had been kidnapped?"; and "Did Miss Boyer witness his slaying?" The *Sentinel* concluded by saying that these questions hadn't been answered and "newspapers from Los Angeles to New York are also asking them."

Late in December, Alexander told the *Sentinel*, "We have definite information that Lisa Boyer is a prostitute." Early in the new year, Klein was quoted as saying that his private detective had turned up evidence indicating that Sam had burst into Franklin's office looking not for Boyer, but for his license and credit cards. "Klein believes the woman, fearing Cooke would harm her, shot him as he shook her demanding she return his clothing and his credit cards. . . . 'It just wasn't Sam's nature to chase women like that,' Klein said." Alexander told the *Amsterdam News*, "We are very encouraged by what we have found, and we intend to push this investigation until the complete truth is known. We are convinced there was foul play involved that has not come fully to light. We feel there are people who were in the motel who have not divulged what they really heard and saw." Plus, there was evidence that "shed new light" on Franklin and Boyer.

On January 11, 1965, a month after Sam's death, the Hollywood vice squad got a tip about some hookers in a local hotel. One officer called and set up a date with a woman who "agreed to perform acts with the officer 'which went considerably beyond normal relations.' " The reputed asking price was $50. The police then raided the place, and the woman turned out to be Lisa Boyer, who was charged with prostitution and ordered to stand trial.

Meanwhile, Barbara Cooke and the twenty-year old Bobby Womack were, according to the *Sentinel*, "dating openly, attending local nightclubs and social events together." Bobby told the papers he'd admired Barbara for a long time but "she never knew." He'd stayed around her "during the crisis. She really needed someone at that time . . ." and then he'd asked her to marry him. Citing his friendship with Sam, Bobby argued that "he would want me to do this," although he admitted that at first, Barbara had been shocked. It had taken her a few weeks to decide, but by late in January—less than two months after her husband had been shot—she was telling columnist Gertrude Gibson about her engagement. Barbara announced they would tie the knot on February 25, two days after the final disposition of Sam's estate.

Sam's producer, Al Schmitt, remembers getting a call from Barbara around this time: she wanted to bring Bobby by to get him a recording contract. "When Bobby walked in, I almost fell over, because he had all Sam's clothes on!" Neither Bobby nor Barbara seemed to understand that the romance might offend some people. "The children are very fond of me," Bobby told the press before the marriage and then chuckled. "Tracey even calls me Daddy. They think I look a lot like Sam." Cooke fans were horrified; even Barbara's mother reacted sourly, telling the *Chicago Defender*, "I don't know anything about those people's business, so I really don't want to say anything." As Curtis Womack recalls, the public didn't really get that his brother Bobby was "a dumb little kid, running around and getting dirty." Inevitably, the gossip mills churned, as people assumed that Bobby and Barbara had had something going on before Sam died. When Bobby assured the press that "we still believe [the shooting] was a setup thing," many whispered that maybe the widow and her young lover had played a part in it.

If Sam Cooke left a will—and many family and friends believe he did—it was never registered. On February 23, Barbara was named administrator of the estate. The next day, she and Bobby hurried to the University Hospital for a blood test; then, TV cameras following, they appeared before a superior court judge to be married. They were refused. Since Bobby wouldn't turn twenty-one for another month, the judge told them he needed written permission from his parents. Barbara—with fourteen-year-old daughter Linda in tow—announced to the assembled reporters that the couple would ask the elder Womacks and then gave Bobby a loving kiss. But the Womacks wouldn't agree. Mrs. Womack was quoted as saying she "wanted no part of it." So Bobby and Barbara waited until early March, when Womack turned twenty-one, and then married in a ceremony so private that brother Curtis heard about it only after the couple had left Los Angeles for their honeymoon.

By this time, according to Allen Klein, the private investigation into Sam's shooting had been ended on Barbara's request. "Look, I've got two little kids," she told him. "It's going to be painful for them. Why don't we forget it." Her other point to Allen was even more forceful. "Will it bring Sam back?" While the answer appears obvious, for a legion of Sam Cooke fans, friends, and his family, it wasn't. Cooke's death had transformed his image. From pop star, former gospel singer, businessman, and civil rights supporter, he'd been turned into an adulterer and rapist, a drunk attacking an old woman, a naked body slumped against the wall of a cheap motel. For those who cared about Sam, every sleazy detail of his last night was vitally important, because proving that story false would reestablish their hero. The answer to Barbara's question was yes. Absolutely. Finding out the truth about Sam's death *would* bring him back.

Chapter
24

By the time the Los Angeles Police Department realized how famous their "dead nigger" was, it had, to all intents and purposes, closed the case: the report had been filed, the autopsy was done, and both Lisa Boyer and Bertha Franklin had been interviewed. It was only after the press started calling that detectives arranged lie detector tests. Then the coroner and the D.A. pushed through a rapid inquest that confirmed the police findings and limited the amount of cross-examination. If the official version of Sam's death is true, it was never proved in court. And there are some large holes in the story.

The contradictions begin immediately. When Lisa Boyer was asked at the inquest when she'd first met Sam Cooke, her answer was: "Well, we spoke to each other on Thursday evening." The ambiguous wording was never questioned. Joan Schmitt's recollection that when she left Martoni's, Sam was sitting in a booth with Lisa Boyer snuggled up next to him, looking as if they already knew each other well, fits with newspaper accounts that they'd been seen "dating" over the last few years.

While J. W. Alexander now says he doubts that—"I think Sam met Lisa Boyer at Martoni's"—Curtis Womack distinctly remembers coming back into town after Sam's death, and Alex saying, " 'We knew this girl from some time' . . . like a groupie-type chick they knew." Cliff White is sure he saw Alex and Lisa Boyer together a while before Sam's shooting. Lou Adler confirms that she "hung around the music areas," and Johnny Morisette, pimping in the area, says, "I don't know whether Sam know Elisha Boyer or not. But I had saw Elisha a lot, up in Hollywood. . . . I used to just see her in them clubs, and she'd always be with them entertainers. Sam could have known her."

Boyer testified that she was introduced to Sam that night at what she called "a party in Hollywood." After the introduction, "he decided to give me his telephone number," which is why it was later found in her pocketbook. The coroner didn't ask where the party was or why Cooke gave her his number. Later that evening, during the "dinner party," according to Boyer, "Mr. Cooke got up and sang. . . ." While it's a stretch to call Martoni's a "Hollywood party," it's even harder to believe Sam got up and sang there: the Italian restaurant had no stage, no band, not even a microphone. Sam's friends immediately suspected that Boyer had made up the story of being seduced by Sam's singing to explain why she would have agreed to go on to PJ's with him and to hide her true occupation.

Boyer told the jury that it was after leaving PJ's, as they drove back down Santa Monica Boulevard, that she began pleading, fruitlessly, for Cooke to take her home. There's nothing in the coroner's inquest that contradicts this abduction story; on the other hand, inquiries meant to question it were disallowed. When Machat tried to ask one of the police officers what Boyer did for a living, the coroner told him, "We are not concerned with the occupation of Miss Boyer, Mr. Macheck." If Boyer was a prostitute, it wouldn't have eliminated the possibility of kidnapping and rape, but it certainly would have raised some doubt in the jurors' minds. And it might have made them wonder what else she wasn't telling.

Scores of interviews with people who knew Cooke have not uncovered one who considers Boyer's abduction story possible. People like Crain, Morisette, Crume—men and women who are willing to admit they partied with Cooke, saw his sexual appetite, his bouts of temper, the strained workings of his marriage—say Boyer's testimony makes no sense. "She said he was kidnapping her," Alexander states. "I know better." Sam's friends point to his signing his own name in the motel's registry as unlikely behavior for a kidnapper and a rapist.

Others say Sam might well have been attracted to Lisa. She was good-looking, he was famously unfaithful, it was late at night, and they'd been drinking. If he knew she was a prostitute, that wouldn't have stopped him, either. "I often said Sam would walk past a good girl to get to a whore," Bumps Blackwell states. "You see, going with a girl that's a little more worldly: then, there ain't no problems." Lou Adler agrees, as does Sam Moore: "Sam loved himself some hookers! He would sleep with them, do whatever. . . . I don't know what it was; he loved them." The way Cliff White looks at it, "Cat's dick gets hard, he's liable to do a whole lot of weird things."

The Hacienda Motel was a one-story, U-shaped complex; you drove into the opening of the U, and the motel manager's office was there on your left. Boyer testified that Sam parked inside the court-yard and then walked back "very fast" to register. When she caught up to him near the registration window, "I told him, 'Please take me home,' and I talked very loudly. . . . While she was walking away, the manager was, he took me by the arm and he dragged me into that room." But Bertha Franklin, also under oath, said there had been no argument: "No, she didn't say anything; she didn't say a word." And the one motel resident who testified said Boyer put up "a little bit of resistance" when they got back to the car and headed to the room, "but not no fight where I could say he dragged her in. . . ." Again, this doesn't establish whether Boyer struggled with Cooke or not, only that the coroner, D.A., and police detectives refused to investigate obvious contradictions in the evidence.

Only Lisa Boyer lived to say what occurred once the two entered their room. The place was tiny, barely big enough to hold a double bed and a little dresser with a cheap lamp. The walls were cracked, the paint chipped; a shade was pulled down over the one window; there was a small bathroom off to the side. It looked and smelled and, through the thin walls, probably sounded like the hookers' motel it was.

Boyer testifies that Cooke locked the door, pushed her onto the bed, and then pinned her down "for a little while." She kept asking him to "please, take me home"; he was "very quiet and very forceful." Then, Boyer told the jury, Sam pulled her up, yanked off her sweater, and ripped off her dress, tearing the zipper in the back. "I knew he was going to rape me. So, I told him, 'Mr. Cooke, may I go to the bathroom, please?' " It seems like an odd request at that moment, but Lisa testified she was looking for a way out. She tried the bathroom window; it was painted shut. Wearing only her slip and bra, she walked back into the bedroom, where Sam had undressed. Boyer says when he went into the bathroom, she grabbed her clothes, shoes, and handbag, and ran.

According to Boyer, she knocked on the manager's door, got scared, and kept going. She "walked" around the corner and then pulled on her sweater and ran about four houses farther up Figueroa. She says it was there she first discovered she was carrying Sam's shirt, pants, sport jacket, and underwear. She threw his clothes aside and, from a phone booth "a couple of steps away," called the cops.

As soon as Sam's friends heard that Lisa ended up with Sam's clothes, many assumed she had robbed him. "Most hookers during that day," says Henry Nash of the Upsetters, "when they would clip you, they would take your pants and perhaps your shoes—but they would always take your pants so that you wouldn't be able to chase them. Standard practice." The Schmitts report that Lisa had seen the wad of money Sam was carrying, and Joan Schmitt says her later research indicated that Boyer was known for ripping off her johns this way, sometimes throwing the pants out the window to her waiting pimp. The private detective hired by Allen Klein stated that "Elisa Boyer is well known among the cheap nightclub hangers-on as being a professional roller."

Bertha Franklin's testimony didn't do anything to convince Sam's friends and fans. She told the jury she was on the phone with the owner of the Hacienda, Evelyn Card, when she excused herself, because "someone knocked on the door." When she checked, no one was there. "A few minutes later," Card testified, she heard "Mr. Cooke ask for his girlfriend and say she was in the office. . . ." The ongoing phone call is an ideal corroboration, and Card's and Franklin's stories match perfectly: two knocks at the door, first nobody there, then Cooke. It isn't, however, what Bertha Franklin originally told the police.

Officer Wallace Cook testified that "Mrs. Franklin was having a telephone conversation with a friend, she received a knock on the door, which was the deceased asking if his lady friend was inside. Mrs. Franklin stated, no, she was not; and, at that time, the deceased left and Mrs. Franklin continued her phone call with her friend." It was shortly after that, the detective says, that Franklin "heard a car drive from the rear portion of the motel parking lot to the front and stop, and, again, the deceased came to the door and started pounding and shouting and asking if his lady friend was inside. . . ."

Did Franklin see and speak to Cooke the first time someone knocked? Then the sequence of events is that Sam, discovering that both his clothes and Lisa are gone, goes to the manager's door, knocks, and asks if the girl is there. Told she isn't, he returns to his car. Then, driving back out of the motel, he stops at the manager's office again. Maybe he's seen Lisa knocking at Franklin's door. Whatever the reason, he becomes convinced enough that Lisa is in the manager's office to shout and finally break down the door. This is the description of a man building to a rage. According to the Franklin/Card version, on the other hand, there's no warning, no nothing, only a man pounding at and then breaking in the door. It's a quick, mindless, maybe drunken fury. Neither the coroner nor the D.A. bothered to discover whether the cop's notes were inaccurate (calling his testimony into question) or whether Bertha's story had changed in the five days between the shooting and the inquest.

"When he walked in," Bertha testified, "he walked straight to the kitchen, and then he came back and went into the bedroom. Then, he came out. I was standing there in [sic] the floor, and he grabbed both of my arms and started twisting them and asking me where was the girl."

From this description, Sam sounds convinced Lisa is there. He doesn't ask Franklin anything; he doesn't race through the place. He walks in, goes straight through the two small rooms, and then comes back to the main room. And Bertha Franklin doesn't make it sound as if she was very frightened. Her boss is right there on the phone, listening, and she doesn't call for help. The Hacienda is a tough motel in a tough neighborhood. According to the *L.A. Sentinel*, earlier in the year Franklin had shot at another resident. She'd also been warned that night by Card that "there had been two colored boys around . . . trying to hold us up." But when a half-naked man breaks down her door, Franklin doesn't reach for the .22 pistol she keeps beside her.

After Sam inspected the apartment, the two "got in a tussle," per Franklin, Sam holding her by the wrists, twisting both arms, and again asking, "Where is the girl?" The fifty-five-year-old woman fought back against the thirty-three-year-old man, till the two of them fell to the floor, knocking over the table. She started kicking and trying to bite him through his overcoat: "biting, scratching, biting, scratching, and everything." Finally, Franklin kicked him back toward the wall by the door where he'd entered. He didn't stop, then, and wonder what he was doing wrestling with a woman his mother's age. He didn't consider where he was or who he was. He jumped right up, Franklin testified, and ran back at her to rejoin the fight. Again, she pushed the young man down. This time she ran over to the TV, grabbed her gun, and shot.

No one established how this middle-aged, slightly overweight woman could have been pushing around a man in his prime. The police testified it was "hard to say" if the apartment was messed up from a fight. And no one asked why Franklin used the gun when she did instead of earlier or later.

The coroner asked Bertha how far Cooke was from her. "He wasn't too far; he was at close range," she answered. Three bullets were fired: one struck the ceiling over the bedroom door and fell onto the couch, the second was never found, and the third entered Cooke in the left chest. The angle of the bullet placed the pistol near Sam's left arm and aimed slightly downward: an awkward but possible position. Gauging by the powder burn, the police figured the gun was about an inch and a half from Sam. No explanation was given as to how she could have missed twice at this range. Or were the first two shots pulled off when Sam was at a distance?

"Lady, you shot me." Those were, according to Bertha Franklin, Sam's last words.

Wounded through his heart and lungs and bleeding profusely, he supposedly ran at Franklin again. Bertha says that this time—though there were three bullets left in the gun—she grabbed a flimsy stick and hit him over the head. Sam's body was eventually found next to the entrance door. The room was full of blood: on the floor, the walls, all over Bertha's turquoise dress. Later, Joan Schmitt examined the police photographs, and they were very gory and "very, very, very hard to look at." The inquest never established why Sam would have been in what sounds like a blind, animal rage. Was he after his money? After the girl? The jury bought the portrait of a rampaging, drunken Negro without needing any further explanation.

The police got their first call at 3:09 A.M. It was Lisa Boyer. She claimed not to know where she was ("probably close to Western. . . . It is pretty dark here"), only that she'd been kidnapped. Evelyn Card put in her call at 3:17. According to her testimony, she called immediately after the shooting. So, in the ten minutes while Boyer waited in her phone booth, Sam Cooke was shot and killed. A half block from the scene, Lisa apparently didn't hear the three shots from the .22—even though Franklin's door, closest to the street, was wide open and hanging on its hinges. Nor could the police produce any other witnesses who heard the shots, including the one motel resident who testified.

Because the official story of Sam Cooke's death was full of gaps, contradictions, and unlikelihoods, people began to fill in almost immediately with their own theories. The timing of the shooting—a year after President Kennedy's and a couple of months before Malcolm X's—only fueled the sense of conspiracy.

The gospel world, almost to a person, believes Sam was executed by the mob. Cooke's old co-lead Paul Foster turns out to be the primary source for this theory. Foster told his fellow singers that a close associate of Sam's found out Cooke was killed across the street from the Hacienda in a club, and Bertha Franklin was paid to take the fall. Foster believes the mob did it: "Sam was working for them; Sam was getting the money." Leroy Crume, thinking back over his conversations with Sam about going to Vegas, tends to agree. Cooke was just hotheaded and proud enough to resist being ordered around, and it was his downfall. "He wouldn't play the game, so you got to be eliminated. That shows other people in the business, hey, we mean business!" That's how Curtis Womack sees it, too. He ties Sam's fight with the union at the Apollo, his success at the Copa, and Charles Cook's stabbing together into the narrative of a man growing too independent for the powers that be.

Other suspects are closer to home. Curtis remembers recording at Chess Records after Sam was killed and listening to musicians openly question how much his brother, Bobby Womack, might have had to do with the shooting. He married the widow so soon afterwards—surely they had something going on; maybe they needed the husband out of the way. And because of Allen Klein's tough-guy reputation, there have been whispers among Sam's cohorts that he was somehow connected to Sam's death.

But the factual evidence doesn't support any of these scenarios. For them to be true, Bertha Franklin has to have been a hit woman, paid to set Sam up and pull the trigger. Or someone else has to have executed Cooke in Franklin's room, using her gun. Or Cooke has to have been shot elsewhere and brought to the Hacienda Motel.

The evidence that Sam died in Bertha Franklin's motel room is pretty convincing. His blood was splattered everywhere, the door was broken in, a bullet was found in the ceiling that matched the gun that killed him—and it was Franklin's gun.

Still, isn't it possible that Bertha Franklin was paid to hit Sam? If so, it seems odd that two months after Cooke's death, she sued his estate for $200,000 in compensation for injuries sustained that night. (She eventually was awarded $30,000.) Would someone hiding undesirable mob connections risk another appearance before a jury?

In the end, the strongest evidence that Sam was set up is the number of his friends who suspect that's what went down.

Part of why people like Cliff White conclude that "the whole thing is strange, strange, strange" is their doubt that Sam would have driven all that way from Hollywood to south L.A. when there were a hundred motels closer by. Sam liked classy places, friends argue; if he was looking for fun with a woman, he would have gone somewhere better and nearer to PJ's. Yet, it turns out Sam knew both the area and the motel.

Just up the block, at 8401 Figueroa, was the Sands Cocktail Lounge. The club had a dance floor, good steaks, and regular variety acts, from ventriloquists to fashion shows. The Prudhomme twins—Sam's friends and co-songwriters—recall seeing him perform there early in his career. According to Johnnie Morisette, Sam's party partner, "That was our stomping ground!" And on Thursday nights, the Sands regularly featured Sam's old SAR act the Sims Twins. According to Bobby and Kenneth Sims, Sam stopped at the Sands the day he was killed and "said he would see us later. He never did because he got shot." If Sam was looking to hear more music at an after-hours place, he might well have headed from Hollywood to the Figueroa area.

Furthermore, Johnnie Morisette confirms newspaper reports that Sam knew Bertha Franklin—an ex-hooker with a "soft spot" for whores, according to Johnnie—and had been in the Hacienda. "Sam," as Morisette puts it, "had a lot of people fooled." Grady Gaines thinks it's likely Cooke knew the place, given that his band—Sam's backup band, the Upsetters—had used the Hacienda as their West Coast base after their breakup with Little Richard. Henry Nash, the band's manager, said the musicians Cooke had been touring with over the last two years "knew the motel very, very well."

Those who admit Sam could have been with Lisa Boyer at the Hacienda but can't buy either the police or the conspiracy version of his death have worked out another way to explain the facts as they understand them.

Sam and Lisa probably knew each other; she, anyway, knew of him. Whether or not she was a hooker wouldn't have concerned Cooke too much; it certainly wouldn't have stopped him from taking her out. After a night of drinking at Martoni's and PJ's, they left Hollywood to hear some more music in south L.A. During the half-hour drive south on the freeway, there was some heavy petting. (Franklin testified that when Sam registered, his tie was loose and his shirttails outside his pants.) They decided to pull into the Hacienda Motel. When

Sam went to the bathroom, Lisa decided to rip him off, grabbed his clothes, and ran. Maybe she figured Sam Cooke wouldn't risk his reputation chasing her; maybe she didn't figure. For whatever reason, Sam became convinced that Bertha Franklin knew where Boyer was. A little high, very pissed off, he broke down the door and was shot.

That, anyway, was the best people could do. It still didn't clear Sam's name—nothing could—but it sounded more like the man they knew. He did have a fierce temper; he did pursue pretty women; he did know and hang out in the "bad" parts of town.

Both women needed an alibi, especially since the corpse was Sam Cooke and a thorough investigation was likely. Franklin got her boss, Evelyn Card, to cover for her, and then they embellished their story with some knocks on the door, wrestling, etc. to make Sam's attack seem more deliberate, the shooting more in self-defense. At the same time, Lisa Boyer decided to say she was abducted to avoid questions of prostitution—which might lead to questions of theft. As it turned out, the alibis weren't all that important; their stories, barely probed, held up in court.

Almost everyone had reasons not to get to the bottom of the shooting. RCA released the single "Shake"/"A Change Is Gonna Come" three days after Sam was buried, and it took off; the *Copa* LP was still on the charts. In fact, as Klein told the press, the phenomenal spurt in Sam's record sales guaranteed his family a $150,000 annual income for the next two years. Barbara Cooke didn't want an investigation that would disturb the children and inevitably pry into her and Sam's private life. Those who believed there was a mob connection didn't want to stir up the mud. It was to the LAPD's advantage to get the case wrapped. And the jurors at the inquest were eager to reach a decision and used to following the police version.

No matter how you explained it, Sam's death had a way of overwhelming his life. For those who believed rock & roll was amoral, Cooke eventually slipped into place beside Jimi Hendrix, Janis Joplin, Elvis Presley: his death another inevitable punishment. Some of Sam's old gospel friends felt much the same way. "If he hadn't have left God," as the Reverend Clay Evans puts it, "left the church, it would never have happened." And when Dickie Freeman of the

Fairfield Four started thinking about the connection between Sam's death and crossing over to pop, he concluded, "Hey, I ain't going over there! I'm scared of it." For those who swore by the image of the worldly, bad-ass soul man, Sam's death was a tragedy like James Dean's: a romantic, outlaw's end. For those, like Ali, who appreciated Sam's politics, the shooting was a murder—and some kind of deliberate silencing. And judging by the lack of follow-up in the white press, the majority saw his death as shocking, perhaps, but not surprising. Behind that Ivy League sweater, the "good Negro" had turned out to be just like all his brothers and sisters. Never mind who killed him; he'd been found half naked, in a cheap motel. Case closed.

Sam's death revealed how various his life had been. That's part of why people saw it—and continue to see it—as mysterious. How could he have been the man with the sweet voice, the innocent smile, and also be out with a hooker? How could he be the assimilated friend to the whites he knew and be cruising Watts? People saw the one side of the man they were allowed to see—the side he could show them—the nightclub crooner or the soul man or the student of black history. Then, in one evening, with one bullet, all those different sides suddenly came together—and collapsed. In a different time, maybe, in a different country, with a different history, people might have looked at the complexities and contradictions his death revealed. They might have decided it was that much more remarkable that he'd been able to create music that crossed boundaries and meant so much to so many different kinds of people. In a different time, maybe, in a different country. But then again, Sam never said a change was here. He said a change was gonna come.

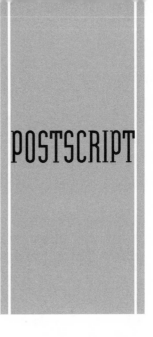

POSTSCRIPT

According to unconfirmed reports, Bertha Franklin moved to Michigan and died some eighteen months after Sam.

Lisa Boyer—also known as Crystal Chan Young, Jasmine Jay, and Elsie Nakama—lived at various addresses in southern California. In 1979, she was found guilty of second-degree murder in the shooting death of her lover, Louis Reynolds. Reynolds had attacked her with a chair. She received an indeterminate sentence of two to five years at the California Institution for Women at Frontera.

For many of those closest to Sam, his death was an abrupt and arbitrary end to their dreams. The small empire that had grown around Sam's talent collapsed. RCA continued to release singles culled from old recordings, but of six, only "Sugar Dumpling" made the Top Forty, in August of 1965. The haphazardly thrown together LPs did equally poorly. L. C. Cook immediately announced he was going to "step into the giant-sized entertainment shoes of his slain brother," went out on the road with the Upsetters for a year or so, and planned to cut a tribute album, but none of it ever amounted to much. S. R. Crain organized a memorial concert to Sam in Chicago, participated in a documentary movie on the Soul Stirrers, and eventually retired to his home in Texas. Cliff White continued to gig around some, playing with various bands and on recordings, before getting off the road for good. At SAR/Derby, as Curtis Womack puts it, "Everything was at a standstill." The Womacks went to Chess, Johnny Taylor to Stax, the Sims to Ray Charles's label, and Johnny Morisette went back to the streets.

Sam's family found the death nearly incomprehensible. Some resented Barbara for marrying so quickly, and many doubted that Sam—with all his business sense—would have left no will to provide for his parents and siblings. At the end of June 1965, four months after their marriage, Barbara and Bobby Womack came to Chicago for the wedding of Sam's niece Gwendolyn Miller. Late the Saturday night of the wedding, Sam's brothers Charles and young David went by the Roberts Motor Inn, where Bobby and Barbara were staying. According to newspaper accounts, the Cook brothers got in an argument over "the eventual disposition of Sam's clothes and other belongings."

As Charles's then wife, Phyllis, remembers it, "Barbara said something smart; Charles just doesn't take it. . . . He hit her in the mouth." Barbara's .38 revolver appeared, and Charles ended up using it to pistol-whip both Sam's widow and her new husband. Barbara later swore out an arrest warrant charging him with battery, assault, and theft. Thirty years later, Charles shows no remorse. "He meant to do that!" says Phyllis. "Yeah, he meant to do that."

Alex was having his own problems with Barbara. As the administrator of Sam's estate, she had become part owner of SAR/Derby, KAGS, and Malloy. As Alex remembers it, she and Bobby came down to the office one day and Barbara said, "Well now, Alex, I've become your partner, and I'm going to go everywhere: I'm not gonna be like Sam . . . and Bobby's gonna take over Sam's office." Then, three weeks after Charles beat her up, she filed papers to dissolve the label and the publishing companies; she argued that Alexander had "excluded" her from the corporations. Alex fought back. He said that a forced sale of the catalog of Sam's songs would lower their value. And he offered to buy Barbara out.

Instead, in April 1966, Barbara sold her half of the publishing to Sam's old producers, Hugo and Luigi. The IRS was auditing Sam's tax returns, and Barbara needed money. "I was out on the coast working," says Luigi, "and I got in touch with her . . . [and] we did buy it from her. Kind of sight unseen." Both the producers decided Cooke's tunes were "long-term meaningful music"—which would translate, of course, into long-term meaningful profits. Right after Barbara sold her half for $103,000, Lou Adler ran into her on a plane and recalls being shocked at how little she'd gotten for Sam's treasured publishing rights. And Alexander was caught totally by surprise. One day, Hugo and Luigi walked into the office and declared, "We're your partners."

It didn't work out. Luigi remembers the corporations were "all mixed up legally with Alexander," and it seemed like more trouble than it was worth. Within a year, the producers sold to Allen Klein, who had "screwed around with the position enough to end up with it." Now, Klein and Alexander started having some problems—"It was gonna be a stalemate," as Alex puts it—plus, J.W. had some tax problems of his own. "So, I said what the hell! I'll just go on and sell it."

In 1968, having made a fortune during the British invasion, Klein was on the verge of what *Variety* called the "music industry's biggest coup": buying Chappell Music for $60 million. By May of 1969, he would become business manager to three of the four Beatles. Despite these other interests, he paid special attention to the Cooke catalog he now controlled completely. "Allen loved Sam Cooke," says Klein's friend Jocko. "I mean, loved him—did you hear what I said? More than just a manager and client relationship: he *loved* Sam Cooke—and Sam loved him. They did every damn thing but kiss."

Perhaps love explains Klein's protective attitude to all things concerned with Cooke. Over the years, he floated various projects about Sam, including movies, books, and Broadway plays, but none came to fruition. Something was always a little wrong. While he let director Spike Lee use "A Change Is Gonna Come" for the climactic moment of the movie *Malcolm X* and donated the proceeds to the United Negro College Fund ("I know this sounds mushy," Klein said, "but I think Sam would have wanted it"), he still refused to have the song acknowledged in the credits or included on the sound track. Klein felt it would have risked "dilution" of Cooke's legacy.

"I wanted to be his champion," says Klein, and the first twenty-five years of his control of Sam's publishing, label, and recordings were marked by a string of lawsuits. Barbara sued KAGS for, among other sums, the unknown quantity of royalties paid to KAGS by Tracey—which is to say, paid by Klein to Klein. She followed that with a suit accusing Klein, as the majority stockholder in Tracey, of "fraud and breach of fiduciary duty" for not issuing half of Tracey's stock to her. Klein successfully denied all charges and eventually settled the suits in his favor. In 1979, Klein's ABKCO Records accused RCA of breach of contract. The settlement in 1984 included an agreement to finally release the live performance tapes from Harlem Square, a compilation LP called *The Man and His Music*, another compilation of Sam's ballad work to be called *Blue Mood*, and the Copa LP.

The Harlem Square recording, especially, provoked renewed interest when it came out in 1985. Rock critics and fans, unaware of the 1973 Specialty release of Sam's live gospel show at the Shrine, announced there was a new, rougher side of Cooke. Younger fans who had written him off as hopelessly compromised and old-fashioned started to reassess. But the *Blue Mood* collection never followed.

Klein then got into it with BMG, the company that had bought RCA. He argued it was prohibited from releasing any Sam Cooke records in the United States except these four. BMG subsequently brought suit against Klein's ABKCO for, among other things, claiming the rights to Sam's old Keen masters. As impressive, critically acclaimed CD collections from artists like Jackie Wilson and Ray Charles were released, Cooke's recordings were squabbled over and tied up in seemingly endless bickering. (ABKCO did, however, release a well-annotated double CD sampling of the SAR/Derby catalog in 1994.)

Sam's musical legacy was most directly transmitted through his daughter Linda. While still in her teens, she did some writing with her stepfather, Bobby Womack, for soul shouter Wilson Pickett, then went on to marry Bobby's youngest brother, Cecil. As Womack and Womack, the couple were a successful songwriting team and dance band through the eighties. But Sam's influence went far beyond family. Artists including Al Green, Rod Stewart, Aretha Franklin, Lou Rawls, Luther Vandross, and Aaron Neville—just to name a few—

have cited Sam as an inspiration and a standard-setter. In 1986, he was among the first ten candidates inducted into the Rock & Roll Hall of Fame; his fellow inductees included Elvis, Little Richard, Chuck Berry, and Fats Domino.

And his songs have continued to be covered. Dr. Hook's version of "Only Sixteen," Herman's Hermits' remake of "Wonderful World," and the Art Garfunkel/James Taylor/Paul Simon version of the same song all charted, as did both the Animals' and Eddie Floyd's "Bring It On Home to Me." Cat Stevens had a hit with "Another Saturday Night," and there were scores of others that indicated Cooke's continuing influence, including a tribute album by the Supremes, Sam and Dave's remake of "Soothe Me," and Otis Redding's "Shake," "Cupid," "A Change Is Gonna Come," and "Try a Little Tenderness." Otis was out front about it: he told an interviewer he wanted "to fill the silent void caused by Sam Cooke's death." (Which only makes it that much more macabre that Otis died in a plane crash four years to the day after Sam's last night on the town.)

In the spring of 1967, Sam's old roommate Lou Adler organized the Monterey International Pop Festival. He not only booked Cooke's heir apparent, Otis (thus breaking him to the white audience), and Lou Rawls, but he earmarked a percentage of the profits to go to the Sam Cooke Memorial Scholarship fund to give ghetto kids musical educations. Sam "showed the way," Adler says. "He broke the barriers down as far as how the young white audience could—not worship—but be fans to a black artist. . . ." Adler still sees Sam's death as a tragedy "to everyone who met him and everyone who was ever going to meet him. . . . I just think he had more to offer than any other artist that's come along." Identify Monterey as one of the seminal moments when rock & roll tried to break through the segregation of genres—Jimi Hendrix applying chitlin-circuit theatrics to psychedelia, Janis Joplin mixing Bessie Smith with patchouli oil and beads, Otis singing to the "love generation"—and Cooke becomes the era's invisible mentor.

Herb Alpert, Lou's old partner, still ranks Sam as "musically . . . in a category by himself." To Bumps Blackwell, Sam was "unique; he was different. . . . Sam was just special. He was more than special."

What amazed Harold Battiste was "the genius of his talent. Of his voice. Of his spirit. I constantly hear, over the years—say like you hear a little bit of Charlie Parker in all saxophone players now—Sam was one of those original, creative persons who left a whole legacy of stuff for singers to use. They can just take a little piece of what he had and make a career out of it!" The soul glissando, the hoarse, intimate delivery, the gospel climax of rock superstars from Madonna to Prince all owe a debt to Sam.

But to go back over his life is also to see how Cooke was *not* special. He came of age in post-Depression America, and his family was part of the great migration into the cities. Like many members of his race, he was shaped by the black church, with its tradition of turning oppression into hope. And like millions of others, Sam wanted his part of America's midcentury economic bonanza. What Cooke had that the dominant culture valued—on top of good looks and a beguiling voice—was the ability to bring a crowd to climax and hold them there. From Rudy Vallee through Bing Crosby to Frank Sinatra, the mainstream had always rewarded white men who could do this. When rock & roll hit, the major labels were still most comfortable with teen idols who looked like Paul Anka, the Everly Brothers, or even Elvis Presley. But Sam and his contemporaries couldn't be denied.

In gospel music, getting Sister Flute was an understood phenomenon: her shrieking and talking in tongues and sobbing didn't upset the church culture; it validated it. To break through was to get free. When Cooke crossed over into the mainstream culture (the single, best-known gospel star to do so), the perception of what he was doing changed. White teenagers reacting as Sister Flute had were seen as a threat: a break*down* in morals and a challenge to the status quo.

Sam Cooke lived his life at the center of cultural change. He was there when gospel music's coded message of hope and rebellion bloomed into the civil rights movement. And his sound—soul music—helped spread that message out into the mainstream culture. When people say Sam couldn't have died as he died, part of what they're saying is that his life meant something different. They hear how often his secular music called on the future, just as his gospel had called on the Lord. "If you ever change your mind . . ."; "What a wonderful world this would be . . ."; "A change is gonna come. . . ." The best of his music cracked through the everyday, made the impossible seem close at hand.

Because Cooke died just as that future was speeding closer—the Watts rebellion erupted a year after his death—it's tempting to read his end as a premonition of how the politics of the sixties eventually played out. But, finally, what Cooke did is more important than how he died. His achievements were all about crossing over: whether it was passing through the restrictive covenants around Bronzeville, going from gospel to pop, integrating the Atlanta fairgrounds on Dick Clark's show, or making it at the Copa. And his stubborn insistence that he could reach everyone remains a goal in a country whose connections and divisions are reflected in its music.

"We had a feeling," J. W. Alexander says of his ex-partner and friend, "that people were people. And so it was a matter of reaching people. We used to use an old saying, a religious saying, 'You try the spirit by the spirit.' So if you give, you receive."

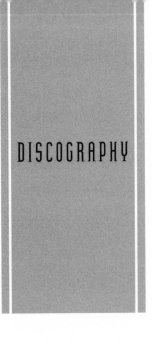

DISCOGRAPHY

This discography is indebted to *The Directory of American 45 RPM Records* by Ken Clee (Stack-o-Wax, 1985); "SAR Records" by Ray Funk, with assistance from John Cordell and Mike Sweeney (*Goldmine*, August 26, 1988, pp. 86–88); *Gospel Records: A Black Music Discography 1943–1969* by Cedric J. Hayes and Robert Laughton (Milford, N.H.: Big Nickel, 1993); *Sam Cooke: The Man Who Invented Soul* by Joe McEwen (Sire Books/Chappell Music Company, 1977); and "Sam Cooke" by Joanne Palmer (*Goldmine*, January 2, 1987, pp. 8–10). Thanks also to Bill Belmont at Fantasy Records, collector Barry Hill, Bernadette Moore at BMG, and collector Opal Nations.

All chart listings here and throughout the book are from Joel Whitburn's *The Billboard Book of Top 40 Hits* (New York: Billboard Publications, 1987) and his *Top R&b Singles: 1942–1988* (Menomonee Falls, Wis.: Record Research, Inc., 1988).

GOSPEL SINGLES (WITH THE SOUL STIRRERS)

Note: Sales figures, rounded to the nearest hundred, are from Specialty's archives and are through December 31, 1957. They are not absolutely accurate but are useful for comparative purposes.

LABEL	TITLE	TOTAL SALES

1951

Spec 802	Peace in the Valley/Jesus Gave Me Water	65,300
Spec 813	Come, Let's Go Back to God/Joy, Joy to My Soul	23,300
Spec 821	I'm Gonna Build on That Shore/ Until Jesus Calls Me Home	13,300

1952

Spec 824	How Far Am I from Canaan?/It Won't Be Very Long	21,300
Spec 835	Just Another Day/Let Me Go Home	22,900

1953

Spec 845	Jesus Paid the Debt/Blessed Be the Name of the Lord	11,300
Spec 851	He'll Welcome Me/End of My Journey	3,800

1954

Spec 859	He's My Friend Until the End/Come and Go to That Land	10,300

Spec 868   Jesus, I'll Never Forget/Any Day   11,800
            Now

1955

Spec 878   Nearer to Thee/Be with Me Jesus   37,000
Spec 882   One More River/I'm So Glad   21,800

1956

Spec 892   Wonderful/Farther Along   21,600
Spec 896   Touch the Hem of His Garment/   27,300
            Jesus, Wash Away My Troubles

1957

Spec 902   In a Few More Days/Pilgrim of   10,600
            Sorrow

1958

Spec 907   Sinner, Run to Jesus/Were You   8,200
            There?

1959

Spec 921   Jesus Bears the Cross Alone   —

1970

Spec 928   Just Another Day/Christ Is All   —

1974

Spec 930   That's Heaven to Me   —

POP SINGLES

Note: Initial asterisk (*) indicates million-sellers according to Joseph Murrells, *The Book of Golden Discs* (London: Barrie & Jenkins, 1978). Some B-sides have chart positions.

LABEL	TITLE	RELEASE DATE	CHART *(pop; r&b)*

1957

Spec 596	Lovable/Forever	1/31	—
Keen 4013	*You Send Me/Summertime	9/7	1;1
Spec 619	*I'll Come Running Back to You/Forever	11/18	18;1
Keen	For Sentimental Reasons/ Desire Me	12/2	17;5 B: 47;17

1958

Spec 627	I Don't Want to Cry/That's All I Need to Know	2/28	—
Keen 4009	You Were Made for Me/ Lonely Island	3/24	39;7 B: 26;10
Keen 2005	Stealing Kisses/All of My Life	7/	—
Keen 2006	Win Your Love/Houseboat	8/25	22;4
Keen 2008	Love You Most of All/Blue Moon	10/	26;12

1959

Keen 2018	Everybody Likes to Cha Cha Cha/Little Things You Do	2/	31;2
Keen 2022	Only Sixteen/Let's Go Steady Again	6/1	28;13
Keen 2105	Summertime/Pt. 2	9/4	—
Spec 667	I Need You Now/Happy in Love	11/9	—
Keen 2105	There I've Said It Again/One Hour Ahead of the Posse	11/	—
Keen 2111	T'Ain't Nobody's Bizness/No One	—	—

1960

RCA 7701	Teenage Sonata/If You Were the Only Girl	2/9	50;22
RCA 7730	You Understand Me/I Belong to Your Heart	3/5	—
Keen 2112	*Wonderful World/Along the Navajo Trail	4/14	12;2
Keen 2117	With You/I Thank God	—	—
RCA 7783	*Chain Gang/I Fall in Love Every Day	7/26	2;2
Keen 2118	So Glamorous/Steal Away	—	—
RCA 7816	Sad Mood/Love Me	11/8	29;23
Keen 2122	Mary Mary Lou/Eee Yi Ee Yi Oh	—	—

1961

RCA 7853	That's It—I Quit—I'm Movin' On/What Do You Say	2/14	31;25
RCA 7883	Cupid/Farewell My Love	5/16	17;20
RCA 7927	Feel It/It's Alright	8/29	—

1962

RCA 7983	*Twistin' the Night Away/ One More Time	1/9	9;1
RCA 8036	Bring It On Home to Me/ Having a Party	5/8	13;2 B: 17;4
RCA 8088	Nothing Can Change This Love/Somebody Have Mercy	9/11	12;2 B: 70;3
RCA 8129	Send Me Some Lovin'/Baby Baby Baby	12/28	13;2

1963

RCA 8164	Another Saturday Night/ Love Will Find a Way	4/2	10;1
RCA 8215	Cool Train/Frankie and Johnny	7/9	B: 14;4
RCA 8247	Little Red Rooster/You Gotta Move	10/8	11;7

1964

RCA 8299	Ain't That Good News/Basin Street	1/22	Hot 11
RCA 8368	Good Times/Tennessee Waltz	7/9	Hot 11 B: Hot 35
RCA 8426	Cousin of Mine/That's Where It's At	9/16	Hot 40 B: Hot 93
RCA 8486	Shake/A Change Is Gonna Come	12/22	7;2 B: 31;9

1965

RCA 8539	Ease My Troublin' Mind/It's Got the Whole World Shakin'	3/23	B: 41;15

| RCA 8586 | When a Boy Falls in Love/ The Piper | 5/18 | — |
| RCA 8631 | Sugar Dumpling/Bridge of Tears | 7/6 | 32;18 |

1966

RCA 8751	Feel It/That's All	1/18	—
RCA 8803	Trouble Blues/Let's Go Steady Again	3/29	—
RCA 8934	Meet Me at Mary's Place/If I Had a Hammer	8/30	—
CHERIE 4501	Darling I Need You Now/ Win Your Love for Me	—	—

LPs

LABEL   TITLE

1957

Keen 2001   SAM COOKE

You Send Me. The Lonesome Road. Tammy. Ol' Man River. Moonlight in Vermont. Canadian Sunset. Summertime. Around the World. Ain't Misbehavin'. The Bells of St. Mary's. So Long. Danny Boy. Lucky Old Sun. (Charted #16, 2 weeks.)

1958

Keen 2003   SAM COOKE ENCORE

Oh, Look at Me Now. Someday. Along the Navajo Trail. Running Wild. Accentuate the Positive. Mary, Mary Lou. When I Fall in Love. I Cover the Waterfront. My Foolish Heart. Today I Sing the Blues. The Gypsy. It's the Talk of the Town.

1959

Keen 2004   **TRIBUTE TO THE LADY**

God Bless the Child. She's Funny That Way. I've Got a Right to Sing the Blues. Good Morning, Heartache. T'Ain't Nobody's Bizness. Comes Love. Lover Girl. Let's Call the Whole Thing Off. Lover Come Back to Me. Solitude. They Can't Take That Away from Me. Crazy in Love with You.

Keen 86101   **HIT KIT**

Only Sixteen. All of My Life. Everybody Likes to Cha Cha Cha. Blue Moon. Win Your Love. Lonely Island. You Send Me. Love You Most of All. For Sentimental Reasons. Little Things You Do. Let's Go Steady Again. You Were Made for Me.

1960

Keen 86103   **I THANK GOD**

I Thank God. You Got to Move.* Jericho Walls.† That's Heaven to Me. Love Lifted Me.† Coming Up Through the Years.* Steal Away. Trust and Obey.† This Friend Jesus.* Deep River. God's Goodness.† Oh, Lord Fix It.* (*Songs by the Original Blind Boys with Clarence Fountain. †Songs by the Gospel Harmonettes.)

RCA 2236   **COOKE'S TOUR**

Far Away Places. Under Paris Skies. South of the Border. Bali Ha'i. The Coffee Song. Arrivederci, Roma. London by Night. Jamaica Farewell. Galway Bay. Sweet Leilani. Japanese Farewell Song. The House I Live In.

KEEN 86106   **WONDERFUL WORLD**

Wonderful World. Desire Me. Summertime. Almost in Your Arms. That's Heaven to Me. No One. With You. Blue Moon. Stealing Kisses. You Were Made for Me. There I've Said It Again. I Thank God. (In Great Britain, Immediate IMLP002; 1966.)

RCA 2236   **HITS OF THE 50's**

Hey There. Mona Lisa. Too Young. The Great Pretender. You, You, You. Unchained Melody. Wayward Wind. Secret Love. The Song from Moulin Rouge. I'm Walking Behind You. Cry. Venus.

1961

RCA 2293   **SWING LOW**

Swing Low, Sweet Chariot. I'm Just a Country Boy. They Call the Wind Maria. Twilight on the Trail. If I Had You. Chain Gang. Grandfather's Clock. Long, Long Ago. You Belong to Me. Goin' Home.

Famous 502   **SAM'S SONGS**

Little Things You Do. Come Love. Lonesome Road. The Gypsy. That's Heaven to Me. Love You Most of All. Canadian Sunset. Solitude. I Thank God. Danny Boy.

Famous 505   **ONLY SIXTEEN**

Only Sixteen. She's Funny That Way. My Foolish Heart. So Long. Mary, Mary Lou. So Glamorous. Crazy in Love With You. When I Fall in Love. Good Morning Heartache. Let's Go Steady Again.

Famous 508   **SO WONDERFUL**

Wonderful World. Summertime. Almost in Your Arms. Tammy. Talk of the Town. You Were Made for Me. Along the Navajo Trail. No One. I Cover the Waterfront. Around the World in 80 Days.

RCA 2392   **MY KIND OF BLUES**

Don't Get Around Much Anymore. Little Girl Blue. Nobody Knows You When You're Down and Out. Out in the Cold Again. But Not for Me. Exactly Like You. I'm Just a Lucky So and So. Since I Met You Baby. Baby, Won't You Please Come Home. Trouble in Mind. You're Always on My Mind. The Song Is Ended.

1962

RCA 2555   **TWISTIN' THE NIGHT AWAY**

Twistin' the Night Away. Sugar Dumpling. Twistin' in the Kitchen with Dinah. Somebody's Gonna Miss Me. A Whole Lotta Woman. The Twist. Twistin' in the Old Town Tonight. Movin' and A'Groovin'. Camptown Twist. Somebody Have Mercy. Soothe Me. That's It—I Quit—I'm Movin' On. (Charted #74, 8 weeks; released Great Britain as Starcall 1034, 1976.)

Famous 509   **YOU SEND ME**

You Send Me. Old Man River. Ee-Yi-Ee-Yi-Oh. With You. Accentuate the Positive. Desire Me. Ain't Misbehavin'. Lucky Old Sun. Today I Sing the Blues. Lonely Island.

RCA 2625   **THE BEST OF SAM COOKE**

You Send Me. Only Sixteen. Everybody Loves to Cha Cha Cha. For Sentimental Reasons. Wonderful World. Summertime. Chain Gang. Cupid. Twistin' the Night Away. Sad Mood. Having a Party. Bring It On Home to Me. (Charted #22, 35 weeks.)

SAR 503   **GOSPEL PEARLS**

That's Heaven to Me. Deep River. I Thank God. Heaven Is My Home.* God Is Standing By.* Pass Me Not.† Steal Away. Must Jesus.* Lead Me Jesus.* Troublin' Mind.† Sometimes.† Somebody.† (*Songs by the Soul Stirrers. †Songs by R. H. Harris and the Gospel Paraders.)

1963

RCA 2673   **MR. SOUL**

I Wish You Love. Willow Weep for Me. Chains of Love. Smoke Rings. All the Way. Send Me Some Lovin'. Cry Me a River. Driftin' Blues. For Sentimental Reasons. Nothing Can Change This Love. Little Girl. These Foolish Things. (Charted #94, 9 weeks.)

RCA 2720   **3 GREAT GUYS**

I Can't Say a Word.* No, No.* I'm Gonna Forget About You. Tenderness. This Endless Night.† Too Late.† Laugh, Laugh, Laugh.* I Remember.* I Ain't Gonna Cheat On You No More. Talkin' Trash. Without Your Love.† Another Day, Another Heartache.† (*Songs by Paul Anka. †Songs by Neil Sedaka.)

RCA 2709   **NIGHT BEAT**

Nobody Knows the Trouble I've Seen. Lost and Lookin'. Mean Old World. Please Don't Drive Me Away. I Lost Everything. Get Yourself Another Fool. Little Red Rooster. Laughin' and Clownin'. Trouble Blues. You Gotta Move. Fool's Paradise. Shake Rattle and Roll. (Charted #62, 19 weeks.)

RCA SP-33-223 **THE NEW SOUND OF THE STARS**
Nobody Knows the Trouble I've Seen. (Compilation with 11 other RCA artists.)

1964

RCA 2899   **AIN'T THAT GOOD NEWS**
Ain't That Good News. Meet Me at Mary's Place. Good Times. Rome Wasn't Built in a Day. Another Saturday Night. Tennessee Waltz. A Change Is Gonna Come. Falling in Love. Home. Sittin' in the Sun. No Second Time. The Riddle Song. (Charted #34, 34 weeks.)

RCA 2970   **SAM COOKE AT THE COPA**
The Best Things in Life Are Free. Bill Bailey. Nobody Knows You When You're Down and Out. Frankie and Johnny. Medley: Try a Little Tenderness/For Sentimental Reasons/You Send Me. If I Had a Hammer. When I Fall in Love. Twistin' the Night Away. This Little Light of Mine. Blowin' in the Wind. Tennessee Waltz. (Charted #29, 55 weeks.)

Spec 2106   **SOUL STIRRERS FEATURING SAM COOKE**
Wonderful. Be with Me Jesus. The Love of God.* Come and Go to That Land. By and By.† He'll Welcome Me. Touch the Hem of His Garment. It Won't Be Very Long. Sinner Run to Jesus. Let Me Go Home. Feel Like My Time Ain't Long. I'm So Glad (Trouble Don't Last Always). (*Lead by Johnnie Taylor. †Lead by R. H. Harris.)

1965

RCA 3367   **SHAKE**
Shake. Yeah Man. Win Your Love for Me. Love You Most of All. Meet Me at Mary's Place. It's Got the Whole World Shakin'. A Change Is Gonna Come. I'm in the Mood for Love. You're Nobody Till Somebody Loves You. Comes Love. I'm Just a Country Boy. Ease My Troublin' Mind. (Charted #44, 23 weeks.)

RCA 3373   THE BEST OF SAM COOKE, VOL. 2

Frankie and Johnny. That's Where It's At. Another Saturday Night. Little Red Rooster. Shake. Baby, Baby, Baby. Ain't That Good News. Cousin of Mine. A Change Is Gonna Come. Tennessee Waltz. Basin Street Blues. Love Will Find a Way. (Charted #128, 8 weeks.)

RCA 3435   TRY A LITTLE LOVE

Don't Cry. Bridge of Tears. I Fall in Love Every Day. You're Always on My Mind. Houseboat. When a Boy Falls in Love. To Each His Own. Tammy. Gypsy. Little Things. You Send Me. (Charted #120, 7 weeks.)

1966

RCA 3517   THE UNFORGETTABLE SAM COOKE

I'm Gonna Forget About You. Wonderful World. I Ain't Gonna Cheat on You No More. Soothe Me. Feel It. One More Time. Sugar Dumpling. It's All Right. With You.

1968

CAMDEN 2264 THE ONE AND ONLY SAM COOKE

Jamaica Farewell. Don't Get Around Much Anymore. Far Away Places. Little Girl Blues. The Song Is Ended (but the Melody Lingers On). Bali Ha'i. Trouble in Mind. They Call the Wind Maria. Swing Low Sweet Chariot. Since I Met You Baby.

RCA 3991   THE MAN WHO INVENTED SOUL

Blowin' in the Wind. (Somebody) Ease My Troublin' Mind. Nobody Knows You When You're Down and Out. Danny Boy. The Great Pretender. Send Me Some Lovin'. I Ain't Gonna Cheat on You No More. Falling in Love. Tain't Nobody's Bizness If I Do. Willow Weep for Me. Try a Little Love.

1969

Spec 2116   THE GOSPEL SOUL OF SAM COOKE WITH THE
              SOUL STIRRERS, Vol. 1

Jesus Wash Away My Troubles. Jesus, I'll Never Forget. Nearer to Thee. One More River. Must Jesus Bear The Cross Alone. Any Day Now. He's

My Friend Until the End. I'm Gonna Build on That Shore. Just Another Day. Someday, Somewhere. Jesus Paid the Debt. Peace in the Valley.

1970

RCA 6027   **THIS IS SAM COOKE**

Frankie and Johnnie. You Send Me. Summertime. Chain Gang. Baby, Baby, Baby. Only Sixteen. Love Will Find a Way. Bring It On Home to Me. Twistin' the Night Away. Feel It. (I Love You) For Sentimental Reasons. Another Saturday Night. Wonderful World. Having a Party. Little Red Rooster. Cupid. Sugar Dumpling. Send Me Some Lovin'. Everybody Loves to Cha Cha Cha.

Camden 2433   **SAM COOKE**

Spec 2119   **THE TWO SIDES OF SAM COOKE**

The Last Mile of the Way. Touch the Hem of His Garment. Jesus Gave Me Water. Were You There. Pilgrim of Sorrow. He's My Guide. I'll Come Running Back to You. I Don't Want to Cry. Lovable. That's All I Need to Know. Forever. Happy in Love.

1971

Cherie 1001   **RIGHT ON**

Win Your Love. With You. Tammy. Deep River. Darling I Need You Now. You Were Made for Me. Summertime. Steal Away. You Send Me. All of My Life. Stealing Kisses. Ol' Man River. There I've Said It Again. Let's Go Steady Again. Summertime Pt. 2. Almost in Your Arms. That's Heaven to Me. Wonderful World. No One (Can Ever Take Your Place). Only Sixteen. I Thank God. Desire Me. Little Things You Do. Love You Most Of All.

Spec 2128   **THE GOSPEL SOUL OF SAM COOKE WITH THE SOUL STIRRERS, Vol. 2**

Christ Is All. Wonderful. Until Jesus Calls Me Home. Come and Go to That Land. Let Me Go Home. I'm So Glad (Trouble Don't Last Always). I'm on the Firing Line. He'll Make a Way. Be with Me Jesus. It Won't Be Very Long. How Far Am I from Canaan. Farther Along.

Spec 2137   **THE ORIGINAL SOUL STIRRERS FEATURING SAM COOKE**

Jesus Gave Me Water. Out on a Hill.* Sinner Run to Jesus. Faith and Grace.† Pilgrim of Sorrow. In a Few More Days. Touch the Hem of His Garment. Feel Like My Time Ain't Long.† The Lord Is My Shepherd†. The Love of God.* By and By.† He'll Welcome Me. (*Lead by Johnnie Taylor. †Lead by R. H. Harris.)

1972

Spec 2146   **THAT'S HEAVEN TO ME** (with the Soul Stirrers)

That's Heaven to Me. I Gave Up Everything to Follow Him. My Lord Done Just What He Said. I'm So Happy. Come, Let Us Go Back to God. I Have a Friend Above All Others. Mean Old World. Joy, Joy to My Soul. All Right Now. Wait on Jesus. Jesus Will Lead Me to That Promised Land. Lord, Remember Me.

TRIP TLP-8030 **THE GOLDEN SOUND OF SAM COOKE**

God Bless the Child. She's Funny That Way. Bells of St. Mary's. Danny Boy. I've Got a Right to Sing the Blues. Foolish Heart. Lonesome Road. Canadian Sunset. Lucky Old Sun. Oh, Look at Me Now. Solitude. Talk of the Town. Moonlight in Vermont. Lover Come Back to Me. I Cover the Waterfront. They Can't Take That Away from Me. When I Fall in Love. Comes Love. Running Wild. Crazy in Love with You.

TRIP 152   **SIXTEEN GREATEST HITS**

Camden 4610 **THE UNFORGETTABLE SAM COOKE**

(Reissue of RCA 3517.)

Spec 2153   **GOSPEL STARS IN CONCERT**

It's Getting Late in the Evening.* Get Away Jordan.* How I Got Over.† I'm Happy Working for the Lord.† Straight Street.‡ Mother Bowed.‡ I Have a Friend Above All Others. Be with Me Jesus. Nearer to Thee. (*Songs by Dorothy Love Coates and the Original Harmonettes. †Songs by Brother Joe May. ‡Songs by the Pilgrim Travelers.)

1974

Camden 0445   **YOU SEND ME**
You Send Me. Hey There. Mona Lisa. Too Young. Cry. The Wayward
Wind. Secret Love. The Gypsy. Venus.

RCA   **THE LEGENDARY SAM COOKE**
DPL3-0107
You Send Me. Cousin of Mine. Little Red Rooster. Sugar Dumplin'. Sad
Mood. Ain't That Good News. Try a Little Tenderness. Feel It. Teenage
Sonata. Having a Party.

1975

RCA-APL-1-   **SAM COOKE INTERPRETS BILLIE HOLIDAY**
0899
(Reissue of Keen 2004.)

1977

VeeJay   **GOSPEL IN MY SOUL**
VJS-18013
(Reissue of SAR 503.)

1979

"51 West"   **MY FOOLISH HEART**
CBS
Canadian Sunset. T'Ain't Nobody's Bizness. The Lonesome Road. Oh,
Look at Me Now. The Bells of St. Mary's. Lover Come Back. Lucky Old
Sun. Danny Boy. When I Fall in Love.

1985

RCA   **LIVE AT THE HARLEM SQUARE CLUB**, 1963
PCD1-5181

Feel It. Chain Gang. Cupid. Medley: It's All Right/For Sentimental Reasons/Twistin' the Night Away. Somebody Have Mercy. Bring It On Home to Me. Nothing Can Change This Love. Having a Party.

1986

RCA   **SAM COOKE—THE MAN AND HIS MUSIC**
PCD1-7127

Touch the Hem of His Garment. That's Heaven to Me. I'll Come Running Back to You. You Send Me. Win Your Love for Me. Just for You. Chain Gang. When a Boy Falls in Love. Only Sixteen. Wonderful World. Cupid. Nothing Can Change This Love. Rome Wasn't Built in a Day. Love Will Find a Way. Everybody Loves to Cha Cha Cha. Another Saturday Night. Meet Me at Mary's Place. Having a Party. Good Times. Twistin' the Night Away. Shake. Somebody Have Mercy. Sad Mood. Ain't That Good News. Bring It On Home to Me. Soothe Me. That's Where It's At. A Change Is Gonna Come.

1991

Spec   **SAM COOKE WITH THE SOUL STIRRERS**
CD-7009-2

Peace in the Valley. It Won't Be Very Long. How Far Am I from Canaan? Just Another Day. Come and Go to That Land. Any Day Now. He'll Make a Way. Nearer to Thee. Be with Me Jesus. One More River. I'm So Glad (Trouble Don't Last Always). Wonderful. Farther Along. Touch the Hem of His Garment. Jesus Wash Away My Troubles. Must Jesus Bear This Cross Alone? That's Heaven to Me. Were You There? Mean Old World. Lord Remember Me. Lovable. Forever. I'll Come Running Back to You. That's All I Need to Know. I Don't Want to Cry.

1992

Spec   **JESUS GAVE ME WATER**
CD-7031-2

Jesus Gave Me Water. Christ Is All. Come Let Us Go Back to God. I'm
On the Firing Line. How Far Am I from Cannan? Jesus Done Just What
He Said. He's My Rock (Wait On Jesus). Joy, Joy to My Soul. I'm Gonna
Build on That Shore. Until Jesus Calls Me Home. Jesus Will Lead Me
to That Promised Land. It Won't Be Very Long. Let Me Go Home.
Someday Somewhere. Jesus Paid the Debt. End of My Journey. He's My
Friend Until the End. I Have a Friend Above All Others. I Gave Up Ev-
erything to Follow Him. Come and Go to That Land. I'm So Happy in
the Service of the Lord. Any Day Now. Jesus, I'll Never Forget. All
Right Now. Pray.

1993

Spec   **THE GREAT 1955 SHRINE CONCERT**
CD-7045-2

(Reissue of Spec 2153 with additional cuts by the Caravans, the Pilgrim
Travelers, Annette May, and Ethel Davenport.)

1994

Spec   **THE LAST MILE OF THE WAY**
CD-7052-2

The Last Mile of the Way. Mean Old World. That's Heaven to Me. Were
You There? (false starts). Were You There? Lord Remember Me. Pilgrim
of Sorrow. He's My Guide. He's My Guide (incomplete). He's My Guide.
The Last Mile of the Way (incomplete). The Last Mile of the Way. Pilgrim of Sorrow. All Right Now. He'll Make a Way. Jesus, I'll Never Forget. Come and Go to That Land. Come and Go to That Land (composite
take). Just As I Am (incomplete). He'll Welcome Me. He's My Friend
Until the End. Jesus Paid the Debt. Jesus Will Lead Me to That Promised Land (incomplete). It Won't Be Very Long. How Far Am I from Canaan? (incomplete). How Far Am I from Canaan? Let Me Go Home.

EPs

LABEL   TITLE

1957

SAR-EP 205   SOUL STRINGS FEATURING SAM COOKE
              Nearer to Thee.
Keen B2001   SAM COOKE, VOL. 1
Keen B2002   SAM COOKE, VOL. 2
Keen B2003   SAM COOKE, VOL. 3

1958

Keen B2006   ENCORE, VOL. 1
Keen B2007   ENCORE, VOL. 2
Keen B2008   ENCORE, VOL. 3

1959

Keen B2012   TRIBUTE TO THE LADY, VOL. 1
Keen B2013   TRIBUTE TO THE LADY, VOL. 2
Keen B2014   TRIBUTE TO THE LADY, VOL. 3

1961

RCA LPC126   SAM COOKE SINGS

1963

RCA 4375   ANOTHER SATURDAY NIGHT
Another Saturday Night. You Send Me. Only 16. Bring It On Home to Me.

SAR SINGLES

Note: Sam Cooke has author credit for songs below followed by asterisk (*) and coauthor credit for those followed by dagger (†).

SAR #   ARTIST   TITLE

1959

| 101 | SOUL STIRRERS | Stand By Me Father† He's Been a Shelter for Me† |

1960

102	KYLO TURNER	I'll Keep Thinking of You/The Wildest Girl in Town
103	SOUL STIRRERS	Wade in the Water†/He Cares
104	JOHNNIE MORISETTE	Never (Come Running Back to You)†/In My Heart†
105	SOUL STIRRERS with Sam Cooke	Nearer To Thee Pt 1.*/Pt. 2.*
106	JOEL PAULEY	That's Why I Cried/Slim Jim
107	JOHNNIE MORISETTE	Always on My Mind/Dorothy
108	SOUL STIRRERS	I'm a Pilgrim/Jesus, Be a Fence Around Me.*
109	L. C. COOKE	Teach Me†/Magic Words†

1961

| 110 | SOUL STIRRERS | Listen to the Angels/Toiling On |
| 111 | PATIENCE VALENTINE | Dance and Let Your Hair Down*/In the Dark |

112	L. C. COOKE	The Lover*/Sufferin'
113	JOHNNIE MORISETTE	Damper/Don't Cry Baby
114	JOHNNIE TAYLOR	A Whole Lotta Woman/Why Why Why
115	?	
116	SOUL STIRRERS	I Love The Lord/I'm Thankful†
117	SIMS TWINS	Soothe Me*/I'll Never Come Running Back to You† (Charted #4 r&b; #42 pop.)
118	WOMACK BROTHERS	Somebody's Wrong/Yield Not to Temptation
119	PATIENCE VALENTINE	I Miss You So/If You Don't Come
120	SOUL STIRRERS	Heaven Is My Home/Lead Me Jesus†
121	JOHNNIE MORISETTE	You Are My Sunshine/Your Heart Will Sing
122	SAM COOKE	Just For You*/Made For Me*
123	?	

1962

124	SOUL STIRRERS	Must Jesus Bear the Cross Alone/God Is Standing By
125	SIMS TWINS	The Right to Love/The Smile†
126	JOHNNIE MORISETTE	Meet Me at the Twisting Place*/Anytime Anyplace Anywhere (Charted #18 r&b; #63 pop.)
127	R. H. HARRIS AND HIS GOS- PEL PARADERS	Pass Me Not/Troublin' Mind
128	CLIFTON WHITE	Dance What You Wanna†/Theme of Tomorrow†
129	JACKIE ROSS	Hard Times/Hold Me†
130	SIMS TWINS	You're Pickin' in the Right Cotton Patch/ Double Portion of My Love

131	JOHNNIE TAYLOR	Rome (Wasn't Built In A Day)*/Never Never
132	VALENTINOS	Looking for a Love/Somewhere There's a Girl (Charted #8 r&b; #72 pop.)
133	JOHNNIE MORISETTE	Sho' Miss You Baby†/Wildest Girl in Town†
134	L. C. COOKE	Tell Me/You're Workin' Out Your Bag*

1963

135	R. H. HARRIS AND HIS GOSPEL PARADERS	Sometimes/Somebody
136	SIMS TWINS	I Gopher You/Good Good Lovin'
137	VALENTINOS	Darling Come Back Home/I'll Make It Alright
138	SIMS TWINS	That's Where It's At†/Movin' and Groovin'†
139	JOHNNIE MORISETTE	Don't Throw Your Love on Me So Strong/ Blue Monday
140	SOUL STIRRERS	Praying Ground/No Need to Worry
141	L. C. COOKE	The Wobble*/Chalk Line†
142	PATIENCE VALENTINE	Unlucky Girl/Arnistine*
143	MEDITATION SINGERS	There Must Be a Place/Behold Your Hand(?)
144	VALENTINOS	She's So Good To Me*/Baby, Lots of Luck
145	SOUL STIRRERS	Free at Last/His Love
146	R. H. HARRIS AND HIS GOSPEL PARADERS	Even Me/Oh Lord, Come and Ease
147	JOHNNIE MORISETTE	I Don't Need Nobody but You/Black Night

1964

148	L. C. COOKE	Put Me Down Easy*/Take Me for What I Am*
149	GUS JENKINS	Right Shake/Don't Get Sassy
150	SOUL STIRRERS	Oh Mary Don't You Weep/Looking Back
151	JOHNNIE MORISETTE	Gotta Keep Smilin' (So Trouble Won't Come)/I'll Never Come Running Back to You*
152	VALENTINOS	It's All Over Now/Tired of Living in the Country* (Charted #94 r&b/pop.)
153	LINDA CARR	Sweet Talk/Jackie,Bobby,Sonny,Bill
154	SOUL STIRRERS	Lead Me to Calvary/Mother, Don't Worry About Me
155	VALENTINOS	Everybody Wants to Fall in Love/Bitter Dreams
156	JOHNNIE TAYLOR	Oh, How I Love You/Run, But You Can't Hide
157	PATIENCE VALENTINE	Woman in a Man's World/Lost and Looking

SAR LPs

Note: Sam Cooke has author credit for songs below followed by asterisk (*) and coauthor credit for those followed by dagger (†).

1961

| 701 | SOUL STIRRERS | JESUS BE A FENCE AROUND ME |

I'm a Pilgrim. Listen to the Angels. Jesus Be a Fence Around Me.* Toiling On. He's Been a Shelter for Me.† Stand By Me, Father.† Must Jesus Bear the Cross Alone? Don't Leave Me. I'm Thankful.† I Love the Lord. He Cares. Wade in the Water.†

| 702 | SOUL STIRRERS | ? |

1962

| 703 | GOSPEL PEARLS | (See Sam Cooke LPs.) |
| 704 | SOUL STIRRERS | ENCORE |

His Love. No Need to Worry. Since I Met the Savior. Praying Ground. Amazing Grace.* Free at Last. Something Here Inside.* Time Brings About a Change. Joy in My Soul. Where Jesus Is.

1994

ABKCO   2231-2   SAM COOKE'S SAR RECORDS STORY
1959–1965

CD-1   *Soul Stirrers:* Wade in the Water. I'm a Pilgrim. Praying Ground. *R. H. Harris and His Gospel Paraders:* Somebody. Sometimes. *Soul Stirrers:* Amazing Grace. *R. H. Harris and His Gospel Paraders:* Pass Me Not. *Soul Stirrers:* Oh Mary, Don't You Weep. Since I Met the Savior. God Is Standing By. Lead Me to Calvary (with Sam Cooke and S. R. Crain). Listen to the Angels Sing. Don't Leave Me Alone. Stand By Me Father. Jesus Be a Fence Around Me. Lead Me Jesus. Free at Last. Looking Back. *R. H. Harris and His Gospel Paraders:* Born Again. Wait on Jesus. *Soul Stirrers:* Time Brings About a Change. Must Jesus Bear the Cross Alone. *The Womack Brothers:* Yield Not to Temptation. Couldn't Hear Nobody Pray. Somewhere There's a God. *Sam Cooke:* That's Heaven to Me.

CD-2   *Sam Cooke:* You Send Me—Demo. Just for You. Somewhere There's a Girl. You Were Made for Me. *Mel Carter:* When a Boy Falls in Love. *The Simms Twins:* Soothe Me. That's Where It's At. *The Valentinos:* Everybody Wants to Fall in Love. *Johnnie Taylor:* Keep On Loving You. I'll Always Be in Love with You. Baby, We've Got Love. *The Valentinos:* Baby, Lots of Luck. *L. C. Cooke:* Put Me Down Easy. *Johnnie Taylor:* Rome (Wasn't Built in a Day). *Billy Preston:* Greazee Pt. I/Pt. II. *The Simms Twins:* I Gopher You. *Johnnie Morisette:* You're Always on My Mind. I Need Lots of Love. Don't Throw Your Love on Me So Strong. Black Night. Damper. *Johnnie Taylor:* You Can Run (but You Can't Hide). *Johnnie Morisette:* Meet Me at the Twisting Place. *The Simms Twins:* Good Good

Loving. *L. C. Cooke:* The Wobble. *The Valentinos:* Lookin' for a Love. I've Got Love for You. Tired of Living in the Country. It's All Over Now.

DERBY

Note: Sam Cooke has author credit for songs below followed by asterisk (*) and coauthor credit for those followed by dagger (†).

1963

100	BUCK FLOYD	Short Short Skirt/Tobacco Road
101	JOHNNIE TAYLOR	Shine Shine Shine/Dance What You Wanna*
1002	BILLY PRESTON	Greazee Pt. 1/Pt. 2
1003	MEL CARTER	When a Boy Falls in Love†/So Wonderful (Charted #30 r&b; #44 pop.)
1004	JEANIE ROBERTSON	Tears of Happiness/Memories
1005	MEL CARTER	Time of Young Love/Wonderful Love
1006	JOHNNIE TAYLOR	(I'll Always Be) In Love with You/Baby, We've Got Love*
1007	MILT GRAYSON	Wayfarin' Stranger/Your Old Standby
1008	MEL CARTER	After the Parting, the Meeting Is Sweeter/ Why I Call Her Mine
1009	THE EXECUTIVES	Falling in Love/Happy Chatter†
1010	JOHNNIE TAYLOR	I Need Lots of Love/Getting Married Soon

DERBY LPs

| 702 | MEL CARTER | WHEN A BOY FALLS IN LOVE |
| ? | BILLY PRESTON | GREAZEE SOUL |

NOTES ON SOURCES

INTERVIEWS

These interviews were conducted by G. David Tenenbaum and Daniel Wolff, in some cases with the assistance of S. R. Crain and Cliff White, in person, over the telephone and in writing, between 1982 and 1994. We are grateful to all for sharing their time and memories—often more than once.

Lou Adler; J. W. Alexander; Muhammad Ali; Andy Allen; Dick Allen; Herb Alpert; Larry Auerbach; Thelma Ballard; Harold Battiste; Dr. Benjamin H. Bendat; Robert "Bumps" Blackwell; Lorenza Brown-Porter; Jerry Brandt; Lonnie Brooks; Jerry Butler; Joyce Caldwell; Earl Calloway; Paul Cantor; Berneice Carter; Johnny Carter; Mel Carter; James "Dimples" Cochran; Bishop M. R. Conic; Reverend Charles Cook; Charles Cook, Jr.; Joey Cook (Nathaniel Brown); Phyllis Cook; Margaret Cranhaw; Luigi Creatore; Leroy Crume; Joan Deary; Joan Dew; Reverend Clay Evans; Ernie Farrell; Johnny Fields; Harry Finfer; Paul Foster; Clarence Fountain; Isaac "Dickie" Freeman; Grady Gaines; Albert "June" Gardner; Greg Geller; John Govan; Florence Greenberg; Frank Guida; René Hall; Joyce Harris; James Hill; Steven Hill; George Jay; Anita Jefferson; Jocko (Douglas Henderson); Ray Johnson; E. Rodney Jones; Tim Jones; Casey Kasem; Bob Keen; Henry Kirkland; Allen Klein; Deano Lappas; Beverley Lee; Reverend Sammie Lewis; Bishop Dwight Arnold "Gatemouth" Moore; Sam Moore; Johnnie Morisette; Edwin J. Mullens;

Scott Muni; Henry Nash; Earl Palmer; Ray Pohlman; Lawrence Pritchard; Beverly and Betty Prudhomme; Jess Rand; Lou Rawls; Nona Ray; Vi Redd; Dora Robinson; Louie Robinson; Rosko (Bill Mercer); Art Rupe; Lee Rupe; Zelda Sands; Bobby Schiffman; Al Schmitt; Wallace Seawell; Sid Sharp; Alex Siamas; Bobby and Kenneth Sims; Charley Cronander Smith; Fred Smith; Purvis Spann; Louis Tate; Sammie Tate; Elizabeth Taylor; Johnny Taylor; Spencer Taylor; Jimmy Tolbert; Juanita Tucker; Albertina Walker; Marion Williams; Curtis Womack; Early Wright.

PROLOGUE

1–4   Unless otherwise noted, this version of Cooke's death is taken from the official transcript of the coroner's inquest held December 16, 1964, in Room 150, Hall of Justice, Los Angeles.

1   Black Muslim newspaper   Gerri Hirshey, *Nowhere to Run: The Story of Soul Music* (New York: Penguin, 1984), p. 106.

4   "Is it true?"   A. S. "Doc" Young, "The Mysterious Death of Sam Cooke," *Chicago Defender*, 12/31/64, p. 6.

4   headlines   *Los Angeles Sentinel*, 12/11/64, p. 1.

5   "fixed up"   Bumps Blackwell interview.

5   got a clue   Young, "Mysterious Death," p. 17.

5   business associate   Allen Klein in *Variety*, 12/16/64, p. 57.

6   "cover-up"   *Afro-American* (Baltimore), 12/19/64, p. 1; *Amsterdam News*, 1/30/65, p. 1; *Forward Times*, 12/26/64; *Chicago Defender*, 12/29/64.

6   vice raid   *Los Angeles Sentinel*, 1/21/65, p. 1.

6   marriage license   Ibid., 2/11/65, p. 1

CHAPTER 1

7   vision   Otho B. Cobbins, ed., *History of Church of Christ (Holiness) U.S.A. 1895–1965*, (New York: Vantage, 1966), p. 24.

8   "nigger burying ground"   Neil R. McMillen, *Dark Journey: Black Mississippians in the Age of Jim Crow* (Chicago: University of Illinois Press, 1990), p. 6.

8   "You shall write . . ."   Cobbins, p. 25.

8 "no idea" Ibid., p. 23.

8 1893 and 1900 Vinson Synan, *The Holiness-Pentecostal Movement in the United States* (Grand Rapids, Mich.: William B. Eerdmans, 1971), p. 53.

8 "Never before" Ibid.

8–9 Holiness history from Cobbins.

10 married in 1887 National Census, 1900.

10 Mother Cook Bishop M. R. Conic interview.

10 her vision Cobbins, p. 381.

10 Alex Reverend Charles Cook interview.

11 "a flame" Eric Lincoln and Lawrence H. Mamiya, *The Black Church in the African American Experience* (Durham, N.C.: Duke University Press, 1990), p. 81.

11 church split see Cobbins.

11 age seventeen Reverend Charles Cook interview.

12 "cotton obsessed" Rupert B. Vance, *Human Factors in Cotton Culture* (Chapel Hill, N.C.: University of North Carolina Press, 1929), p. 266, quoted in William Ferris, *Blues from the Delta* (New York: Da Capo, 1978).

12 Handy Ibid., p. 87.

12–13 Lomax Alan Lomax, *The Land Where the Blues Began* (New York: Pantheon, 1993), p. 58.

13 over eighty Negro churches C.P.J. Mooney, ed., *The Mid-South and Its Builders* (Memphis: Mid-South Biographical and Historical Association, 1920), n.p.

15 twenty-three people killed Viv Broughton, *Black Gospel: An Illustrated History of the Gospel Sound* (Dorset, England: Blandford, 1985), p. 36.

15 "the attempt" McMillen, p. 237.

15 *Clarion-Ledger* Ibid.

16 150,000 Negroes Ibid., p. 262.

16 November 15, 1923 Marriage license, Coahama County.

16 Mound Bayou McMillen, pp. 186–90.

17 "public work" Sam Cooke birth certificate.

CHAPTER 2

19   by a mid-wife   Birth certificate.

20   as early as 1927   Robert Palmer, *Deep Blues* (New York: Penguin, 1981), p. 107.

20   "You ain't supposed"   Ferris, p. 81.

20   sacred music outsold the blues   Broughton, pp. 42, 49.

20   Mahalia   Ibid., p. 53.

22   "more by education"   Nicholas Lemann, *The Promised Land: The Great Black Migration and How It Changed America* (New York: Knopf, 1991), p. 37.

22   "lynching"   Charles S. Johnson, *Growing Up in the Black Belt: Negro Youth in the Rural South* (Washington, D.C.: American Council on Education, 1941), p. 318.

22   Mullens   Mooney, p. 230, and E.J. Mullens III interview.

23   more than three-quarters   Johnson, p. 110.

23   nearly tripled   Lemann, p. 16.

24   90 percent   David K. Fremon, *Chicago Politics Ward by Ward* (Bloomington and Indianapolis: Indiana University Press, 1988), p. 29.

24   Church of Christ   Cobbins, p. 175.

24   the Murphys   Chicago phone book, 1928–29.

25   "past grandeur"   Louis Wirth and Maraget Furez, *Local Community Fact Book (1938)* (Chicago: Chicago Recreation Commission, 1938), n.p.

25   local   John Govan interview.

25   Objective statistics   Wirth and Furez.

25   one local   Berneice Carter interview.

25   Doolittle Elementary   James R. Grossman, *Land of Hope: Chicago, Black Southerners, and the Great Migration* (Chicago: University of Chicago Press, 1989), p. 254.

26   one contemporary   Jerry Butler interview.

26   "And boy"   Margurite Belafonte, "Eye to Eye with Sam Cook," *Amsterdam News*, 12/21/1957, p. 11.

26   Chicago Heights   Cobbins, p. 198.

27   65,000 ... "Rows of automobiles"   St. Clair Drake and Horace R. Cayton, *Black Metropolis: A Study of Negro Life in a Northern City* (New York: Harper & Row, 1970), pp. 618, 417.

28   "My family was poor"   Ernestine Cofield, *"Sam Cooke's Big Decision"* (hereafter referred to as Cofield 2), *Chicago Defender*, 10/25/58, p. 14.

29   Reynolds Metal   Reverend Charles Cook interview.

29   one visitor   S. R. Crain.

29   "His religious background"   Thelma Ballard interview.

29   "tear down fences"   Cofield 2.

30   climb up on a tub   Ernestine Cofield, *Close Look at Sam Cook* (hereafter referred to as Cofield 1), *Chicago Defender*, 10/18/58, p. 11.

30   "wonderful boy"   *Chicago Defender*, 12/16/64, p. 3.

31   In 1942   Program for Chicago funeral.

31   "the beginning of the end"   Cobbins, p. 44.

33   "only in the urban milieu"   Joseph R. Washington, Jr., *Black Sects and Cults* (New York: Anchor/Doubleday, 1973), p. 80.

33   the Rhumboogie   William Barlow, *Looking Up at Down: The Emergence of the Blues Culture* (Philadelphia: Temple University Press, 1989), p. 329, Mike Rowe, *Chicago Blues: The City and the Music* (New York: Da Capo, 1975), pp. 43, 63, 79.

33   "going astray"   Drake and Cayton, p. 637.

34   Leonard and Phil Chess   Rowe, pg. 65

34   "the astonishing thing"   Thomas Lee Philpott, *The Slum and the Ghetto: Neighborhood Deterioration and Middle-Class Reform, Chicago, 1880–1930* (New York: Oxford University Press, 1978), p. 130.

34   Ku Klux Klan   Ibid., pp. 186, 196.

35   "unnecessary"   Drake and Cayton, p. 121.

35   the *Defender*   Ibid., p. 749.

35   Richard Wright   Ibid., p. xiii.

CHAPTER 3

37   "sixth-graders"   Drake and Cayton, p. 516.

37   " 'abandon all hope' "   Dianne M. Pinderhughes, *Race and Ethnicity in Chicago's Politics: A Reexamination of Pluralist Theory* (Chicago: University of Illinois, 1987), p. 218.

38   three thousand more children   Mary J. Herrick, *The Chicago Schools: A Social and Political History* (Beverly Hills and London: Sage Productions, 1971), p. 270.

38   "all Negroes"   Pinderhughes, p. 158.

38   solo   *Sunday News*, 7/16/61.

38   His teachers   *Chicago Defender*, 12/14/64, p. 6.

38   yearbook   *The Phillipsite*, June 1948.

39   "personable and aggressive"   *Chicago Defender*, 12/14/64, p. 6.

39   "noticed the girls"   Cofield 1.

39   "like the Ink Spots"   Belafonte, p. 11.

40   110,000   Arnold Richard Hirsch, *Making the Second Ghetto: Race and Housing in Chicago: 1940–1966* (Ph.D. thesis, University of Illinois, 1978), p. 23.

40   Flash fires   Harold M. Mayer and Richard C. Wade, *Chicago: Growth of a Metropolis* (Chicago: University of Chicago Press, 1969), p. 381.

40   "We are out to fight"   *Chicago Defender*, 10/13/45, p. 1.

40   more a social club   Cofield 1.

41   The way Sam told it   *Sunday News*, July 16, 1961, p. 4.

42   "Nobody knows"   *Sepia*, June 1958, p. 20.

43   "how to meet people"   Kip Lornell, *Happy in the Service of the Lord: Afro-American Gospel Quartets in Memphis* (Chicago: University of Illinois Press, 1988), p. 85.

43   "You got five dudes"   Louie Robinson, "Lou Rawls," *Ebony*, October 1978, p. 116.

44   Soul Stirrers   S. R. Crain. For Stirrers' history in general, see Broughton; Ray Funk, "The Soul Stirrers," *Rejoice!*, Winter 1987, pp. 12–20; and Tony Heilbut, *The Gospel Sound: Good News and Bad Times* (New York: Simon & Schuster, 1985), as well as various liner notes on CDs listed in discography.

45   Willie Johnson   quoted in Broughton, p. 63.

45   one historian   Ibid., p. 62.

46   Lomax   Funk, "Soul Stirrers."

46   the first   Heilbut, p. 83.

46   By 1938   Broughton, p. 58.

48   R. H. Harris has said   Heilbut, p. 92.

CHAPTER 4

49   big Mother's Day program   *Chicago Defender*, 5/1/48.

50   Georgia   S. R. Crain; Charles Cook, Jr., interview.

50   Everybody knew   Horace Coon, "Dynamite in Chicago Housing," *Negro Digest*, April 1951, p. 7.

51   September 26, 1948   *Chicago Defender*, 9/18/48, p. 27.

53   That summer, one reporter   *Chicago Defender*, 7/10/48, p. 3.

53 The official program *Michigan Chronicle*, 2/12/1949, p. 22.

53 a picture Ibid., 2/19/1949, n.p.

54 C. L. Franklin Jeff Todd Titon, *Give Me This Mountain: Reverend C. L. Franklin Life History and Selected Sermons* (Champaign: University of Illinois Press, 1989), pp. 19–29.

55 Memphis For background, see Lornell; Margaret McKee and Fred Chisenhall, *Beale Black and Blue: Life and Music on Black America's Main Street* (Baton Rouge: Louisiana State University Press, 1981); and Louis Cantor, *Wheelin' on Beale* (New York: Pharos, 1992).

55 "failed repeatedly" *Chicago Defender*, 7/10/48, p. 3.

55 "custom of 150 years" McKee and Chisenhall, pp. 6–7, 85.

55 James Darling Lornell, p. 44.

56 WDIA For detailed history, see Cantor.

56 "They are businessmen" McKee and Chisenhall, p. 93.

56 Dwight "Gatemouth" Moore Moore interview; Cantor; *Memphis World*, 1/11/49, p. 1, and 3/1/49, p. 3.

58 Spirit of Memphis For extensive history, see Lornell.

58 Brewster see Bernice Johnson Reagon, ed., *We'll Understand It Better By and By: Pioneering African American Gospel Composers* (Washington and London: Smithsonian Institution Press, 1992), pp. 185–254.

58 "lectured" Ibid., p. 201.

59 to advertise *Indianapolis Recorder*, 5/14/49, p. 6.

60 Jackie Ross For more information, see Robert Pruter, "Jackie Ross: She's Not Selfish at All!" *It Will Stand* #29, Spring 1983, pp. 6–8.

CHAPTER 5

64 "art almost immune" Heilbut, p. 82.

64 September 24, 1950 *Chicago Defender*, 9/16/50, p. 33.

70 a friend Leroy Crume interview.

70 "I seen him" Broughton, p. 68.

71 "They used to call us" Liner notes for the Pilgrim Travelers, *Walking Rhythm*, Specialty CD-7030-2, 1991.

72 "the guiding force" *Philadelphia Tribune*, 1/4/58, p. 8.

72 "I had a wonderful time" *Tan*, April 1958, p. 23.

73 an old picture *Los Angeles Sentinel*, 1/4/51, p. 1a-6.

73 Specialty For an overview, see Arnold Shaw, *Honkers and Shouters: The Golden Years of Rhythm and Blues* (New York: Collier, 1978).

73 In 1930 Barlow, p. 334.

73 Central Avenue Stanley Robertson, "The Rise and Fall of Central Avenue," *Los Angeles Sentinel*, 6/25/59, p. 6.

73 increased by 70 percent Keith E. Collins, *Black Los Angeles: The Maturing of the Ghetto* (Sacramento, Cal.: Century Twenty-one, 1980), pp. 5–23.

74 Rupe had been raised Unless otherwise noted, information on Art Rupe is from Shaw, pp. 179–94, and Rupe interview.

74 "I looked" Shaw, p. 182.

75 Sam Phillips Colin Escott with Martin Hawkins, *Good Rockin' Tonight: Sun Records and the Birth of Rock 'n' Roll* (New York: St. Martin's, 1991), p. 32.

75 specialize Shaw, p. 183.

75 The big band scene Ed Ward, Geoffrey Stokes, and Ken Tucker, *Rock of Ages: The Rolling Stone History of Rock & Roll* (New York: Rolling Stone Press/Summit Books, 1986), p. 38.

75 "a freak" Rob Finnis, liner notes to Little Richard boxed set, Specialty CD-8508.

75 "made two institutions" Charlie Lange, liner notes, *Roy Milton*, Specialty CD-7004.

76 "Actually" "The Specialty Story," *Hit Parader*, June 1969.

76 "the fervor" Art Rupe interview.

77 27,000 copies Specialty files at Fantasy Records.

79 "very intense guy" Interview with Art Rupe in Specialty files.

80 Art reassured him Letter in Specialty files.

81 "as an art form" Art Rupe interview.

81 "[W]e want to thank you" Letter in Specialty files.

CHAPTER 6

84 itinerary From Claude A. Barnett papers, Associated Negro Press, Chicago Historical Society.

84 Mother's Day *Chicago Defender*, 5/5/51, p. 39.

85 "Women became" Heilbut, p. 85.

85 400,000 votes *Chicago Defender*, 11/3/45, p. 6.

87 $1,000 white nylon Ibid., 7/14/51, p. 2.

87 Thomas Dorsey Ibid., 8/11/51, p. 2.

88   Between 1947 and 1957   Martin Feldstein, ed., *The American Economy in Transition* (Chicago: University of Chicago Press, 1980), p. 1.

88   "Deliver Us From Evil"   *Los Angeles Sentinel*, 2/1/51, p. A-7.

91   "juicy"   *Chicago Defender*, 3/8/52, p. 22.

91   Clara Ward   *Courier*, 7/26/52, magazine section, p. 4, in Barnett Collection, Chicago Historical Society.

91   "I felt"   Art Rupe interview.

91   Lillian Cumber   Letters in the Barnett Collection, Chicago Historical Society.

93   "quartet chicken"   Edwin Smith, *Rejoice!*, 2–3/1992, pgs. 3–6

94   Morisette   Tim Schuller, "The Johnny Two-Voice Story: Johnnie Morisette," *Living Blues*, Winter 1980–81, pp. 20–26.

95   Jesse Whitaker   Lawrence N. Redd, *Rock Is Rhythm and Blues: The Impact of Mass Media* (Detroit: Michigan State University Press, 1974), p. 157.

95   "[h]e went down"   Patrick and Barbara Salvo, "The Bobby Womack Story," *Black Music*, January 1975, pp. 60–62; Curtis Womack interview.

96   During the summer   *Chicago Defender*, 7/21/51, p. 1.

97   Thurgood Marshall   Ibid., 7/7/51, p. 1.

97   Christmas night   Ibid., 1/5/52, p. 1.

97   Alan Freed   Ward, Stokes, and Tucker, p. 70.

97   so shy   Lee Rupe interview.

CHAPTER 7

101   He wrote Crain   Letter in Specialty files.

101   "Sam started as a bad imitation"   Heilbut, p. 88.

103   "breaking attendance records"   *Los Angeles Sentinel*, 6/25/53, p. A-6.

105   Dolores Elizabeth Milligan   Joey Cook interview.

106   the population   *Our World*, April 1953, pp. 15–21.

108   *Billboard*   Joel Friedman in *Billboard*, 2/6/54, p. 13.

109   *Variety*   Redd, p. 30.

109   grossed $125,000   Ibid., p. 33.

109   Charles Keil   Quoted in Shaw, p. 92.

110   Anthony Heilbut   Heilbut, p. 124.

111   San Francisco   Ibid., p. 125.

111   "Reverend Cheeks" *Rejoice!*, February/March 1992, pp. 3–6.

112   Rawls Lou Rawls interview.

113   James Cone James H. Cone, *The Spirituals and the Blues* (New York: Seabury, 1972), p. 320.

113   "to be themselves" Wyatt Tee Walker, *Somebody's Calling My Name: Black Sacred Music and Social Change* (Valley Forge, N.Y.: Judson Press, 1979), p. 143.

113   "the most vaudevillian" Taylor Branch, *Parting the Waters: America in the King Years 1954–63* (New York: Simon & Schuster, 1988), p. 267.

114   "As a participant" Walker, p. 183.

CHAPTER 8

115   "like a basketball team" Interview with Art Rupe in Specialty files.

115   Willie Webb Cobbins, pp. 176, 199.

117   "I trust" Letter in Specialty files.

117   Blackwell Rob Finnis, liner notes; Blackwell interview.

117   August of 1952 *Los Angeles Sentinel*, 8/7/52, p. B-3.

118   As Rupe Art Rupe interview.

118   The tape Finnis, liner notes.

118   Jesse Belvin See Jim Dawson, "Jesse Belvin," *Goldmine*, 12/5/86, pp. 16–17; Steve Propes, liner notes to *Jesse Belvin: The Blues Balladeer*, Specialty CD-70003.

119   In July *Los Angeles Sentinel*, 7/21/55, p. 7.

121   Brother Joe May Ibid., 9/17/55, p. 7.

122   J.W. announced Ibid., 10/8/55, p. 6.

123   renewal time in February Specialty files.

123   Till *Chicago Defender*, 9/17 & 10/1/55, p. 4.

124   Thurgood Marshall *Afro-American* (New Jersey), 10/8/55, p. 1.

124   "electrified audiences" *Los Angeles Sentinel*, 3/29/56, p. 10.

CHAPTER 9

129   "A Friend" Letter in Specialty files.

130   "[W]e most certainly" Ibid.

131   "first battle of song" *Atlanta Daily Word*, 7/15/56, p. 3.

133   the famous Apollo See Ted Fox, *Showtime at the Apollo* (New York: Holt, Rinehart & Winston, 1983).

133   larger fees *Amsterdam News*, 3/10/56, p. 15.

134   Bill Cook Ibid., 9/8/56, p. 11.

134   April of 1956 Redd, pp. 40–41.

135   Negro columnist *Los Angeles Sentinel*, 1/11/51, p. A4.

135   Negro dj's Ward, Stokes, and Tucker, p. 128.

135   "Frankly" *Tan*, April 1958, p. 24.

135   "a lot of things" Ibid.

136   Cosimo Matassa's See John Broven, *Rhythm & Blues in New Orleans* (Gretna, La.: Pelican, 1978).

136   author Rick Coleman Liner notes to Little Richard boxed set, Specialty CD-8508.

137   Bumps would write J.W. Letter in Specialty files.

139   *Billboard* agreed *Billboard*, 3/9/57, p. 26.

139   cabled Art Rupe Cable in Specialty files.

139   Whitaker's estimation Redd, p. 163.

140   "an interesting case" *Billboard*, 3/9/57, p. 26.

CHAPTER 10

143   "The Only Music" Letter in Specialty files.

143   by mid-'56 Specialty files.

145   a contract Ibid.

145   Hall on rhythm guitar These and all subsequent personnel listings come from recording notes, courtesy Carmen Fanzone, American Federation of Musicians Union.

148   terms for Blackwell's Specialty files.

150   the release Ibid.

150   court documents *Robert A. Blackwell v. John Siamas, etc.*, Case #743709, California Superior Court, Los Angeles, 4/15/60.

152   Calumet Park *Los Angeles Sentinel*, 8/1/57, p. 2.

152   Levittown Ibid., 8/15/57, p. 2.

152   Roy Hamilton   Ibid., 7/25/57, p. 8.

152   McPhatter   Ibid., 9/5/57, p. 8.

152   LaVern Baker   Ibid., p. 9.

152   Mahalia   Ibid., 7/4/57, p. 6.

154   "We sold eighty thousand"   Marc Elliot, *Rockonomics: The Money Behind the Music* (Toronto: Franklin Watts, 1989), p. 39.

155   Louis Armstrong   *Michigan Chronicle*, 9/28/57, Section 2, p. 5.

155   Little Rock NAACP   Ibid., 10/26/57, p. 1.

156   As Cooke later told   *Amsterdam News*, 12/21/57, p. 11.

156   *Billboard* highlighted   *Billboard*, 10/21/57.

158   "I still don't know"   *Sepia*, June 1958.

CHAPTER 11

162   *Ebony*   *Ebony*, May 1951, p. 62.

162   "Hi Sweet"   Letter in Specialty files.

163   Back in August   Specialty files.

166   "New!"   *Billboard*, 11/23/57.

167   "the NEW"   *Billboard*, 12/2/57.

167   Sullivan show   See Museum of Television and Radio, Media #070293 C*361.

168   *Sepia*   *Sepia*, June 1958, pp. 16–20.

169   Connie Bollings   *Philadelphia Tribune*, 3/25/58, p. 1.

170   Frank Sinatra   Daniel P. Szatmary, *Rockin' in Time: A Social History of Rock-and-Roll* (New York: Prentice-Hall, 1991).

170   "music with a beat"   Stanley Robertson, "How Sam Cooke Sends 'Em," *Los Angeles Sentinel*, 3/6/58, p. B-9.

171   Jules Podell   *New York Times*, 9/15/44, and obituary 9/29/73.

173   "old friends"   *Variety*, 3/12/58, p. 70.

173   "About halfway through"   *New York World Telegraph and Sun*, 2/6/64.

173   "handsome young Negro"   Ibid.

173   In Los Angeles   *Los Angeles Sentinel*, 3/20/58, p. 8.

CHAPTER 12

175   paternity suit   *Philadelphia Tribune*, 4/1/58, p. 1.

176   "the most formidable"   *Norfolk Journal*, 3/8/58, p. 15.

176   "almost enough"   *Billboard*, 2/24/58, p. 6.

176   Phil Everly   Roger White, *The Everly Brothers: Walk Right Back* (London: Plexus, 1984), p. 39.

176   "a rock 'n' roll star"   Ibid., p. 44.

176–177   Feld's tour the year before   *Billboard*, 9/27/57, p. 79.

177   "We won't say"   *Amsterdam News*, 4/21/56, p. 11.

177   "I know it is bound"   Ibid., 12/21/57, p. 11.

178   Sam and LaVern   *Los Angeles Sentinel*, 4/17/58, p. 4.

178   "show-stopper"   *Billboard*, 4/21/58, p. 7.

178   "enthusiasm for Sam"   *Atlanta World*, 5/27/58.

178   "Get that blues singer"   Heilbut, p. 90.

179   "sensational swoon swinger"   *Atlanta World*, 5/27/58.

179–180   Early in the tour   *Billboard*, 4/21/58, pg. 7.

180   Alan Freed's tour   Ward, Stokes, and Tucker, p. 175.

181   Dolores testified   *Sam Cook v. Dolores Cook*, #0529553, California Superior Court, Los Angeles, 11/15/57.

182   John told journalist   *Los Angeles Sentinel*, 7/24/58, p. 8.

182   the President   Ibid., 5/15 & 5/22/58.

183   lacked "sincerity"   *Variety*, 9/3/58, p. 55.

184   The magazines   *Sepia*, January 1960, pp. 34–37.

184   "Gert"   *Los Angeles Sentinel*, 11/6/58, p. 3; 12/17/64, p. 1.

184–185   *Dick Clark's*   See Dick Clark and Richard Robinson, *Rock, Roll & Remember* (New York: Thomas Y. Crowell, 1976), pp. 133–36.

185   "an aura"   *Billboard*, 10/20/58, p. 5.

187   stopped to check   *Chittenden County Times* (West Memphis, Arkansas), 11/14/58, p. 1.

CHAPTER 13

190   "a public hospital"   *Ebony*, October 1978, p. 118.

195   "Even when I"   Liner notes to *Tribute* LP.

197   March 21   *Fresno Bee*, 3/23/59, p. 1.

198   "God in His infinite wisdom"   *Amsterdam News*, 4/25/59, p. 16.

198   "the lull in rock"   See Steve Chapple and Reebee Garofaro, *Rock & Roll Is Here to Pay* (Chicago: Nelson-Hall, 1977).
199   "ran the audience wild"   *Amsterdam News*, 4/25/59, p. 16.
201   In Charlotte   *Atlanta Daily World*, 6/14/59, p. 5.
201   Mack Charles Parker   *Los Angeles Sentinel*, 5/28/59, p. 1; 6/25/59, p. 4–   .
202   Shuttlesworth   Ibid., 6/11/59, p. 1.
202   "if the South's cause"   Ibid., 6/17/59, p. 1.
202   "NEGRO REVOLT"   *Amsterdam News*, 7/4/1959, p. 1.

CHAPTER 14

203   "initial entry"   *Variety*, 7/8/59, p. 87.
205   "joy"   *Sepia*, January 1960, p. 34.
206   "whirlwind courtship"   *Chicago Defender*, 10/17/59, p. 1.
206   "revisiting their old haunts"   *Sepia*, January 1960, p. 34.
206   a summons   *B. Wolf v. Rex. Productions, Inc.*, Los Angeles Superior Court, 3/16/60.
207   "hottest rumor"   *Billboard*, 11/9/59, p. 2.
207   Wexler   Hirshey, p. 107.
208   "a source of ready cash"   Dorothy Wade and Justine Picardie, *Music Man: Ahmet Ertegun, Atlantic Records, and the Triumph of Rock 'n' Roll* (New York and London: Norton, 1990), p. 257.
213   "winner"   *Billboard*, 2/15/60, p. 10.

CHAPTER 15

215   syndicated piece   *New York Journal-American*, 8/5/60; *Pittsburgh Courier*, 10/8/60, p. 28.
216   February 1, 1960   Branch, p. 276.
216   outside the established   See Howell Raines, *My Soul Is Rested: The Story of the Civil Rights Movement in the Deep South* (New York: Penguin, 1977), p. 80.
216   Little Rock   Dawson in *Goldmine*; *Los Angeles Sentinel*, 2/18/60, p. 1.
217   "hoping for a boy"   *Los Angeles Sentinel*, 2/18/60, p. 2-C.
218   Freed   Ward, Stokes, and Tucker, pp. 206–14.

219   "collective payola"   *Billboard*, 1/8/60, p. 1.

219   Al Benson   Ibid., 1/11/60, p. 1.

219   "the horse's tail"   Ibid., 1/8/60, p. 8.

219   Johnny Otis   *Los Angeles Sentinel*, 6/23/60, p. 4A.

221   "spins aplenty"   *Billboard*, 4/4/60, p. 57.

221–222   "devastating effect"   *Amsterdam News*, 5/7/60, p. 1.

223   Birmingham   *Los Angeles Sentinel*, 7/21/60, p. C-1.

223   Larry Williams   *Amsterdam News*, 7/30/60, p. 17.

224   Kilgallen   *New York Journal American*, 8/5/60.

225   Kilgallen column   Ibid.

CHAPTER 16

230   "so hypnotic"   François Postif in *Jazz Hot*, December 1960, pp. 26–27 (translation by author).

231   McPhatter   *Amsterdam News*, 7/9/60, p. 15.

232   "Oreatha"   *Los Angeles Sentinel*, 1/19/61, p. C-3.

233   "just beautiful"   Phyl Garland, *The Sound of Soul* (Chicago: Henry Regnery, 1969), p. 199.

233   forbade it   Chris Cory in *Time*, June 3, 1968.

233   "With Sam"   Ibid.

233   "gospel roots"   Fox, p. 237.

235   "deluxe limited"   *Los Angeles Sentinel*, 4/6/61, p. C-2.

238   West Indies   *Cash Box*, 3/18/61, p. 41.

238   May 4   Raines, p. 111.

240   "unusual honor"   *Cash Box*, 7/15/61, p. 28.

240   "I want to sing"   *Sunday News*, 7/16/61.

241   "The teeners"   *Billboard*, 11/6/61, p. 3.

242   hitting nationally   *Cash Box*, 9/9/61, p. 16.

242   first small ad   Ibid., 9/23/61, p. 16.

CHAPTER 17

243   October 19, 1961   *Wolf v. Siamas*.

244   small piece   *Cash Box*, 11/25/61, p. 36.

245   "That gave me"   Chris Roberts, "Doesn't That Gospel Music Just Swing!" *Melody Maker*, 10/20/62, p. 6.

245   an interviewer   *Dick Clark Show*, 4/4/64.

245   "sparkling"   *Cash Box*, 1/20/62.

246   "riding high"   Ibid., 1/27/62, p. 28.

247   RCA's earnings   Ibid., 4/28/62.

249   two white officers   *Los Angeles Sentinel*, 5/3/1962, p. 1.

251   early July   *Afro-American* (Baltimore), 7/14/62, p. 4.

251   "Westcoasters"   *Los Angeles Sentinel*, 7/26/1962, p. 16a.

251   numbers raid   *Afro-American* (Baltimore), 11/18/1962, p. 13

251   "The first five-hundred-dollar bill"   Heilbut, p. 125.

252   "Hi, Jerry"   *Afro-American* (Baltimore), 9/1/62.

253   lynch mobs   Branch, pp. 638–40.

253   Gibson   *Los Angeles Sentinel*, 11/7/57, p. 9.

254   author Charles White   Charles White, *The Life and Times of Little Richard: The Quasar of Rock* (New York: Harmony, 1984), pp. 111–18.

254   "So fast"   Roberts in *Melody Maker*, p. 6.

255   "First thing"   *Black Music*, January 1970.

256   "rockinest group"   Liner notes, Little Richard boxed set, Specialty.

256   invited women   *Variety*, 11/7/62.

256   *Tonight Show*   *Amsterdam News*, 11/17/62, p. 19.

CHAPTER 18

259   J.W., for one   *Los Angeles Sentinel*, 2/28/63, p. A-16.

259   Scepter Records   *Chicago Defender*, 12/11/62.

260   Smokey Robinson   Nelson George, *Where Did Our Love Go?: The Rise and Fall of the Motown Sound* (New York: St. Martin's, 1985), p. 67.

261   announced special guest   *Los Angeles Sentinel*, 12/27/62, p. 8B.

262   Harlem Square Club   See Peter Guralnick's liner notes, RCA PCD1-5181, 1985.

267   Pat Boone   Roberts in *Melody Maker*, p. 6.

268   throwing Jimmy's ax   Harry Shapiro and Caesar Glebbeck, *Jimi Hendrix: Electric Gypsy* (New York: St. Martin's, 1990), p. 75.

268   "I'd have learnt more"   Ibid., p. 71, quoting *Rave*, June 1967.

269   accountant   Interview with Allen Klein, *Playboy*, 11/71, p. 104.

269   "a very poor student"   Loraine Alterman, "Portrait of 'Klein,' " *Melody Maker*, 2/19/72, p. 15.

269   "I was clerking"   Ibid.

270   *Rockonomics*   Elliot, p. 40.

270   "When I met Sam"   *Los Angeles Sentinel*, 1/21/65, p. A-5.

271   "I started out"   Alterman, p. 15.

CHAPTER 19

273   Jimmy Travis   Branch, p. 717.

273   McPhatter   Reprinted from *Norfolk Journal and Guide*, in *Philadelphia Tribune*, 4/30/63, p. 16.

273   King   Branch, p. 709.

274   "It amazes me"   *Pittsburgh Courier*, 4/13/63, p. 13.

274   Tall Paul   See Branch, pp. 755–803, for description of Birmingham march.

274   "first time"   Ibid., p. 775.

274   Pittsburgh   *Variety*, 5/8/63.

275   Allen Klein   Robert Hilburn, "Sam Cooke—Our Father of Soul," *Los Angeles Times*, 2/16/86, p. 62.

275   "stars of soul music"   Branch, p. 792.

275–276   the mid-point   Ibid., p. 825.

276   "The heart"   Ibid., p. 824.

277   pair of mink stoles   *Los Angeles Sentinel*, 6/20/63, p. 18A.

277   Gibson   Ibid.

277   usually covered   *Los Angeles Sentinel*, 6/20/63, p. 1.

277   "several minutes"   Louie Robinson, "Death Shocks Singer's Fans," *Jet*, 12/31/65.

CHAPTER 20

282   Blueflame Lounge   *Chicago Defender*, picture files.

282   "manse buzzed"   *Los Angeles Sentinel*, 8/29/63, p. 16A.

283   unresolved litigation   *BMG Music v. ABKCO Music and Records, Inc.*, New York Supreme Court, #1047-92, 1/10/92.

283   When Alex registered Tracey   List of Officers, Directors and3 Agents, 10/14/63, State of Nevada.

283   IRS eventually audited   *Barbara Cooke v. Allen Klein et al.*, California Superior Court, Los Angeles, #951 036, 7/23/71.

283   "controlled and dominated"   *BMG v. ABKCO.*

283   same techniques   Philip Norman, *Symphony for the Devil: The Rolling Stones Story* (New York: Linden Press/Simon & Schuster, 1989), p. 156.

283   solely owned and operated   Ibid., p. 272.

283–284   The cover   *Cash Box*, 12/1/63, cover.

284   the local paper   *Louisiana Weekly*, 9/28/63, p. 22.

284   the mayor   Ibid., 10/5/63, p. 1.

285   "Negro Band Leader"   *New York Times*, 10/9/63, p. 29.

286   new attendance record   *Amsterdam News*, 11/23/63, p. 17.

286   L&M   *Ebony*, November 1963, p. 34.

286   Jack Paar's show   *Amsterdam News*, 11/23/63, p. 17.

286   Howard Bingham   Thomas Hauser, *Muhammad Ali: His Life and Times* (New York: Simon & Schuster, 1991), p. 286.

286   Frank Schiffman   *Amsterdam News*, 11/30/63, p. 17.

287   "tan population"   *Los Angeles Sentinel*, 11/30/63, p. 1.

287   Malcolm wrote   Ibid.

288   Battiste   For A.F.O. and New Orleans history, see Broven, p. 161.

289   "I hate to see"   Ibid., p. 164.

CHAPTER 21

293   From 1955 to 1963   Ward, Stokes, and Tucker, p. 272.

293   Sam told a New York reporter   William Peper, "Sam Cooke Sings the Blues, Too," *New York World Telegraph and Sun*, 2/6/64.

294   Klein's perspective   Hilburn, p. 62.

294   "I got a big ego"   Peper.

294   a press release   Billboard, 2/15/64, p. 40.

295   "the world's greatest"   Video of Clay/Liston fight, courtesy Allen Klein.

295   "Once he got by"   *Los Angeles Sentinel*, 2/27/64, p. A-11.

296   A. S. Young   Ibid., 3/12/64, p. D-3.

296   "the champion of racial segregation"   Ibid., 3/26/64, p. B-3.

296   Columbia Records studio   *New York Times*, 3/4/64, p. 44.

296–297   Klein had gone to London   Norman, p. 154.

297   at least one critic   Ibid., p. 126.

298   so blatant   J. W. Alexander interview.

298   *American Bandstand*   *Dick Clark Show*, 4/4/64.

299   By now, the business end   J.W. signed papers for Klein to become "sole and exclusive administrator and selling agent" for KAGS on 8/14/63, courtesy A. Klein.

301–302   Up at the Warwick Hotel   And subsequent quotes: Ray Coleman, "Sam Seeks a New Twist," *Melody Maker*, 7/4/64, p. 7.

302   "Who's the Biggest Cook?"   *Amsterdam News*, 6/27/64, p. 17.

302   Despite the fact   *New York Times*, 6/17/64.

303   tight black tapered pants   *Amsterdam News*, 7/4/64, p. 16.

305   "to open up Mississippi"   *Eyes on the Prize* video.

306   "stands the test"   *New York Times*, 7/7/64.

306   "solid headliner"   *Variety*, 7/1/64, p. 57.

306   "swinging"   *Billboard*, 7/4/64, p. 12.

306   "best voice"   *Amsterdam News*, 7/4/64, p. 16.

306   "I want to go to Las Vegas"   Don Paulsen in *Rhythm and Blues Magazine*, July 1964, reprinted as liner notes on *Sam Cooke at the Copa* LP.

CHAPTER 22

310   wooden mallets   *Variety*, 8/5/64, p. 55.

310   "looked more appropriate"   *Afro-American* (New Jersey), 7/25/64, p. 1.

310   King declared   David Garrow, *Bearing the Cross: Martin Luther King, Jr., and the Southern Christian Leadership Conference* (New York: William Morrow, 1986), p. 344.

310   "You'll get your freedom"   Howard Zinn, *A People's History of the United States* (New York: Harper & Row, 1980), p. 453.

311   "Blues Revue"   *Chicago Defender*, 8/15–21/64, n.p.

312   The premier   *Shindig* premier, Museum of Television and Radio, #070728 B*404.

316   According to Barbara   Chicago Defender, 2/6/65, p. 1.

CHAPTER 23

323   "demonstrating"   *Los Angeles Sentinel*, 12/17/64, p. 4A.

323–324   Klein issued a statement   *Variety*, 12/16/64.

324   "Many, even the men"   *Chicago Defender*, 12/16/64, p. 12.

324   for a comparison   *Chicago Defender*, 12/14/64, p. 3.

324   *Chicago Defender*   Ibid., pp. 1, 3.

325   Kilgallen   *New York Journal-American*, 12/15/64.

325   sergeant in charge   *Chicago Defender*, 12/16/64, p. 3.

325   trying to find her   *Los Angeles Sentinel*, 12/17/64, p. D-1.

325   coroner's inquest   Account following from official transcript.

328   the foreman of the jury   Dr. Benjamin H. Bendat interview.

328   on-the-street interviews   *Chicago Defender*, 12/16/64, p. 11.

329   The scandal   Ibid., 12/18/64, p. 1.

329   "A few white people"   *Afro-American* (New Jersey), 12/26/64, p. 1.

330   "I don't like the way"   *Jet*, 12/31/64, p. 64.

330   had seen him and Lisa Boyer   *Los Angeles Sentinel*, 12/17/64, p. D-1.

330   Kilgallen   *New York Journal-American*, 12/17/64.

330   Warren Commission's report   Lee Israel, *Kilgallen* (New York: Delacorte, 1979), p. 392.

331   "long lines"   *Afro-American* (New Jersey), 12/26/64, p. 1.

331–332   The service began   *Los Angeles Sentinel*, 12/24/64, p. 1.

332   Gibson read a eulogy   Ibid., p. D-1.

332   Dr. A. B. Charles   Ibid., p. A-4.

333   "Nation Seeks Answers"   Ibid., 12/24/64, p. 1.

333   Alexander told   Ibid., 1/21/65, p. 1.

334   Klein announced   Ibid.

334   Alexander told   *Amsterdam News*, 1/9/65, p. 3.

334   January 11, 1965   *Chicago Defender*, 3/6/65, p. 1.

334   "dating openly"   Quoted in *Amsterdam News*, 2/6/65, p. 1.

335   Bobby told the press   *Chicago Defender*, 2/6/65, p. 1.

335   On February 23   *Los Angeles Sentinel*, 2/26/65, p. 1.

335   The next day   Ibid., 3/4/65, p. 1.

335   According to Allen Klein   Hilburn, p. 62.

CHAPTER 24

340   The private detective   Report courtesy Allen Klein.

342   Franklin had shot   *Los Angeles Sentinel*, 12/17/64, p. 1.

344   she sued his estate   Ibid., 4/1/65, p. 1.

345   regularly featured   Ibid., 12/10/64, ad, entertainment section.

346   Klein told the press   Ibid., 1/21/65, p. 1.

POSTSCRIPT

349 In 1979 *People of the State of California* v. *Crystal Chan Young,* #A076500, 8/30/77.

349 "step into the giant-sized" *Chicago Defender,* 12/26/64, p. 2.

349 memorial concert   Ibid., 1/23/65, p. 2.

350 Roberts Motor Inn *Amsterdam News,* 7/3/65, p. 1.

350 she filed papers   Trial Brief, California Superior Court, Los Angeles, #P 491 858, 12/22/66.

351 $103,000   see Petition for Ex Parte Order Authorizing Sale of Securities, California Superior Court, Los Angeles County, #P 491 858, 4/11/66.

351 "biggest coup" *Variety,* 2/7/68, p. 47.

351 "dilution" David Hinckley in *New York Daily News,* quoted in *Washington Post,* 12/5/92.

352 BMG *BMG v. ABKCO.*

353 "to fill the silent void" Arnold Shaw, *The World of Soul: Black America's Contribution to the Pop Music Scene* (New York: Cowles, 1970), p. 245.

SELECTED BIBLIOGRAPHY

Alberston, Chris. *Bessie.* New York: Stein & Day, 1982.

Baldwin, James, *Just Above My Head.* New York: Dial, 1979.

Barlow, William. *Looking Up at Down: The Emergence of the Blues Culture.* Philadelphia: Temple University Press, 1989.

Branch, Taylor. *Parting the Waters: America in the King Years 1954–63.* New York: Simon & Schuster, 1988.

Broughton, Viv. *Black Gospel: An Illustrated History of the Gospel Sound.* Dorset, England: Blandford, 1985.

Broven, John. *Rhythm & Blues in New Orleans.* Gretna, La.: Pelican, 1978.

Busnar, Gene. *The Rhythm and Blues Story.* New York: J. Messner, 1985.

———. *It's Rock 'n' Roll.* New York: J. Messner, 1979.

Cantor, Louis. *Wheelin' on Beale.* New York: Pharos, 1992.

Chapple, Steve, and Reebee Garofaro. *Rock & Roll Is Here to Pay.* Chicago: Nelson-Hall, 1977.

Charles, Ray, and David Ritz. *Brother Ray: Ray Charles' Own Story.* New York: Dial, 1978.

Clark, Dick, and Richard Robinson. *Rock, Roll & Remember.* New York: Thomas Y. Crowell, 1976.

Cobbins, Otho B., ed. *History of Church of Christ (Holiness) U.S.A. 1895–1965.* New York: Vantage, 1966.

Collins, Keith E. *Black Los Angeles: The Maturing of the Ghetto.* Sacramento, Cal.: Century Twenty-one, 1980.

Cone, James H. *The Spirituals and the Blues.* New York: Seabury, 1972.

Davis, Mike. *City of Quartz.* New York: Vintage, 1992

Drake, St. Clair, and Horace R. Cayton. *Black Metropolis: A Study of Negro Life in a Northern City.* New York: Harper & Row, 1970.

Duncan, Otis Dudley, and Beverley Duncan. *The Negro Population in Chicago: A Study of Residential Succession.* Chicago: University of Chicago Press, 1957.

Elliot, Marc. *Rockonomics: The Money Behind the Music.* Toronto: Franklin Watts, 1989.

Escott, Colin, with Martin Hawkins. *Good Rockin' Tonight: Sun Records and the Birth of Rock 'n' Roll.* New York: St. Martin's, 1991.

Fahey, John. *Charlie Patton.* London: November Books, 1970.

Feldstein, Martin, ed. *The American Economy in Transition.* Chicago: University of Chicago Press, 1980.

Ferris, William. *Blues from the Delta.* New York: Da Capo, 1978.

Fox, Ted. *Showtime at the Apollo.* New York: Holt, Rinehart & Winston, 1983.

Fremon, David K. *Chicago Politics Ward by Ward.* Bloomington and Indianapolis: Indiana University Press, 1988.

Garland, Phyl. *The Sound of Soul.* Chicago: Henry Regnery, 1969.

Garrow, David. *Bearing the Cross: Martin Luther King, Jr., and the Southern Christian Leadership Conference.* New York: William Morrow, 1986.

George, Nelson. *Where Did Our Love Go?: The Rise and Fall of the Motown Sound.* New York: St. Martin's, 1985.

———. *The Death of Rhythm and Blues.* New York: Pantheon, 1988.

Gourse, Leslie. Unforgettable: *The Life and Mystique of Nat King Cole.* New York: St. Martin's, 1991.

Grossman, James R. *Land of Hope: Chicago, Black Southerners, and the Great Migration.* Chicago: University of Chicago Press, 1989.

Guralnick, Peter. *Sweet Soul Music: Rhythm and Blues and the Southern Dream of Freedom.* New York: Harper & Row, 1986.

Haralambos, Michael. *Soul Music: The Birth of a Sound in Black America.* New York: Da Capo, 1974.

Harris, Michael W. *The Rise of Gospel Blues: The Music of Thomas Andrew Dorsey in the Urban Church.* New York: Oxford University Press, 1992.

Haskins, James. *Black Music in America: A History Through Its People.* New York: Thomas Y. Crowell, 1987.

Hauser, Thomas. *Muhammad Ali: His Life and Times.* New York: Simon & Schuster, 1991.

Hayes, Cedric J., and Robert Laughton. *Gospel Records: A Black Music Discography 1943–1969.* Milford, N.H.: Big Nickel, 1993.

Heilbut, Tony. *The Gospel Sound: Good News and Bad Times.* New York: Simon & Schuster, 1985.

Herrick, Mary J. *The Chicago Schools: A Social and Political History.* Beverly Hills and London: Sage Productions, 1971.

Hirsch, Arnold Richard. *Making the Second Ghetto: Race and Housing in Chicago, 1940–1966.* Ph.D. thesis, University of Illinois, 1978.

Hirshey, Gerri. *Nowhere to Run: The Story of Soul Music.* New York: Penguin, 1984.

Hurst, Walter E., and William Storm Hale. *The Music Industry Book (How to Make Money in the Music Industry).* Hollywood: Seven Arts Press, 1963.

Israel, Lee. *Kilgallen.* New York: Delacorte, 1979.

Johnson, Charles S. *Growing Up in the Black Belt: Negro Youth in the Rural South.* Washington, D.C.: American Council on Education, 1941.

Johnson, James Wedlon, and J. Rosamond Johnson. *The Books of American Negro Spirituals.* New York: Viking, 1951.

Keil, Charles. *Urban Blues.* Chicago: University of Chicago Press, 1966.

Lemann, Nicholas. *The Promised Land: The Great Black Migration and How It Changed America.* New York: Knopf, 1991.

Lincoln, Eric, and Lawrence H. Mamiya. *The Black Church in the African American Experience.* Durham, N.C.: Duke University Press, 1990.

Lomax, Alan. *The Land Where the Blues Began.* New York: Pantheon, 1993.

Lornell, Kip. *Happy in the Service of the Lord: Afro-American Gospel Quartets in Memphis.* Chicago: University of Illinois Press, 1988.

Lovell, John. *Black Song: The Forge and the Flame: The Story of How the Afro-American Spiritual Was Hammered Out.* New York: Macmillan, 1972.

Marsh, Dave. *The Heart of Rock & Soul: The 1001 Greatest Singles Ever Made.* New York: New American Library, 1989.

Mayer, Harold M., and Richard C. Wade. *Chicago: Growth of a Metropolis.* Chicago: University of Chicago Press, 1969.

McEwen, Joe. *Sam Cooke: The Man Who Invented Soul: A Biography in Words and Pictures.* Sire Books/Chappell Music Company, 1977.

McKee, Margaret, and Fred Chisenhall. *Beale Black and Blue: Life and Music on Black America's Main Street.* Baton Rouge: Louisiana State University Press, 1981.

McMillen, Neil R. *Dark Journey: Black Mississippians in the Age of Jim Crow.* Chicago: University of Illinois Press, 1990.

Mooney, C.P.J., ed. *The Mid-South and Its Builders.* Memphis: Mid-South Biographical and Historical Association, 1920.

Murray, Albert. *The Omni-Americans: Black Experience and American Culture.* New York: Vintage, 1970.

Norman, Philip. *Symphony for the Devil: The Rolling Stones Story.* New York: Linden/Simon & Schuster, 1989.

Oliver, Paul, Max Harrison, and William Bolcom. *The New Grove Gospel, Blues and Jazz*. New York: Norton, 1980.

Oliver, Paul. *The Meaning of the Blues*. New York: Collier, 1972.

Otis, Johnny. *Upside Your Head: Rhythm and Blues on Central Avenue*. Wesleyan: Wesleyan University Press, 1994.

Palmer, Robert. *Deep Blues*. New York: Penguin, 1981.

Philpott, Thomas Lee. *The Slum and the Ghetto: Neighborhood Deterioration and Middle-Class Reform, Chicago, 1880–1930*. New York: Oxford University Press, 1978.

Pinderhughes, Dianne M. *Race and Ethnicity in Chicago's Politics: A Reexamination of Pluralist Theory*. Chicago: University of Illinois Press, 1987.

Raines, Howell. *My Soul Is Rested: The Story of the Civil Rights Movement in the Deep South*. New York: Penguin, 1977.

Reagon, Bernice Johnson, ed. *We'll Understand It Better By and By: Pioneering African American Gospel Composers*. Washington and London: Smithsonian Institution Press, 1992.

Redd, Lawrence N. *Rock Is Rhythm and Blues: The Impact of Mass Media*. Detroit: Michigan State University Press, 1974.

Ricks, George Robinson. *Some Aspects of the Religious Music of the United States Negro*. New York: Arno, 1977.

Riedel, Johannes. *Soul Music Black and White: The Influence of Black Music on the Churches*. Minneapolis: Augsburg House, 1975.

Roberts, John Storm. *Black Music of Two Worlds*. New York: Morrow, 1972.

Rowe, Mike. *Chicago Blues: The City and The Music*. New York: Da Capo, 1975.

Schwerin, Jules. *Got to Tell It: Mahalia Jackson Queen of Gospel*. New York: Oxford University Press, 1992.

Shapiro, Harry, and Caesar Glebbeck. *Jimi Hendrix: Electric Gypsy*. New York: St. Martin's, 1990.

Shaw, Arnold. *Honkers and Shouters: The Golden Years of Rhythm and Blues.* New York: Collier, 1978.

————. *The Rockin' '50s: The Decade That Transformed the Pop Music Scene.* New York: Hawthorn, 1974.

————. *The World of Soul: Black America's Contribution to the Pop Music Scene.* New York: Cowles, 1970.

Shore, Michael, with Dick Clark. *The History of "American Bandstand."* New York: Ballantine, 1985.

Sloan, John W. *Eisenhower and the Management of Prosperity.* Kansas City: University Press, 1991.

Southern, Eileen, ed. *Readings in Black American Music.* New York: Norton, 1971.

Synan, Vinson. *The Holiness-Pentecostal Movement in the United States.* Grand Rapids, Mich.: William B. Eerdmans, 1971.

Szatmary, Daniel P. *Rockin' in Time: A Social History of Rock-and-Roll.* New York: Prentice-Hall, 1991.

Titon, Jeff Todd. *Give Me This Mountain: Reverend C. L. Franklin Life History and Selected Sermons.* Champaign: University of Illinois Press, 1989.

Wade, Dorothy, and Justine Picardie. *Music Man: Ahmet Ertegun, Atlantic Records, and the Triumph of Rock 'n' Roll.* New York: Norton, 1990.

Walker, Wyatt Tee. *Somebody's Calling My Name: Black Sacred Music and Social Change.* Valley Forge, N.Y.: Judson Press, 1979.

Ward, Ed, Geoffrey Stokes, and Ken Tucker. *Rock of Ages: The Rolling Stone History of Rock & Roll.* New York: Rolling Stone Press/Summit Books, 1986.

Washington, Joseph R., Jr. *Black Sects and Cults.* New York: Anchor/Doubleday, 1973.

White, Charles. *The Life and Times of Little Richard: The Quasar of Rock.* New York: Harmony, 1984.

White, Roger. *The Everly Brothers: Walk Right Back.* London: Plexus, 1984.

Wirth, Louis, and Maraget Furez. *Local Community Fact Book* (*1938*). Chicago: Chicago Recreation Commission, 1938.

Wright, Richard. *Native Son.* New York: Harper & Row, 1940.

Zinn, Howard. *A People's History of the United States.* New York: Harper & Row, 1980.

ACKNOWLEDGMENTS

I want to thank my three collaborators for their enormously dedicated work; Nancy Nicholas, who has helped at every stage of this project, from conception to rewrite, *and* had the good sense to pass her Sam Cooke records on to her little brother; Owen Laster, for his dedication and patience; Dave Marsh, who was my university; all those who were interviewed, but especially Zelda Sands and J. W. Alexander, who went out of their way to make connections to Sam's circle of friends; Becky Arntzen and Mike Rausch, for a year in their garage; Amos and Lorenzo, for growing up with this project; and Marta Renzi, for making it possible.

—DANIEL WOLFF

This book is dedicated to the memory of my parents, who gave me the skills, values, and courage to succeed in life. To Mr. Isaiah Rogers, whose sense of humor, compassion, and innate wisdom I will cherish forever. To Gary Urwin, a very special friend whose lone voice of encouragement in the beginning and exceptional writing talent made it possible for me to fulfill my dream of contributing to the Sam Cooke story. To Sam Cooke's cadre of close friends and colleagues (affectionately referred to by Sam as "the Sam Cooke Family," including S. R. Crain, Clifton White, Zelda Sands, J. W. Alexander, and Johnnie Morisette), who were incredibly lucky to be an integral part of Sam Cooke's life. After becoming friends with each of them, I can state without qualification that Sam Cooke was equally lucky to have them as part of his "family." To Lionel and Barbara

Williams; Cameron, Yvette, Alexander, and Camille Jolly; Arnold and Elizabeth MacMahon; David Berkovitz; Kim Kelly; Gunther and Marcet Kahn; Audrey and Ivan Schiff; David Small; Vivian Alston; Greg Berk; Linda Elerath; and Gail Solo. And to Daniel Wolff—as far as I am concerned, he is Moses in shepherding this project to its fruition.

—David Tenenbaum

I owe too much to too many people. I thank them all.

—S. R. Crain

To Bumps Blackwell, without whom the whole thing would not have come about.

—Clifford White

Additional thanks to Jack Bart; Bill Belmont; Dorothy Love Coates; Steven Crain; Chick Crumpacker; the Reverend Eric Cummings; Bruce Eglauer; Carmen Fanzone; Marty Faye; Ted Fox; Ray Funk; Florence Gaines; Robert Gordon; Sid Graves, the Delta Blues Museum; Paula Guibault; Peter Guralnick; R. H. Harris; Tony Heilbut; Lee Hildebrandt; James "Pookie" Hudson; Ralph Kaffel; Iris Keitel; Joe Killian; Grelun Landon; Lee at Martoni's; Kip Lornell; Lorene Lortie; Linda Clifton Lowe; Joyce McRae; Bernadette Moore; Jim O'Neil; Sid Ordauer; Don Pitts; Robert Pruter; the Rhythm and Blues Foundation; Sandy Rosoff; Bruce Scavusso; Tony Scherman; the staff at the Schomburg Center for Research in Black Culture; Melissa Schwartz; Joel Selvan; Eddie Shore; Norris A. Solomon, Esquire; Jane Stevens; Linda Stotereau; Randy Van Horne; Billy Vera; Katrina Vinegardner; Wade Walter; Selma Williams; Shirley Williams; Charles Wolf; Paula Wolff; Joe Yore; Dick Young; Irwin Zucker.

INDEX